Contests for Corporate Control

Contests for Corporate Control

Corporate Governance and Economic Performance
in the United States and Germany

MARY O'SULLIVAN

OXFORD
UNIVERSITY PRESS

OXFORD
UNIVERSITY PRESS

Great Clarendon Street, Oxford OX2 6DP

Oxford University Press is a department of the University of Oxford.
It furthers the University's objective of excellence in research, scholarship,
and education by publishing worldwide in

Oxford New York

Athens Auckland Bangkok Bogotá Buenos Aires Calcutta
Cape Town Chennai Dar es Salaam Delhi Florence Hong Kong Istanbul
Karachi Kuala Lumpur Madrid Melbourne Mexico City Mumbai
Nairobi Paris São Paulo Singapore Taipei Tokyo Toronto Warsaw

with associated companies in Berlin Ibadan

Oxford is a registered trade mark of Oxford University Press
in the UK and in certain other countries

Published in the United States
by Oxford University Press Inc., New York

British Library Cataloguing in Publication Data

Data available

Library of Congress Cataloging in Publication Data

O'Sullivan, Mary,
Contests for corporate control: corporate governance and economic performance in the
United States and Germany / Mary O'Sullivan.
p. cm.
Includes bibliographical references and index.
1. Corporate governance—United States. 2. Corporate governance—Germany.
3. Corporations—United States. 4. Corporations—Germany. 5. Industrial management—
United States. 6. Industrial management—Germany. 7. United States—Economic conditions.
8. Germany—Economic conditions. I. Title.
HD2741. O76 2000   658.4—dc21   99-086830
ISBN 0–19–829346–1

1 3 5 7 9 10 8 6 4 2

Typeset in Garamond 3
by Best-set Typesetter Ltd., Hong Kong
Printed in Great Britain
on acid-free paper by
Biddles Ltd.
Guildford & King's Lynn

Acknowledgements

My interest in the subject of corporate control dates back more than a decade. Growing up in Ireland, a country that was heavily dependent on foreign direct investment for jobs, exports, and growth, I found myself wondering about the process through which major corporations made decisions that had repercussions for the economic and social development of regions and nations. The relationship between business organization and the process of economic development in Ireland still interests me, and indeed has become an integral part of my research agenda as an academic, but in the process of intellectual development that led to the writing of this book I became convinced of the importance of understanding the evolution of corporate control in the leading advanced industrial economies.

The Dublin of the late 1980s, with unemployment running into the high teens, had little in common with what has become in the late 1990s, with the emergence of the Celtic Tiger, Europe's party capital. Like so many Irish people before me my first job took me abroad, in my case to London in 1988 to pursue a career with McKinsey and Company. It was there that I developed a fascination with all aspects of financial economics, an interest that I was to pursue in a more academic setting when McKinsey sponsored me to undertake a Master of Business Administration (MBA) at Harvard Business School.

I arrived at HBS in 1990. The great wave of financial restructuring that became known as the Deal Decade had collapsed. Serious questions were being raised about its impact on the productive capabilities of the American corporate economy. The Japanese system of corporate governance was the toast of the international community. If ever there was a time to go to HBS, it was then, because there was scope for debate about the merits and shortcomings of different economic systems for delivering growth, employment, and, at least in some classes, equity.

Three professors at HBS stand out for their influence on my intellectual development during my MBA studies and, in particular, for encouraging me to pursue a Ph.D. in Economics. One was Richard Vietor, whose encouragement of classroom debate and refusal to tolerate nonsense, no matter how eloquently delivered, made his classes among the most stimulating and thought-provoking that I have enjoyed. William Sahlman, an expert in entrepreneurial finance, ran one of the most challenging analytical courses at the school, and constantly reminded us how much we did not know about the techniques of financial analysis and their application, as well as some of their limits. Finally, but undoubtedly most important in persuading me of the value of a Ph.D., was Michael Jensen.

Jensen's course at HBS was one of the most popular electives in the school. His course was essentially a sustained argument for the merits of shareholder value as a principle of corporate governance. As a teacher and a writer he was highly persuasive, and he convinced many MBA students of the merits of leveraged buyouts and hostile raids for enhancing economic performance. I greatly enjoyed Jensen's course although there were central elements of his thesis that I found troubling. As will be evident from the arguments contained in this book, that discomfort has burgeoned into outright disagreement with proponents of shareholder value. Yet the journey from there to here has been a long one, and Michael Jensen played an important role in my embarking on it by encouraging my questions, by suggesting that I pursue further studies in economics to develop my understanding of corporate control and economic development, and by recommending me for the Ph.D. programme in Business Economics at the Harvard Economics Department.

The transition from one school to another, although they were both part of the same university, was a shock to the system. From the initial 'math camp' it was clear that what mattered to the economists was analysis, not debate, and general principles rather than anecdotes. To someone who had spent two years on an MBA programme, reading more cases than I care to remember and listening to classroom discussions that were often higher in confidence than in content, the shock was initially a refreshing one. Finally, I had an opportunity to develop my capabilities to analyse the principles underlying the operation and evolution of economic systems in a rigorous, scientific way.

The gloss took some time to wear off because the intensity of the programme was such that there was little time to stand back from what we were learning to consider its value. One incident does stand out in my mind, however, as sowing the first seeds of doubt about the relevance of what I was being taught. At the end of three months of an intensive Microeconomics course, the professor paused after a fifteen-line equation and asked what economic intuition it supported. The class was silent. He asked again, this time giving us a hint. 'When prices go up . . .', he said, waiting for us to finish the sentence, but no one responded. Apparently, our training was too advanced to grasp the inverse relationship between price and quantity that every introductory class on economics teaches!

It was not, however, until we had the final few weeks of instruction in Microeconomics by Steve Marglin that I began to see the systematic biases in the course material for what they were. At the time Marglin was allotted approximately four weeks to teach everything that did not fall under the umbrella of neoclassical economics. Thus we got our first taste, and for most students their last, of Schumpeter, Marx, and Keynes, and anyone else who had the temerity to throw off the traces of mainstream economic thought.

I remember leaving Harvard for the summer, having completed my general exams, in a state of great confusion. I spent the ensuing few months reading like a maniac trying to understand where the course material fitted in with the evolution of economic thought. That challenge continues to preoccupy me to this day but what I could quickly see even then was that what I was getting at the Harvard Economics Department as the cutting edge of scientific endeavour in economics was only the tip of the iceberg of what economic thinkers have learned. I focused in particular on the economics of the corporate economy and found that although I was enrolled in an institution that had been home to some of the most original thinkers in the field, their legacy had been systematically erased.

When I returned to Harvard, I began working with Steve, and he was to become my thesis adviser as well as my most important mentor for the duration of my doctoral studies. It is to him, and especially his interest in savings and investment, that I owe my recognition of the importance of corporate resource allocation to economic outcomes. With his guidance and support I felt ambitious enough to attempt to challenge on economic grounds the dominant paradigm in the corporate governance debates.

Other members of the Harvard Economics Department also provided me with important intellectual support at various stages of my work. Oliver Hart stands out among them for his guidance. A number of fellow-students in the department also made a major difference to my intellectual development and social life as a graduate student, especially Sanjay Reddy and Jeff Bernstein.

As a student in Business Economics, I was permitted to rope in non-economists on my committee, and I exploited that opportunity to gain access to my other two advisers, Joe Bower of HBS and Roberto Unger at Harvard Law School. I had known Joe since my MBA years, and I had often talked with him about my work. His own earlier research in corporate resource allocation meant that he was a great source of advice for me in my work on corporate governance and was a natural choice of adviser for me. I became acquainted with Roberto Unger's work through a course on 'Firms, Workers, and Governments' that he taught at Harvard Law School with another law professor, David Charny. Coming from economics, at a time when neoliberal thinking was in the ascendant, and many of my fellow graduate students were trotting off to Moscow to bring, as they saw it, the good news of the market economy to the Russian masses, I found Unger's approach to be a breath of fresh air. I was already committed to being a critical economist, but Unger's contentious and original arguments constantly alerted me to the dangers of economic determinism that are common to many schools of economic thought. In both Harvard Business School and Harvard Law School I also found kindred spirits among the student population. Jonathan West and Kerry Rittich deserve special mention as colleagues and friends.

Indeed, the great benefit of doing a Ph.D. at Harvard was precisely the opportunity that it gave me to engage in cross-disciplinary research. It was certainly a challenge, often a headache, and I sometimes wondered whether it would lead anywhere, but I was never in any doubt that to understand the issues with which I was concerned disciplinary boundaries had to be traversed. I was encouraged in my efforts by the time that I spent at the Center for European Studies (CES) at Harvard. I am very grateful to Charlie Maier and Abby Collins for their support and also to the other scholars with whom I came into contact while I was there, first as a graduate student and later as a Faculty Affiliate. A constant reminder of the complexity of the corporate economy, but also of the possibilities of cross-disciplinary discussion, was the Business History seminar at Harvard Business School. There I had the pleasure of getting to know scholars in the field of business history like Alfred Chandler,

Thomas McCraw, and Takashi Hikino, who were based at HBS, as well as other distinguished scholars who came to give seminars there.

It was through the Business History seminar that I came into contact with Bill Lazonick, an economist, who had once been a colleague of Steve Marglin in the Harvard Economics Department. He had since moved first to Barnard College at Columbia University and subsequently to the University of Massachusetts Lowell to contribute to the building of that university's capabilities in the study of regional economic and social development. I was planning to write a term paper on the history of the cotton industry in Lancashire, and I was told that I should contact Bill, who had long attended the Business History seminar and was a well-known expert in the history of the textile industry.

Bill had also made a name for himself as a critical economist and was less than thrilled to get a call from someone who, as a graduate student in economics, was likely to be enamoured with what he had described as 'the myth of the market economy'. Our inauspicious first contact was, however, to evolve into a long-term collaboration in the study of business organization and comparative economic development that is still going on. Many of the ideas developed in this book owe an immeasurable debt to my work with Bill and to our discussions together.

Through Bill I also came into contact with a number of scholars who regularly attended a Friday afternoon seminar at UMass Lowell including Beth Almeida, Mike Best, Bob Forrant, Erin Flynn, Ann Frost, Qiwen Lu, William Mass, Phil Moss, and Chris Tilly as well as the Vice-Chancellor of the university, Fred Sperounis, and the Chancellor, William Hogan. The number of students that attended this seminar from Harvard and MIT was testament to the quality of the discussions that one could find there as well as the dearth of similar debates in Cambridge. Many of the people I met through these seminars continue to play important roles in my intellectual life.

It is only as one writes an acknowledgements section that one realizes just how many people have had an identifiable influence on one's thinking in the years that go into the development of a book. Keith Smith played a crucial role in supporting, both intellectually and financially, the early stages of my research on corporate governance. In particular, he provided funding through the STEP (Studies in Technology, Innovation, and Economic Policy) Group for me to spend a summer in Oslo working on my thesis. I benefited greatly from my time there and especially from my interaction with other researchers at STEP. In a variety of other academic venues, comments on my work by Franco Amatori, Alice Amsden, Ron Blackwell, Kristine Bruland, Youssef Cassis, Zhiyuan Cui, Andrea Colli, Ronald Dore, Lou Ferleger, Martin Fransman, Patrick Fridenson, Lou Galambos, Les Hannah, Philippe Haspeslagh, Gary Herrigel, Ulrich Jürgens, Henry Mintzberg, Jonathan Story, Kazuo Wada, Christian Weller, and Jonathan Zeitlin all deserve special mention.

Fellowships from Harvard Business School, the Harvard Graduate School of Arts and Sciences, and the Center for European Studies at Harvard have permitted time for research and writing. My work on corporate governance was funded for a number of years by the Levy Institute, where I am a Research Fellow. The European Commission has also provided me with financial support, first through TSER project No.

SOE1-CT95-1004 on 'Innovation Systems and European Integration', directed by Charles Edquist from Linköping University in Sweden, and more recently through TSER project No. SOE1-CT98-1114 on 'Corporate Governance, Innovation, and Economic Performance in the EU', co-directed by Bill Lazonick and me from the European Institute of Business Administration (INSEAD).

Three years ago I was appointed an assistant professor at INSEAD. I initially had serious reservations about taking a faculty position there given that most business schools do not consider it their responsibility to engage in critical discussions of corporate control. In this respect INSEAD is no different, even if some individuals there recognize the importance of educating students to think critically about the economic and social roles that their business careers accord them. What does distinguish INSEAD, however, is its commitment to admitting a truly international student body. Given the diversity of the students that attend the school, it is hard to stifle debate about the strengths and weaknesses of different systems of corporate governance even if one wanted to (as indeed many do). For someone who places a high value on intellectual debate, perhaps due to the cantankerous Irishwoman in me but also because I have seen what happens without a serious commitment to it in many economics departments, a wide variety of students is a constant joy. I would like to acknowledge the crucial role that my MBA students have played in pushing me to refine my ideas on corporate governance when I thought that I had lost the energy to go any further. They have persuaded me that serious debates about economic efficiency and equity can happen at business schools.

I would also like to extend a special thanks to Valérie Bouland and Michèle Plu, who have worked with me since my arrival at INSEAD and who have helped me more times than I can remember in the process of getting this book to press. David Musson from Oxford University Press was largely responsible for my deciding to write this book and, throughout its development, he struck the perfect balance between patience and persistence. T. W. Bartel did an excellent job of copy-editing the manuscript and Sarah Dobson was a great help in getting the book through to publication.

My family have by now had just about enough of this book but it certainly would not have been finished without their encouragement and support. They also made sure that when I took the manuscript and myself too seriously for my own good they were around to make sure I laughed myself out of whatever dilemma I had created for myself. Special gratitude is due to my parents not only for all of the help that they gave me while I wrote the book but for what they've put up with for a lot longer than that. To them I dedicate this book in the year that they both turned sixty. There was a point at which they thought they might be seventy before it finally appeared on their bookshelf, and I am more than happy to have proven them wrong.

On a more sombre note, however, I would like to pay tribute to my great friend, Qiwen Lu, for the great conversations and wonderful times that we had together over the last six years. Qiwen was a Ph.D. student in Sociology at Harvard when I was there but we actually met at UMass Lowell. Since then we have moved along similar paths, finishing our doctorates around the same time and getting our first jobs in the same place. We both contracted with Oxford University Press to publish books, me this one on corporate governance, he a forthcoming one on high-technology indigenous companies in China. In August 1999 as we both put the finishing touches to our manuscripts, Qiwen died as he underwent surgery, leaving behind his wife Lily and his two daughters, Mindy and Jessie, as well as many friends who, like me, loved and respected him. In death as in life Qiwen reminds me of how much I have and how little I deserve.

Contents

List of Figures

List of Tables

Introduction

The question of how corporations should be governed to enhance corporate and economic performance has been widely discussed in the last two decades in the United States and Britain. Until recently, the subject of corporate governance has attracted much less attention on the European continent, in Asia, and in other parts of the world. By the late 1990s, however, corporate governance had become a major, and highly contentious, issue in all of the advanced economies and, increasingly, in developing countries as well. International organizations, including the OECD, the World Bank, and the IMF, have devoted increasing attention to corporate governance as a topic of global concern.

Contemporary debates about corporate governance stem, in part, from the recognition by economists of the centrality of corporate enterprises for allocating resources in the economy. In most economies, corporate enterprises play a critical role in shaping economic outcomes through the decisions that they make about investments, employment, and trade. That is, an economy's performance is importantly related to the process through which corporate revenues are allocated. Retained earnings—undistributed profits and capital consumption allowances—have always provided, and continue to provide, the financial resources that are the foundations of investments in productive capabilities. How major corporations allocate their vast revenues is a matter of strategic choice, and the strategic choices of corporate decision-makers can have profound effects on the performance of the economy as a whole.

Economic analysis is focused on resource allocation—what is to be produced, how it is to be produced, and for whom it is to be produced. To address these issues, economists strive to find answers to the following types of question: 'How should these resource allocation decisions be made? Who should make these decisions? How can those who are responsible for making these decisions be induced to make the right decisions? How are they to know what and how much information to acquire before making the decisions? How can the separate decisions of the millions of actors—decision makers—in the economy be controlled?' (Stiglitz 1994: 13)' Corporate governance is concerned with the institutions that influence how business corporations allocate resources and returns. Specifically, *a system of corporate governance shapes who makes investment decisions in corporations, what types of investments they make, and how returns from investments are distributed.* My interest in corporate governance, like that of most economists, is with its implications for economic outcomes at the enterprise and societal levels. The central focus of this book is the relationship between systems of corporate governance and the economic performance of corporate enterprises themselves and the economies in which they are embedded.

In approaching corporate governance from the perspective of economic analysis, I will ignore studies of corporate governance that either do not deal with economic performance, or make unsubstantiated assumptions about its generation. There is, for example, a substantial body of literature, emanating primarily from management studies, that is concerned with issues such as the composition of boards of directors, the process through which the remuneration of senior executives and directors is determined, the voting rights of shareholders, and the ethical status of corporate behaviour. While these studies deal with corporate enterprises and the manner in which they are controlled, they are not, at least as a general rule, embedded in an economic theory of the firm. Given my central concern with the governance of corporate resource allocation and its implications for corporate and economic performance, my main theoretical interest is in exploring the strengths and weaknesses of economic theories that (1) recognize the importance, for better or worse, of the corporation for resource allocation in the economy and (2) seek to justify their arguments concerning how corporations should be governed in terms of the implications for economic performance.

The starting point for my analysis of corporate resource allocation and its governance is a concern with the *dynamics* of enterprise and economic performance. Central to the process through which successful enterprises and economies improve their performance over time, as well as relative to each other, is a phenomenon that can broadly be termed 'innovation'. Innovation is the process through which productive resources are developed and utilized to generate higher-quality and/or lower-cost products than had previously been available. In this book, therefore, the concept of innovation is used in a general sense to include all activities that enterprises and economies undertake to deliver higher-quality and/or cheaper products. The term 'innovation', as employed herein, has, therefore, a distinctly commercial connotation. In particular, it is not reducible to technological novelty and indeed, may refer to processes that do not entail technological development.

A relevant theory of resource allocation must incorporate an understanding of the central characteristics of the innovation process. By providing a foundation on which wealth can be accumulated by more and more people over a prolonged period of time, innovation can mitigate conflicts among different interest groups over the allocation of resources and returns: an increase in the living standards of one interest group does not have to come at the expense of another. Of course, a theory of corporate governance should not be exclusively concerned with innovative economic behaviour. The process of adaptation through which firms live off the resources that they have developed in the past is a necessary and important dimension of the economic behaviour of all successful enterprises and economies. So too in dynamic economies firms and entire nations may have to confront the problem of exit from certain business activities. But the economics of adaptation and exit in a world in which other firms continue to innovate can only be analysed within a theoretical perspective that systematically deals with the economics of innovation.

What is striking about the contemporary debates on corporate governance, however, is that the leading theories advanced in these discussions are not rooted in a systematic theory of innovation. The Anglo-American debates on corporate governance have been largely confined to shareholder theory, the dominant perspective, and stakeholder theory, its main challenger. To the extent that corporate governance is commanding increased attention in other parts of the world, the issues are currently being framed in terms that are largely derivative of the Anglo-American debates (see, for example, OECD 1999). Both theories of corporate governance recognize the fact that, in practice, 'residual returns' that cannot be attributed to the productivity of any individual factor are generated by business enterprises and persist for sustained periods of time. Indeed, it is with the allocation of these residual returns that they are centrally concerned. The focus of these theories is on the distribution of residuals, and how this affects corporate performance, rather than on how these residuals are generated through the development and utilization of resources.

The neglect of innovation by both of these theories can be traced to their reliance, for an understanding of the relationship between resource allocation and economic performance, on the dominant methodology and ideology of economics, as embodied in what can broadly be described as 'neoclassical economics'. Neoclassical theory is used herein to refer to that body of economic thought that uses the theory of the perfect market economy, whether explicitly or implicitly, as the benchmark for economic efficiency. That description is a wide net since most of contemporary economics, and, in particular, most of the so-called 'market imperfections' literature, falls within it. The problem with neoclassical theory as the foundation for understanding how corporations should be governed to generate economic performance in a dynamic environment is that it was never designed to deal with the innovation process, let alone the role of corporate resource allocation in that process.

In historical perspective, the overwhelming concern of the architects of neoclassical theory with the analysis of the economics of market exchange was pursued at the expense of the economic analysis of innovation and the productive sphere of the economy more generally. In their quest to understand the economic properties of exchange economies, neoclassical economists developed a concept of resource allocation as reversible, individual, and optimal. The assumption of reversibility means that the allocation of resources today has no effect on the allocation of resources tomorrow. The assumption of individuality means that each economic actor can develop his resources as he sees fit, without coordinating them with the decisions and actions of other individuals. Finally, the assumption of optimality means that the allocation process entails a choice among alternative economic outcomes, given market and technological conditions.

By virtue of these assumptions, neoclassical economics excluded the critical characteristics of innovative resource allocation that have been highlighted in the burgeoning literature on the subject. Indeed, a stylized characterization of the way in which resources are allocated to the development and utilization of resources directly contradicts the neoclassical conception. In particular, economists of innovation have emphasized that resources are allocated through a process that is (1) developmental—resources must be committed to irreversible investments with uncertain returns; (2) organizational—returns are generated through the integration of human and physical resources; and (3) strategic—resources are allocated to overcome market and technological conditions that other firms take as given. These characteristics of innovative resource allocation were excluded from the standard analytical framework of neoclassical theorists for good reason. The problem with incorporating one or more of these dimensions of innovative resource allocation was that they threatened the equilibrating mechanism in exchange economies and, as a consequence, the normative implications of the neoclassical theory of the market.

There have, of course, long been attempts by heterodox economists to introduce one or more of the characteristics of resource allocation that I have highlighted into the framework of economic analysis. The leading theories of economic performance that have resulted from these attempts are suggestive of the critical implications for a theory of governance of alternative concepts of resource allocation. The limitation of most of these theories, however, is that they integrate only one, or at best, two of the characteristics of innovative resource allocation. Yet, it is only by taking all of these characteristics together that one can see the profound implications that they have for the governance of corporate enterprises. On the one hand, neoclassical economists, in assuming resource allocation to be reversible, individual, and optimal, consider the ideal system of economic governance to be one that supports market control over the allocation of economic resources. In contrast, the developmental, organizational, and strategic characteristics of resource allocation imply the need for organizational control.

To date, research on the relationship between the process of innovation and corporate governance has been limited because the leading perspectives advanced in the contemporary debates on corporate governance—the shareholder and stakeholder theories—have largely ignored the requirements that the developmental, organizational, and strategic characteristics of resource allocation place on the governance of corporations if they are to be innovative. In relying on concepts of resource allocation that are, to a greater or lesser degree, borrowed from neoclassical economics, neither of these theories of governance provides an analysis of the economics of innovation. Given its overwhelming concern with the analysis of the economics of market equilibrium, neoclassical theory is a highly inappropriate microeconomic foundation for a rigorous and relevant theory of corporate governance.

As an alternative to the shareholder and stakeholder perspectives, I develop an organizational control theory of corporate governance that can provide a framework for analysing the institutional conditions that support the innovation process.[1] That the resource allocation process which generates innovation is developmental, organizational, and strategic implies that, at any point in time, a system of corporate governance supports innovation by generating three conditions—*financial commitment*, *organizational integration*, and *insider control*—that, in combination, ensure organizational control over the development and utilization of resources. Without governance institutions that support organizational control over knowledge and money, business enterprises cannot generate innovation through strategic investment in organizational learning processes. However, that organizational control is supported by a system of corporate governance at a point in time does not imply that innovation

---

[1] The institutional analysis that forms the foundation for this perspective owes much to my collaborative work with William Lazonick on the theory and history of comparative industrial development. See Lazonick and O'Sullivan (1996, 1997b, 1997c, 1997d).

will in fact occur. The relationship between organizational control and innovation is complicated by (1) the dynamics of organizational control and, in particular, the effect of enterprise development on the integration of strategists with the learning processes that generate innovation; (2) differences in what constitutes innovation given variations in the nature of competition across business activity and within business activity over time; and (3) the dynamics of institutional change.

My empirical analysis of the operation and evolution of actual systems of corporate governance shows how the organizational control theory can be used to analyse the relationship between institutions of corporate governance, innovation, and corporate performance. Given that corporations have long been important players in the advanced industrial economies, and that many of the institutions that shape corporate resource allocation today emerged with the rise of corporate economies, empirical analysis that sheds insight on the workings of corporate governance systems must be historical. The significant differences in systems of corporate governance, not only over time, but also across place, implies, moreover, that there is considerable value to be derived from studying systems of corporate governance in comparative as well as historical perspective.

In this book I focus, in particular, on a comparison of the historical development of systems of corporate governance in the United States and Germany. Given the pervasive influence of the US system as a model of corporate governance in contemporary academic and policy debates, I have undertaken an especially detailed historical analysis of the evolution and influence of governance institutions in that country. That study reveals the value of the organizational control framework for understanding the economics of corporate governance in the US. Just as important, it highlights the serious deficiencies of alternative theoretical treatments of the contemporary US system that have often led to what, in historical perspective, are serious misunderstandings of its essential elements.

For example, the alignment of strategic managers with public stockholders is now typically regarded as a defining feature of the US system of corporate governance. However, in historical perspective, shareholder control over the allocation of American corporate resources stands out as a recent development. For most of the twentieth century public stockholders exercised little, if any, control over the allocation of corporate revenues. To explain how the US corporate economy could have flourished under such a governance regime, as well as to appreciate the limits of a system of corporate governance that concentrated control over corporate resource allocation in the hands of an elite of salaried managers, is an important challenge for any economic theory of corporate governance.

Similarly, the German system of corporate governance, and in particular the role of the major German commercial banks in that system, has often been characterized in various theories of corporate governance in ways that are difficult to support with empirical analysis. Once again, the use of the organizational control perspective as a guide to understanding how the German system of corporate governance evolved, as well as the changing role of the banks and other groups within that system, is a fertile source of theoretical critiques and insights. In the 1980s, for example,

Deutsche Bank, Dresdner Bank, and Commerzbank were frequently characterized as 'patient capitalists' that provided support for the allegedly long-term perspectives of German corporate managers. Yet, in the 1990s, these financial enterprises, and Deutsche Bank in particular, are at the forefront of introducing shareholder value to Germany. To understand the changing motivation and behaviour of these financial enterprises demands a more rigorous empirical inquiry into the critical elements of the German system of governance than, for example, the shareholder theory or the oft-cited 'patient capital' characterization offers.

The comparative historical analysis of systems of corporate governance sheds light not only on how institutions influence corporate resource allocation but also on the foundations for the widespread concern with the subject of corporate governance. As I have already noted, corporate enterprises are central to the process of resource allocation in all advanced industrial economies, and, on those grounds alone, should be central to any analysis that purports to understand how these economies generate performance. Yet, corporate enterprises have long played an important role in these economies. Nor, indeed, are debates on corporate governance entirely new. In the US and Germany, in the early years of the century, there was considerable discussion of the implications of the emergence of corporate economies. In the early 1930s the question of how corporations should be governed to generate economic prosperity once again came to the fore. Debates on corporate governance have, however, occurred sporadically and have tended to be stimulated by changes in corporate behaviour and the systems of corporate governance that shaped it. The contemporary discussions on the subject are no exception to the general pattern. What has contributed to widespread contemporary concern with issues of corporate governance not only in the economics profession but also among policy-makers, labour organizations, corporate managers, and financiers is the reality, or anticipation, of significant changes in systems of corporate governance around the world.

It is, therefore, no surprise that the current debate on corporate governance first raised its head in the United States. It was in this country that, confronted by productive and financial pressures that emerged in the 1970s and 1980s, corporate enterprises began to show marked changes in their strategies towards the allocation of financial and human resources. At that time, as has been the case throughout the twentieth century, a relatively small number of giant corporations, employing tens of thousands or even hundreds of thousands of people, dominated the economy of the United States. On the basis of capabilities that had been accumulated over decades, these corporations generated huge revenues. These corporations tended to retain both the money that they earned and the people that they employed, and they reinvested in physical capital and complementary human resources. Retentions in the forms of earnings and capital consumption allowances provided the financial foundations for corporate growth, while the building of managerial organizations to develop and utilize productive resources enabled investments in plant, equipment, and personnel to succeed.

In the 1960s and 1970s, however, the principle of 'retain and reinvest' began running into problems for two reasons, one having to do with the growth of the corporation and the other having to do with the rise of new competitors. Through internal growth and through merger and acquisition, corporations grew too big, with too many divisions in too many different types of businesses. The central offices of these corporations were too far from the actual processes that developed and utilized productive resources to make informed investment decisions about how corporate resources and returns should be allocated to enable strategies based on 'retain and reinvest' to succeed. The massive expansion of corporations that had occurred during the 1960s resulted in poor performance in the 1970s, an outcome that was exacerbated by an unstable macroeconomic environment and by the rise of new international competition, especially from Japan.

As major US manufacturing corporations struggled during the 1970s with these very real problems of excessive centralization and innovative competition, a group of American financial economists developed an approach to corporate governance based on agency theory. Trained, as virtually all American economists are, to believe that the market is always superior to organizations in the efficient allocation of resources, these economists were ideologically predisposed against corporate—that is, managerial—control over the allocation of resources and returns in the economy. Agency theorists posited that in the governance of corporations, shareholders were the principals and managers were their agents. They argued that, because corporate managers were not disciplined by the market mechanism, they would opportunistically use their control over the allocation of corporate resources and returns to line their own pockets, or at least to pursue objectives that were contrary to the interests of shareholders. Given the entrenchment of incumbent corporate managers and the relatively poor performance of their companies in the 1970s, agency theorists argued that there was a need for a takeover market that, functioning as a market for corporate control, could discipline managers whose companies performed poorly. The rate of return on corporate stock was their measure of superior performance, and the maximization of shareholder value became their creed.

In addition, during the 1970s the quest for shareholder value in the US economy found support from a new source—the institutional investor. The transfer of stockholding from individual households to institutions such as mutual funds, pension funds, and life insurance companies made possible the takeovers advocated by agency theorists and gave shareholders much more collective power to influence the yields and market values of the corporate stocks they held. Institutional investors became central participants in the hostile-takeover movement of the 1980s. The ideology of the market for corporate control lent powerful support to the claim that such takeover activity was beneficial to the corporations involved and indeed to the US economy as a whole. Takeovers, it was argued, were needed to 'disgorge the free cash flow' from companies. The exchange of corporate shares for high-yield debt forced liquidity on the acquired or merged companies. These takeovers also placed managers in control of these corporations who were predisposed toward shedding labour and selling off physical assets if that was what was needed to meet the corporation's new financial obligations and, indeed, to push up the market value of the company's stock. For those engaged in the market for corporate control, the sole measure of corporate performance became the enhanced market capitalization of the company after the takeover.

If the attempts to engage in corporate governance reform on the principle of creating shareholder value had been confined to the takeover movement of the 1980s, the rise of shareholder value as a principle of corporate governance might have met a rapid demise in the US with the stock market crash of 1987. Instead the US stock market made a rapid recovery, and since that time has had the longest bull run in its history. Increasingly during the 1980s, and even more so in the 1990s, support for corporate governance according to the principles of creating shareholder value came from an even more powerful and enduring source than the takeover market. By the 1980s the deregulated financial environment and the rise of the institutional investor as a holder of corporate stocks encouraged top managers to align their own interests with external financial interests rather than with the interests of the productive organizations over which they exercised control. Manifesting this alignment was the explosion in top-management pay, while the other side of the same coin was the shift in the strategic orientation of top management from 'retain and reinvest' to 'downsize and distribute'. In the name of 'creating shareholder value', top managers downsize the corporations they control, with a particular emphasis on cutting the size of the labour forces they employ and on distributing corporate revenues through dividends and stock buybacks. With the cooperation of top corporate managers, therefore, shareholder value had by the 1990s become a firmly entrenched principle of US corporate governance.

In Germany in recent decades the institutional foundations of the post-war system of organizational control have proved to be more enduring than in the United States. Nevertheless various pressures have built up on the German system of corporate governance that are bringing the issue of corporate governance to the fore in policy debates. Some of these pressures emanate from sources external to the operation of the domestic corporate economy, such as the processes of European integration and German reunification. The more powerful pressures, however, reflect financial and productive challenges that are integrally related to the evolving political economy of the German corporate sector, as was also the case in an earlier period in the US. First, growing systematic pressures for financial liquidity are rooted in the rising level of savings generated by the country's post-war economic success, pressures that are likely to grow as the trend toward intergenerational dependence increases in Germany. A second formidable challenge to the German system of organizational control is that posed by international competition, especially emanating from Japan. The Japanese competitive challenge is fundamentally an organizational one, since it confronts the social foundations on which German enterprises have successfully competed in the past, even in high-quality niches in which they have previously been unrivalled.

The confluence of these pressures has focused considerable attention in Germany on the subject of corporate governance. Some prominent German corporate managers have been calling for an increased focus in corporate resource allocation on 'shareholder value', even if it comes at the expense of social cohesion. The rhetoric of shareholder value, as invoked by German managers, has not gone unchallenged. German labour representatives have, in the post-war period, had a significant voice in the governance of German corporate enterprises and some of them have publicly expressed their disquiet with talk of shareholder value and the ideology of casino capitalism of which, they allege, it is a harbinger. Of course, many Germans, and continental Europeans in general, are sanguine about the possibilities of these types of behaviour taking hold among German managers. And, within German companies, even those that are most strident in their proclamations of their conversion to shareholder value, corporate resource allocation processes are only beginning to be overhauled to accord with its logic.

Nevertheless, it is dangerous to dismiss such rhetoric as grandstanding or faddish. The analysis that will be presented here suggests that the confluence of structural changes in the financial and productive spheres has created the conditions under which a formidable challenge to the extant system of German corporate governance might be mounted. Moreover, the US experience of corporate governance in recent decades is an instructive one. Today the United States is regarded as a bastion of liquid financial markets. Yet, one of the most important lessons that the recent history of American corporate governance teaches us is that, in the face of unprecedented productive and financial challenges to an extant system of corporate governance, 'organization men' can be induced to be, at least with appropriate incentives for self-enrichment, ardent proponents of shareholder value.

Given the motivation for concern with corporate governance it is clear why the subject has attracted so much attention outside of academia. This concern makes the subject more exciting and dynamic than many of the issues deemed interesting only within the arcane world of economics. Yet, the danger associated with the contemporary relevance of corporate governance issues is that intellectual debate is confined within the boundaries defined by dominant political interests. Comparative-historical analysis of systems of corporate governance can, however, serve as an important antidote to such a politicization of the analysis of governance, at least in its worst extremes, by shedding light on the evolving politics of the social systems that shape corporate resource allocation.

Of particular importance in bringing issues of corporate governance to the fore in national debates in the United States and Germany has been the rising power of domestic financial interests. In both countries, financial assets have been accumulating at a rapid pace, partly because these economies have been successful in creating and distributing wealth but also due to the ageing of their populations. There are substantial differences across countries in the nature and timing of these trends, as well as in the way that they have affected the corporate economy, but in both the United States and Germany, they have led to an increase in the pressure for higher returns on corporate securities from those who are fortunate enough to have financial assets.

Financial interests are, of course, not alone in having a vested interest in the debate on corporate governance, although they do stand out for their influence in the global economy today. Whatever the political power of different interest groups, and there remain substantial differences across countries in the politics of corporate governance, as the comparison of the United States and Germany shows, what needs to be kept in mind is the question of whether the popularity of a particular theory of corporate governance, in the popular and the academic literature, is mainly a product of its analytical power and empirical support or rather a function of its acceptability in a particular political context.

Politics also enters the discussion of the relationship between corporate governance and innovation through another door. Throughout the book I will speak of innovation as if (1) what is a high-quality and low-cost product can be taken as an objective fact and (2) it is a self-evidently desirable goal toward which a society would want to develop its institutions of governance. I do so in order to engage, on their own terms, with the dominant perspectives on corporate governance and to show that even if we accept these terms the leading perspectives rest on foundations that bear little relation to the reality of corporate economies. In making that claim, however, I invoke theoretical arguments and empirical evidence that call into question more fundamental claims, especially about consumer sovereignty, that mainstream economists have traditionally relied on to justify the primacy in economic systems of the pursuit of material wealth. In a world in which corporations exercise organizational control over the allocation of resources and returns, and in turn have an important influence on consumer demand and technological options, these claims are much less plausible. I make no attempt to deal with these issues in the current work but they must be analysed in any theory of corporate governance that purports to deal comprehensively with the role of the corporation in the economy.

More generally, my theoretical and empirical analysis of corporate governance and economic performance is not intended to be a definitive statement on the subject. There is scope for much debate even on the issues that I do deal with, such as the precise characteristics of innovative resource allocation across industry and over time. Debates on these issues are needed, as well as additional empirical research that seeks to explore the dimensions of the innovation process and its relationship to institutions of corporate governance.[2] Yet intellectual progress on these issues cannot be made without a common recognition of the importance of innovation in analysing the relationship between corporate governance and economic performance. The contemporary debates on governance have blocked the path to theoretical and empirical development along these lines by neglecting the economics of innovation. The objective of my book is to show the potential value of breaking with that neglect by explicitly linking the economics of innovation and corporate governance in a synthetic analytical framework.

---

[2] For an example of an empirical research project on these issues, see the 'Corporate Governance, Economic Performance, and Innovation' project co-directed by William Lazonick and Mary O'Sullivan and funded by the European Commission (www.insead.fr/cgep).

1

Innovation, Resource Allocation, and Governance

1.1. Introduction

Given the centrality of the process of innovation to the performance of dynamic economies, the types of corporate governance that will promote economic performance can only be determined within a conceptual framework that integrates an analysis of the economics of innovation. In section 1.2, I briefly review the theoretical and empirical research on the economics of innovation to identify the key stylized facts of the process through which resources are developed and utilized in the economy. Specifically, I characterize innovation as a process that is cumulative, collective, and uncertain. In section 1.3 I argue that these characteristics imply that innovation requires an allocation process that is (1) developmental—resources must be committed to irreversible investments with uncertain returns; (2) organizational—returns are generated through the integration of human and physical resources; and (3) strategic—resources are allocated to overcome market and technological conditions that other firms take as given.

In section 1.4, the critical characteristics of innovative resource allocation are contrasted with neoclassical resource allocation, which is reversible, individual, and optimal. The assumption of reversibility means that the allocation of resources today has no influence on the allocation of resources tomorrow. The assumption of individuality means that the allocation of resources permits each economic actor to develop and utilize his productive resources as he sees fit, quite apart from the decisions and actions of other individuals in the economy. Finally, the assumption of optimality means that the allocation process entails a choice among alternative economic outcomes, given market and technological constraints.

That neoclassical economists subscribe to such a concept of resource allocation must be understood in light of their intellectual project to develop a theory of market exchange and its normative implications even to the extent that it came at the cost of the economic analysis of the productive sphere of the economy. In particular, the critical characteristics of innovative resource allocation were excluded from the standard analytical framework of neoclassical theorists, largely because they threatened the normative implications of the theory of the market economy. As a result, the neoclassical concept of resource allocation precludes any understanding of the investment process, which by developing and utilizing productive resources can, if successful, yield residual returns.

There are, however, continuing attempts by heterodox economists to introduce one or more of the characteristics of resource allocation that I have emphasized to a theory of economic performance. The arguments put forward, in particular by transaction cost, Austrian, and evolutionary economists, are suggestive of the important implications of the developmental, organizational, and strategic characteristics of innovative resource allocation for the governance of economic activity. Yet it is only by taking all of these characteristics of innovative resource allocation together, something that none of these theories does, that one can see the profound implications that they have for the governance of corporations. Whereas neoclassical economists, in assuming resource allocation to be reversible, individual, and optimal, consider the ideal system of economic governance to be one that supports *market control* over the allocation of economic resources, the developmental, organizational, and strategic characteristics of innovative resource allocation imply the need for *organizational control* over the allocation of resources in the economy. These relationships between resource allocation and corporate governance are discussed in section 5.

1.2. Characterizing Innovation

There have long been economists who have recognized that innovation is central to the dynamic process through which economies develop, but it is only in recent decades that the economics of innovation has attracted widespread academic attention. There is now an extensive body of research on innovation from which we can glean an understanding of the defining features of the process. What follows is not a comprehensive review of the literature on the economics of innovation. Rather, it is a stylized characterization of innovation, based upon that literature, as a process that is cumulative, collective, and uncertain (see, for example, Pavitt 1994).

1.2.1. Cumulative

By definition, underlying the innovation process is a learning process; if we already knew how to generate higher-quality, lower-cost products then the act of doing so would not require innovation. As Christopher Freeman notes:

The picture which emerges from numerous studies of innovation in firms is one of continuous interactive learning. Firms learn both from their own experience of design, development, production and marketing . . . *and* from a wide variety of external sources at home and abroad—their customers, their suppliers, their contractors . . . , and from many other organisations—universities, government laboratories and agencies, consultants, licensors, licencees and others. (Freeman 1994: 470)

How the economist conceives of knowledge, the way it is acquired through learning, and its use in the decisions that shape the learning process thus has an important influence on his understanding of the economics of innovation. A central finding of the literature on innovation is that the learning that generates higher-quality and/or lower-cost products occurs through a process that is cumulative.

Thorstein Veblen eloquently described the phenomenon of cumulative learning almost a century ago; through the experience of innovating, he argued, the learners accumulate a 'common stock' of knowledge:

The complement of technological knowledge . . . held, used, and transmitted in the life of the community is, of course, made up out of the experience of individuals. Experience, experimentation, habit, knowledge, initiative, are phenomena of individual life, and it is necessarily from this source that the community's common stock is all derived. The possibility of its growth lies in the feasibility of accumulating knowledge gained by individual experience and initiative, and therefore it lies in the feasibility of one individual's learning from the experience of another. But the initiative and technological enterprise of individuals, such for example as shows itself in inventions and discoveries of more and better ways and means, proceeds on and enlarges the accumulated wisdom of the past. Individual initiative has no chance except on the ground afforded by the common stock, and the achievements of such initiative are of no effect except as accretions to the common stock. And the invention or discovery so achieved always embodies so much of what is already given that the creative contribution of the inventor or discoverer is trivial by comparison. (Veblen 1904: 328)

When the learning process is cumulative, through innovation—through the process of generating higher-quality and/or lower-cost products—new innovative opportunities become apparent that are not readily identifiable or exploitable by those who do not have access to the 'common stock of knowledge'.

The cumulative dimension of the innovation process is prominent in evolutionary economics, a literature that is greatly influenced by the work of Richard Nelson and Sidney Winter (Nelson and Winter 1977, 1982). In their book *An Evolutionary Theory of Economic Change*, they criticized the neoclassical treatment of production, which conceptualizes productive opportunities as analogous to a book of blueprints from which economic actors choose technologies that minimize costs at prevailing market prices. As suggested by the blueprints metaphor, neoclassical orthodoxy assumes that knowledge of feasible technical methods is objective, widely available, and useful to many different economic actors, and that there is a sharp distinction between deciding what technique to use and operating that technique. Nelson and Winter contended that 'blueprints' are, in fact, only a small part of what is needed to develop and utilize technologies and that the choice set of production possibilites and the choosing are generally inextricably intertwined. Firms are really only familiar with techniques that they are currently using rather than with those that are potentially available.

Drawing on Herbert Simon's notion of decision-making heuristics, they proposed a theory of firm decision-making based on the concepts of 'routines' and 'search'. By 'routine' they meant all regular and predictable behaviour patterns of firms; a routine is the capability of an organization for 'a smooth sequence of coordinated behaviour that is ordinarily effective relative to its objectives, given the context in which it normally occurs' (Nelson and Winter 1982: 73). They contended that an enterprise could be understood as a hierarchy of practised organizational routines which define lower-order organizational skills and how these are coordinated, as well as higher-order decision procedures for choosing what is to be done at lower levels (Nelson and Winter 1982; Nelson 1991: 61–74). Nelson and Winter argued that a firm would use routines tomorrow that are similar to those that it relies on today; routines are therefore heritable. Organizations 'remember' routines over time by exercising them and the routines which organizations have acquired experience in practising comprise the 'organizational capabilities' of the firm—the set of things that an organization is capable of doing well (Nelson and Winter 1982: 99).

In an article entitled 'In Search of Useful Theory of Innovation', Nelson and Winter (1977) also introduced the concepts of 'technological regimes', and 'natural trajectories' that are specific to these regimes, to capture the cumulative dimension of the innovation process. Building upon these ideas, and drawing on the language of the history of science (especially the work of Thomas Kuhn (1962)), Giovanni Dosi defined a 'technological paradigm' as 'a "pattern" of solution of *selected* technological problems, based on *selected* principles derived from natural sciences and on *selected* material technologies' (Dosi 1982: 152; emphasis in the original). Such a paradigm embodies strong prescriptions on the directions of technical change to pursue and those to neglect; he described as a 'technological trajectory' 'the pattern of "normal" problem-solving activity' that occurs within any particular technological paradigm. (Dosi 1982: 152). Dosi contended that it is 'the paradigmatic cumulative nature of technological knowledge that accounts for the relatively ordered nature of the observed patterns of technological change' (Dosi 1988: 1129).

1.2.2. Collective

What distinguishes collective learning from individual learning are the ways in which learning by individuals in the collective process is affected by the concomitant learning of others and integrated as new, collective knowledge. The vitality of a collective learning process is critically dependent on the creativity and experience of the individuals who participate in it. But through their integration into a process of collective learning, individual learners have possibilities for learning that are not available to outsiders to that process. Relations among people open up new opportunities for learning beyond the individual's direct experience of work and personal creativity. These social relations permit the transmission of the knowledge of individual learners—their creativity and experience—but also its transformation through the conveyor's interaction with the learning of another. Knowledge is thus shared and transformed through collective learning. When collective learning is based on and embedded in the social relations among its participants, it is neither reducible to the knowledge of the individuals or insiders that generated it nor easily replicable by other collectivities. That is, through their participation in a collective process of learning the insiders acquire knowledge that is specific to the social process that generates it.

Joseph Schumpeter, an economist generally regarded as the leading theorist of innovation in Western economic thought, emphasized the importance of understanding how 'the entrepreneurial function may be and often is filled co-operatively' (Schumpeter 1949: 71). That Schumpeter underlined the collective character of innovation towards the end of his life is particularly notable given the character of his earlier work on innovation and economic development; in *The Theory of Economic Development*, Schumpeter's first treatise on the subject, his analysis of the process of innovation revolved around the individual entrepreneur. By 1928, however, he considered that a shift from nineteenth-century 'competitive capitalism' to twentieth-century 'trustified capitalism' had occurred (Schumpeter 1928: 361–86). In *Capitalism, Socialism and Democracy*, published in 1942, he sought to explain the increasingly collective foundations of the innovation process. He argued that the economy had passed into a stage where the 'perfectly bureaucratised giant industrial unit' had succeeded in rationalizing and routinizing the process of innovation, thus rendering redundant the social function of individual entrepreneurship. Technological progress did not falter with the demise of the entrepreneur but it increasingly became the business of 'teams of trained specialists who turn out what is required and make it work in predictable ways'. In 1949, in 'Change and the Entrepreneur', one of the last articles that Schumpeter wrote, he emphasized the need for more research into the collective foundations of innovation:

the entrepreneurial function need not be embodied in a physical person and in particular in a single physical person. Every social environment has its own ways of filling the entrepreneurial function . . . the entrepreneurial function may be and often is filled co-operatively. With the development of the largest-scale corporations this has evidently become of major importance: aptitudes that no single individual combines can thus be built into a corporate personality; on the other hand, the constituent physical personalities must inevitably to some extent, and very often to a serious extent, interfere with each other. In many cases it is difficult or even impossible to name an individual that acts as the 'entrepreneur' in a concern. The leading people in particular, those who carry the titles of president or chairman of the board, may be mere coordinators or even figure-heads; and again a very interesting field of research opens up into which I do not wish to go, however, since this problem is in no danger of being forgotten. (Schumpeter 1949: 71)

Ten years after these words were written, a book entitled *The Theory of the Growth of the Firm* was published which made an important contribution to our understanding of the collective foundations of innovation. Its author, Edith Penrose, an economist at Johns Hopkins University, made the process of collective learning central to her theory of enterprise development. Specifically, she argued that enterprises developed and utilized productive resources on the basis of knowledge generated through managerial teamwork:

Businessmen commonly refer to the managerial group as a 'team', and the use of this word implies that management in some sense works as a unit. An administrative group is something more than a collection of individuals; it is a collection of individuals who have had experience working together, for only in this way can 'teamwork' be developed. Existing managerial personnel provide services that cannot be provided by personnel newly hired from outside the firm, not only because they make up the administrative organisation which cannot be expanded except by their own actions, but also because the experience they gain from working within the firm and with each other enables them to provide services that are uniquely valuable for the operations of the particular group with which they are associated. (Penrose 1959: 46)

A central analytical distinction in Penrose's work is that between productive resources and the services that they yield. 'Resource' is the collective term for a bundle of potential services and it can generally be defined independently of its use: 'it is never the *resources* themselves that are the "inputs" in the production process but only the *services* that resources can render' (Penrose 1959: 25; emphasis in original). The services yielded by resources are a function of the manner in which they are used and/or the combination of other resources with which they are used. In particular, Penrose argued, the productive services that resources yield in use in the enterprise are a function of the experience and knowledge accumulated by the collectivity that manages the enterprise. Managerial services are the only type of productive services that every firm, as an administrative organization, uses, and since managers determine how productive resources are allocated among different uses their experience influences the services that all resources render.

Planning the activities of the firm, and in particular the new opportunities that it is to undertake, requires, in Penrose's words, 'the co-operation of many individuals who have confidence in each other, and this, in general, requires knowledge of each other' (Penrose 1959: 47). Penrose argued that managers acquire common understanding through the experience of working together:

when men have become used to working in a particular firm or with a particular group of other men, they become individually and as a group more valuable to the firm in that the services that they can render are enhanced by their knowledge of their fellow-workers, of the methods of the firm, and of the best way of doing things in the particular set of circumstances in which they are working. Individuals taking over executive functions new to them will find that many things are problems merely because of their relative unfamiliarity. As executives become more familiar with their work and succeed in integrating themselves into the organisation under their control, the effort required of them [in existing activities] will be reduced and their capacity will therefore become less completely used, while at the same time that capacity will itself have increased through experience and general growth in knowledge. (Penrose 1959: 52)

Experience acquired through managerial teamwork, through the cooperation of individual managers in a social process, is specific to the managerial collectivity of which they are members. The capabilities that managers acquire through the experience of working together are not readily transferable to different social contexts:

Much of the experience of businessmen is frequently so closely associated with a particular set of external circumstances that a large part of a man's most valuable services may be available only under these circumstances. A man whose past productive activity has been spent within a particular firm, for example, can, because of his intimate knowledge of the resources, structure, history, operations, and personnel of the firm render services to that firm which he could give to no other firm without acquiring additional experience. (Penrose 1959: 54)

The collective experience of the managerial group is thus the basis for the generation of a unique set of managerial services that permit the allocation of resources in ways that improve the performance of the firm in existing productive activities. The experience of managerial teamwork also contributes to the capacities of individual team members to identify new possibilities for action and to conceive of ways in which they could be undertaken by the firm, thus creating unique innovative opportunities for the firm (Penrose 1959: 99; see also 52 ff.):

The experience gained is not only of the kind just discussed which enables a collection of individuals to become a working unit, but also of a kind which develops an increasing knowledge of the possibilities for action and the ways in which action can be taken by the group itself, that is, by the firm. This increase in knowledge not only causes the productive opportunity of a firm to change in ways unrelated to changes in the environment, but also contributes to the 'uniqueness' of the opportunity of each individual firm. (Penrose 1959: 52–3)

In confining her analysis of the learning organization to managerial organization, Penrose restricted the applicability of her theoretical framework to enterprises in which only the creativity and experience of managers are integrated with the collective learning process. Her theory failed to take account of the possibilities for integrating the capabilities of other employees of the enterprise with a process of collective learning because it ignored 'the importance of teamwork and knowledge creation to the organization of non-managerial teamwork' (Best 1990: 134). Penrose did not provide an explicit theoretical rationale for her exclusive focus on managers. Indeed, her bias was most likely a subconscious reflection of the empirical foundations of her theory rather than a deliberate theoretical position; her arguments were informed primarily by her analysis of US industrial enterprises, in which, as I will discuss in greater detail in Chapters 3 and 4, participation in collective learning was largely confined to the managerial class. The limitations of Penrose's analysis of collective learning is that she made the historical and social peculiarities of American industrial development an integral element of her theoretical framework.

In contrast, Michael Best argued on the basis of empirical evidence concerning the Japanese production system and the Third Italy that Penrose's concept of the learning firm must be extended to include the possibility of 'the integration of thinking and doing within the labor process itself' if it is to be applicable beyond 'the archetypal American Big Business' (Best 1990: 134). Similarly, the comparative historical research of another contemporary economist, William Lazonick, is an important corrective to the Penrosian focus on managerial learning. Lazonick argues, like Penrose, that the sustained competitive advantage of an enterprise depends on its success in building a collective learning process that can generate the skills and knowledge required to develop and utilize productive resources in distinctive ways (Lazonick 1991: 83). Unlike Penrose's services, however, Lazonick's organizational capabilities can be based on the learning of other members of the organization besides managers. An important theme in his book *Competitive Advantage on the Shop Floor*, a comparative historical analysis of economic development in Britain, the United States and Japan, is that the strategic extension of the organizational learning process to integrate shop-floor workers as well as managers can contribute to the competitive advantage of enterprises (Lazonick 1990).

1.2.3. Uncertain

To innovate is perforce to confront uncertainty (Schumpeter 1996: 85; Kline and Rosenberg 1986). As G. L. S. Shackle put it:

the businessman is not merely the helpless victim of uncertainty. He is at all times actively promoting it. For he hopes to discover and apply new knowledge, knowledge of natural principles or market possibilities, and in so far as knowledge is genuinely new it must subvert in some degree what has been accepted as knowledge hitherto. New knowledge is in part destructive of old knowledge. The businessman desires, and strives, to gain advantage over his rivals by innovation, by novelty in products or technology. The fact that a field for such innovation exists is itself a proof that business uncertainty is inescapable. Businessmen compete with each other largely by policies which directly create uncertainty. Innovation is the chief means of business success. There is in consequence a compulsion upon businessmen to search for possibilities of innovation and thus to bring about the evolution of society's productive system as a whole. (Shackle 1970: 21–2)

The meaning of uncertainty as it is used in the literature on innovation must be distinguished from that which has become pervasive in neoclassical economics under the influence of the Arrow–Debreu model of general equilibrium under uncertainty. Arrow describes uncertainty as it is used in neoclassical theory in the following terms:

Uncertainty means that we do not have a complete description of the world which we fully believe to be true. Instead we consider the state of the world to be in one or another of a range of states. Each state of the world is a description which is complete for all relevant purposes. Our uncertainty consists in not knowing which state is the true one. (Arrow 1974: 34)

For neoclassical economists, following Arrow, uncertainty is parametric; the economic agent does not know which state of a range of possible states is the true one.

In the literature on innovation, in contrast, the emphasis is on structural or radical uncertainty.[1] Economic agents are uncertain not just about which possible state will obtain but about which ones are even possible. To assume that the environment in which economic decisions are made can be characterized as a set of mutually exclusive but collectively exhaustive possible states of the world (Arrow and Debreu 1954; Arrow 1974)—an environment that is closed and deterministic—is to obscure how, through the process of innovation, new states of the world are revealed and even created. Kline and Rosenberg describe the innovation process as follows:

When one does innovation . . . [o]ne starts with problem A. It looks initially as if solving problem A will get the job done. But when one finds a solution for A, it is only to discover that problem B lies hidden behind A. Moreover, behind B lies C, and so on. In many innovation projects, one must solve an unknown number of problems each only a step toward the final workable design—each only a shoulder that blocks the view of further ascent. The true summit, the end of the task, when the device meets all the specified criteria, is seldom visible long in advance. (Kline and Rosenberg 1986: 297–8)

---

[1] For general discussions of the difference between parametric and structural or radical uncertainty see Shackle (1972); Loasby (1976); O'Driscoll and Rizzo (1985); Langlois (1986).

From this perspective, the future state of the world cannot be defined until it is discovered through the process of innovation (Rosenberg 1994: 53–4). The uncertainty inherent in the innovation process thus unfolds over time as economic agents innovate. As Gerard O'Driscoll and Mario Rizzo (1985) put it in their analysis of *The Economics of Time and Ignorance*,

The dynamic conception of time . . . is time perceived as a flow of events. Implicit in this idea of a flow is that of novelty or true surprise. The individual's experience of today's events makes tomorrow's perceptions of events different than it otherwise would be. As an individual adds to the stock of his experience, his perspective changes and so both the present and the future are affected by the past flow of events. Flows, however, are continuous, and hence the individual's perspective changes right up to the moment of any experience. This renders perfect prediction of the experience impossible . . . Choices made in real time are thus never made with complete knowledge (either deterministic or stochastic) of their consequences. (O'Driscoll and Rizzo 1985: 3)

Given macroeconomic conditions, an enterprise that attempts to innovate confronts two types of uncertainty: productive uncertainty and competitive uncertainty. Productive uncertainty exists because business enterprises that undertake innovative strategies have to develop the productive capabilities of the resources in which they have invested before these resources can generate returns. The learning process may not be successful. Competitive uncertainty exists because even when a business enterprise is successful in generating a product that is higher quality and/or lower cost than it had previously been capable of producing, it may not gain competitive advantage and generate returns, because a competitor, pursuing an alternative approach to innovation, may be even more successful at doing so.[2]

1.3. Innovative Resource Allocation

The stylized characterisation of innovation as cumulative, collective, and uncertain that I have outlined may be challenged on the basis of future theoretical and empirical research. Yet to the extent that it represents a summary of our current understanding of innovation, it can provide us with a foundation on which to consider the implications of innovation for the way in which corporations allocate resources. Many of the decisions that influence the extent to which innovation occurs in an economy are decisions about the allocation of resources. To permit an individual or group to learn, resources must be expended to make available the materials and machines with which they work. Investments must also be made in the development of their knowledge and abilities. Finally, resources are required to give learners incentives to devote their effort, experience, and creativity to the learning process. That innovation is collective, cumulative, and uncertain implies that resources are allocated to innovation through a *process* that is, at once, (1) developmental—resources must be committed to irreversible investments with uncertain returns; (2) organizational—returns are

---

[2] The terminology of 'productive' and 'competitive' uncertainty comes from Lazonick (1991: 199–202). A similar distinction, between technological and market uncertainty, is made in Freeman (1974).

generated through the integration of human and physical resources; and (3) strategic—resources are allocated to overcome market and technological conditions that other firms take as given.

1.3.1. *Developmental*

The cumulative and uncertain characteristics of innovation imply that innovative resource allocation is a developmental process. That is, it involves irreversible commitments of resources today for uncertain returns in the future. To commit resources to innovation means forgoing their exchange while the learning process is under way. What one learns changes how one conceives of the problem to be addressed, the possibilities for its solution, and the appropriate direction for further learning. The withdrawal of some of the learners or physical resources from the learning process before it is complete may endanger the success of the entire undertaking.

The scale of innovative investment thus depends not only on the size of the investment in productive resources and in the abilities and incentives of learners, but also on the duration of the investment necessary to sustain that process over the period during which learning occurs (Freeman 1974; Kline and Rosenberg 1986: 298–300; Teece 1986; Lazonick 1991: ch. 3; Lazonick and O'Sullivan 1996; Freeman and Soete 1997: chs. 10 and 11). The returns to these developmental investments are highly uncertain and the investments that will result in the development of higher-quality and/or lower-cost products cannot be known in advance (Schumpeter 1996: 85). Given the uncertainty inherent in the innovation process, a failure to generate returns at any point in time may be a manifestation not of a failed innovative strategy, but of the need to commit even more resources to an ongoing learning process.

1.3.2. *Organizational*

In an economy characterized by collective and cumulative learning, innovation and hence economic development cannot occur without social organization, that is, without individuals interacting with each other in groups to achieve common goals. The way work is organized—how it is divided and integrated—within an economy shapes the extent to which, and the manner in which, knowledge is generated within it. Learning is influenced by what a person does—his experience—as well as the creativity with which that experience is shaped through the specification of the problems that he attempts to solve. How work is divided influences the scope that individuals have to learn because it shapes what they do and the autonomy they have in doing it. How work is integrated shapes the way in which people interact in the performance of their work and the working relationships that they establish with each other. The organization of work thus shapes the opportunities for the transmission and transformation of knowledge in a process of collective learning. How work is organized determines the identity of the *insiders*—those whose experience and creativity is integrated into a process of organizational learning—and the identity of the *outsiders*—those whose creativity and experience are dispensable to that process, even though they may supply their effort to the enterprise (Maurice, Sellier, and Silvestre 1986; Lane 1989; Clark and Fujimoto 1991; Jorde and Teece 1990; Best 1990; Lazonick 1991; Lundvall 1992; Funk 1992; Susman 1992; Penrose 1995; Edquist 1997).

To the extent that an enterprise successfully innovates—generates new knowledge through learning that allows it to deliver products to customers at prices which they are willing to pay—it can build and sustain a competitive advantage. Rivals cannot secure the same level of productivity from resources as can the advantaged organization unless they replicate or surpass the capabilities that it has developed. Nor can rivals, without equivalent productivity, afford to reward these resources to the same extent (Penrose 1995; Teece, Pisano, and Shuen 1997: 524–6; Lazonick and O'Sullivan 1996).

If they successfully learn to innovate, business organizations can thus develop integrated structures of abilities and incentives for their participants that cannot be replicated through the market coordination of economic activity. If a competing organization commits resources to replicating the advantages that the incumbent has already accumulated—a time-consuming and expensive process—it will not secure privileged access to specific organizational knowledge. To innovate, the competitor must shape a process of organizational learning that renders obsolete, as a basis for competition, the incumbent's cumulative history of collective learning. One can certainly find examples of innovations that engender radical shifts in product and/or process technologies and render outmoded the previous learning trajectory in that industry. These shifts are, however, rare and are seldom attributable to the efforts of a single enterprise.[3]

That the process of resource allocation is organizational means that there is substantial ambiguity in the relationship between innovative investments and returns. First, given the collective nature of the innovation process, it is not possible to closely link individual contributions to a joint outcome (Teece, Pisano, and Shuen 1997; Alchian and Demsetz 1972). Secondly, the cumulative dimension implies ambiguity in the relationship between investments and returns over time; if a return is generated in period 10 it will not be clear to what degree it is because of contributions made by participants in period 10, period 9, or even period 1.

1.3.3. Strategic

All three characteristics of innovation—its cumulative, collective, and uncertain dimensions—imply that resources are allocated to generating innovation through a process that is strategic. Economic actors who strategically allocate resources are, in essence, attempting to change the technological and market conditions that they face, rather than taking them as given data determined by forces beyond their control. Strategic decisions are thus a creative response to existing conditions. There are, as

---

[3] For a debate on radical and continuous change, see Tushman and Anderson (1988) and Pavitt (1988). For empirical studies, see Miyazaki (1995) and McKelvey (1996).

a result, no objective guidelines for making these decisions, nor for resolving disputes, about the allocation of resources to the learning process. To strategically shape the organization of work in an innovative way requires the visualization of a range of potentialities that were previously hidden and that are now believed to be accessible. In *The Theory of Economic Development* Schumpeter described strategic decision-making in the following terms:

> As military action must be taken in a given strategic position even if all the data potentially procurable are not available, so also in economic life action must be taken without working out all the details of what is to be done. Here the success of everything depends upon intuition, the capacity of seeing things in a way which afterwards proves to be true, even though it cannot be established at the moment, and of grasping the essential fact, discarding the unessential, even though one can give no account of the principles by which this is done. Thorough preparatory work, and special logical analysis, may under certain circumstances be sources of failure. (Schumpeter 1996: 85–6)

Innovative strategy is thus inherently subjective in that it relies on the perception of the decision-maker.

But innovative strategy involves more than one decision based on an interpretation of a particular set of conditions at a given point in time. It is a process of decision-making that occurs as the uncertainty inherent in the innovation process unfolds over time. As a consequence, it is experiential as well as interpretative. The basis for strategic decision-making shifts as learning occurs through the process of innovating. The fruits of learning may, for example, render unattainable the solution that the learning process is designed to achieve and necessitate a restructuring and redirection of the learning process. By contrast, learning may make possible, through the discovery of new means, the attainment of ends that were previously considered impossible.

1.4. Innovative versus Neoclassical Resource Allocation

The dimensions of innovative resource allocation stand in stark contrast to the standard neoclassical concept of resource allocation as reversible, individual, and optimal. The neoclassical assumption of reversibility means that the allocation of returns today has no influence on the allocation of resources tomorrow. That the allocation of resources to the process of innovation is developmental, however, means that how resources are allocated today creates the possibilities for developing and utilizing productive resources tomorrow. The neoclassical assumption of individuality—a prime attribute of the market mechanism—means that the allocation of resources permits each economic actor to develop and utilize his productive resources as he sees fit, quite apart from the decisions and actions of other individuals in the economy. But when learning is collective and cumulative, the allocation of resources and returns to the process of innovation must be organizational; to generate innovation, large numbers of economic actors with different functional capabilities and hierarchical responsibilities must cooperate in the development and utilization of productive resources. They must engage in organizational learning, and they must integrate their skills and efforts to achieve common goals. The neoclassical assumption of optimality means that the allocation process entails a choice among alternative economic outcomes, given market and technological constraints. But the distinguishing feature of the allocation process which generates innovation is that it seeks to transform existing market and technological conditions. The corporate strategies that allocate resources to innovation confront and seek to overcome the uncertainty inherent in the transformation of markets and technologies.

The neoclassical reliance on a concept of resource allocation as reversible, individual, and optimal reflects the primacy of exchange as the key economic activity in neoclassical theory. The bias of neoclassical economists towards exchange as the critical activity of economic actors, to the exclusion of any concern with innovation and the productive sphere more generally, has deep roots in the development of economic thought. With the marginal revolution, and the subsequent replacement of classical by neoclassical economics as the mainstream orthodoxy from the late nineteenth century, the focus of economic analysis shifted dramatically. For classical economists the sphere of production served as the critical basis for their theories of growth, distribution, and value. In contrast, the marginalists took the endowment of productive resources as given and focused on the development of a theory of the behaviour of consumers who traded goods that they possessed for goods that they preferred, that is, a theory of pure exchange. The central proposition advanced in the marginal revolution was that the exchange value or price depended on the marginal increment of utility. If an individual is assumed to maximize his 'utility', and he takes his resource endowment and market prices as given, he will engage in exchange up to the point at which the marginal utility of each commodity he possesses equals its market price.

Although originally conceived of as a theory of market price, the significance of neoclassical theory to the development of economic thought in the twentieth century was that it went beyond its origins to become a theory of the allocation of scarce resources to alternative uses. In the absence of possibilities for the development of productive resources, the only way to achieve improvements in economic performance was through a process of mutually beneficial exchange. Specifically, when two or more individuals can exchange resources that they currently have for resources that they would prefer, without making anyone in the economy worse off, then the efficiency of the economy as a whole can be enhanced. As the twentieth century unfolded the scope of mainstream economic enquiry narrowed to focus on the conditions that promoted the exploitation of all mutually beneficial trading opportunities and that, as a result, ensured the optimal utilization of existing productive resources. To this end, neoclassical economists articulated a theory of the market economy in which the perfection of capital, labour, and product markets was supposed to lead to optimal economic outcomes.

The shift from classical to neoclassical economics thus resulted in the usurpation of production by exchange as the activity that was deemed central to the generation of economic value. Indeed, the early formulations of neoclassical price theory completely ignored production and focused exclusively on the forces that shaped economic demand. Yet, the centrality of production in classical economics meant that for the 'revolutionaries' to succeed it was crucial to extend the model of pure exchange to include the sphere of production. Beginning in the 1880s there was a variety of attempts to integrate production with, or more precisely to subordinate it to, consumption in the theory of exchange (Mirowski 1989: 295, 293–310). The synthesis that, at least in the early decades of neoclassical economics, was to become the most widely accepted of the attempts to generalize price theory to incorporate production was Alfred Marshall's integration of the concept of the supply curve, based on marginal productivity analysis, into the theory of market exchange. In contrast to many of the marginalists, who tended to be hostile to classical theories of production, Marshall seemed, with the introduction of the supply curve, to retain the classical concern with production. Thus, he gave the impression that a reconciliation had been achieved between utility and cost theories. Market price, he argued, was determined by the simultaneous interaction of the spheres of consumption and production: 'We might as reasonably dispute whether it is the upper or the under blade of a pair of scissors that cuts a piece of paper, as whether value is governed by utility or cost of production' (Marshall 1948: 348).

Although it is for his scissors of demand and supply that Marshall is now remembered by most neoclassical economists, he was well aware of the limitations of the 'statical theory of equilibrium' for understanding economic reality:

The theory of stable equilibrium of normal demand and supply helps indeed to give definiteness to our ideas; and in its elementary stages it does not diverge from the actual facts of life, so far as to prevent its giving a fairly trustworthy picture of the chief methods of action of the strongest and most persistent group of economic forces. But when pushed to its more remote and intricate logical consequences, it slips away from the conditions of real life. In fact we are here verging on the high theme of economic progress; and here therefore it is especially needful to remember that economic problems are imperfectly presented when they are treated as problems of statical equilibrium, and not of organic growth. For though the statical treatment alone can give us definiteness and precision of thought, and is therefore a necessary introduction to a more philosophic treatment of society as an organism, it is yet only an introduction.

The Statical theory of equilibrium is only an introduction to economic studies; and it is barely even an introduction to the study of the progress and development of industries which show a tendency to increasing return. Its limitations are so constantly overlooked, especially by those who approach it from an abstract point of view, that there is a danger in throwing it into definite form at all. (Marshall 1948: 461)

Yet, the critical problem with the Marshallian theory of statical equilibrium was that although it purported to integrate a theoretical analysis of the production process, it could not deal with certain dimensions of the process of production that seemed empirically important. The problems of 'reconciling process and equilibrium', as Brian Loasby put it, sparked a vigorous debate among post-Marshallians in the years after their master's death in 1923 (Loasby 1989: 61). Their discussion focused, in particular, on the inconsistency between increasing and/or diminishing returns and the theory of statical equilibrium.

In his famous 1926 article, 'The Laws of Returns under Competitive Conditions', Piero Sraffa brought the debate to a head when he laid out these problems with Marshallian analysis and suggested two ways out of the dilemma. One option was to abandon the assumption of perfect competition and assume that firms can set prices within margins, or as Sraffa put it, to turn to the theory of monopoly. Alternatively, economists could save the theory of prices by abandoning Marshall's partial equilibrium for Walras's general equilibrium framework. Increasing returns would then have to be assumed away if equilibrium prices were to be achieved.

Joan Robinson followed Sraffa's first suggestion with the publication of her *Economics of Imperfect Competition* in 1933; in it she referred to Sraffa's article 'as the fount from which my work flows, for the chief aim of this book is to attempt to carry out his pregnant suggestion that the whole theory of value should be treated in terms of monopoly analysis' (Robinson 1933: p. xiii). In doing so she did not abandon Marshallian static equilibrium but rather attempted to make 'the economics of imperfect competition' consistent with it by invoking the concept of the 'optimum size of firms'. She borrowed this idea from E. A. G. Robinson, who argued in *The Structure of Competitive Industry*, first published in 1931, that, with increases in the firm's output, internal economies of scale would give way to internal diseconomies of scale because of a managerial limit (Robinson 1931: ch. 3). The constraint imposed by the managerial limit and the increasing costs that resulted for firms beyond a certain scale—depicted in the familiar U-shaped cost curve—meant that even when conditions in the product markets are imperfect the competitive system could be in equilibrium. From the 1930s the U-shaped cost curve became a central element of the orthodox treatment of the firm among students of partial equilibrium analysis.

Yet, the equilibrium that the introduction of the U-shaped cost curve allowed did not prove very attractive to many neoclassical economists, because it lacked the precise properties claimed earlier for the perfectly competitive process. In the words of Phyllis Deane:

[Joan Robinson's theory] blew a great hole in the normative implications of neo-classical analysis by showing that the natural tendencies of the market do not inevitably lead to an optimal distribution of scarce resources. The notions of consumer's sovereignty and maximum productivity which could be attached to analyses based on the assumption of perfect competition sat uneasily in an analysis based on the contrived variety of products in an imperfectly competitive market. (Deane 1978: 153)

As a result, even as polite a reconciliation of demand and supply as Joan Robinson's could not satisfy mainstream neoclassical economists.[4] Ruder suggestions by those concerned with the process of economic development, such as Allyn Young, Joseph Schumpeter, and Nicholas Kaldor—all of whom argued that it was statical equilibrium theory that should be dumped or at least pushed to the sidelines in

---

[4] It was only later that Joan Robinson declared that she had taken a 'wrong turning' in analysing the economics of imperfect competition on the basis of static assumptions. It would have been more fruitful, she later contended, to build on Marshall's theory of economic development. See 'Joan Robinson's "Wrong Turning"', Ch. 5 in Loasby (1989).

economics—proved even less palatable. The leading neoclassical theorists instead marched down the second of Sraffa's suggested avenues. If increasing returns posed a problem for perfect competition and the optimality conditions that it implied, then increasing returns would have to go!

The formalization of economic theory that took place in the decades following World War II was based on Walrasian, not Marshallian, theory. Whereas Marshall attempted to integrate a theory of exchange with one of production by exploring the costs of production which lie behind the supply curve, in Walrasian general equilibrium theory all economic activity was collapsed into exchange. Since increasing returns were incompatible with the existence of a perfectly competitive equilibrium, they were eliminated from the model by assuming that the production possibility set of firms was convex. Indeed, the concept of a firm had no real meaning in the Walrasian model. Instead, there was a set of feasible production plans. An economic actor chooses from this set the production plan that maximizes his welfare and exchanges inputs and outputs in a spot market to realize his optimal plan.

With the mathematization of general equilibrium theory by Arrow and Debreu in the 1950s (Arrow and Debreu 1954; Debreu 1959), microeconomists increasingly relied on the assumption of constant returns to scale because of its adaptability in theoretical proofs of the existence of competitive equilibria. The characteristics of the process of production were regarded as peripheral to the theoretical apparatus of neoclassical economics. Their consideration was cordoned off into the field of industrial organization, which was, as Mirowski puts it, 'by general consensus an elephant's graveyard of little theoretical consequence' (Mirowski 1989: 328). The history of the neoclassical treatment of production is summarized well by Pasinetti:

> In dealing with production, whenever anything came to light that was not quite consistent with the model of pure exchange, the typical reaction has been to modify the production side of the picture, i.e. to introduce into the theory of production all the assumptions that are necessary to restore its consistency with the preconceived model of pure exchange. (Pasinetti 1977: 26)

The most important legacy of the subordination of production to exchange in neoclassical theory was the effect that it had on the dominant concept of resource allocation in mainstream economic thought. From the characterization of exchange as a spot, arm's-length, and certain, or at least estimable, activity flowed a concept of resource allocation as reversible, individual, and optimal.

Whatever the virtues of the neoclassical characterization of resource allocation as the foundation for an analysis of exchange (and its merits even for this purpose have been contested by, for example, Friedrich von Hayek and his successors, the Austrian economists), the characterization is extremely confining for those who are interested in the economics of production, primarily because it is inimical to any concept of productive investment. It is the weakness of neoclassical theory in this regard that has been the source of the fundamental controversies over capital, interest, and profit that have reared their heads on several occasions during the twentieth century. There have been repeated attempts by neoclassical economists over the last century to avoid these problems by appealing to some 'self-evident' characteristic of the production process as the basis for altering one of the neoclassical characteristics of resource allocation. Yet, in making these appeals new theoretical problems are created that resemble those encountered by Marshallian economics in the 1920s and 1930s. To take one step toward the reality of the process of production is to take one step away from general equilibrium theory and, more importantly, its normative implications.

Most neoclassical theorists have thus tended to focus on exchange and, in doing so, to confine their analysis to the optimal utilization of existing productive resources. As a result, neoclassical economics lacks any concept of the investment process, which by developing and utilizing productive resources can, if successful, yield residual returns. To analyse the significance for resource allocation of an innovation process that is cumulative, collective, and uncertain is to understand why neoclassical economists have for so long excluded the process of innovation from their theoretical frameworks. Any one of these characteristics alone poses a significant challenge to the normative implications of neoclassical theory. The implications of the cumulative nature of economic activity for neoclassical theory illustrate the general point.

1.4.1. Cumulation and Neoclassical Theory

The challenge that a cumulative process of economic change poses to neoclassical economics was outlined very clearly by Allyn Young, an influential American economist, in the 1920s. In the US during this period mainstream economists were, as in Britain, increasingly focusing on the articulation of a static theory of price determination and less and less concerned with the process of economic development. In 1921, Frank Knight published an influential book, *Risk, Uncertainty, and Profit*, based on his doctoral dissertation of 1916, in which he defined the concept of perfect competition in precise terms and argued that for the purposes of economic analysis a sharp separation should be made between the 'static' and 'dynamic' problems. The static problem was the allocation of a given stock of productive resources in accordance with known wants using existing technology and methods of business organization. The dynamic problem was one in which one or more of the fundamental conditions of the static state was changed. Knight regarded the Marshallian concept of increasing returns as falling within the dynamic area and he contended that it was, therefore, logically inconsistent to use it, as Marshall had, in static price theory. As mainstream economists increasingly assumed away the problem of increasing returns they generally invoked Knight's distinction between the static and the dynamic, and focused on the former rather than the latter.

Young supervised Knight's doctoral thesis but he disagreed with his student on the importance of equilibrium economics to an analysis of economic activity. Young believed that the real challenge for economists who wanted to understand the foundations of economic performance was to analyse the process of economic change. In 1928, when he wrote 'Increasing Returns and Economic Progress', Young contended that to deal with the dynamics of economic performance, economists had to confront both the endogeneity of the process of economic change to the economic system and its cumulative character:

the counter forces which are continually defeating the forces which make for economic equilibrium are more pervasive and more deeply rooted in the constitution of the modern economic system than we commonly realise. Not only new or adventitious elements, coming in from the outside, but elements which are permanent characteristics of the ways in which goods are produced make continuously for change. Every important advance in the organisation of production, regardless of whether it is based upon anything which in a narrow or technical sense would be called a new 'invention' or involves a fresh application of the fruits of scientific progress to industry, alters the conditions of industrial activity and initiates responses elsewhere in the industrial structure which in turn have a further unsettling effect. Thus change becomes progressive and propagates itself in a cumulative way. (Young 1928: 533)

Young argued that, given these characteristics of dynamic economies, equilibrium economics was of little use in studying economic progress and indeed acted as a barrier to its analysis: 'No analysis of the forces making for economic equilibrium, forces which we might say are tangential at any moment of time, will serve to illumine this field, for movements away from equilibrium, departures from previous trends, are characteristic of it' (Young 1928: 528). More fundamentally, Young's emphasis on the cumulative nature of economic change challenged the device invoked by neoclassical economists to evade the problem of economic progress by confronting Knight's basic premise that the static and dynamic were conceptually separate. However, the concerns that Young raised, like those of other economists concerned with the process of economic development, were largely ignored by the mainstream of the economics profession, especially with the formalization of economic theory in the decades after World War II.

It was in the context of the formalization of equilibrium economics that Nicholas Kaldor revived the issues raised by Allyn Young in a fundamental attack on 'The Irrelevance of Equilibrium Economics' (1972) as expounded by Walras and developed by mathematical economists of his own generation, on the grounds that it was 'barren and irrelevant as an apparatus of thought to deal with the manner of operation of economic forces, or as an instrument for non-trivial predictions concerning the effects of economic changes, whether induced by political action or other causes' (Kaldor 1972: 1237). Indeed, he went further to argue that the powerful attraction of the habits of thought engendered by 'equilibrium economics' had become a major obstacle to our understanding of the economy. Thus he argued that 'without a major act of demolition—without destroying the basic conceptual framework—it is impossible to make any real progress' (Kaldor 1972: 1237).

For Kaldor, as for Young, the fundamental problem with equilibrium economics was that it could not deal with economic change that 'propagates itself in a cumulative way' (Young 1928: 533; Kaldor 1972: 1244–8), a fact which he made incontrovertible by his clear articulation of the consequences of abandoning the axiom of constant returns to scale and dealing with the reality of 'endogenous and cumulative change':

When every change in the use of resources—every reorganisation of productive activities—creates the opportunity for a further change *which would not have existed otherwise*, the notion of an 'optimum' allocation of resources—when every particular resource makes as great or greater contribution to output in its actual use as in any alternative use—becomes a meaningless and contradictory notion: the pattern of the use of resources at any one time can be no more than a link in the chain of an unending sequence and the very distinction, vital to equilibrium economics, between resource-creation and resource-allocation loses its validity. The whole view of the economic process as a medium for the 'allocation of scarce means between alternative uses' falls apart—except perhaps for the consideration of short-run problems, where the framework of social organisation and the distribution of the major part of available 'resources,' such as durable equipment and trained or educated labour, can be treated as given as a heritage of the past, and the effects of current decisions on future development are ignored. (Kaldor 1972: 1245–6; emphasis in original)

Yet, Kaldor's arguments, forceful as they were, suffered a similar fate among mainstream economists to those of Young. In seeking to explain the neglect by neoclassical economists of the issues raised by Kaldor it is notable that in a recent introduction to a book on *The Return to Increasing Returns* James Buchanan did not question their relevance to an understanding of real economies. To the contrary, he welcomed recent attempts to incorporate increasing returns in economic models. Buchanan sought to account for the 'oversight' by mainstream economists of Kaldor's critique of equilibrium economics on political grounds, although the guilty party in his account would seem to have been Kaldor rather than those who ignored him![5] Yet, in light of the historical development of neoclassical theory, this explanation seems insufficient because it does not account for the neglect of Young's critique. Young was perhaps the most respected neoclassical economist of his generation and while his politics may have been somewhat to the left of Buchanan's, that still left him closer to Samuelson than to Kaldor. The real problem with these arguments was not their source so much as their implications for the entire framework of neoclassical theory. It was surely the challenge that endogenous and cumulative change posed to the bedrock of the neoclassical analysis of economic performance, as well as the normative implications that derived from it, that made it so unpalatable to mainstream economists.

1.4.2. *Alternative Concepts of Resource Allocation*

There continues to be dissatisfaction among economists with the neoclassical concept of resource allocation as the basis for analysing the performance of real economies. Whereas the focus by Young and Kaldor on cumulative change led them to a

---

[5] 'Kaldor's influence did not, however, extend much beyond the boundaries of Cambridge itself. This fact is, I think, explained by the complexities introduced by the entanglements that arise when ideological commitment is seen to be directing inquiry and analysis. Kaldor lived and worked through the decades when the whole neoclassical enterprise was interpreted by many socialist scholars to be little more than an elaborated defense or apology for capitalist economic organization. And Kaldor himself seemed to be more interested in undermining the normative implications of neoclassical economic theory than he was in working out the analysis itself, divorced from those implications' (Buchanan 1994: 8).

particular concern with the developmental aspect of resource allocation, other economists have focused on the other dimensions of innovative resource allocation that I have emphasized (see Table 1.1). The strategic and organizational dimensions of resource allocation prove just as problematic for neoclassical theory as cumulativeness, even when their normative implications are considered in isolation from one another, but especially when they are considered together.

In industrial organization, for example, the dominant theoretical framework in use after the war was the structure–conduct–performance (S–C–P) analysis, in which the performance of firms was deemed to be a function of their conduct, which was in turn shaped by the industrial structure in which they operated. The S–C–P model assumed the existence of market imperfections, such as barriers to entry, in an attempt to provide more realistic accounts of industrial organization than the perfectly competitive model. Nevertheless, these imperfections were regarded as exogenously determined. In particular, since business enterprises could not influence the structure in which they operated through the strategic allocation of resources, traditional industrial organization (IO) economics remained close to the spirit of neoclassical resource allocation.

The introduction of game-theoretic methods to IO, however, led to a major reorientation of the field and, in particular, to an emphasis on the possibilities for strategic action by firms to alter the industrial structure in which they operated. Game-theoretic models of strategic action in IO generally invoked some 'market imperfection' or 'market failure' to allow for the possibility of strategic action. In many cases, these assumptions implied some appeal to other dimensions of resource allocation, such as irreversibility and indivisibility (Antonelli 1997), that are close to the developmental and organizational characteristics which I have highlighted (Antonelli 1997). Yet these characteristics were generally introduced in an opportunistic way, depending on the problem to which any particular model was addressed, leading to a lack of consistency in the treatment of resource allocation from one model to another. Moreover, when these characteristics were introduced they were usually treated as separable from strategic decision-making; they were not integrated into a holistic treatment of resource allocation in which, for example, the strategy and organization of an enterprise were interdependent.

The failure to develop a concept of resource allocation that was fundamentally dif-

TABLE 1.1 Alternative Concepts of Resource Allocation

	Developmental	Organizational	Strategic
Neoclassical	No	No	No
Young/Kaldor	Yes	No	No
Game-theoretic IO	No	No	Yes
Transaction cost	No	Yes	No
Austrians	Yes/No	No	Yes
Evolutionary	Yes	Yes	No

ferent from that which informed neoclassical theory is what accounted for the tendency of these models to fall back on the theory of the market economy as the benchmark for superior economic performance. In this theory, perfect markets allocate scarce resources to their optimal uses. The invocation of the 'perfect' market economy as the ideal form of economic organization had the effect of distorting economists' understanding of the organization of dynamic economies. From the perspective of innovation, the most critical 'market imperfections' that conventional economists cite—imperfections in financial markets, labour markets, and product markets—may not be imperfections at all but rather improvements in social organization that foster technological innovation and economic development (Lazonick and O'Sullivan 1996).

Three schools of economic thought—transaction cost, Austrian, and evolutionary economics—have attempted to make a sharper break with neoclassical theory than the market imperfections approach. These theories have done so, each in its own distinctive way, both by moving farther away from the neoclassical concept of resource allocation and, more importantly, by abandoning the neoclassical ideal as a benchmark for superior economic performance. There is, therefore, much to be learned from these theories about the implications for economic governance of alternative concepts of economic activity and resource allocation.

Transaction cost economics (TCE) was inspired by the ideas expressed by Ronald Coase in his article on 'The Nature of the Firm' more than a half-century ago. Coase pointed out that, notwithstanding the assumption of neoclassical theory that the allocation of resources is coordinated through a series of exchange transactions on the market, in the real world we find that a considerable proportion of economic activity is organized in firms. Why, he asked, is the price system so often supplanted by firms? What is the economic explanation for the existence of firms and what determines which economic activities will be undertaken within firms instead of through markets (Coase 1937)?

Coase contended that 'the main reason why it is profitable to establish a firm would seem to be that there is a cost of using the price mechanism' (Coase 1937: 21). Within a firm, Coase argued, the price mechanism is suppressed because resource allocation is undertaken in response to the orders of the boss: '[o]utside the firm, price movements direct production, which is co-ordinated through a series of exchange transactions on the market. Within a firm, these market transactions are eliminated and in place of the complicated market structure with exchange transactions is substituted the entrepreneur-coordinator, who directs production' (Coase 1937: 19). Thus the 'transaction costs' of using the price mechanism—'the costs of negotiating and concluding a separate contract for each exchange transaction' (Coase 1937: 22)—can be reduced by coordinating economic activity within firms on the basis of the authority exercised by their entrepreneur-coordinators: 'the operation of a market costs something and by forming an organisation and allowing some authority (an entrepreneur) to direct the resources, certain marketing costs are saved' (Coase 1937: 22).

Coase's contention that the firm can be understood as a mechanism to economize on the transaction costs of using the price mechanism is the central foundation of

TCE. The approach attempts to explain the existence of firms in terms of the imperfections of markets and, in particular, in terms of the transaction costs of market exchange. As in neoclassical economics, exchange is accorded primacy as the central economic activity in TCE, the difference being that TCE considers that certain types of exchanges can take place in firms in ways that economize on transaction costs. In other words, in terms of the nature of the activities that they perform, there is no difference in TCE between firms and markets.

TCE is, in its essence, an attempt to understand business organizations in terms of the logic of exchange. Yet, in developing Coase's ideas into a theoretical framework that can be used to analyse economic organization, contemporary transaction cost economists, most notably Oliver Williamson, have found it necessary to appeal to phenomena that are exogenous to the sphere of exchange. Coase argued that the main costs of transacting through the market were likely to rise with the term of the contract but he did not present a systematic analysis of the nature and origins of transaction costs. Williamson, in contrast, has developed a typology based on transactional attributes to explain the sources of transaction costs and the way in which they differ across different types of exchanges (Williamson 1985).

Williamson identifies three critical transactional attributes: asset specificity, uncertainty, and frequency. Of these, he singles out asset specificity as the critical determinant of transaction costs and states that 'the absence of asset specificity would vitiate much of the theory's content' (Williamson 1985: 56). Asset specificity, as Williamson uses the term, 'refers to durable investments that are undertaken in support of particular transactions, the opportunity cost of which investments is much lower in best alternative uses or by alternative users should the original transaction be prematurely terminated' (Williamson 1985: 62). The significance of asset specificity from Williamson's point of view is that when transactions are supported by investments in durable, transaction-specific assets, the parties to the transaction experience 'lock-in' effects. Thus a fundamental transformation occurs so that a condition of bilateral supply results from investments in specific assets even if, at the outset, a large-numbers bidding condition prevailed: '[f]aceless contracting is thereby supplanted by contracting in which the pairwise identity of the parties matters' (Williamson 1985: 62). When a commitment of resources to specific assets has been made, Williamson argues, the identity of the transacting parties matters, in contrast to neoclassical economics, where buyers and sellers are faceless or anonymous. If asset specificity is absent, parties have no continuing interest in the identity of one another so arm's-length, discrete contracts undertaken through the market mechanism will work effectively, as neoclassical economists contend. When asset specificity is high, however, there is a need for an alternative form of economic governance if resources are to be efficiently allocated. The alternative, Williamson argues, is the hierarchical firm.

The value of the TCE framework, as expounded by Williamson, is its explicit recognition that one's characterization of economic activity and resource allocation, has critical implications for one's analysis of the governance structures that enhance economic performance. There is, however, an important limitation of Williamson's particular theory of governance that stems from his treatment of asset specificity, the crucial variable in determining transaction costs, as a black box. The condition of asset specificity enters the TCE framework as a variable that is exogenous to the various governance structures that Williamson analyses. Yet, it seems more plausible, especially given what we know from the economics of innovation, that asset specificity is generated endogenously by certain types of organizational arrangements but not by others. Indeed, it is arguably inherent in an innovative strategy; innovative enterprises purposefully attempt to generate the condition in order to build a sustainable competitive advantage (see, e.g., Dierickx and Cool 1989). To accept this proposition would require an analysis of the dynamic interaction between asset specificity (as well as other technological and market conditions) and organization, which I have suggested is necessary to a thorough understanding of the foundations of corporate performance in dynamic economies. To explore the developmental and strategic dimensions of the process of resource allocation that could shape such a dynamic interaction would in turn demand an acceptance of the existence of a sphere of economic activity that is fundamentally different from exchange. That recognition would, however, fundamentally undermine the analytical framework of TCE, in which, with its focus on the transaction as the basic unit of economic analysis, it is critical that the transactional attributes, and indeed the transaction itself, be invariant from one governance structure to another. Only in this way can a comparison be made among these structures in terms of their capacity to economize on the costs of undertaking a given transaction (Dow 1987: 13–38).

The failure of TCE to go beyond the neoclassical preoccupation with exchange in its search for an alternative theory of resource allocation is echoed in the approach taken by the Austrian school of economics (for useful surveys, see O'Driscoll and Rizzo 1985; Kirzner 1997: 60–85). Austrian economics traces its origins to Friedrich Hayek's analysis of *The Use of Knowledge in Society* (1945). Hayek contended that '[a]ny approach, such as that of mathematical economics with its simultaneous equations, which in effect starts from the assumption that people's knowledge corresponds with the objective facts of the situation, systematically leaves out what is our main task to explain' (Hayek 1945: 90–1). It was their assumption of complete knowledge that led neoclassical economists to focus on the way in which preferences and means were matched in the economy. For Hayek, in contrast, a crucial feature of economic activity was 'the unavoidable imperfection of man's knowledge and the consequent need for a process by which knowledge is constantly communicated and acquired' (Hayek 1945: 90). He argued that the economic problem which society faced was inextricably linked to the dispersion of knowledge and that the manner in which knowledge is transmitted was central to any theory explaining the economic process:

The peculiar character of the problems of a rational economic order is determined precisely by the fact that the knowledge of the circumstances of which we must make use never exist in concentrated or integrated form, but solely as the dispersed bits of incomplete and frequently contradictory knowledge which all the separate individuals possess. The economic problem of society is thus not merely a problem of how to allocate 'given' resources—if 'given' is taken to mean given to a single mind which deliberately solves the problem set by those 'data'. It is rather a problem of how to secure the best use of resources known to any of the members of the society, for ends whose relative importance only these individuals know. Or, to put it briefly, it is a problem of the utilization of knowledge which is not given to anyone in its totality. (Hayek 1984: 212)

Hayek drew a distinction between scientific knowledge, in the sense of knowledge of general rules, and knowledge of the particular circumstances of time and place, by which he meant knowledge of people, of local conditions, and of special circumstances. With respect to specific knowledge he argued that every individual generally has some advantage over others because of the unique information that he possesses and the fact that circumstances are always changing. He contended that the relative importance of the two kinds of knowledge determines how planning—the complex of interrelated decisions about the allocation of our available resources—is to be done and who is to do it. He identified three alternative governance structures for allocating resources. First, central planning could be undertaken by one authority for the whole economic system. Secondly, competition could facilitate 'decentralised planning by many separate persons'. Hayek also recognized a third possibility, albeit without much enthusiasm: '[t]he halfway house between the two, about which many people talk but which few like when they see it, is the delegation of planning to organised industries, or, in other words, monopolies' (Hayek 1984: 213).

Hayek attached particular importance to the knowledge of the particular circumstances of time and place and emphasized its close connections with the process of economic change. Thus, he concluded, resources had to be allocated in a decentralized manner:

If we can agree that the economic problem of society is mainly one of rapid adaptation to changes in the particular circumstances of time and place, it would seem to follow that the ultimate decisions must be left to the people who are familiar with these circumstances, who know directly of the relevant changes and of the resources immediately available to meet them. We cannot expect that this problem will be solved by first communicating all this knowledge to a central board which, after integrating all knowledge, issues its orders. We must solve it by some form of decentralisation. (Hayek 1984: 217)

There still remained the problem of coordinating the resource allocation decisions of decentralized economic agents. 'The man on the spot' may be familiar with his own time and place but his resource allocation decisions needed to be coordinated with all of the other decisions being made by other decentralized agents. Hayek argued that 'in a system in which the knowledge of the relevant facts is dispersed among many people, prices can act to coordinate the separate actions of different people in the same way as subjective values help the individual to co-ordinate the parts of his plan' (Hayek 1984: 218).

Taking their lead from Hayek, the Austrian economists identify the 'marvel of the market' as the ideal mechanism for the allocation of resources in the economy. Their concept of the ideal market is, however, substantially different from the neoclassical perfect market. Indeed, the Austrians have been among the most incisive critics of neoclassical economics as a theoretical framework for understanding what happens in market economies. For the Austrians, competition is a process of discovery. As that process unfolds, economic agents acquire knowledge that permits the mutual adjustment of their resource allocation plans. Austrian economists contend that neoclassical economics misrepresents the role of the market by focusing on equilibrium states to the neglect of the dynamics of the market process. For Hayek, 'which goods are scarce goods, or which things are goods, and how scarce or valuable they are— these are precisely the things which competition has to discover' (Hayek 1984: 256). Hence 'the absurdity of the usual procedure of starting the analysis with a situation in which all the facts are supposed to be known. This is a *state* of affairs which economic theory curiously calls "perfect competition". It leaves no room whatever for the *activity* called competition, which is presumed to have already done its task' (Hayek 1984: 257; emphasis in original).

Related to the differences between Austrians and neoclassicals in their understanding of markets are alternative concepts of individual decision-making. For the Austrians, drawing on Mises, the entrepreneur is the driving force behind the discovery process that occurs through the market (Mises 1949). The uncertainty of the dynamic economic process and the incomplete knowledge of economic agents continually open up new opportunities in the economy for agents who are willing to learn from the changes in their economic circumstances. The Austrians emphasize the subjectivity of what Israel Kirzner has described as 'entrepreneurial discovery' (Kirzner 1985, 1989: ch. 2). What an economic actor learns depends on his changing experience—on the evolution in the particular circumstances of his time and place—as well as his creativity in perceiving and/or responding to these changes (O'Driscoll and Rizzo 1985: 3).

For the Austrians, entrepreneurial or strategic decision-making cannot be understood as maximizing choice, as the optimal adjustment of means to ends. The latter concept of rationality presupposes some framework of means and ends within which optimization takes place. It also implicitly assumes that the framework for the decision corresponds to the objective facts of the situation and that, as a consequence, it can be defined independently of the decision-maker (Langlois 1986: 225–55). To portray individual decision-making as an exercise in constrained maximization 'robs human choice of its essentially open-ended character, in which imagination and boldness must inevitably play central roles' (Kirzner 1997: 64). The essence of entrepreneurial learning, in contrast, is the perception of new alternatives and possibilities. It is, as a result, interpretative and therefore subjective, rather than 'rational' and objective. The differences between the Austrian and neoclassical concept of decision-making are particularly striking in their treatment of uncertainty (Shackle 1992; Loasby 1976; O'Driscoll and Rizzo 1985; Langlois 1986: 22). As Kirzner put it:

Even though standard neoclassical theory deals extensively with decision making under (Knightian) risk, this is entirely consistent with absence of scope for the qualities of imagination and boldness, because such decision making is seen as being made in the context of known probability functions. In the neoclassical world, decision makers know what they are ignorant about. One is never surprised. For Austrians, however, to abstract from these qualities of imagination, boldness, and surprise is to denature human choice entirely. (Kirzner 1997: 64)

That the Austrians make the strategic and developmental dimensions of resource allocation central to their economic theory leads them to a substantially different understanding of the ideal economic system than that promulgated by neoclassical economists: 'the Austrians understand that whatever social efficiency may be achieved in the market economy [it] is not achieved at all by its participants behaving as if they were agents in a perfectly competitive equilibrium state—but precisely by their behaving entrepreneurially and (dynamically) competitively, under conditions of disequilibrium' (Kirzner 1997: 78). Their exclusive focus on the 'marvel of the market', however, has led the Austrians, like their neoclassical counterparts, to neglect the economics of business organization. The Austrians have thus far failed to integrate a theory of the firm into their conceptual framework.

That they have failed to come to terms with the possibility that resource allocation can be organizational as well as individual stems from their a priori assumption that entrepreneurial discovery, or learning, is an individual process. When learning relevant to innovation is an individual act, as they assume, it can be done external to organizations by the individuals themselves. The individual can then sell the improved skills, machines, or materials at the going market price (which may include what economists, following Alfred Marshall, call 'quasi-rents'). When learning is collective, however, large numbers of economic actors with different functional capabilities and hierarchical responsibilities must cooperate in the development and utilization of productive resources. The allocation of resources to the process of innovation must then be organizational. The Austrians, however, provide no scope for collective learning in their theoretical framework.

The failure of Austrian economics to integrate a theory of the firm into their conceptual framework has been the source of concern for economists operating in the Austrian tradition, and some of them have sought insights on the matter from economists who have attempted to deal with organizational learning by firms. In their influential survey of Austrian theory, for example, Gerald O'Driscoll and Mario Rizzo strongly advocated the evolutionary approach taken by Richard Nelson and Sidney Winter, even going so far as to suggest that Nelson and Winter might have inadvertently laid the foundations for a dynamic Austrian theory of the firm (O'Driscoll and Rizzo 1985).

In contrast to the Austrian economists, the evolutionary economists make central to their analysis of economic change the cumulative and collective action that is undertaken by firms. For evolutionary economists, unlike their neoclassical, transaction cost, and Austrian counterparts, the economic activity that is undertaken by firms is not reducible to exchange; firms can build organizational capabilities that are not available on the market. As discussed in section 1.2.1 above, Nelson and Winter contend that groups of people in business organizations learn how to undertake tasks as members of a collectivity, they practise these tasks together, and they remember them over time. Nelson and Winter assert that much of the knowledge that underlies effective performance in firms is tacit knowledge of the organization which is not consciously known or articulable by anyone in particular. The limits on the articulation of organizational knowledge, they claim, like those associated with individual skills, are rooted in 'the 'whole versus parts' problem of reconciling an exhaustive account of details with a coherent view of the world' (Nelson and Winter 1982: 125). But the limits on the articulation of organizational knowledge are more severe 'because although attending to details is something that can be shared and decentralised, the task of achieving a coherent view of the world is not' (Nelson and Winter 1982: 125). Organizational capabilities take time to cumulate and the returns that enterprises can reap from competing on the basis of their learned routines are uncertain. Fundamental to evolutionary economics, therefore, is the recognition of the organizational and developmental dimensions of resource allocation as opposed to the neoclassical concept of resource allocation as individual and reversible.

Moreover, evolutionary economists rely on a different concept of decision-making than the concept of maximizing choice which lies at the heart of neoclassical theory. Whereas optimizing choice carries connotations of deliberation, Nelson and Winter emphasize the automaticity of behaviour; although the exercise of organizational routines may involve choices, they are often made automatically or instinctively without any awareness that a choice is being made. The knowledge underlying organizational behaviour, they argue, is, to a large extent, tacit. Nevertheless, the difference between the concepts of decision-making in neoclassical and evolutionary economics should not be overemphasized. There is also an important degree of automaticity in the neoclassical model given the extent to which the behaviour of economic actors is assumed to be constrained by the market and technological conditions that they face. Thus, although actors are regarded as rational, with the capacity to make optimal decisions, the actual decision that they make is, in the standard neoclassical theory, determined for them by the given parameters of the decision problem that they confront (Latsis 1972; Langlois 1986: 230–41).

In fact, the deficiencies of the evolutionary characterization of economic action for understanding innovative firm behaviour are closely related to its emphasis on automaticity of decision-making to the neglect of strategic action. A critical insight from Austrian theory, in particular, is that the experience through which the learner acquires knowledge can be actively or strategically shaped. Strategy is, however, a concept that is absent from the evolutionary theory of economic change. Although Nelson and Winter recognized that routines can be changed, the process through which change is brought about is itself routinized, rather than strategic. In an article entitled 'Why do Firms Differ, and How does it Matter?' Nelson recognized the deficiencies of this approach for dealing with the process of innovation. He argued that the original Nelson and Winter formulation was handicapped by its insufficient attention to strategy, by which he meant 'the set of broad commitments made by a firm that define and rationalise its objectives and how it intends to pursue them' (Nelson 1991: 61–74). Nelson thus underlined the need for evolutionary economists to integrate an analysis of the strategic dimension of resource allocation with its organizational and developmental characteristics.

Yet, such a synthesis is difficult to achieve within the theoretical framework of evolutionary economics because of its dependence on the concept of routines for understanding organizational learning. The temptation, as exemplified in recent attempts to develop a dynamic capabilities theory of the enterprise, is to add creativity at the apex of the enterprise hierarchy.[6] Top managers exercise their creativity in selecting alternative routines but those who inhabit the rest of the organization are required to accept and follow orders for routinized behaviour decreed from above. Such an approach echoes the hierarchical segmentation of thinking and doing assumed in models of business organization that have long proved popular in American business enterprises and business schools.

Unfortunately, to attempt to deal with the strategic dimension of resource allocation by adding strategic action to routinized organizations is to obscure rather than illuminate the implications of innovative resource allocation for corporate governance. Specifically, it ignores the influence that purposeful decisions have on who is permitted to learn in the organization, what they are required to do, and how they are encouraged to do so on behalf of the organization, as well as the effects on strategic action of the social relations that strategists have with learners. In short, it ignores the economic significance of the social process through which strategists and learners cooperate and conflict in the generation of organizational learning.

It is apparent from the review of these various strands of the economic literature that alternative conceptions of resource allocation to that which forms the bedrock of neoclassical analysis have critical implications for a theory of the governance institutions that shape resource allocation in the economy. Although each of these alternative theories focuses on one or two of the dimensions of resource allocation that I have emphasized, none of them comes to terms with the implications of taking all three of these characteristics at once. Yet, it is only by taking together the developmental, organizational, and strategic characteristics of innovative resource allocation that one can see the profound implications that the economics of innovation has for the governance of corporations.

1.5. Resource Allocation and Corporate Governance

The implications for corporate governance of a concept of resource allocation as a developmental, organizational, and strategic process as opposed to a reversible, individual and optimal transaction are manifold. That the resource allocation process which shapes innovation is developmental, organizational, and strategic places requirements on the governance of corporations if they are to be innovative. These requirements not only differ from those suggested by a concept of resource allocation as reversible, individual, and optimal; they are, in fact, contradictory to it.

---

[6] For a selection of articles on the dynamic capabilities theory of the firm, see *Industrial and Corporate Change*, 3(3) (1994).

To the extent that resource allocation is reversible, individual, and optimal, the optimal utilization of existing productive resources is achieved, as neoclassical economists argue, in a market economy in which capital, labour, and product markets are perfect. From the neoclassical standpoint, therefore, an ideal system of economic governance is one that generates the institutional conditions that support resource mobility in the economy and that, in combination, ensure *market control* over the allocation of economic resources (see Figure 1.1).

In contrast, that the resource allocation process which generates innovation is developmental, organizational, and strategic implies that, at any point in time, a system of corporate governance supports innovation by generating three conditions— *financial commitment*, *organizational integration*, and *insider control*—that, respectively, provide the institutional support for (1) the commitment of resources to irreversible investments with uncertain returns; (2) the integration of human and physical resources into an organizational process to develop and utilize technology; and (3) the vesting of strategic control within corporations in the hands of those who, as insiders, have the incentives and abilities to allocate resources to innovative investments (see Figure 1.2). In combination, financial commitment, organizational integration, and insider control support *organizational control* in contrast to *market control* over the critical inputs to the innovation process: knowledge and money (Lazonick 1991: ch. 1, 1992; Lazonick and O'Sullivan 1996, 1997b, 1997c, 1997d).

Without governance institutions that support organizational integration, financial

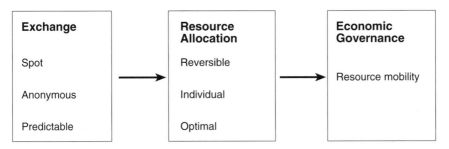

FIG. 1.1 The logic of market control

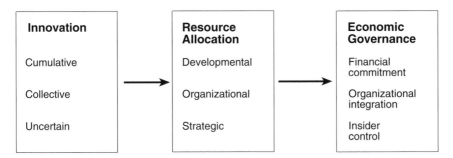

FIG. 1.2 The logic of organizational control

commitment, and insider control, or more precisely, without the organizational control over knowledge and money that these conditions support, business enterprises cannot generate innovation through strategic investment in collective learning processes. However, as will be discussed in Chapter 2, that organizational control is supported by a system of corporate governance does not imply that innovation will in fact occur. The relationship between a system of corporate governance and innovation is complicated by the complexity inherent in the innovation process.

Innovation is defined relative to the competitive environment in which it occurs. Whether certain products are considered higher quality and lower cost, and hence innovative, depends on the quality and cost of competitive offerings. To the extent that the competitive environment differs across industry and over time, social conditions that supported the generation of higher-quality and/or lower-cost products in one industry at a particular time may prove unsuitable as a basis for innovation in another industry at the same time, or in the same industry at another time. To recognize the need to bring the analysis of innovative enterprise into the corporate governance debates is thus only the beginning of the task of understanding the relationship between corporate governance and innovation. A research agenda that seeks to understand this relationship requires comparative studies of resource allocation and the competitive performance of corporate enterprises in particular industries operating in different social environments.

1.6. Conclusion

To date, research on the relationship between the process of innovation and corporate governance has been limited because, as I shall discuss in the next chapter, the leading perspectives advanced in the contemporary debates on corporate governance—the shareholder and stakeholder theories—have largely ignored the requirements that the developmental, organizational, and strategic characteristics of resource allocation place on the governance of corporations if they are to be innovative. These theories do not systematically integrate an analysis of the economics of innovation. Instead, they cling to a concept of resource allocation that is at variance with what we know about the allocation of resources in innovative enterprises.

The limitations of the shareholder and the stakeholder arguments in this regard can, as I argue in the next chapter, be traced to their reliance on neoclassical theory for an understanding of economic performance. Neoclassical economists, as I have underlined in this chapter, have been primarily concerned with developing a theory of value, and thus with the analysis of the economics of market equilibrium. A rigorous and relevant theory of the firm played no role in the advancement of this theoretical agenda. Thus neoclassical economics cannot provide the microfoundations for a rigorous and relevant theory of corporate governance.

2

Transforming the Debates on Corporate Governance

2.1. Introduction

The Anglo-American debates on corporate governance that have taken place over the last two decades have been largely confined to shareholder theory, the dominant perspective, and stakeholder theory, its main challenger. Both theories of corporate governance recognize the fact that, in practice, 'residual returns' that cannot be attributed to the productivity of any individual factor are generated by business enterprises and persist for sustained periods of time. Indeed, it is with the allocation of these residual returns that they are centrally concerned. The focus of these theories is on the recipients of the residual, and how this affects corporate performance, rather than on how these residuals are generated through the development and utilization of resources.

The shareholder theory of corporate governance is discussed in section 2.2. I argue that the theory precludes an understanding of the nature of corporate governance required for innovation due to its failure to incorporate a systematic analysis of innovation, and more generally, of production, in its conceptual framework. Rather, taking its lead from neoclassical economics, as discussed in section 2.3, it regards economic activity as synonymous with exchange and, as a result, conceives of resource allocation as a transaction that is reversible, individual, and optimal. From this point of view, the perfection of capital, labour, and product markets leads to optimal economic outcomes; for superior economic performance, nothing should inhibit the free flow of economic resources from one use to another. The proponents of shareholder theory argue, by extrapolation from the neoclassical theory of the economy, that the ideal system of corporate governance is one that promotes *market control* in the corporate economy. Yet, the virtues of market control rest on assumptions about resource allocation that are inimical to any plausible concept of productive investment, and in particular to any concept of investment undertaken by business enterprises. As a result, I contend that there are serious problems associated with the arguments that financial economists make to justify the claims of shareholders to returns generated by corporate enterprises.

Given the difficulties encountered in providing plausible economic explanations for the returns that shareholders actually receive, it is hard to see what intellectual grounds there would be for demanding even higher shareholder returns. Yet, in their guise as proponents of shareholder theory, this is precisely what many financial economists have been arguing. And since the 1980s, the ability of shareholders to extract higher yields on the stocks that they hold, especially in US and British corporations, has been greatly enhanced. With the increased power of shareholders, some economists and politicians have contended that there are other 'stakeholders', besides shareholders, who have a claim to corporate residual returns.

In the academic arena, one of the most sophisticated proponents of the stakeholder argument is Margaret Blair, an economist at the Brookings Institution, and I focus on her arguments in my discussion of the stakeholder theory of corporate governance in section 2.3. In her recent book, *Ownership and Control: Rethinking Corporate Governance for the Twenty-first Century* (Blair 1995), Blair argues that a critical dimension of the economic process that generates wealth is that individuals invest in their own 'human capital'. To some extent the assets that are developed through these investments are 'firm-specific' and, as a result, those who make these investments bear some of the risk of the corporation's doing well or badly. Blair contends that the governance of corporations should recognize the central importance of these investments in human assets to the success of the enterprise and the prosperity of the economy.

In recognizing the importance of investments that are specific to particular firms, Blair moves away from the neoclassical concept of resource allocation as a reversible transaction. Latent in her argument is a recognition of the importance of the production process. Yet, lacking any explicit theory of production, Blair introduces the assumption of firm-specificity as a *deus ex machina* that leaves her without theoretical support for her central assumption that investments in firm-specific assets generate quasi-rents. It seems plausible, at least in any kind of dynamic economy, that even if firm-specific investments generate quasi-rents at a point in time, these rents may no longer be forthcoming when technological, organizational, and competitive conditions change. Lacking any analysis of these conditions and their relationship to the process of productive investment—that is, in failing to link corporate governance to the dynamics of the innovation process—the stakeholder argument risks encouraging different groups to lay claim to shares of corporate revenues, as has increasingly been the case with shareholders, whether or not their contributions to the generation of these revenues make those returns possible on a sustainable basis.

In relying on concepts of resource allocation that are, to a greater or lesser extent, borrowed from neoclassical economics, neither of these theories of governance integrates an analysis of the economics of innovation. To do so, a theory of corporate governance must come to terms with the reality of a resource allocation process that is developmental, organizational, and strategic. Thus it must explain how, at any point in time, a system of corporate governance generates institutional conditions that support (1) the commitment of resources to irreversible investments with uncertain returns; (2) the integration of human and physical resources into an organizational process to develop and utilize technology; and (3) the vesting of strategic control within corporations in the hands of those with the incentives and abilities to allocate resources to innovative investments. It must also provide a framework for analysing the relationship between institutions of corporate governance and innovation across different business activities, and within business activities, over time. Section 2.4 describes an organizational control theory that demonstrates the implications of innovation for corporate governance. It thus provides an alternative to the shareholder and stakeholder theories for thinking about the institutions that shape corporate resource allocation and their implications for economic performance.

2.2. The Shareholder Theory of Corporate Governance

Advocates of the shareholder view contend that shareholders are the 'principals' in whose interests the corporation should be run even though they rely on others for the actual running of the corporation. When corporations are run to maximize shareholder value, it is argued, the performance of the economic system as a whole, not just the interests of shareholders, can be enhanced. In making this claim, advocates of shareholder theory portray residuals as rewards for critical economic functions that shareholders perform. Specifically, shareholder returns are regarded as incentives for risk-bearing and waiting.

That shareholders have title to residual claims because they are the residual risk-bearers in the corporate enterprise is widely accepted not only in financial economics but among many mainstream economists. As equity investors, it is argued, shareholders are the only economic actors who make investments in the corporation without any contractual guarantee of a specific return. As 'residual claimants', shareholders thus bear the risk of the corporation's making a profit or loss and have an interest in allocating corporate resources to their 'best alternative uses' to make the residual as large as possible. Since all other 'stakeholders' in the corporation will receive the returns for which they have contracted, the 'maximization of shareholder value' will result in superior economic performance not only for the particular corporation but also for the economy as a whole.

It is regarded as economically efficacious for shareholders to bear the residual risk in the corporation. As a class, they are better equipped to bear risk than managers and workers, because they are not tied to the firms in which they hold shares. Consequently, shareholders can diversify their investment portfolios to take advantage of the risk-minimization possibilities of grouping or consolidating different types of risk. As Fama and Jensen put it: 'the least restricted residual claims in common use are the common stocks of large corporations. Stockholders are not required to have any other role in the organization; their residual claims are alienable without restriction; and, because of these provisions, the residual claims allow unrestricted risk sharing among stockholders' (Fama and Jensen 1983: 303). The financial theory of risk-bearing thus hinges on 'a separation of decision management and residual risk-bearing' in the corporation. This separation permits optimal risk allocation in the corporate economy; indeed, that the corporate form facilitates this allocation is the financial economist's key explanation for the growth and persistence of the corporate enterprise with diffuse shareholding.

The risk allocation advantage comes, however, at a cost in terms of incentives within the corporation: '[s]eparation and specialisation of decision management and residual risk bearing leads to agency problems between decision agents and residual claimants. This is the problem of the separation of ownership and control that has long troubled students of the corporation' (Fama and Jensen 1983: 312). The governance problem of the modern corporation, as financial economists conceptualize it, is that those who bear the residual risk—the shareholders or 'principals'—have no assurance that the corporate managers or 'agents' who make decisions that affect shareholder wealth will act in shareholder interests. The costs that result from the exercise of managers' discretion to act other than in the best interests of their principals, as well as the expenses of monitoring and disciplining them to prevent the exercise of that discretion, are described as 'agency costs'.

The central preoccupation of financial economists who work on corporate governance has been the analysis of mechanisms that mitigate the agency problem between shareholders and managers. One possibility is to use compensation contracts to create direct incentives for managers to act in shareholders' interests, but this leads to less than optimal risk-sharing (Murphy 1985; Baker, Jensen, and Murphy 1988; Jensen and Murphy 1990; Hart 1995). Thus, other mechanisms for governing corporations, including boards of directors, proxy fights, large shareholders, hostile takeovers, and corporate financial structure, have been proposed (see, for example, Jensen and Ruback 1983; Jensen 1986; Scharfstein 1988; Jensen 1988; Grossman and Hart 1988; Morck, Shleifer, and Vishny 1989). There has been much discussion within financial economics about the efficacy of these mechanisms for mitigating agency problems in the corporate economy.[1] What has been absent from these internal debates, however, is any discussion of the assumptions that underlie the basic framework within which corporate governance issues are analysed, despite the fundamental questions that persist in economics about the nature of profits and interest.[2]

The basic foundation for the treatment of resource allocation in financial economics is Irving Fisher's theory of investment, articulated in its most complete form in his book *The Theory of Interest* (1930). In Fisher's own words:

The theory of interest bears a close resemblance to the theory of prices, of which, in fact, it is a special aspect. The rate of interest expresses a price in the exchange between present and future goods. Just as, in the ordinary theory of prices, the ratio of exchange of any two articles is based, in part, on a psychological or subjective element—their comparative marginal desirability—so, in the theory of interest, the rate of interest, or the premium on the exchange between present and future goods, is based, in part, on a subjective element, a derivative of marginal desirability; namely, the marginal preference for present over future goods. This preference has been called time preference, or *human impatience*. The chief other part is an objective element, *investment opportunity*. (Fisher 1930: 61–2; emphasis in original)

For Fisher it was the interaction of these two conditions, human impatience and investment opportunity, that determined the rate of interest.

---

[1] For a review of the corporate governance literature in financial economics, and an internal critique of the various mechanisms of governance, see Hart (1995) and Shleifer and Vishny (1997).

[2] In the interests of brevity, I focus only on these issues as they are manifested in the finance literature. They have, however, been the subject of repeated 'capital controversies' in mainstream economics since the late 19th century although they have not, as yet, been resolved. For an introduction to these debates, see Harcourt (1972).

In developing Fisher's theory of the market determination of interest rates, economists in the 1950s and 1960s extended it to include an equilibrium analysis of risk. Many economists, including Fisher himself, had long attributed differences in the returns on securities to the differential risk of their income streams. In extending the Fisherite model, the objective was to develop an explanation of these differences by analysing how the market 'priced' risk. Drawing on the Arrow–Debreu theory of general equilibrium, and the concept of expected utility on which it is based, as well as a host of additional heroic assumptions about preferences and probabilities, it was argued that a linear relationship—the 'market line'—should be observed between the return on a financial asset and its risk, as measured by its contribution to the total risk of the return on an efficient market portfolio. From this perspective, the expected return on a risky security was considered to be a combination of a risk-free rate of interest and a risk margin linked to the covariance between the security's returns and the return on the market portfolio (Debreu 1959; Markowitz 1959; Arrow 1964; Hirshleifer 1965; Sharpe 1964; Lintner 1965a, 1965b; Mossin 1966). Accordingly, in the words of Jan Mossin, one of the key contributors to the extension of the Fisherite model, 'we may think of the rate of return of any asset as separated into two parts: the pure rate of interest representing the "price for waiting," and a remainder, a risk margin, representing the "price of risk"' (Mossin 1966: 774). It is this logic that is at the heart of modern finance theory and, as a result, the shareholder theory of governance; shareholders' returns are compensation for both waiting and risk-bearing.

'Waiting' was a key element in Fisher's explanation of interest as a return to capital; in responding to socialists who think of 'interest as extortion' (Fisher 1930: 51), he claimed that

capitalists are not . . . robbers of labor, but are labor-brokers who buy work at one time and sell its products at another. Their profit or gain on the transaction, if risk be disregarded, is interest, a compensation for waiting during the time elapsing between the payment to labor and the income received by the capitalist from the sale of the product of labor. (Fisher 1930: 52)

For Fisher, that the act of waiting brought forth a return to capital was inherent in the technique or the 'objective facts' of production. In *The Theory of Interest*, he repeatedly emphasized the importance of productivity in the determination of interest to correct a widespread interpretation of his theory as one in which impatience was considered to be the sole determinant of the rate of interest. In a review of Fisher's earlier work in the *American Economic Review*, for example, one critic had contended that

[t]he most striking fact about this method of presenting his factors is that he [Fisher] dissociates his discussion completely from any account of the production of wealth. From a perusal of his *Rate of Interest* and all but the very last chapters of his *Elementary Principles* (chapters which come after his discussion of the interest problem), the reader might easily get the impression that becoming rich is a purely psychological process. It seems to be assumed that income streams, like mountain brooks, gush spontaneously from nature's hillsides and that

the determination of the rate of interest depends entirely upon the mental reactions of those who are so fortunate as to receive them . . . The whole productive process, without which men would have no income streams to manipulate, is ignored, or, as the author would probably say, taken for granted. (Seager 1912: 835–7)

Fisher railed against this criticism on the grounds that he was not only cognizant of the fact that the 'technique of production' entered into the determination of the rate of interest but that it was a central element in his analysis (Fisher 1913: 610). He took pains to distinguish himself from economists who 'still seem to cling to the idea that there can be no *objective* determinant of the rate of interest. If subjective impatience, or time preference, is a true principle, they conclude that because of that fact all productivity principles must be false' (Fisher 1930: 181–2; emphasis in original). Fisher argued that in ignoring the influence of the technique of production on the interest rate their proposed solutions were indeterminate. He considered that the rate of interest was determined by an interaction between time preference and investment opportunity. When asked to which school of interest theory he belonged, 'subjective or objective, time preference or productivity', Fisher thus replied: 'To both.' In fact, he claimed that '[s]o far as I have anything new to offer, in substance or manner of presentation, it is chiefly on the objective side' (Fisher 1930: 182).

Fisher's conceptualization of the determination of interest owed much to that of Eugen Böhm-Bawerk. Indeed, he dedicated his *Theory of Interest* to the Austrian economist (and to John Rae), 'who laid the foundations upon which I have endeavored to build'. Böhm-Bawerk preceded Fisher in arguing that it was the interaction between time preference and the productivity of investment that gave rise to interest. The former he took to be a general characteristic of the average man. To explain the latter, he introduced the concept of the 'roundabout process of production'. Böhm-Bawerk argued that a given quantity of goods yielded a larger physical product when those goods passed through more stages of production, that is, when they were used first to make intermediate products and then to produce consumer goods. The generation of higher productivity was, from his perspective, inextricably tied to the extension of the time during which an investment was tied up in the production process.[3]

As Joseph Schumpeter described it, the critical problem with Böhm-Bawerk's roundaboutness argument was that it 'would, in itself, not account for any persistent surplus from the continued repetition of a process of a given "length," once it has been introduced and the whole economy is adapted to it; it is only the successive "extensions" of the period which would keep interest alive even if there were no other reason for its survival' (Schumpeter 1951: 930). Indeed, it was precisely the limitations of Böhm-Bawerk's theory of interest, as well as other economists' attempts to explain interest within a theoretical framework in which technological and market conditions were taken as given, that led Schumpeter to develop his own theory of

---

[3] For an introduction to the writings of Böhm-Bawerk, see 'Eugen von Böhm-Bawerk', ch. 6 in Schumpeter (1951).

interest. The central foundation of that theory was an analysis of innovation, the process through which resources are developed as well as utilized, and its implications for resource allocation (see, for example, Schumpeter 1939, 1996).

The mainstream of the economics profession did not, however, follow Schumpeter's lead. In fact, notwithstanding the problems with Böhm-Bawerk's theory, a watered-down version of it—a concept of interest as the result of the interaction of time preference with the productivity of investment—became the most widely accepted theory of interest among neoclassical economists, with Fisher as the most influential exponent of this perspective. Although Fisher took issue with certain elements of Böhm-Bawerk's theory, as Schumpeter observed, 'whatever may be said about Böhm-Bawerk's technique, there was no real difference between him and Fisher in fundamentals' (Schumpeter 1951: 232).[4] What is certainly true is that Fisher provided no alternative theory of production to replace that of Böhm-Bawerk. Indeed, he regarded such a theory as unnecessary for his purposes: 'it does not seem to me that the theory of interest is called upon to launch itself upon a lengthy discussion of the productive process, division of labor, utilization of land, capital, and scientific management. The problem is confined to discover how production is related to the rate of interest' (Fisher 1930: 473). But lacking a theory of production, and specifically one that integrated an analysis of the development and utilization of resources, Fisher could not provide an adequate explanation of the return to capital.[5] Only through an analysis of what that process entails, and the conditions under which it succeeds or fails, can we even begin to consider its implications for resource allocation.

Yet, immanent in Fisher's work is at least the recognition that value creation and value distribution are importantly related. In emphasizing the importance of production to resource allocation, his work might well have induced his followers to open the black box of production to uncover the principles of the process through which productive resources are developed and utilized. Instead his epigones in financial economics attempted to nail that box shut. At best, they regarded the productive sphere as nothing more than an extension of neoclassical price theory. At worst, they attempted to colonize production further by asserting that investment decisions in the productive sphere should be made according to the dictates of financial markets (Fama and Miller 1972: 108–43). In both cases their analytical frameworks were based on a concept of economic activity as the allocation of scarce resources to alternative uses where the productive capability of these resources, and the alternative uses to which they can be allocated, are given. By imposing this static concept of resource allocation on their analysis of interest and capital, they thus lost even the

[4] In a discussion of Fisher (1930), Joseph Schumpeter noted that most of it was 'splendid wheat . . . with very little chaff in between'. However, he went on to say that '[t]he criticism of Böhm-Bawerk's teaching on the 'technical superiority of present goods' in § 6 of chapter XX must, I fear, be classed with the chaff. By that time it should have been clear that, whatever may be said about Böhm-Bawerk's technique, there was no real difference between him and Fisher in fundamentals': see 'Irving Fisher's Econometrics', ch. 8 in Schumpeter (1951); quotation from p. 232.

[5] It is surely for this reason, and notwithstanding his distaste for 'naïve productivity theories' that consider interest to express the physical productivity of land, or nature, or of man, that Fisher ended up relying to a great extent on examples of natural production to illustrate his theory.

limited appreciation in Fisher's work of the developmental nature of the resource allocation process.

Modern financial economists are, as a result, truly guilty of that of which Fisher was accused: of providing 'an explanation of distribution as completely divorced from the explanation of production, as though incomes "just growed"'' (Seager 1912: 837). They analyse why it is that portfolio investors would demand a return on the securities that they hold without ever posing the question of why such a return might be forthcoming in the economy. Without a theory of why investment can be expected to generate a return to capital in the form of interest, financial economists give the impression 'that the determination of the rate of interest depends entirely upon the mental reactions of those who are so fortunate as to receive them' (Seager 1912: 835–7). And they compound Fisher's problem by adding another stream of capital income to interest—a risk premium—without ever explaining why a return to risk-bearing might be generated in the real economy. There are, of course, risks inherent in the process of production, but to say that the process is one that is risky does not imply that bearing risk is the key activity involved in generating a return.[6]

How returns to investment are generated within the economy cannot be understood without analysing the process through which resources are developed and utilized. Financial economists make no attempt to deal with innovation and its implications for resource allocation. Instead, following Fisher, and neoclassical economists in general, they take investment opportunities as given. Then, as proponents of shareholder theory, they try to justify why shareholders are entitled to lay claim to the rewards that these investments generate.

Financial economists' analysis of the returns to shareholders is not only theoretically suspect but also empirically questionable. It is to Adolf Berle that we owe perhaps the most eloquent statement of the empirical vacuity of the economic rationale for the returns that shareholders receive. In 1968, in his preface to the revised edition of *The Modern Corporation and Private Property*, the classic analysis of corporate control that he co-authored with Gardiner Means, Berle called into question the justification for shareholder wealth:

Now, clearly, this wealth cannot be justified by the old economic maxims, despite passionate and sentimental arguments of neoclassic [*sic*] economists who would have us believe the old system has not changed. The purchaser of stock does not contribute savings to an enterprise, thus enabling it to increase its plant or operations. He does not take the 'risk' of a new or increased economic operation; he merely estimates the chance of the corporation's shares increasing in value. The contribution his purchase makes to anyone other than himself is the maintenance of liquidity for other shareholders who may wish to convert their holdings into cash. Clearly he cannot and does not intend to contribute managerial or entrepreneurial effort or service.

This raises a problem of social ethics that is bound to push its way into the legal scene in the next generation. Why have stockholders? What contribution do they make, entitling them

---

[6] Indeed, an analysis of innovation shows that the uncertainty inherent in it does not correspond to the diversifiable risk of financial economics. It cannot be reduced through consolidation or grouping but is, in its essence, non-insurable (Knight 1971: 197–232).

to heirship of half the profits of the industrial system, receivable partly in the form of dividends, and partly in the form of increased market values resulting from undistributed corporate gains? Stockholders toil not, neither do they spin, to earn that reward. They are beneficiaries by position only. Justification for their inheritance must be sought outside classic economic reasoning. (Berle 1968: pp. xxii–xxiii)

Berle's observation of the lack of empirical justification for the claims by shareholders to the returns from productive investment is as true today as it was in the late 1960s. To recapitulate, in calculating the expected returns to shareholders, financial economists include two types of income streams: interest and a risk premium. The economic rationale for shareholders' entitlement to interest is based on the assumption that they have financed investment in the productive assets of the enterprises in which they hold shares. Their entitlement to the residual is based on the premise that they bear risk commensurate with that return. Both of these arguments can be called into question on empirical grounds.

That public shareholders invest in productive assets is a notion that actually has little basis in the history of successful industrial development in the United States or any other advanced industrial economy (Lazonick and O'Sullivan 1997*b*, 1997*c*). The stock market has not served as an important source of funds for long-term business investment. Rather, it has enabled original owners of highly successful enterprises to cash out of their firms, while leaving resource allocation under the control of the organizations that have given such ventures their competitive advantages as going concerns. Shareholders in these economies generally invest their money in the securities issued by successful enterprises on the basis of investments in productive assets that have already been made. In other words, public shareholders do not 'wait' until the developmental investments that these companies make bear fruit but buy shares in these companies after they have paid off. In the US, for example, this is reflected in the fact that the market for industrial securities only came into existence at the turn of the century, due to decisions to 'go public' made by a number of owner-controlled companies that had grown to commanding positions within their respective industries since the 1860s (Navin and Sears 1955; Chandler 1977; Lazonick and O'Sullivan 1997*c*). Once a business generates a steady stream of revenues—once it has made the transition from new venture to going concern—the most important sources of finance are retained earnings and depreciation allowances, that is retentions. The financing of investment on the basis of retentions, a practice that was and continues to be pervasive in all of the advanced industrial countries, uses a portion of the surplus revenues generated by previous enterprise activities to finance investment in new activities (Corbett and Jenkinson 1996).

In permitting the separation of asset ownership and managerial control, the stock market, and the portfolio investors who participate in it, clearly play a critical role in the development of the corporate economy, especially in the US, but it is not primarily a financing role. The key contribution of a liquid market for industrial securities is that it allows the link between the preferences of successful entrepreneurs for consumption and saving to be separated from the productive process. That the mechanism of the liquid stock market is the most economically efficient way to achieve this goal should not be taken for granted. More to the point, how shareholders should be compensated for their participation in this process is not at all obvious and certainly cannot be explained by appealing to arguments about waiting.

Empirical evidence also calls into question the risk-bearing justification for shareholder returns. That shareholders bear the risk associated with the corporate enterprise is so widely accepted among financial economists that it is often just asserted as if it were a self-evident fact. However, as Margaret Blair recently observed, it is not at all self-evident. The presence of limited liability and the reality of incomplete contracts for all suppliers of inputs to the corporate enterprise, she argues, renders suspect the assumption that shareholders bear all of the residual risk. As discussed in section 2.3 below, Blair uses this insight as the starting point for her own theory of stakeholder governance.

But even when financial economists have attempted to evaluate their own theories with reference to empirical evidence, especially their theories of asset pricing, the risk-bearing explanation has proven problematic. The total real return—capital gain plus dividends—on American equities exceeded that on short-term US treasury bills by an average of 6.1 percentage points per annum between 1926 and 1992 (Siegel 1994: 20). The difference between the return on stocks and 'risk-free' assets like t-bills is often called the 'equity risk premium' because it is thought to reflect equity holders' compensation for additional risk associated with stocks. But the equity premium has been declared a 'puzzle' because the measured risk of equity returns is not high enough to justify premia of the order of 6 per cent without resorting to unreasonable assumptions about risk aversion among portfolio investors (Mehra and Prescott 1985; Kocherlakota 1996; Siegel and Thaler 1997). When mean reversion—a characteristic of the real returns on stocks but not of fixed income assets—is considered, the puzzle deepens. Although the annual standard deviation of real t-bill rates of returns is approximately 6.14 per cent compared with 18.15 per cent for real equity returns, the standard deviation of annual rates of return on t-bills over 20-year periods is 2.86 per cent, which is greater than the comparable figure of 2.76 per cent for stocks. As Siegel and Thaler observe in their recent review of the equity premium literature,

This analysis suggests that the equity premium is even a bigger puzzle than has previously been thought. It is not that the risk of equities is not great enough to explain their high rate of return; rather, for long-term investors, fixed income securities have been riskier in real terms. By this reasoning, the equity premium should be negative! (Siegel and Thaler 1997: 195)

Financial economists have encountered similar puzzles and anomalies in their attempts to use the risk calculus to account for differential returns among stocks. Expected returns are commonly estimated on the basis of the capital asset pricing model (CAPM). The CAPM estimates the expected returns on securities as a positive linear function of risk as measured by their market beta (the slope in the regression of a security's return on the return from the market portfolio) (Sharpe 1964;

Lintner 1965*a*, 1965*b*). There is, however, little empirical support for the CAPM. Analyses of cross-sections of realized average returns on US common stocks have revealed that market betas have little explanatory power (Banz 1981; Reinganum 1981; Breeden, Gibbons, and Litzenberger 1989; Fama and French 1992).

The response to this anomaly by some financial economists has been to search for other factors in these regressions that have more power. The list of identified variables is now extensive, and includes size, book-to-market equity, earnings–price ratio, cash flow–price ratio, and previous sales growth (see, for example, Fama and French 1996). These factors have been generated by mining the data for correlations, and the 'multifactor' models of asset pricing based upon the relationships that have emerged from these analyses have been criticized, even within financial economics, as essentially atheoretical, because none of the identified factors are linked to existing economic explanations of asset pricing.

There are, of course, ongoing attempts to explain all of these empirical anomalies in asset pricing within the framework of financial theory. Yet, lacking as it does any concept of innovation and its implications for resource allocation, it is difficult to see how such a theory could ever explain the high returns to shareholders that have been sustained for almost a century. More than half of the real returns on equities have been realized by shareholders in the form of dividends,[7] paid out by corporations during a period in which wages have continually increased and output prices fallen. Without an understanding of how the pie has been expanded in the real economy, financial economists' puzzles (or blindspots?) are unlikely to disappear. Nevertheless, the logic of the productive process holds little interest for most proponents of shareholder theory.

The subordination of the process of innovation, and of production more generally, to a theory of market exchange is, as I have pointed out in the previous chapter, not exclusive to financial economics but forms part of a more general trend in mainstream economic thought. The predominant attitude among neoclassical economists is to favour the sanctity of exchange over production. The analytical limitations of neoclassical economics for dealing with production and investment are problematic for anyone concerned with the analysis of dynamic economies but they are especially confining for students of the corporate allocation of resources. In particular, neoclassical economics has no theory of the business enterprise that generates returns that are not market-determined, nor does it have a theory of the distribution of these returns. It thus provides no direct guidance on the generation or allocation of the persistent profits of dominant enterprises, with which the participants in contemporary debates on corporate governance are centrally concerned.

Yet, rather than confronting the challenge of providing plausible explanations of how corporate residuals are generated, proponents of shareholder theory have concentrated their energies on analysing institutional mechanisms that increase the control exercised by financial markets over the allocation of corporate resources and

---

[7] For the period 1921–95 US stocks earned a real compound return of 8.22%, of which 4.84% can be attributed to dividend payments (Goetzmann and Jorion 1997: 23).

that, as a result, allow the corporate economy to mimic as closely as possible the perfect-market ideal of neoclassical economics. They advocate, in particular, the alignment of managerial incentives with the dictates of the markets through the use of stock-based rewards, the use of the market for corporate control to enable shareholders to take over companies and replace managers who do not act in accordance with the demands of financial markets, and the distribution of corporate returns to shareholders to allow the markets to reallocate these resources in ways that maximize shareholder value.[8]

Most neoclassical economists recognize that in the real world markets are not perfect, that the unimpeded flow of resources from one use to another does not, even as a general rule, actually occur. Within financial economics, an influential body of literature exists on information asymmetries and the consequent impossibility of capital markets working perfectly (for a discussion, see Chapters 5 and 6). Yet this literature does not constitute a fundamental break with the concept of resource allocation that underlies neoclassical theory and particularly with the central idea in neoclassical economics that exchange is the key activity in a well-functioning economy. Moreover, the benchmark for superior economic performance employed in the economics of imperfect markets remains the theory of the market economy, in which perfect markets allocate scarce resources to alternative uses. As a result, these adjustments have failed to take into account what we know about the innovation process and to come to terms with the fact that much of what we know, in fact, directly contradicts the neoclassical concept of resource allocation.

2.3. The Stakeholder Perspective

Notwithstanding the fundamental problems with the theoretical framework that financial economists bring to the analysis of corporate governance, shareholder theory remains dominant in the governance debates. Yet, as shareholders have flexed their muscles to demand greater control over the allocation of corporate resources, there have been various attempts to develop an intellectual response in the form of a stakeholder theory of governance. The stakeholder perspective is more often expounded as a political position than as an economic theory of governance. Indeed, many of its proponents rely on sweeping and unsubstantiated assumptions about the foundations of economic success. For example, in their recent edited volume of essays on 'stakeholder capitalism', Gavin Kelly, Dominic Kelly, and Andrew Gamble identify the key challenge for proponents of stakeholder governance as reconciling in practice the competing claims of economic efficiency and social justice; they take it as given that '[i]ndividuals well endowed with economic and social capabilities will be more productive; companies which draw on the experience of all of their stakeholders will be more efficient; while social cohesion within a nation is increasingly seen as a requirement for international competitiveness' (Kelly, Kelly, and Gamble 1997: 244).

---

[8] For a more detailed discussion of these arguments, see Chs. 5 and 6.

It is rare in this literature to find someone who has gone beyond such (rather hopeful) statements to analyse how the allocation of returns to different stakeholders affects economic performance. An important exception is the recent work by Margaret Blair (1995). I focus on her arguments in my analysis of stakeholder theories of governance because she has attempted to embed them in a framework of economic analysis. To concentrate on instrumental stakeholder theories is not to devalue the importance of the politics of corporate governance but to emphasize the importance of a cogent economic theory of governance as a foundation for an understanding of its politics.

Blair emphasizes the need for an analysis of corporate governance that is based on 'a broader range of assumptions about how wealth is created, captured, and distributed in a business enterprise' (Blair 1995: 15). She does not challenge the claim of the shareholder perspective that shareholders are 'principals'; she accepts that shareholders have 'residual claimant' status because she believes that they invest in the productive assets of the enterprise and bear some of the risk of its success.[9] But she argues that the physical assets in which shareholders allegedly invest are not the only assets that create value in the corporation. Human assets create value as well. Individuals invest in their own 'human capital' and to some extent their skills are specific to the firm for which they work. As a result, they bear some of the risk associated with the enterprise:

in most corporations, some of the residual risk is borne by long-tenured employees, who, over the years, build up firm-specific skills that are an important part of the firm's valuable assets, but which the employees cannot market elsewhere, precisely because they are specific to the firm. These employees have contributed capital to the firm, and that capital is at risk to the extent that the employees' productivity and the wages they could command at other firms are significantly lower than what they earn in that specific firm. (Blair 1995: 15)

Because employees with firm-specific skills have a 'stake' that is at risk in the company, Blair argues that they should be accorded 'residual claimant' status alongside shareholders (Blair 1995: 238). In other words, in allocating corporate returns, the system of corporate governance should recognize the central importance of individuals' investments in human assets to the success of the enterprise and the prosperity of the economy.

Blair's analysis of firm-specific skills owes much to Gary Becker's theory of investments in on-the-job training. Becker contended that many workers increase their productivity by learning new skills and perfecting old ones on the job, that on-the-job training is costly, and that the nature of training—and, in particular, its relationship with the activities of the firm that undertakes it—has an important influence

[9] Blair emphasizes this in several places in her book, e.g. 'I do not advocate governance changes that are intended to disenfranchise the shareholders or give total control to employees or to any other stakeholder. Instead I stress that the goals of directors and management should be maximising total wealth creation by the firm. The key to achieving this is to enhance the voice of and provide ownership-like incentives to those participants in the firm who contribute or control critical, specialised inputs and to align the interests of these critical stakeholders with the interests of outside, passive shareholders' (Blair 1995: 22).

on the process through which resources are allocated to training (Becker 1975). Specifically, he argued that the costs of 'general training'—training useful in many firms besides those providing it—and the profit from its return will be borne, not by the firms providing it, but by the trainees themselves. In contrast, Becker contended that it is plausible, at least as a first approximation, that the costs of 'specific training'—training that increases productivity more in the firms providing it—and the returns that it generates will be borne by employers because 'no rational employee would pay for training that did not benefit him' (Becker 1975: 28). The analysis of specific training is complicated, however, by the potential for a 'hold-up problem' between employer and employee. Becker reasoned that

[i]f a firm had paid for the specific training of a worker who quit to take another job, its capital expenditure would be partly wasted, for no further return could be collected. Likewise, a worker fired after he had paid for specific training would be unable to collect any further return and would also suffer a capital loss. (Becker 1975: 29)

To overcome this problem, Becker considered that the costs of, and returns to, specific training would be shared between employer and employee, the balance being largely determined by the likelihood of labour turnover. On the basis of his analysis of workers' incentives to quit and firms' incentives to lay off, Becker concluded that 'rational firms pay generally trained employees the same wage and specifically trained employees a higher wage than they could get elsewhere' because '[f]irms are concerned about the turnover of employees with specific training, and a premium is offered to reduce their turnover because firms pay part of their training costs' (Becker 1975: 31). To the extent that employees pay a share of the costs of specific training, he argued, the wage effects would be similar to those for general training: employees would pay for this training by receiving wages below their current (opportunity) productivity during the training period and higher wages[10] at later periods when the return was collected (Becker 1975: 31–2).

By making the concept of firm-specific investment central to their arguments, both Becker and Blair move away from the neoclassical idea of resource allocation as reversible. However, Becker, and Blair in turn, maintains the neoclassical assumptions that resource allocation is individual and optimal. Investments in, and returns from, productive resources are assumed to attach to individuals, even when these factors of production are combined in firms.[11] All economic agents are assumed to optimize their objectives subject to market and technological constraints that shape the specificity of investments and the returns that they generate. The role of eco-

---

[10] Not higher than their marginal productivity at that time but higher than what they received during the training period, and also higher than the wages of those without this training, because their marginal productivity is higher.

[11] It is this assumption that allows it to link up with an individualistic leftist political ideology. Gavin Kelly, Dominic Kelly, and Andrew Gamble, for example, argue that stakeholding 'contains the seeds of a post-Thatcher, post-Labourist project for the left which has a strong individualist dimension with its emphasis upon autonomy, rights and obligations, as well as a radical critique of the institutional obstacles to the creation of a more meritocratic and just society and an efficient economy. It is the potential of stakeholding to combine an individualist agenda with an active state which makes it a novel and dynamic idea and one appropriate for the times' (Kelly, Kelly, and Gamble 1997: 239).

nomic governance is to get factor returns 'right' so that the individual actors are induced to make the 'firm-specific' investments that the enterprise requires.

In Becker's human capital theory, as in neoclassical theory more generally, optimal resource allocation takes place through the market. Specifically, he argues that the appropriate incentives for investments in training, whether it is general or specific, will be provided through wage adjustments in competitive labour markets. Thus, from Becker's standpoint, market control represents the ideal system of economic governance even when firm-specific investments are taken into consideration.

Blair, in contrast, claims that when investments are firm-specific 'competitive markets are of little use in determining how to allocate the rents and risk associated with those investments' (Blair 1995: 267). She argues that there is a need to supplement the market with institutions that govern how corporations allocate their returns to ensure that employees have adequate incentives to commit resources to investments in firm-specific assets:

if stakeholders are defined to mean all those participants who have substantial firm-specific investments at risk, then this idea is actually a reasonable and appropriate basis for thinking about corporate governance reforms. Far from abandoning the idea that firms should be run for all the stakeholders, contractual arrangements and governance systems should be devised to assign control rights, rewards, and responsibilities to the appropriate stakeholders—the parties that contribute specialised inputs. (Blair 1995: 274)

Blair displays considerable caution in prescribing corporate governance reform— indeed she claims that, at least in the US, 'there is no need for radical changes in the law or the tax code, or in the structure of existing regulatory institutions' (Blair 1995: 324)—since she believes that 'because US corporation law, contract law, and securities law readily accommodate most experiments in new organisational forms, many new governance structures are emerging on their own' (Blair 1995: 277). Nevertheless, she does suggest some specific reforms of the extant US system of corporate governance to correct 'institutional biases in the allocation of risk and control that may discourage investments in human capital' (Blair 1995: 277). Her recommendations include the introduction of mechanisms to encourage boards to act as representatives of all the important stakeholders in the firm, the development of new measures of investment and wealth creation that include investments and returns to human capital, the promotion of employee ownership, and the encouragement of more mobile employee benefits.[12]

The introduction of the concept of firm specificity, while it does not represent a complete break with the neoclassical concept of resource allocation, is certainly an attempt to render it less hostile to production and productive investment. Yet, the concept of firm specificity is a black box in these theories. Becker implicitly recognizes that firms differ in assuming that training can be specific, in that it increases productivity more in the firm providing the training than in other firms. He does not, however, provide any explanation of the sources of these differences or, as a result,

---

[12] For the details of these and other recommendations, see 'Conclusions and Recommendations', ch. 9 in Blair (1995).

any analysis of the source of returns to firm-specific skills. Becker argues that invest-ments in training will be undertaken when investors, be they firms or employees, expect them to generate a return. But he treats the characteristics of different train-ing options—the degree to which they are general or specific—as well as their expected returns as factors exogenous to the economic process with which he is con-cerned (for a critique, see Eckaus 1963).

Blair, at least, recognizes the need for an analysis of what she calls 'wealth cre-ation' (Blair 1995: 232–4, 240 ff., 327–8) in order to make the case for a corporate governance process that allocates returns to firm-specific human assets, but she pro-vides no theory of the process that generates higher-quality and/or lower-cost prod-ucts. She merely asserts that investment in firm-specific assets can generate residuals without specifying under what conditions (technological, organizational, and com-petitive) such increased returns are generated. Thus, like Becker, she fails to go beyond the neoclassical preoccupation with static resource allocation. The returns to all participants (productive factors) in the enterprise—in such forms as wages, rent, and interest—remain strictly determined, as they are in the neoclassical model, by technological and market forces that are external to the operation of the enterprise and human control more generally.

There are economists of innovation who have argued that the characteristic of firm specificity is an outcome of organizational learning processes through which resources are developed and utilized in the economy (see, for example, Penrose 1995; Best 1990; Lazonick 1991). Yet, given the change inherent in the process of innovation, the organizational requirements of innovative investment strategies differ over time as learning within and outside the enterprise develops. Thus the firm-specific skills that result from continued innovation are constantly evolving. Firm-specific skills that were at one time part of a process that enhanced economic performance may fail to do so in another era and may even retard it. To focus on firm-specific skills as the critical dimension of the process of wealth creation is to ignore the dynamics of the innovation process. Linked to a theory of governance, such a perspective may well encourage the entrenchment of the claims of economic actors who have participated in and benefited from wealth creation in the past, even when the integration of their skills is no longer a viable basis on which the economy can generate the returns to meet these claims. That is, the stakeholder theory risks becoming a de facto theory of corporate welfare.

An additional problem with Blair's argument is the lack of clear-cut empirical evi-dence to support her central assumption that employees make significant, value-creating investments in their own human capital. To support this claim, Blair points to evidence from the US labour market that shows 'that employees accumulate valu-able firm-specific skills if they stay with the same employer for an extended period' (Blair 1995: 263):

Firstly, wages typically rise with job tenure by more than they would be expected to rise solely as a result of the employee's increased general experience. These higher wages are generally taken as evidence that the employee becomes more productive as he accumulates firm-specific human capital. Second, job turnover rates (both layoffs and quits) typically fall with job tenure. This is also construed as evidence that employees accumulate firm-specific human capital that makes them more valuable to the firm and the jobs more valuable to the workers . . . The third piece of evidence is the fact that the costs of being laid off are typically larger for workers with more tenure. If workers had only generic skills that they could easily take with them to the next job, labor markets would not be expected to exhibit any of these three features. (Blair 1995: 263–5)

She goes on to argue that

because employees are promised a share in the rents, most economists believe that employees also share in the costs of firm-specific training, perhaps by accepting wages that are below what they might earn elsewhere during the early months and years that they work for a given employer and perhaps only by sacrificing the opportunity to learn special skills and share in the rents in some other enterprise. (Blair 1995: 255)

That higher returns can be attributed to firm-specific capital is, to use Blair's term, construed from the fact that high returns seem to be positively correlated with employment tenure. That employees make the investments which allegedly generate these returns requires an even greater leap of faith; we must rely on the belief that because employees were rewarded, they must have made the investments that generated these rewards. In fact, the evidence is just as consistent with the view that firms made these investments: Becker's model predicted that rational employers would pay workers a premium over the market wage precisely to reduce their turnover. He also argued that firms would be reluctant to lay off workers with specific skills unless there was a permanent decline in demand, which would be consistent with workers with long tenure incurring high costs of layoff.

In truth, Blair's argument seems particularly implausible as applied to US blue-collar workers. The notion that they reaped supernormal returns on the basis of investments that they made in their own firm-specific human capital clashes with much of what we know about the jobs that these workers did in the companies in which they were employed. Labour historians have provided extensive documentation of the process, which evolved over more than a century, through which the blue-collar workforce was systematically excluded from any meaningful role in the productive process in all of the leading sectors of American industry (Montgomery 1987; Brody 1993; see also Gordon, Edwards, and Reich 1982 and Lazonick 1990). Increasingly, as the century unfolded, and certainly in the post-war period, blue-collar workers were denied opportunities to participate in organizational learning processes through which they could develop firm-specific skills; that privilege was reserved for the managerial class (Chandler 1977; Lazonick 1990).

The managers of US corporate enterprises proved themselves vehemently hostile to initiatives taken by some union leaders after World War II to allow workers to participate in the allocation of corporate resources. Once these attempts were rebuffed, American unions did not, in general, challenge the principle of management's 'right' to control the development and utilization of productive capabilities (Harris 1982). In practice, however, the *quid pro quo* for union cooperation was that seniority be a prime criterion for promotion along well-defined job structures, thus giving older workers best access to a succession of jobs paying gradually higher hourly wage rates.[13] It seems more plausible, in light of US business history, that it was this labour–management accord, rather than shop-floor workers' firm-specific skills, that provided the institutional basis on which the dominant industrial corporations were compelled to share the gains of post-World War II prosperity.

The stakeholder theory of governance provides no theoretical basis for dealing with this reality. In particular, the assumption that resource allocation is individual and optimal, and that the firm is, as a result, nothing more than a combination of physical and human assets that for some reason—labelled 'firm-specificity'—happen to be gathered together, precludes an understanding of the economic foundations of strategic control by one group of people over the learning opportunities of others.

2.4. The Organizational Control Theory

The central problem with both the shareholder and the stakeholder theories of corporate governance is that their roots in neoclassical theory lead them to focus exclusively on the governance structures that facilitate the optimal utilization of existing productive resources and to systematically neglect the governance of the process through which resources are developed as well as utilized in the economy. In the absence of possibilities for the development of productive resources, the only way to achieve improvements in economic performance is through a process of mutually beneficial exchange. It is the primacy of exchange as the key economic activity in neoclassical economics, as I observed in Chapter 1, that accounts for its characterization of resource allocation as reversible, individual, and optimal. To the extent that resource allocation is reversible, individual, and optimal, as it is in the neoclassical economy, the optimal system of economic governance is one that generates the institutional conditions that support the free flow of economic resources from one use to another.

The shareholder theory of corporate governance is an attempt to directly apply the neoclassical benchmark for optimal governance to the corporate sphere. Proponents of shareholder theory do not question whether the mobility of resources is an appropriate benchmark for the corporate economy notwithstanding the fact that since the 1920s, if not before, the very existence of the corporation as a central and enduring entity in the advanced economies has prompted a number of economists to question the relevance of neoclassical theory for understanding the most successful economies of the twentieth century (Veblen 1923; Berle and Means 1932; Schumpeter 1975; Galbraith 1967). Instead, they remain uncritically wedded to the tenets of neoclassical theory and, in particular, have failed to go beyond the exclusive concern of neoclassical economics with the allocation of resources given individual preferences and technological opportunities. To transcend the static analysis would be to recognize that what we know about the economics of innovation challenges the assumption

---

[13] For an extended discussion of US labour–management history, see Ch. 3.

that exchange relations are the central economic interactions in a dynamic economy and the neoclassical characterization of resource allocation as individual, optimal, and reversible.

The stakeholder perspective, as advanced by Blair, also conceives of resource allocation as individual and optimal. Investments in, and returns from, productive resources are assumed to attach to individuals, even when these factors of production are combined in firms. All economic agents are assumed to optimize their objectives subject to market and technological constraints that shape the specificity of investments and the returns that they generate. The role of economic governance is to get factor returns 'right' so that the individual actors are induced to make the firm-specific investments that the enterprise requires. In Becker's human capital theory, optimal resource allocation takes place through competitive markets, but Blair argues that when investments are firm-specific there is a need for additional institutional support to bolster the incentives of economic actors to make firm-specific investments in their human capital.

Although Blair maintains the neoclassical assumptions that resource allocation is individual and optimal, she moves away from the notion of reversibility by making the concept of firm-specific investment central to her argument. Yet, firm-specificity is a black box in her theory and its introduction does not allow her to go beyond the neoclassical preoccupation with static resource allocation. Economic agents take technological and market conditions as given and do not act strategically to shape the environment in which they operate.

Neither of the leading perspectives on corporate governance incorporates a systematic analysis of innovation in their analytical frameworks. Rather, each depends on a concept of economic activity that, to a greater or lesser extent, is derivative of the neoclassical theory of static resource allocation. Yet, in assuming that the process of resource allocation is individual and optimal, and, at least from the perspective of shareholder theory, reversible, these theories of governance directly contradict the findings of a large body of research on the innovation process, which show that it requires an allocation process which is developmental, organizational, and strategic. The shareholder and stakeholder theories of governance have thus fostered a neglect of the important implications of the economics of innovation for the governance of corporations. As an alternative to these theories, I put forward the organizational control hypothesis in the previous chapter as a framework for exploring the implications of innovation for corporate governance. I shall now develop in greater detail the implications of the organizational control argument for the theoretical and empirical analysis of corporate governance.

2.4.1. *The Logic of Organizational Control*

As I noted in Chapter 1, that the resource allocation process which generates innovation is developmental, organizational, and strategic implies that, at any point in time, a system of corporate governance supports innovation by generating three conditions—*financial commitment*, *organizational integration*, and *insider control*—that provide the institutional support for, respectively, (1) the commitment of resources to irreversible investments with uncertain returns; (2) the integration of human and physical resources into an organizational process to develop and utilize technology; and (3) the vesting of strategic control within corporations in the hands of those who, as insiders, have the incentives and abilities to allocate resources to innovative investments. In combination, financial commitment, organizational integration, and insider control support *organizational control* in contrast to *market control* over the critical inputs to the innovation process: knowledge and money.

One condition, financial commitment, is that institutions support the ongoing access of a business organization to the financial resources required to undertake and sustain the development and utilization of productive resources until such time as these resources can generate returns that provide the financial liquidity which allows the enterprise to survive. Financial commitment permits not only the strategic allocation of resources to organizational learning, but also the appropriation of product market revenues by the innovative enterprise. How these revenues are allocated, and in particular the extent to which the returns from successful innovative investments are strategically channelled into future innovative activities, is critical for sustaining a strategy of continuous innovation. Only through continued investment can the depreciation or obsolescence of existing productive resources—skills, knowledge, and physical assets—be counterbalanced by the development of new skills, knowledge, and physical resources in order to sustain the competitive advantage of the learning collectivity.

Another condition, organizational integration, is that social institutions support the incentives of participants in a complex division of labour to commit their skills and efforts to the pursuit of the goals of enterprises rather than selling their human capital on the open market. To some extent the collective and cumulative character of the learning process constrains individuals to commit their skills to the investing organization. In addition, however, the prospects of sharing in the gains of successful innovation by the investing organization can lead even mobile participants to forgo the lure of the market and remain committed to the pursuit of organizational goals.

The final condition, insider control, ensures that control over the allocation of corporate resources and returns is in the hands of decision-makers who are integrated with the learning process that generates innovation. Innovative resource allocation is strategic and, therefore, interpretative and experiential, so decision-makers must have control of resources if they are to commit them to a developmental process in accordance with their evaluation of the problems and possibilities of alternative learning strategies. They also require control in order to keep resources committed to the innovative strategy until the learning process has generated the higher-quality, lower-cost products that enable the investment strategy to reap returns. Thus, inherent in the process of innovation, in the need to commit resources to undertake it and the uncertainty of returns from innovative investments, is a need for control of resources by the decision-makers who shape the innovative process (Schumpeter 1996; Lazonick and O'Sullivan 1996).

If those who exercise control over resources are to have the abilities and incentives to make innovative investments, they must be integrated with the organization that generates learning and innovation. Strategists must be aware of what the learning process is generating if, in shaping or reshaping it, they are to take account of the opportunities for, and threats to, innovative success that learning reveals. When the basis for the generation and transmission of learning is an organizational process, strategic decision-makers need to be integrated into the network of relations that underlies it; that is, they must be insiders to the learning process to allow strategy and learning to interact in the process of innovation. When strategists are members of the learning collectivity, they can become privy to some of the knowledge that the collectivity generates, and can use it as a basis for organizing the work that members of the collectivity undertake. The integration of strategy and learning facilitates a developmental interaction of strategy and learning in which strategic decisions actively shape the direction and structure of learning and the knowledge continually generated through learning informs strategy.

The integration of strategic decision-makers with the organizational learning process enhances not only the abilities of strategists to develop innovative investment strategies, but also their incentives to do so, because they see their own goals as being furthered through investment in a learning process that is both collective and cumulative. When strategists are insiders to the learning process that sustains innovation, the value of their learning is specific to the collectivity that generates it. The innovative success of that collectivity therefore enhances the strategists' own success. There is, in contrast, no systematic basis for ensuring that outsiders to the organizational learning process will have the incentives and abilities to promote innovation. To the extent that they exercise strategic control—be they managers within the enterprise, financial shareholders, or other stakeholders—they are likely to pose a threat to the ongoing innovative success of the enterprise.

2.4.2. Organizational Control and Innovation

Without governance institutions that support organizational integration, financial commitment, and insider control, or more precisely, without the organizational control over knowledge and money that these conditions support, business enterprises cannot generate innovation through strategic investment in cumulative and collective learning processes. However, that organizational control is supported by a system of corporate governance does not imply that innovation will in fact occur, because the relationship between organizational control and innovation is an evolving one that is influenced by three types of dynamics. First, the relationship between corporate governance and innovation is complicated by the dynamics of organizational control and, in particular, by the effect of enterprise development on the integration of strategists with the learning processes that generate innovation. Secondly, the relationship is influenced by the nature of competition, and, specifically, by variations in the investment strategies and organizational learning that generate innovation across business activity and, within business activity, over time. Finally, it is complicated by the dynamics of institutional change.

The Dynamics of Organizational Control   To the extent that an enterprise innovates it can build a competitive advantage and thus appropriate supernormal profits. How returns from innovative investments are distributed and, in particular, the extent to which they are reinvested in the incentives and abilities of incumbent insiders influences the further development of the enterprise. In a successfully innovative enterprise, the use of a portion of the surplus revenues generated by previous enterprise activities to deepen or extend the innovation process permits the constant renewal and enhancement of its competitive advantage. The uncertainty inherent in the innovation process means that attempts to further develop an extant learning process can fail in the same way that a new venture can prove unsuccessful. In contrast to a new venture, however, enterprises that have become going concerns through innovation in the past will have developed and utilized resources that they can live off, at least for a while, in the event of innovative failure.

Absent an investment strategy of continuous innovation, the learning collectivity's existing resources—the knowledge of the incumbent insiders and the productive assets in which they are embedded—will depreciate or obsolesce as new learning, materials, and machines are developed by competing learning collectivities. If the enterprise fails to innovate through reinvestment, it will forego its privileged access to knowledge about how to produce higher-quality and/or lower-cost products, and, as a result, its ability to appropriate a return in competition with more innovative enterprises. Without the control of resources that these returns provide, the insiders will ultimately lose the capacity to set an innovative strategy for learning.

The critical economic rationale for reinvestment in continuous learning by incumbent insiders is the presence of cumulation advantages in their learning process. That the learning process is cumulative means that through the experience of innovating—through the process of generating higher-quality and/or lower-cost products—new innovative opportunities become apparent to insiders that are not readily identifiable or exploitable by outsiders. When the learning process is cumulative 'the very process of operation and of expansion are intimately associated with a process by which knowledge is increased' (Penrose 1995: 56). Thus an internal inducement is created to firm expansion: 'the growing experience of management, its knowledge of the other resources of the firm and the potential for using them in different ways, create incentives for further expansion as the firm searches for ways of using the services of its own resources more profitably' (Penrose 1995: xii). Through the process of expansion on the basis of its unique productive services the firm can potentially reap what Penrose calls 'economies of growth', which are 'internal economies available to an individual firm which make expansion profitable in particular directions. They are derived from the unique collection of productive services available to it, and create for that firm a differential advantage over other firms in putting on the market new products or increased quantities of old products' (Penrose 1995: 99).

That the learning process is cumulative, that there is the potential for the realization of Penrosian economies of growth, does not, however, ensure that they will be realized. The implications for economic performance of the growth of the firm depends not only on the extent of cumulation advantages but also on the process through which these advantages are pursued and, in particular, on how this process affects the relationship between strategy and learning in the corporate enterprise as a whole. If cumulation advantages can be pursued only by involving a wider group of insiders in the enterprise's learning process, the increased scope and complexity of the extended learning process will eventually overwhelm the capacity of existing strategists to remain integrated with it. To the extent that strategists try to maintain both the originating learning unit and the offspring that it spawns as elements of a unitary strategic entity, thereby encouraging a segmentation of strategy and learning in the enterprise, they are likely, as outsiders to the organizational learning process or at least important elements thereof, to impede rather than promote the innovative success of the enterprise.

That strategists in the originating enterprise will overextend themselves in this manner should not, however, be taken for granted. They may instead be willing to devolve control over the extended learning process to those who are integrated with it. Since cumulation advantages are based on and embedded in the social relations of the originating enterprise, the devolution of strategic control over the pursuit of these advantages, when it is successful, is likely to be gradual. Otherwise the strategy of the originating enterprise will be disturbed by changes in the strategic focus of the newly independent offspring. Initially, the hierarchical relationship between enterprise and offspring may be transformed into a horizontal one so that strategic control over the offspring's learning process is shared between parent and offspring strategists. But as the offspring develop and utilize resources to generate innovation in the activities in which they compete, they will evolve along different organizational trajectories than those of the originating unit. As these trajectories pull farther apart, the sharing of strategic control across businesses will constrain rather than enhance the innovative capabilities of both units. In the long run the offspring may be spun off as independent enterprises that sink or swim on the basis of the innovative capabilities that their own autonomous strategies and organizational learning processes generate. At this point, as Penrose put it, 'their fruits may remain in existence and be enjoyed by society even if separated from the tree that bore them—a subsequent reduction in the size of the firm need not lead to increased costs of production or distribution of any of its existing products' (Penrose 1995: 98).

The risk that incumbent strategists may become segmented from the learning process which generates innovation is even greater when enterprises enter businesses in which there are few opportunities for them to develop or exploit the advantages of cumulative learning. Yet, as Penrose herself recognized, there may be certain forces at work in the economy that could induce firms to diversify without any prospects of reaping economies of growth. She emphasized, for example, the inclinations of some entrepreneurs towards empire building to amass their individual fortunes and build their personal power base. The corporate enterprise is only a means to an end for 'these abnormal and expansive temperaments' and its success, and even survival, is generally inextricably linked to the personal abilities and ambitions of the empire builder. Consequently, she regarded the expansion of these empires as a phenomenon that was not very amenable to economic analysis (Penrose 1995: 182–9) and one that, in the absence of any suitably persuasive sociological or psychological theory of empire building, must be studied on a case-by-case basis. She was, however, highly sceptical of the long-run economic merits of expansion beyond an enterprise's 'impregnable bases' of organizational learning:

The profitability and even survival of a firm which fails to concentrate on the intensive development of any of its existing fields, and instead jumps from one type of production to another in response to changes in external conditions, depends entirely on the ability of its entrepreneurs to make shrewd financial deals, to judge correctly market changes, and to move rapidly from one product to another in response thereto. Individual fortunes have been made in this manner, but no enduring industrial organisation is ever *maintained* by this type of adaptation or growth, although it may have been a characteristic of the early years of some firms. Sooner or later such 'firms' either break up or settle down to the exploitation of selected fields. (Penrose 1995: 131; emphasis in original)

Yet, as in the case of cumulative expansion, the problems of strategic segmentation need not necessarily arise even in the case of unrelated diversification. It all depends on the relationship of the strategists with the learners. Once again, if those at the apex of a conglomerate are willing to leave strategic control in the hands of those who are integrated with the learning processes that generate competitive success in the various businesses, an integration of strategy and learning may be preserved. Unless the integration is institutionalized, however, it will be vulnerable to strategists who seek to make a reality out of the illusion of a unitary control structure for the corporate enterprise as a whole.

The Dynamics of Competition   Whether certain products are considered higher quality and lower cost, and hence innovative, depends on the quality and cost of competitive offerings. In other words, innovation is defined relative to the competitive environment in which it occurs. Particular types of organizational integration, financial commitment, and insider control may, once instituted, either promote or constrain innovation in a business enterprise depending on the business activity in which that enterprise is engaged and the competitive environment in which it operates.

First, since at any point in time the competitive environment varies across business activities, so too do the organizational and financial requirements of innovative investment strategies. Such differences in the content of innovation across business activities mean that certain types of organizational control that promote innovation in one business activity may fail to support, and even constrain, innovative capability in other activities that depend on different types of learning processes. For example, in industries such as pharmaceuticals, in which value added comes mainly from research, design, and marketing, investments in narrow and concentrated skill bases of scientists, engineers, and patent lawyers form the basis of successful corporate performance. In other industries, such as automobiles, value added is dependent to a greater extent on manufacturing processes and, at least since the Japanese competitive challenge, the leading automobile companies have had to make investments that integrate shop-floor workers in organizational learning processes in order to maintain their competitive positions. Given these types of differences in the strategies and learning that generate innovation, one would expect to see, as the empirical evidence discussed in Chapters 3 to 6 will suggest, substantial variations in innovative capability across business activities when we hold the governance conditions constant.

Secondly, within a given business activity the strategies and learning that generate innovation change over time. To the extent that the competitive environment evolves to generate more powerful strategies and learning processes, social conditions that supported the generation of higher-quality and/or lower-cost products in an earlier era may eventually become unsuitable as the basis for innovation. New competitive challenges prove particularly threatening when they come from foreign enterprises that develop and utilize productive resources with the support of different social institutions. For example, though skill bases within the managerial structures of the enterprise enabled the US automobile companies to be the dominant mass producers from the 1920s to the 1960s, the successful challenge of the Japanese automobile producers has relied on broader skill bases that include both managerial and shop-floor employees.

Since the organizational and financial requirements of innovation vary across business activity, as well as with the emergence of new competitive challenges, over time, we should not expect that governance institutions which supported innovation in one activity and era will be an appropriate basis for the generation of higher-quality, lower-cost products in another activity and era. To the contrary, the historical success of these institutions in supporting the abilities and incentives of insiders to one type of learning process may become a barrier to effective responses to new competition by supporting claims to resources by stakeholders whose contributions to the corporate economy no longer generate returns.

Once corporate enterprises conform to existing types of organizational integration, financial commitment, and insider control, it will be very difficult for them to overcome these conditions even when they become a constraint on innovation. But when competitive challenges are sufficiently threatening that they call into question the very survival of an enterprise, and/or when a particular enterprise has a unique organizational history that gives their strategists incentives and abilities that distinguish them from decision-makers in other firms, those who control corporate enterprises may be willing to exert the substantial effort required to reshape institutionalized practices. There is, however, no assurance that insiders, who have benefited from an existing system of organizational control, will be motivated to reshape governance institutions in ways that revitalize the innovation process. To the contrary, they may well have incentives to promote change that protects their interests but is inimical to meeting the new competitive challenges.

The Dynamics of Institutional Change   The relationship between organizational control and innovation is subject to one additional complication: the institutions of governance are themselves subject to change. That organizational control has been instituted in a corporate economy does not, therefore, imply that it will persist. Institutional transformation may occur in response to pressures that are directly related to the change inherent in the innovation process. In historical perspective, it is also evident that governance institutions come into existence and evolve in response to social pressures that are unrelated to the dynamics of the innovation process.

Of particular importance in recent decades as a source of pressure for the transformation of existing systems of corporate governance has been the growth of intergenerational dependence. In virtually all of the advanced economies, growing life expectancy and a decline in fertility below that which is required for the replacement of the population have contributed to a 'double' ageing process. Pressures from the labour market, especially the striking trend towards early withdrawal from the labour force in most of the advanced industrial economies, have exacerbated the rising intergenerational dependence induced by these demographic changes (World Bank 1994).

In all of the advanced industrial economies, the incomes of present and future retirees are highly dependent on the pension fund accumulations of corporate employees, tax revenues from corporations and their employees, and, increasingly, financial returns to corporate securities in household savings portfolios. When corporations are successful in their innovative investment strategies they can generate an expanding number of well-paid and stable employment opportunities along with the surpluses that, directly and indirectly, can support the retirement system. A conflict between corporate employment and retirement income potentially arises, however, when, on the employment side, corporate decision-makers face a new competitive environment in which investments in productive resources do not generate the returns that they have reaped in the past, and, on the retirement side, retirees (both present and future) demand higher incomes, want them sooner rather than later, and live longer.

The pressures that intergenerational dependence have brought to bear on corporate governance differ markedly across countries due to the considerable variations across countries in ageing trends and in the organization of pension systems (see, for example, Turner and Watanabe 1995). In general, however, with the rise of intergenerational dependence, there has been a tendency for retirement incomes to become an ever-increasing burden on employment incomes. In a growing number of countries, the economic impacts of intergenerational dependence are already, or likely in the near future to be, mediated by the stock market, a trend that has played an important role in bringing the issue of corporate governance to the fore in recent years.

2.4.3. The Institutional Foundations of Organizational Control

An understanding of the complex and evolving relationship between organizational control and innovation is a necessary precursor to any attempt to understand how corporations should be governed to enhance economic performance. But the actual outcomes of the interaction between a particular system of corporate governance and innovative behaviour cannot be determined in the abstract. Rather, they must be studied with reference to the evolving comparative and historical realities of enterprises and institutions.

Organizational integration, financial commitment, and insider control represent conditions that vary substantially across social environments. Reflected in the operation of employment, financial, and legal institutions, these social conditions constitute norms according to which business enterprises seek to make strategic decisions concerning the allocation of resources to productive transformation in their enterprises and the allocation of returns from it. A variety of social organizations, including international bodies, nation states, regions, and, indeed, enterprises themselves, contribute to the generation of the institutions that govern the corporate allocation of resources.

The initiatives to introduce directives that apply common company law and worker participation standards throughout the European Union are examples of attempts by an international organization to directly influence the systems of corporate governance in its member states. Regional institutions have also played an important role in shaping the corporate allocation of resources and returns in societies, such as Italy and Germany, in which there is a sufficent decentralization of political power to allow regions, leading examples being Baden-Württemberg and Emilia-Romagna, substantial autonomy from the nation state. Corporate enterprises themselves may also generate institutionalized practices through their own unique organizational histories to the extent that the norms which they generate in their development foster distinctive patterns of resource allocation.

Notwithstanding the importance of international organizations, local communities, and enterprises at certain times and in certain places in generating governance institutions, in comparative historical perspective it is clear that national institutions of corporate governance have exercised an especially dominant influence on the strategies that corporate enterprises have pursued to develop and utilize productive resources. Thus, in analysing the institutional foundations of organizational control in the chapters that follow, I take the nation state as my primary unit of analysis. Specifically, in the following six chapters I show how the organizational control framework can be used as a basis for analysing the historical evolution of corporate governance systems in the US and the former West Germany.

In each country, a characteristic feature of the organizational transformation of the nation's enterprises that led to the rise of the corporate economy was a managerial revolution that involved the integration of teams of salaried administrators and technologists. What both of these systems had in common, therefore, was investment in managerial learning and the organizational structures that were its basis. These salaried managers were trained by the enterprises for which they worked, rotated through different jobs, and encouraged to make their careers by climbing the hierarchy of the corporation.

There were significant differences between the US and Germany in the manner in which corporate enterprises secured the financial resources that they required to pursue innovative investment strategies, but in both cases they ultimately relied on a separation of equity ownership from managerial control. The institutions that brought about and sustained this 'separation of ownership and control' checked the influence of, and indeed transcended, the very traditions of private property on which 'free-enterprise' capitalism ostensibly rests.

Despite these similarities in the US and German systems of corporate governance, there were considerable national differences in the social institutions that influenced the allocation of corporate resources. For example, after the war the patterns of organizational integration in US and German corporate enterprises diverged substantially. In German corporate enterprises skill formation and learning on the shop floor became integral to the strategy and structure of the enterprise as a whole. In the US case, in contrast, the shop-floor investment strategy has been to substitute machines and materials for the knowledge and initiative of workers. As the twentieth century unfolded, such differences developed into distinctive trajectories of corporate development that were reflected in variations in technological evolution and product-market strategies, and ultimately in differences in the competitive performance of US and German enterprises in various business activities (Lazonick and O'Sullivan 1996).

2.5. Conclusion

In this chapter I have argued that the leading theories advanced in the contemporary Anglo-American debates on corporate governance are subject to serious limitations as frameworks for understanding how corporations should be governed to generate economic performance. The critical weaknesses of both theories can be traced to their reliance on neoclassical theory for an understanding of economic performance and, in particular, to its concept of resource allocation. Neoclassical theory, given its overwhelming concern with the analysis of the economics of market equilibrium, has failed to develop a dynamic theory of the firm that could provide the microfoundations for a rigorous and relevant theory of corporate governance.

Proponents of shareholder and stakeholder governance alike have thus had to improvise substantially within the neoclassical framework to develop their theories of corporate governance. They have focused, in particular, on developing 'explanations' for the claims of different interest groups to the residuals but they have not provided plausible explanations of how residuals are generated. Given the ad hoc nature of this project it is not surprising that it suffers from major problems of internal consistency, which explains how there can be such a vigorous debate between perspectives rooted in what is, broadly speaking, the same basic theory. What is worse is that in improvising in this fashion, the proponents of shareholder and stakeholder theories alike have failed to go beyond the exclusive concern of neoclassical economics with exchange rather than production. As a result, they have remained trapped within a theoretical framework that analyses the allocation of resources given preferences and technological opportunities to the neglect of the process through which resources are developed as well as utilized.

To deal with the economics of innovation, a theory of corporate governance must come to terms with the reality of a resource allocation process that is developmental, organizational, and strategic. I have put forward the organizational control hypothesis as a framework for exploring these issues. As noted earlier, the fact that the resource allocation process which generates innovation is developmental, organizational, and strategic implies that, at any point in time, a system of corporate governance supports innovation by generating three conditions—*financial commitment*, *organizational integration*, and *insider control*—which, respectively, provide the institutional support for developmental, organizational, and strategic resource allocation. Over time, the relationship between organizational control and innovation is complicated by the dynamics of organizational control, by the nature of competition across and within business activities over time, and by the dynamics of institutional change. In the chapters that follow I show how the organizational control perspective can be used to analyse the evolving reality of corporate governance in the US and the former West Germany.

3

The Foundations of Managerial Control in the United States

3.1. Introduction

In the past two decades there has been a noticeable shift in US corporate behaviour away from a strategy of retaining both people and money within corporate enterprises towards releasing them onto labour and capital markets. To account for such actions, US corporate managers have proclaimed that the prime, if not only, responsibility of the corporation is to 'create value for shareholders'. For their success in 'maximizing shareholder wealth', these strategic managers receive ample, and often exorbitant, personal rewards, even as most other corporate employees experience lower earnings and less employment stability (see Chapters 5 and 6). This alignment of the interests of the strategic managers of US public corporations with the demands of the stock market is now typically regarded as a defining feature of the market-oriented US system of corporate governance.

In historical perspective, however, market control over the allocation of US corporate resources stands out as a recent phenomenon. For most of this century, salaried managers have exercised control over resource allocation by US corporate enterprises. In this chapter, I describe the lengthy and complex historical process through which the institutional foundations of managerial control emerged in the US corporate economy. I focus, in particular, on the role of the integration of managers as members of business organizations, the diffusion of share ownership, the changing interaction between the stock market and the public corporation, and the transformation of corporate law in facilitating the separation of beneficial ownership of corporate stock from strategic control over the allocation of corporate resources.

Until the rise of institutional investment, which will be discussed in Chapter 5, public stockholders exercised little, if any, control over the allocation of corporate revenues. This lack of control was a feature of public stockholding that portfolio investors not only accepted but favoured. The market in industrial securities evolved in the United States to effect the separation of stock ownership from strategic control because it offered American households liquidity but did not require commitment. Once the market in industrial securities came into existence, American households were willing to hold shares in publicly traded corporations only because their 'ownership' stakes did not entail any commitments of their time, effort, or additional funds to ensure the success of the company. A general willingness to leave control over the allocation of corporate revenues with managers stemmed in part from the limited-liability protection that public stockholders enjoyed. But, for any particular company, this abdication of control derived from the confidence of public stockholders that the equities they held were liquid, and hence could be sold on the stock market at any time.

It was not only shareholders who, in the US corporate economy, were rendered outsiders to the process through which resources were developed and utilized in US corporations. Increasingly, blue-collar workers were excluded from active participation in corporate innovation processes. Although they supplied their effort to corporate enterprises, their experience and creativity were increasingly dispensable to the competitive advantages of these business organizations. Work was organized within corporations in ways that ensured that managers were the key insiders to learning processes that generated corporate innovation. Although in the wake of the Second World War, some trade unionists made a number of attempts to gain some direct influence over the allocation of corporate resources, they met a wall of opposition from US corporate managers, who were intent on preserving their 'right to manage'.

The growing trend towards managerial control over corporate resource allocation was recognized from the early decades of the twentieth century and there was anxious discussion in certain quarters about its implications for politics and economics. Initially, however, the corporation was dealt with primarily as a problem of antitrust. It was not until the Great Depression that the issue of corporate governance took centre stage and there was much debate around this time about the types of institutions that were appropriate to shaping who made corporate investment decisions, what kinds of investments they made, and how the returns from successful investments were distributed. Yet, notwithstanding these debates, as well as attempts during the New Deal era to make the 'princes of industry' accountable to stakeholder agencies outside the firm, managers retained considerable control over corporate resource allocation. The reality of managerial control in US corporations sat very uncomfortably with the rhetoric of individualism and private property in US society. In light of the disjunction between rhetoric and reality, it is perhaps not surprising that the real issues at stake with respect to the governance of US corporations were rarely dealt with explicitly at law or anywhere else in the public sphere. Ultimately, the fact that a persuasive defence of managerial control was not forthcoming was one reason why it became vulnerable, as I will discuss in Chapter 5, to contests for corporate control by outsiders.

3.2. The Historical Foundations of Managerial Control

Launched on the basis of 'inside' capital provided by the entrepreneur, family members, friends, and business associates, the companies that became successful in the late nineteenth century did so by reinvesting earnings to build productive organizations—as is the case today in the transition from new venture to going concern (Chandler 1977). But a problem of the transfer of ownership of the company arose when the financial value of the company, and the managerial organization that was required to run it, had grown beyond the capacity of a single person or even a small group of partners. Even the owner-entrepreneur's family members would likely be ill-suited to run a company that relied on organizational learning for its competitive advantage. The transfer of ownership particularly became a problem when the original owner-entrepreneurs and their backers were ready to retire, as was the case with the post-Civil War generation of entrepreneurs in the 1890s (Navin and Sears 1955: 108). The emergence of a market for industrial securities permitted the original owner-entrepreneurs to sell the company (often to retire from the industrial scene) while leaving intact the managerial organization that had given the company its competitive advantage as a going concern.

In the United States in this century, the liquidity of equities traded on the stock market, and the consequent possibility for separating ownership and control, has derived from the fact that the market in industrial securities arose *as a result of* the growth of dominant enterprises during the last decades of the nineteenth century. The growth of these enterprises made possible the rise of a market in industrial securities, not vice versa (Lazonick 1992). A market in industrial (as distinct from railroad and government) securities in the United States only came into existence in the late 1890s and early 1900s as a number of owner-entrepreneur companies which had grown to dominant positions in their industries in the decades after the Civil War decided to go public (Navin and Sears 1955). As Thomas Navin and Marian Sears put it in their classic article, 'The Rise of a Market in Industrial Securities, 1897–1902': 'the very term 'industrials', meaning securities of industrial companies, did not come into use until the end of the [1890s]' (Navin and Sears 1955: 106).

3.2.1. *The Organizational Integration of Corporate Managers*

In the late nineteenth and early twentieth centuries, the United States, like Germany and Japan, experienced a transformation in the social organization of its business enterprises. A characteristic feature of this transformation was the creation within enterprises of teams of salaried line and staff personnel to organize the production and distribution of goods and services. Managerial organization proved critical to competitive strength in business activities in which there was a combination of a growing complexity of technology and an increasing scale and scope of market opportunities. Technological advances, mainly in metalworking, chemistry, and electrical engineering, themselves often the result of prior organizational transformations, created the potential for new technological applications and further technological development. To exploit that potential demanded organizational transformation, and the US enterprises that emerged as dominant in markets based on these technologies increasingly made high fixed-cost investments to integrate human and physical resources into organizations that could develop and utilize productive resources to generate higher-quality and/or lower-cost products. The high fixed costs that resulted from these strategic investments in organization and technology created pressures to capture markets to achieve high levels of production throughput (Chandler 1977). The extension of the US market made possible by the development of transportation and communication networks facilitated the spreading out of these costs over a large output. To take advantage of the opportunities for mass distribution, and to effectively integrate production and distribution, required further organizational innovation (Chandler 1977; see also Best 1990; Kogut 1992; Lazonick,1990; von Tunzelmann 1995: 203–12).

Especially in industries in which technological innovation and access to mass markets required unprecedented developmental investments, the most successful business enterprises were those that committed resources to building managerial organizations. Technological advances and market opportunities were neither exogenous to, nor independent of, the business organizations that were set up to gain access to them. Rather, they were themselves the outcomes of prior organizational change, increasingly generated, as the twentieth century unfolded, by dominant business enterprises on the basis of investments in organizational learning. These investments were made not only in the capabilities of those directly involved in production and distribution, but also in the learning of those employed in the research and development laboratories set up by US corporate enterprises in the science-based industries, and in marketing capabilities in the consumer industries that developed in the 1920s (Reich 1985; Smith 1990; Olney 1991). Yet organizational learning, though it was strategically fostered in different functional areas in these dominant US enterprises, was increasingly confined to the management structure.

In the metalworking industries, which exerted a decisive influence on the development of the mass-production industries, craft control over production had predominated in the nineteenth century. Craft workers in these industries 'exercised an impressive degree of collective control over the specific productive tasks in which they were engaged and the human relations involved in the performance of those tasks' and they 'drew strength from [their] functional autonomy on the job, from the group ethical code that they developed around their work relations, and from the organizations they created for themselves to protect their interests and values'. The skills and knowledge that these workers possessed—their 'mass of rule-of-thumb or traditional knowledge'—made their experience and creativity indispensable to the success of the enterprises that employed them (Montgomery 1987: 13).

Yet in the development of mass-production methods, the prevailing managerial ideology in the United States was to break craft control over work organization on the shop floor. By dispensing with the need for shop-floor skills in the development and utilization of technology, enterprises concentrated organizational learning in the managerial structure (Lazonick 1990: ch. 7). In *The Fall of the House of Labor* in a chapter entitled 'White Shirts and Superior Intelligence', the labour historian David Montgomery describes how the process worked to transform a situation in which '[t]he manager's brain [was] under the workmen's cap' into one in which managers were no longer reliant on the workmen's knowledge (Montgomery 1987: 215). The application of Frederick Winslow Taylor's principles of scientific management to the organization of production led to an extreme hierarchical and functional division of labour for shop-floor workers in a wide range of industries. In the process, these workers were rendered outsiders to the processes of learning that generated innovation in these industries.

The minute subdivision of shop-floor tasks was carried to an extreme at the Ford Motor Company. When the Highland Park plant was built in 1910 to produce the Ford Model T, the world's first mass-production automobile, it was regarded around the world as the production showcase of the industry. Using methods of time-and-motion study developed by Taylor, jobs were narrowly subdivided into precisely specified activities, and Ford combined task standardization with mechanization to produce the assembly line. In this system of production, shop-floor workers were required to perform their assigned tasks and were required not to exercise any initiative in so doing. In hiring workers, Ford had 'no use for experience' and wanted 'machine-tool operators who have nothing to unlearn, who have no theories of correct surface speeds for metal finishing, and will simply do what they are told to do, over and over again, from bell-time to bell-time' (Arnold and Faurote 1919: 41–2).

In deskilling shop-floor work, Ford conformed to the more general trend in US industry at the time. By the 1920s craft control had been defeated, and, in the process, in most of the major mass-production enterprises, shop-floor workers found themselves excluded from the organizational learning processes that generated competitive advantage. Responding to, and reinforcing, the segmented system of skill formation that emerged in dominant US industrial enterprises in the early twentieth century, a highly stratified educational system evolved that effectively separated out future managers from future workers even before they entered the workplace. Thus a deep social gulf was created between managers as 'insiders' and workers as 'outsiders' in the employment relations of US industrial enterprises.

Until the last decade of the nineteenth century, a formal system of higher education was relatively unimportant for the development and utilization of productive resources, in part because US industry was only beginning to make the transition from the machine-based first industrial revolution, in which shop-floor experience remained important, to the science-based second industrial revolution, in which systematic formal education was a virtual necessity. From the late nineteenth century, however, the system of higher education became central to supplying technical and administrative personnel to the burgeoning bureaucracies of US industrial enterprises (Noble 1977; Servos 1980; Nelson and Wright 1995: 144–8; Lazonick 1990: 229–32).

The evolution of the General Electric Student Engineering Program, generally described as 'the Test' because trainee engineers served a one- to two-year apprenticeship with the company as testers of company apparatus, is illustrative of the increased reliance on formal education as a source of white-collar workers. The GE Test Program grew rapidly from less than 40 entrants in 1892 to more than 500 by 1907 and increasingly relied on college-trained graduates; by 1900 only one-tenth of the admittees came from a shop background. Initially, General Electric relied, in its selection process, on the recommendations of engineering professors. From 1906, however, the company began sending its own recruiter to the campuses of the top engineering schools. In 1911 its recruitment effort was more systematically organized to serve General Electric's needs when it was placed in the charge of the newly established Education Committee, which included Charles Steinmetz, the Vice-

President of Engineering, and Magnus Alexander, the head of training programmes at General Electric's Lynn plant (Wise 1979: 171–7).

Industrial enterprises increasingly recruited their managers from institutions of higher education that adapted their offerings to cater to these enterprises' organizational and technological needs (Noble 1977; Servos 1980: 531–49; Lazonick 1986; Chandler 1990: 83). Subsequent in-house training and on-the-job experience developed the specialized productive capabilities of these employees. Job rotation and cross-training facilitated the integration of specialist activities, while enabling the most successful specialists to become transformed into 'generalists' with greater responsibility and authority for strategically allocating resources to the enterprise's organizational learning process. That the allocation of corporate resources could increasingly be vested in the hands of career managers who had the ability and incentive to make investments in productive capabilities relevant to their enterprises was facilitated by the separation of equity ownership from strategic control over the allocation of corporate resources and returns that took place in the early decades of the twentieth century.

3.2.2 The Diffusion of Share Ownership

The importance of Wall Street—the major New York investment banks and the New York Stock Exchange—to industrial investment in the twentieth century arose from the way it structured the separation of stock ownership from strategic control. The term 'industrial securities' may have appeared at the end of the 1890s but it took Wall Street some three decades of marketing and trading industrial securities before any but the wealthiest households or the most speculatively minded individuals viewed industrial stocks as sufficiently liquid to be worthy of purchase. In the 1890s and early 1900s initial 'public' offerings, floated by Wall Street investment bankers, went to a relatively small circle of wealthy individuals (including the companies' original owner-entrepreneurs and their families) and financial institutions, particularly insurance companies and the underwriting investment banks themselves. Of the $6.2 billion of industrial common and preferred stock issued during the peak of the merger movement between 1898 and 1902, 49 per cent was privately placed in exchange for the assets or securities of merged companies, and another 45 per cent was issued by companies to their own stockholders as dividends, for cash, or for other unknown purposes. Only 6 per cent of the stock issued was sold to the general public (Nelson 1959: 94).

To ensure themselves an income from industrial securities that might be difficult to market, these early portfolio investors favoured preferred shares or bonds rather than common stocks. Indeed, in many initial offerings, common stocks were distributed as a bonus to the purchasers of preferred stocks or to the promoters and investment banks for their services (Flynn 1934: 140). As the market for industrial securities developed, these stockholders were able to sell off some of their portfolios of preferred and common stocks to the public.

Over time, as the companies listed on the New York Stock Exchange continued to thrive, and as wealthy individuals and institutional investors sold off some of their portfolios, shareholding became more dispersed and the threat of outside interference by substantial stockholders decreased. From the late 1910s through the 1920s, the dispersion of stockholding increased rapidly. The sale of Liberty Bonds during World War I brought the savings of a whole new tier of American households into the securities markets. After the war, Wall Street sought to capture these savings through sales of preferred stocks that were marketed as having the security of bonds (Carosso 1970: 250). The record $1.5 billion in corporate stock issues (over half of which were preferreds) in 1919 was double the value issued in 1916, the previous peak year (US Bureau of the Census 1976: 1005–6). The average annual rate of increase in the number of book stockholders in US corporations was 12 per cent in the period from 1917 to 1920 as compared with 4 per cent from 1900 to 1917 and 5 per cent from 1920 to 1928 (Means 1930: 566).

During the 1920s many of the leading industrial companies made the availability of company stock for purchase by employees one element in an emerging welfare capitalism; by 1928 there were more than 800,000 employee stockholders (Means 1930: 568). Companies also sold shares to customers, the result of which, according to Gardiner Means, was the addition of one million new stockholders between 1920 and 1928 (Means 1930: 569). During the 1920s, the marketing of stock became a highly developed industry in itself, with institutional forms of stockholding, such as the investment trust, becoming wildly popular among small-scale investors (Carosso 1970: Ch. 14; Baskin and Miranti 1997: 196). Stock splits also became common as a way of making shares more accessible to households further down the income scale (Dewing 1934: 98).

The stock market boom of the late 1920s brought crowds of new people into the market, many of them borrowing to buy stocks on margin in attempts to get rich quickly. In 1927 an unprecedented $1.7 billion of new stock was issued, but that amount doubled the next year, and doubled again in 1929. In the process, common stocks gained wide acceptance. In 1927 the amount of common stock issued was only 65 per cent of preferred stock issued; in 1929, it was 300 per cent (US Bureau of the Census 1976: 1006; see also Ciccolo and Baum 1985: 87).

In 1900, there were an estimated 4.4 million stockholders on the books of US corporations, holding an average of 140 $100 par value shares. By 1910, the number of book stockholders had increased to 7.5 million, with their average holdings down to 87 shares. In 1920, these figures were 12 million and 57 shares respectively, and by 1928, 18 million and 51 shares (Berle and Means 1932: 56). In so far as in the later years, stockholders held more diversified portfolios, the actual number of stockholders may have increased somewhat less than fourfold between 1900 and 1928. But it is clear that, over the first three decades of this century, the distribution of stocks became increasingly dispersed.

For companies listed on the New York Stock Exchange, which quickly became the exchange of preference for all of the leading US industrial enterprises, stockholders' expectations concerning liquidity reflected the stages of development and the financial condition of the types of companies in which they acquired shares. These companies were going concerns that before their public offerings had established themselves as dominant enterprises in their particular industries. By developing and utilizing productive resources under owner-entrepreneurs, these companies had already acquired the capacity to generate high levels of profit on a regular basis. Once these companies went public, their high levels of profits made possible continuous dividend payments, which further convinced stockholders of the liquidity of their stock. By refusing to cut dividends except under the direst circumstances, corporate managers ensured that stockholders would not challenge their control over the allocation of corporate revenues.

Wall Street helped to create confidence in the liquidity of corporate stock by identifying, and actively promoting, companies that had already acquired the productive base to generate a consistent stream of profits. Ever more stringent requirements for listing on the New York Stock Exchange built public confidence in the stock market, which, in bringing in new buyers of stocks, added further to the liquidity of the market (Hurst 1970; see also Michie 1987). From the second decade of the century, public confidence was further bolstered by the securities ratings services of Moody's and Standard and Poor's, whose own businesses were based on their reputations for impartiality and credibility (Harold 1938: ch. 2).

Most important, however, in laying the foundation for a highly liquid market in industrial stocks in the first decades of the twentieth century was the emergence, from the last decades of the nineteenth century, of the dynamic industrial enterprises that, through the superior development and utilization of productive resources, had gained distinct competitive advantage in an era before a liquid market in industrial securities even existed. These companies, some of which still maintain dominant market shares, had by the 1920s made the United States the most powerful industrial nation in the world.

As stocks became more widely held, the possibility diminished that any group of stockholders could challenge managerial control of corporate resources. Most corporate stock, whether preferred or common, carried voting rights, but the very dispersion of stockholding with voting rights made it all the more difficult for any small group of stockholders to use these rights to challenge managerial control. Corporate managers were more concerned about diluting the control of holders of preferred shares, rather than holders of common shares, because preferred stockholders, behaving more like creditors than speculators, tended to scrutinize managerial actions and performance more closely when dividend payments were missed. As a result, there was a tendency over the first decades of the century to dilute the power of preferred stockholders by granting common stockholders more votes per dollar of stock. In the 1920s US corporations found that they could dilute shareholder power even more directly through the issue of non-voting stock (Sears 1929: 90–1).

These practices led to a public protest against the disenfranchisement of the stockholder, fuelled by *Main Street and Wall Street*, a book published in 1927 by Harvard professor William Z. Ripley. Ripley's arguments had an important influence on a young legal scholar, Adolf Berle, whose analysis of corporate control, co-authored with Gardiner Means, was to become the classic work on the subject soon after it was published in 1932. Berle taught corporation finance on a part-time basis at Harvard Business School from 1925 to 1928, and it was there that he got to know Ripley. By that time, Berle had already published a series of articles on corporation finance and Ripley had drawn on Berle's research in his 1927 book (Schwarz 1987: 52).

In his early articles, Berle was predominantly concerned with the increasing use by corporate managers of devices to increase their power at the expense of shareholders. He discussed, *inter alia*, the use of non-par stock to dilute the value of existing stock and the recourse to non-voting stock to concentrate control in the hands of management (Berle 1925: 43–63, 1926: 673–93). Berle called for new 'equitable controls' to counter managerial attempts to accumulate power but he did not, at this point, regard federal regulation as necessary for the task. Rather, he looked to three other mechanisms to redress the balance of power between shareholders and managers: 'an association of interested investment bankers, stock exchange regulation of markets, and the organized market power of institutional stockholders whose interests coincided with individual stockholders' (Schwarz 1987: 53).

As Jordan Schwarz put it in his biography of Adolf Berle, '[c]onsidering that all his research pointed to the corporation's genius for evading market checks, Berle's proposals for remedy seem conservative and even disingenuous' (Schwarz 1987: 53). But there was some evidence that Berle's remedies might have had merit. In response to the protest stirred up by Ripley's book, for example, the Governors of the New York Stock Exchange, ever eager to maintain public confidence in the holding of stock, approved a resolution of their Committee on Stock Listing (without devising a definite policy) that 'in the future the committee in considering applications for the listing of securities will give careful thought to the matter of voting control' (Stevens 1926: 365). However, when the New York Stock Exchange subsequently required that listed stock carry voting rights, the result was not to increase shareholder power but, by maintaining public confidence in the holding of stock, to foster the further dispersion of stockholding. Ironically, it thus became all the more difficult, as Berle and Means later famously argued, for a small group of stockholders to challenge managerial control.

3.2.3. *The Stock Market and the Public Corporation*

Wall Street built its business on the basis of the enduring success of major US corporations but, contrary to the conventional wisdom, it did not fund their long-term investment to any significant degree. The reality is that in the United States the stock market is not, and never has been, an important source of funds for long-term business investment by major corporations. Throughout the twentieth century, corporate retentions and corporate debt, not equity issues, have been the main sources of funds for business investment.

Estimates of the sources of funds of US non-financial corporations (based on a sample of 50 major companies), presented in Table 3.1, show that, from the late 1920s through the mid-1970s, retentions (undistributed profits and capital con-

TABLE 3.1 Sources of Funds of US Non-financial Corporations, 1927–1987 (% of all net sources)

Period	Retentions[a]	Net debt issues	Gross stock issues	Net stock issues
1927–30	80.8	1.4	28.8	17.8
1931–35	123.1	−23.1	34.6	0.0
1936–41	73.3	13.3	21.3	13.3
1942–47	74.8	12.6	19.4	12.6
1948–53	80.9	15.5	6.4	0.0
1954–59	81.1	9.4	14.2	9.4
1960–65	78.3	10.4	15.1	11.3
1966–71	66.2	21.6	15.1	12.9
1972–77	73.6	19.2	12.0	7.2
1982–87	79.1	3.2	10.1	3.1

[a] Undistributed profits + capital consumption allowances.

Sources: 1927–1977: Ciccolo and Baum (1985: 86), based on samples of 50 large companies for each period; 1982–1987: Hall (1994: 139), based on the 100 largest manufacturing companies.

sumption allowances) were never less than 66 per cent of all sources over any five- or six-year period. Net equity issues were less than 18 per cent, reaching close to that level only in the period 1927–30, when companies sold large amounts of common stock to speculators in the bull market of 1928 and 1929 (Ciccolo and Baum 1985). For the period 1982–7, for the 100 largest US manufacturing corporations, new equity issues were 10.1 per cent of gross sources of funds and 3.1 per cent of net sources of funds. The gross and net figures for retained earnings were 51.5 per cent and 79.1 per cent, and for new debt 30.2 per cent and 3.2 per cent (Hall 1994: 139; Corbett and Jenkinson 1996: 77).

Even these figures do not tell the whole story of the limited role of equity issues in funding investment in new productive assets. New corporate equity issues have generally been used, not to finance investment in new productive assets, but to transfer financial claims over existing assets or to restructure corporate balance sheets. The ownership transfer may be an initial public offering (IPO), in which case share ownership is transferred from the original owner-entrepreneurs and their venture capital partners to a public stockholder. High levels of IPO activity, therefore, do not necessarily indicate that households and institutional investors are funding a wave of innovative investment. Rather, in absorbing the IPOs, these portfolio investors are paying the entrepreneurs who built the businesses for a claim on the enterprise's future earnings, based on investments in productive capabilities that have already been made. Whether any of the money realized from an IPO ends up committed to new innovative investment strategies, either in the issuing company or some other new venture, is at the discretion of those who control corporate resource allocation in the newly public enterprise and the original owner-entrepreneurs whose shares have been liquidated in part or in full. It is not inherent in the IPO transaction itself.

TABLE 3.2 Security Transactions of 84 Large US Manufacturing Companies, 1921–1939

Year	Own securities sold	Own securities retired (millions of dollars)	A&S[a] securities purchased	Retired	Purchased (as percentage of sold)	Retired+purchased
1921	415	142	192	34	46	81
1922	222	170	69	77	31	108
1923	407	109	290	27	71	98
1924	146	130	61	89	42	131
1925	392	274	189	70	48	118
1926	446	163	192	37	43	80
1927	474	306	113	65	24	88
1928	273	185	224	68	82	150
1929	1,256	680	586	54	47	101
1930	375	159	291	42	78	120
1931	234	169	183	72	78	150
1932	140	255	54	182	39	221
1933	46	188	98	409	213	622
1934	127	179	53	141	42	183
1935	114	278	39	244	34	278
1936	245	307	36	125	15	140
1937	601	180	47	30	8	38
1938	424	76	50	18	12	30
1939	143	105	95	73	66	140

[a] Affiliates and subsidiaries.

Source: Koch (1943: 97).

The ownership transfer may also occur for the purpose of one company acquiring another company. Typically, the acquiring company issues new stock of its corporation to exchange for the existing stock of the acquired company, the stock of which is then retired (Koch 1943). In the aftermath of the acquisition, the acquiring company may make substantial investments in the acquired company, but once again the equity issue does not provide the source of such investment financing. In the 1920s US industrial corporations undertook a wave of acquisitions for purposes of both vertical integration and diversification. During the first half of the 1920s the number of mergers and acquisitions averaged 447 per year; during the second half of the 1920s, 917 per year (US Bureau of the Census 1976: 914). Unlike the merger movement of the turn of the century, which contributed to the rise of a market in industrial securities, the acquisition movement of the 1920s was able to make use of what was by then a highly liquid market in corporate stocks. The existence of the liquid stock market made the stockholders of the acquired firms willing to accept the stock of the acquiring corporations as payment for their equity holdings.

Funds raised through equity issues may also be used to restructure the corporate balance sheet. During the 1920s, Wall Street issued large amounts of corporate stock, much of which, especially in the late 1920s, was used to pay off debt. Table 3.2 shows the relative amounts of their own securities that a sample of 84 large US manufacturing corporations issued and retired, as well as the amount of affiliates' and subsidiaries' securities that these companies purchased from 1921 through 1939. For these same 84 manufacturing companies, the total amount of funds that they retained over the period 1921–9 just equalled their total fixed capital expenditures (Koch 1943: 81). The data strongly suggest that throughout the 1920s companies were issuing securities to retire securities and purchase other companies. Of the $1.26 billion of securities sold in 1929, for example, US Steel sold $150 million of common stock to partially fund the retirement of $394 million in debt (Koch 1943: 95).

3.2.4. The Transformation of Corporate Law

By the late 1920s the de facto power of managers to strategically allocate corporate resources had been greatly enhanced. Meanwhile, from the nineteenth century, corporation law had evolved to extend the privileges accorded to corporate enterprises and to increase managerial control over the operation of these enterprises. Thus developments in corporate law bolstered and enhanced the trend evident in the evolution of more informal institutions of corporate governance.

Until the middle of the nineteenth century, state legislatures awarded corporate charters on a case-by-case basis primarily for the conduct of activities that had some special value for the community, such as the provision of transportation, water, or banking services. From the 1830s, the demand for charters for manufacturing companies increased and as corporate charters were awarded for the carrying on of a wider variety of businesses, state legislatures throughout the US shifted from granting special charters to legislation that made incorporation generally available to most business enterprises (Hurst 1970: 13–57). The implications of the shift were profound: 'As long as corporations had been viewed as joint public and private enterprises, haggling over powers and benefits remained a matter of charter interpretation, and the states reserved the right to the final word. However, the enactment of general incorporation statutes obscured the public's contribution and dissolved the image of a corporation as a venture both public and private' (Kaufman, Zacharias, and Karson 1995: 17).

From then on many restrictions on what corporations could do were progressively eliminated or loosened. As Lawrence Friedman put it: 'in 19th-century law, where there was a corporate will, there was generally a corporate way, at least eventually' (Friedman 1973: 454). Corporations were also accorded new privileges, the most striking of which was the extension to them of constitutional protection of property. The Fourteenth Amendment of 1868 prohibited a state from depriving any 'person' of life, liberty, or property without due process of law. The purpose of the amendment had been to strengthen the rights of former slaves. In its *Santa Clara* decision of 1886, however, the Supreme Court extended its reach considerably in determining that corporations were persons within the meaning of the Fourteenth Amendment. As such the states were required to treat their property as they would the private property of ordinary 'persons'. As a result, attempts by states to regulate corporate activities could be challenged on the grounds that they violated the property rights of corporations (Friedman 1973: 455–9; Hurst 1970: 65–9; Kaufman *et al*. 1995: 18–21).

From the 1890s until the 1930s the bias towards enabling, rather than restraining, corporate action became increasingly accentuated not only in constitutional law but also in general incorporation statutes. In the earlier part of the nineteenth century, the courts' application to corporations of the doctrine of *ultra vires*—actions deemed to be outside the powers of the corporation—meant that the powers delegated to the directors and officers of the corporation had been held to strict judicial standards of accountability. It was the doctrine of *ultra vires* that was used, for example, to dissolve the trusts of the 1880s. In 1889, however, the New Jersey Corporation Law rescued these corporate consolidations by allowing one corporation to hold shares in another. In general, the incorporation statutes, introduced by states in the 'race to the bottom' sparked by the New Jersey statute, gave corporation directors and managers *carte blanche* to do virtually whatever they wanted, and the doctrine of *ultra vires* met its gradual demise as an influence on corporate activities (Horwitz 1977: 77–9).

The states also proved willing to introduce other legal reforms when corporations began the process of consolidation that snowballed into the Great Merger Movement, despite the fact that some of these reforms substantially undermined the rights of shareholders, the traditional bearers of private property in the corporation. Of particular significance as a potential obstacle to corporate consolidation was the common law rule, applied throughout the 1880s, that required the unanimous consent of the shareholders to undertake fundamental change in corporate activities. Following the lead of New York in 1890, a number of states introduced statutes that permitted corporations to merge with majoritarian rather than unanimous consent. As Morton Horwitz has observed: 'The shift to majority rule in fact made the merger movement legally possible. It not only made consolidations much easier to effect; it also dealt the final blow to any efforts to conceptualize the corporation as a collection of contracting individual shareholders' (Horwitz 1977: 89).

The diminution of the legal constraints on the operations of corporate enterprises and the increasing privileges extended by law to them reflected a more general historical process in the United States that transformed the framework of the law to support developmental change, often at the expense of existing individual property rights that might stifle such change (Horwitz 1977, 1992; Sklar 1988). From the late nineteenth century, as laws evolved to relax restraints on, and extend privileges to, corporate enterprises, they not only enabled the activities of these enterprises but also contributed to the ongoing shift in the balance of corporate control by legitimizing the exercise of that control by 'the active insiders' (Hurst 1970: 70).

As the development and utilization of productive resources became less dependent on individual enterprise, and more reliant on learning processes within managerial organizations, especially in the nation's most technologically dynamic industries, laws that were responsive to the perceived needs of the process of economic development weakened the property rights of individuals, who were outsiders to organizational learning processes, and increasingly vested control over corporate resources in the hands of corporate managers. The most important power accorded to corporate managers by statutes and through the courts was the power to declare or withhold dividends.[1] As one commentator described the legal situation,

The board of directors declare the dividends and it is for the directors, and not the stockholders, to determine whether or not a dividend shall be declared. When, therefore, the directors have exercised this discretion and refused a dividend, there will be no interference by the courts with their decision, unless they are guilty of a willful abuse of their discretionary powers, or of bad faith or of a neglect of duty. It requires a very strong case to induce a court of equity to order the directors to declare a dividend, inasmuch as equity has no jurisdiction, unless fraud or breach of trust is involved. (Cook 1913: 447)

As decision-makers integral to the organizational learning process, strategic managers were implicitly deemed by the courts to be the agents of developmental change, and the transformation of corporate law from the late nineteenth century supported managerial rights to allocate corporate resources to generate such change. In his analysis of *The Legitmacy of the Business Corporation in the Law of the United States*, Hurst contends that although the competitive chartering of corporations in a number of states led to an overwhelming bias towards enabling corporate activities, the generality of the new legal pattern and its stability over time suggests that it reflected more than a response to the pecuniary needs of individual states. He argues that it also reflected a broad and growing consensus in legal and other elite circles in the United States from the 1890s that large-scale organization was the new factor of production and that it needed to be developed if economic prosperity was to be enhanced (Hurst 1970: 74–5).

3.3. Managerial Control and the Great Depression

The consolidation of organizational control over the allocation of corporate resources certainly contributed to an unprecedented development of the US corporate economy. By the First World War, US enterprises had built the foundations for competitive advantage in mass-production industries. During the 1920s, while the mass producers consolidated their market dominance, a number of corporations that had been building their capabilities over the previous decades gained leading competitive positions in critical new industries, particularly in consumer durables, chemicals, and electrical manufacturing (Chandler 1977; Lazonick 1990: 241–2; Nelson 1990: 117–32; Nelson and Wright 1995: 129–63).

The strengthening of the productive capacity of US corporate enterprises was hailed by many business leaders and politicians as the foundation for an era of unprecedented prosperity for US citizens. The ideology of progress in the US during this period no longer promised prosperity for the average American citizen solely on the basis of the wages that he earned through his participation in the production

[1] Early cases that established the principle of managerial discretion include *St. John* v. *Erie R.R.*, 22 Wall 136 (1875); *Union Pacific R.R.* v. *US*, 99 US 402 (1879); *Warren* v. *King*, 108 US 380 (1882); *Chaffee* v. *Rutland R.R.*, 36 N.J. Eq. 233 (1882).

process. The citizen as consumer became an increasingly important figure on the US political scene and the benefits of the economic expansion of the 1920s were frequently packaged in terms of what it delivered to him.

Increases in the consumption of consumer durables were certainly spectacular during the 1920s; expenditures (in 1929 dollars) rose to an annual average of $7.06 billion from 1919 to 1928 compared with $4.29 billion from 1909 to 1918. Sales of automobiles increased from around 8 million in 1920 to more than 23 million in 1929, encouraged by, and supportive of, the spectacular expansion of the US automobile industry (Lebergott 1976). The proportion of US households with electric lighting also increased dramatically, from 35 per cent in 1920 to 68 per cent in 1930 (Lebergott 1976: 355), and corporate enterprises like GE and Westinghouse made major investments in organizational capabilities to generate a steady flow of innovative electrical products to these households.

Yet, notwithstanding the ideology of prosperity during the 1920s and the general economic trends, the gains from the economic expansion were unevenly distributed.[2] Although the share of total manufacturing income paid in salaries increased from 17 per cent to 18.3 per cent, and capital's share advanced from 25.5 per cent to 29.1 per cent, the share received by workers fell from 57.5 per cent in 1923–4 to 52.6 per cent in 1928–9 (Bell 1940: 29). Real weekly earnings for production workers in manufacturing increased by 14.5 per cent from 1919 to 1929 but rose by only 4.5 per cent during the period of prosperity from 1923 to 1929. These averages conceal considerable variation among different groups of blue-collar workers, with some groups gaining little during the prosperity decade (Stricker 1983: 14–15). Moreover, notwithstanding low average levels of unemployment in the economy as a whole, the threat of job loss remained real for many workers due to disability, downturns in the fortunes of a particular enterprise or industry, and temporary economy-wide recessions in 1924 and 1927 (Stricker 1983: 18–22).

At a small number of corporations with progressive employment policies, the 1920s saw the introduction of organizational initiatives, including systematic promotion and pay policies, grievance procedures, and employee representation, designed to provide stable and remunerative employment to their workers (Slichter 1929; Jacoby 1985, 1997; Lazonick 1990: ch. 8). General Electric was a leader among these 'welfare capitalists'. Its experience during the 1920s and 1930s illustrates some of the limitations of even the most ambitious attempts to make managerial control the foundation for sustainable prosperity in the 1920s.

3.3.1. The Limits of Corporate Liberalism: General Electric and Trustee Managers

Gerard Swope and Owen Young, the two men who jointly assumed the mantle of GE's leadership in 1922, were products of the managerial revolution that had occurred in the US corporate economy; the control that they exercised was based not

---

[2] For discussions of inequality and the consumer economy, see Leven et al. 1934; see also Cowan 1983.

on ownership but on their pursuit of professional careers.[3] Swope and Young had strong opinions about the implications of the separation of share ownership from managerial control for the nature and scope of corporate management's responsibilities.

Young, sometimes called 'Mr Outside', took responsibility for representing GE before the stockholders and the public. In the keynote speech that he gave at the dedication ceremony for the new Baker buildings at Harvard Business School in 1927, Young summarized his philosophy, which some business leaders regarded as a dangerously radical perspective on corporate management, when he said that the modern corporation had become a public institution and its managers 'trustees'. The managerial challenge, in his view, was to govern the relations between 'those who have invested their savings and those who have invested their lives', because although they were partners in a common enterprise they were also enemies fighting for the fruits of their common achievement:

Take our own company. It is made up of three parts. There is Capital—no, I'd rather speak of that as people. Let us speak in terms of people—human beings. There are, perhaps, 20,000 of these—small investors, widows with small legacies, school teachers, employees, a few large investors—but all people . . . They supply the things we need—the insentient things, such as machinery, tools and raw materials with which we are to work.

Then there's another group of people—a large group—made up of 100,000 other people. In that group are engineers, eminent scientists, skilled laborers, common laborers. Clerks, stenographers and the like—all people . . . all eager to work and to realise something on the investment they, too, are prepared to make—their labor . . .

Now we have these two groups brought together—the one supplying the means of production and the other the power of production by means of the third group of people who are cooperating to make a going institution. This third group . . . is the management, which is the smallest, and whose sole purpose is to make these two other groups function together adequately to produce something that is of value—that is of real service to the world. (quoted in Tarbell 1932: 155)

Young rejected the concept of managers 'as the paid attorneys of capital' and their task as that of squeezing from labour 'its last ounce of effort and last penny of compensation' (quoted in Tarbell 1932: 155). He summarized his view of shareholders

---

[3] Swope was an MIT-trained electrical engineer who started his career in 1895 as an employee of Western Electric, the manufacturing subsidiary of American Telephone and Telegraph. By 1899 he was managing the company's plants in St Louis. By 1913 he had risen to the rank of vice-president. He remained with Western Electric until 1919, when he took up GE's offer to become director of its international operations. Owen D. Young grew up on a modest farm in upstate New York and worked his way through college and law school. He then landed a job with a Boston law firm that specialized in working with companies and local governments in setting up electrical utilities and street railways. In the course of his work, Young represented the Boston engineering company Stone & Webster against GE in disputes over the right to install electrical utilities and railways in Texas. He performed so well as GE's adversary that he came to the attention of Charles Coffin, GE's President. In 1912 he was appointed head of GE's legal department. Besides counselling GE on matters of antitrust and patents, Young distinguished himself, and came to public attention, through his participation in President Woodrow Wilson's Second Industrial Commission. Held in 1919, this commission sought to set a post-war agenda for cooperation between employees and employers.

in asserting his disagreement with the call by William Ripley to give them greater control over corporate enterprises:

Stockholders know nothing about the business nor do they care anything about it . . . They are only [buying or] selling a commodity . . . if it does not yield them adequate returns, they sell their shares . . . The carrying on of the business of the corporations, especially those doing big business, should be in the hands of those who are making that business the business of their lives . . . this is my answer to all those, including Professor Ripley, who are demanding money control of corporations and likewise my answer to the socialists who are demanding community control. (quoted in Case and Case 1982: 371–2)[4]

Young went on to say that

[t]he men who do the business of the General Electric Company, and I mean to include in that all men who think of that business as their business (not simply floaters looking for a day's work), are seeking on the one side to obtain their capital—that is to say, their tools—at the lowest cost . . . On the other side, these men have the job of using these tools so as to make the product which, because of its excellence and cheapness, will command the market. That position not only gives them business today, but insures them business tomorrow. The margins which result from the exercise of their mental and physical effort in that undertaking, in my mind, should belong to them . . . (quoted in Case and Case 1982: 371)

He summarized his aspirations for the future of the corporate economy in the following terms:

I hope the day may come when these great business organisations will truly belong to the men who are giving their lives and their efforts to them, I care not in what capacity. Then they will use their capital truly as a tool and they will all be interested in working it to the highest economic advantage. Then an idle machine will mean to every man in the plant who sees it an unproductive charge against himself. Then we shall have zest in labour, provided the leadership is competent and the division fair. Then we shall dispose, once and for all, of the charge that in industry organisations are autocratic and not democratic. Then we shall have all the opportunities for a cultural wage which the business can provide. Then, in a word, men will be as free in cooperative undertakings and subject only to the same limitations and chances as men in individual businesses. Then we shall have no hired men. That objective may be a long way off, but it is worthy to engage the research and efforts of the Harvard Business School. (quoted in Case and Case 1982: 374)

Gerard Swope was less inclined to philosophical statements than Young. As 'Mr Inside' at General Electric, he took responsibility for production, sales, credit, personnel, prices, research, and engineering, Although he and Young took broad policy decisions together, they agreed that in general Swope would do as much as possible and Young as little as he could (Loth 1958: 131). Nevertheless, Swope shared many of Young's views on corporate control although he placed more emphasis than the lawyer on the instrumental value of stakeholder governance in increasing the productive efficiency and the competitive strength of GE.

---

[4] Josephine Young Case was Owen Young's daughter and her husband, Everett Case, had been Young's assistant.

Young and Swope became well known in the 1920s in American business circles as influential exponents of the philosophy of corporate liberalism. Within GE, they supported some important changes in GE's labour policies. One of their most significant contributions, if not their own initiative, was their support for the establishment of works councils in company plants. In 1918, management and the unionized workers at the Lynn plant reached an impasse in their negotiations with each other about wages and working conditions. The War Labor Board intervened and set up a 'plan of representation' that empowered elected worker representatives to negotiate with management on all issues that affected their working lives, including wages. The plan attracted a high level of participation from workers and their productivity increased. As wages rose steadily in the early 1920s, the Lynn workers remained committed to the plan and lost interest in their unions. Swope thus decided to make the Lynn plan part of company policy. Eventually a similar works council was accepted by the workers at Schenectady (Tarbell 1932: 149). The council was preoccupied in its earlier sessions with the 'rattling of old skeletons and shouting of old slogans' (Tarbell 1932: 149) but when it settled down to business it managed to make some important changes in labour policies. It was agreed that piece rates be tried out in the Schenectady plant and in six months wages were one and a half times what they had been. The council also changed workers' investment and pension schemes by organizing a securities corporation—the General Electric Employees Securities Corporation—run by an equal representation of workers and management. The company owned the capital stock and took the risk of market fluctuations. Thirty thousand employees invested in the savings plan, and although its investments were diversified at the beginning of the 1930s, it was the largest single investor in GE. A pension plan was also worked out by the council.

Critics of corporate liberalism contended that it was paternalistic and that corporate managers used works councils—derogatorily described as 'company unions'—as a means of keeping the real unions out. Swope and Young attempted to counter charges of paternalism against these schemes by insisting that both the company and the employee make contributions. Sometimes this policy worked against the introduction of these plans. For example, Swope and Young proposed an unemployment compensation plan to the works council in 1924 that required a small weekly contribution from everyone in the company, as well as a contribution from the corporation itself. At the time, the prospect of unemployment seemed remote and the plan was rejected because, as Swope recognized, workers saw it as just another scheme to deduct something from their wages (Loth 1958: 156). In 1930, in the midst of the Great Depression, the works councils were asked to reconsider the plan and, for obvious reasons, they adopted it.

Under the leadership of Swope and Young, GE expanded the existing employee benefits programmes and introduced new ones such as profit sharing, mortgage assistance, and a corporate pension plan. The interest of senior GE managers in the new personnel policies had originally been to lower quit rates, reduce labour discontent, and stifle unionization attempts. Yet, once put in place, the value of making these policies integral to a more formal, long-term commitment to the company's non-managerial employees, in order to win their loyalty, became apparent. Managers wanted these employees to think of themselves as valuable company resources to whom the company had an abiding commitment, in the form of employment stability and long-term material rewards, and from whom the company expected regular and conscientious work. While other companies cut back benefit programmes to non-managerial employees as labour unrest faded, GE maintained, and generally strengthened, its programmes.

The labour policies developed at GE during the 1920s were not unique in American industry but they were certainly enlightened relative to the practices of many corporate employers. Yet the concept of corporate management espoused by Swope and Young, progressive as it may have been for its time, was, from the point of view of workers' involvement in the production process, extremely limited. In particular, it did not contemplate any attempt to break down the organizational segmentation between managers and workers that had evolved in GE, as it had in the other leading sectors of US industry.

From the foundation of General Electric in 1892 the company had made strategic investments in the development of a powerful managerial organization that allowed it to develop and sustain a formidable competitive advantage in the electrical industry. The company's early innovative success was dependent on the learning of managers and engineers but it also relied on the experience of the skilled workers employed in the company's heavy apparatus plants, where production was dependent on a relatively high proportion of skilled machinists and other types of craftsmen (Wise n.d.: 201). These men comprised a small aristocracy of labour within GE and their skills were integral to the organizational learning process that generated the company's competitive advantage. To produce the high-quality, custom-designed products that were demanded in the apparatus business, management of necessity had to invest in developing the knowledge of these workers and in integrating it with that of managers and engineers.

With the exception of this small aristocracy of labour, however, the company made no major commitments to investments that would integrate the vast majority of shop-floor workers as insiders to the corporate learning process. For Swope and Young, it was taken for granted that managers were the insiders on whom the success of the corporation depended. Workers were stakeholders in the enterprise, just as shareholders were, but managers were regarded as the ones with the expert knowledge required to run the business in a way that could satisfy the interests of all. From their perspective, workers supplied effort and managers used their knowledge to coordinate that effort with other inputs to the business. Swope and Young considered employee welfare to be related to issues of economic security and cultural opportunities rather than control over work organization and resource allocation. With respect to their scheme of works councils, for example, the historian of General Electric, George Wise, notes that

concepts of workplace democracy, or a genuine interest in workers' hopes, fears, and attitudes, had no place in the scheme. In their more candid moments, even enlightened leaders such as Swope . . . said frankly that it was the job of management to manage, and the job of workers to do as they were told. 'If you could guarantee conditions of autocracy, there isn't any doubt it would be the best form of organization,' Swope said in an address to the company's management in 1923, 'for there is no doubt that the manager could run the business better than any democratic conclave.' The only purpose for even a little bit of democracy was to help the management identify management talent: 'the best way of guaranteeing a succession of good managers is to have them grow in the open.' (Wise, n.d.: 280–1, quoting from Speech to Camp Emmons, Association Island, 1923)

Swope and Young were unwilling or unable to see that workers could be integrated as insiders to the organizational learning process, if resources were committed to the strategic development of their skills and knowledge, and strategic control over the allocation of resources that shaped the organization of their work was, to some extent, devolved to them. Ironically, given their rhetoric, Swope and Young not only failed to break down the organizational segmentation that they inherited, they also presided over changes in corporate strategy which had the effect of drawing the lines of exclusion between management and workers much more starkly than had been the case in the company's early decades. The most important of these changes was their strategy of diversification into appliances.

In the mass-production industry of consumer appliances it was self-evident to contemporary US managers that workers were the outsiders and managers the insiders to the collective learning process which generated innovation and competitive advantage. The diversification into appliances transformed the skill balance of shop-floor work within GE. With the company's expansion into consumer appliances, semi-skilled and unskilled jobs were created in even greater numbers. In the 1920s and 1930s, refrigerators were the most important appliances produced by GE and the nature of work undertaken within the refrigerator plants was starkly different from that conducted in the apparatus plants:

[R]efrigerator buildings resembled auto factories more than other sections of electrical plants. The product was large and complex but standard; jobs were learned easily; if the line broke down for any length of time, hundreds or even thousands of people were forced to stop their labor. The resemblance was reflected in the workers' behavior and consciousness. As in auto factories, line speed up was the greatest grievance. The remedies were brief spontaneous strikes and the 'skippy'—that is, the tactic of simply letting every third or fourth box move down the line uncompleted. When unfinished refrigerators jammed up at the end of the line, supervisors realised they had to cut the speed. (Schatz 1983: 34)

Refrigerator workers had much to complain about, especially as compared with the aristocracy of labour in the apparatus plants, but, as Ronald Schatz notes, during the 1920s and early 1930s, 'They seldom became plant-wide union leaders . . . for their grievances were untypical and their perspective comparatively restricted. They were isolated in separate buildings and paid by the hour rather than by incentives, as most electrical workers were. Union leaders who did emerge from refrigerator buildings were usually nonproduction workers' (Schatz 1983: 34). As consumer appliances became increasingly important to GE's overall business, however, the mix of shop-floor work for the company as a whole changed substantially. The behaviour and consciousness of the labour force that performed this work evolved in response, as did that of the managerial collectivity who supervised work and strategically shaped its organization (Schatz 1983; O'Sullivan 1998).

3.3.2. The Onset of the Great Depression

The Great Depression focused a spotlight on the lines of exclusion in the GE organization, as it did throughout American industry. The limitations of the philosophy espoused by Swope and Young, and corporate liberalism in general, were thrown into stark relief. When the US stock market came tumbling down in October 1929, the price of GE's stock joined other industrials in a free fall. As production declined and unemployment climbed nationwide, Swope reacted by putting a company-funded unemployment compensation plan into effect and claimed that GE's powerful financial position could insulate the company from the massive layoffs occurring elsewhere. However, by October 1930 managers at GE plants were requesting authorization to dismiss low-productivity workers and Swope agreed that layoffs were necessary. By early 1932, as the Depression deepened, GE was making only one-quarter of the electrical products it produced four years earlier, and its revenues no longer covered expenses (Wise n.d.: 286–92). Notwithstanding the rhetoric of Swope and Young about their being trustees for labour as well as capital, the company cut wages and work hours and preserved dividends to stockholders.

GE was highly selective in its layoff policy. In choosing who to keep on the payroll it announced the identity of the insiders and outsiders in loud and clear terms. Great pains were taken to keep the aristocracy of labour with the company, in contrast to the low-skilled mass-production workers, particularly in the appliance business, who were considered dispensable. GE also tried to insulate its expenditures on industrial research during the Depression, with top managers arguing that pure science and innovation remained critical to GE's success, and that continuity in the pursuit and application of new knowledge was of the essence (Wise n.d.: 301). There were layoffs in the research laboratories but they tended to affect administrative staff disproportionately. The commitment to research by GE's managers was publicly bolstered when the 1932 Nobel Prize for chemistry was given to a GE scientist, Irving Langmuir, for his research on surface chemistry, in the first award by the Nobel Committee for scientific work outside a university.

In the US corporate economy, in general, the Great Depression resulted in massive declines in sales, capacity utilization, and employment, especially for the large manufacturing enterprises which sold in the durables markets and which, free from debt, could cut back production without fear of bankruptcy (Chandler 1970: 23, 36). But, given the sound financial condition of the major industrial corporations coming out of the 1920s, they were largely able in the 1930s to maintain their productive capabilities. Having invested in the skills of managerial employees, the corporations sought to keep their managerial organizations intact. Generally, the more valuable the employees as productive resources, the more reluctant were the corporations to part company with them. Indeed, during the 1930s, industrial corporations continued to augment their R&D capabilities. The research laboratories of US manufacturing enterprises employed 2,775 scientific and engineering personnel, or 0.56 research professionals per thousand manufacturing employees, in 1921; 10,927 professionals or 1.93 per thousand in 1933; and almost 28,000 professionals or 3.5 per thousand in 1940 (Mowery 1981, 1986). Moreover, according to a study of 16 of the 50 largest firms in the US in 1937, the decade from 1929 to 1939 was more fruitful in terms of product innovation than the 1920s (Thorp and Crowder 1941: 661).

Within the major industrial corporations, it was the shop-floor workers who were particularly affected by massive cutbacks in employment because, in times of crisis, most of the industrial corporations deemed shop-floor workers to be dispensable. Production employment in manufacturing fell by 31 per cent between 1929 and 1933. By 1933, wages and salaries in US manufacturing had fallen to 48.6 per cent of their 1929 levels (Chandler 1970: 36). The automobile industry was among the industries worst affected. In 1929, Detroit automobile companies employed 475,000 workers; 125,000 were laid off in 1930 and 100,000 more in 1931. By then two-thirds of the Detroit labour force was unemployed (Rothschild 1974: 36). In 1933 wages and salaries in the automobile and automobile equipment industry were a mere 35.9 per cent of their 1929 level (Chandler 1970: 36).

The economic hardship experienced by workers, as measured by the availability of work, reached a high point in 1932 and 1933 as the unemployment rate reached 23.6 per cent and then 24.9 per cent of the labour force compared with only 3.2 per cent in 1929. But high levels of unemployment, although they declined from these peaks, persisted for the rest of the 1930s. It was not until 1941, thanks to the wartime economy, that unemployment fell below 10 per cent of the labour force (Chandler 1970: 5–6).

The Depression also had a serious impact on corporate profitability; as Table 3.3 shows, corporate profits before tax in 1930 were just over one-third of their 1929 level and by 1931 the corporate sector as a whole had run into losses. The impact was, however, unevenly distributed, with smaller corporations suffering much more than larger ones; one study found that in 1931 and 1932 corporations with net assets of $50 million or more recorded net profits as a group whereas those with fewer assets recorded losses (Chandler 1970: 28). What was also striking was the extent to which corporations maintained dividends despite the profit downturn; total dividend payments plummeted by 65 per cent from 1929 to 1933 but the rate of decrease was

TABLE 3.3 US Corporate Profits, 1929–1933 (millions of US dollars)

	1929	1930	1931	1932	1933
Profits before tax	9,628	3,322	−780	−3,017	151
Taxes	1,369	842	498	385	521
Profits after tax	8,259	2,480	−1,278	−3,402	−370
Dividends paid	5,813	5,490	4,088	2,565	2,056
Undistributed profits	2,446	−3,010	−5,366	−5,967	−2,426

Source: Chandler (1970: 27).

still lower than that of corporate profits after tax. To sustain dividends, therefore, corporations had to eat into their undistributed profits (Chandler 1970: 28).

3.4. New Deals, Old Deals

If economic prosperity in the 1920s had insulated corporate management from challenges to the legitimacy of their control over corporate resources, when it disappeared there were plenty who sought to hold corporate managers accountable for its loss. Ordinary Americans had been promised economic prosperity as workers and consumers in the 1920s but these promises looked like illusions in the 1930s. In his presidential acceptance speech in 1932, Franklin D. Roosevelt suggested that a central cause of the Depression was that corporations had allocated resources without due attention to the interests of workers, stockholders, and consumers:

In the years before 1929 we know that this country had completed a vast cycle of building and inflation . . . Now it is worth remembering and the cold figures of finance prove it that during that time there was little or no drop in prices . . . although these same figures proved that the cost of production fell very greatly; corporate profit resulting from this period was enormous . . . the consumer was forgotten . . . the worker was forgotten . . . and the stockholder was forgotten.

What was the result? Enormous corporate surpluses piled up . . . Where did those surpluses go? . . . Chiefly in two directions: first, into new and unnecessary plants which now stand stark and idle; and, second, into the call money market of Wall Street . . .

Then came the crash. You know the story. Surpluses invested in unnecessary plants became idle. Men lost their jobs; purchasing dried up; banks became frightened and started calling loans. Credit contracted. Industry stopped. Commerce declined and unemployment mounted. (quoted in Tugwell 1968: 256)

These statements of Roosevelt on the problem of corporate control echoed something of the tone of discussions that took place in the early 1930s as the economic and social implications of the US system of corporate governance became subject to renewed scrutiny. It seemed to some political elites that it might be an opportune time to challenge unilateral managerial control over the allocation of corporation resources and returns.

3.4.1. The Governance of the Modern US Corporation

Undoubtedly the most influential analysis of 'the modern corporation' and its governance during this period was that of Adolf Berle and Gardiner Means (1932). The research project that resulted in *The Modern Corporation and Private Property* began in 1927 when Berle received a grant from the Social Science Research Council (SSRC). The SSRC was funded by the Laura Spelman Rockefeller Foundation, which counted William Ripley and Edward Filene, the well-known retailer and welfare capitalist, among the members of its organizing committee (Berle and Jacobs 1973: 20). Berle hired Means, who had just completed a master's degree in economics at Columbia, and with whom he had roomed earlier in his life, to work with him on the study of the modern corporation. As the project leader, Berle was not obliged to recognize Means as a co-author but he noted that 'Gardiner Means contributed so much through his statistical studies that I considered his name should appear on the title page' (Berle and Jacobs 1973: 21).

In the opening chapters of their book, Berle and Means contended that a growing concentration of economic power and an increased dispersion of stock ownership had made the 'quasi-public' corporation—'a corporation in which a large measure of separation of ownership and control has taken place'—central to the organization of economic activity in the United States.[5] The evolution of a 'corporate system', they argued, had created an unprecedented problem of corporate governance:

> In its new aspect the corporation is a means whereby the wealth of innumerable individuals has been concentrated into huge aggregates and whereby control over their wealth has been surrendered to a unified direction. The power attendant upon such concentration has brought forth princes of industry, whose position in the community is yet to be defined. The surrender of control over their wealth by investors has effectively broken the old property relationships and has raised the problem of defining these relationships anew. The direction of industry by persons other than those who have ventured their wealth has raised the question of the motive force back of such direction and the effective distribution of the returns from business enterprise. (Berle and Means 1932: 2)

Berle and Means observed that, depending on whether one considered the modern corporation from the intellectual tradition of law or from economics, one was led to a different solution to the problem of corporate governance. The lawyer's solution was to apply the traditional logic of property to the modern corporation. Those in control of corporate resources would thus be required to act as trustees for the shareholders. As such they would be expected to allocate corporate resources and returns for the sole benefit of the shareholders. Berle and Means contended that the traditional logic of property remained the pillar on which corporate law in the US rested, notwithstanding the fact that corporate law in the US had evolved from the second half of the nineteenth century to broaden the powers of management to the point where 'princes of industry' could use them against the interests of the shareholders. To the extent that the courts had failed to enforce the rights of shareholders as owners of the corporation it was not because they had succumbed to a different logic of governance. Their failure, Berle and Means argued, reflected a practical problem; the incompetence of the courts to challenge managerial decisions with regard to the operation of an enterprise led them to permit managers wide discretion in the allocation of corporate resources.

The economist's solution to the governance problem, in contrast, stemmed from the application of the traditional logic of profits to the corporation. Berle and Means characterized that logic in the following way: 'profits act as a return for the performance of two separate functions. First, they act as an inducement to the individual to risk his wealth in enterprise, and, second, they act as a spur, driving him to

---

[5] Berle and Means were certainly not the first scholars to highlight this separation. See, for example, Lippmann (1914).

exercise his utmost skill in making his enterprise profitable'. (Berle and Means 1932: 341). In the modern corporation, they contended, the functions of risk and control were separated and were, in general, undertaken by different groups of people. From this point of view, only a 'fair return' should be paid to the shareholders to compensate them for risk-bearing while the remainder of the profits should go to the controlling group to induce them to their greatest effort in running the corporation. Berle and Means concluded that 'the corporation would thus be operated financially in the interests of control, the stockholders becoming merely the recipients of the wages of capital' (Berle and Means 1932: 344).

The traditional logics of law and economics thus led to directly opposing solutions to the problem of corporate governance. Berle and Means argued that if these were the only options, the view that the corporation should be run in the interests of shareholders was the preferable one:

Changed corporate relationships have unquestionably involved an essential alteration in the character of property. But such modifications have hitherto been brought about largely on the principle that might makes right. Choice between strengthening the rights of passive property owners, or leaving a set of uncurbed powers in the hands of control therefore resolves itself into a purely realistic evaluation of different results. We might elect the relative certainty and safety of a trust relationship in favor of a particular group within the corporation, accompanied by a possible diminution of enterprise. Or we may grant the controlling group free rein, with the corresponding danger of a corporate oligarchy coupled with the probability of an era of corporate plundering. (Berle and Means 1932: 355)

Berle and Means were not content, however, with the conclusion that corporations should be run in the interests of shareholders. They argued that one was only led to it because of the deficiencies of the traditional logics of law and economics for dealing with the modern corporation. Underlying the conventional thinking of scholars in both fields was a concept of economic life, derived from classical economics, that bore little relation to the reality of the US economy in the early 1930s. In particular, it failed to provide a conceptual apparatus that could serve as the foundation for a serious legal and economic analysis of the public corporation (Berle and Means 1932: 345).

The differences between the modern corporate economy and that analysed by the classical economists were, Berle and Means believed, differences of kind rather than degree. The application of a logic rooted in the old reality to the contemporary situation was, as a result, likely to lead to perverse outcomes. Of particular concern to them was that the logic led to a neglect of the transformation of property that had taken place with the development of the corporate economy:

One traditional attribute of ownership is attached to stock ownership; the other attribute is attached to corporate control. Must we not, therefore, recognise that we are no longer dealing with property in the old sense? Does the traditional logic of property still apply? Because an owner who also exercises control over his wealth is protected in the full receipt of the advantages derived from it, must it *necessarily* follow that an owner who has surrendered control of his wealth should likewise be protected to the full? May not his surrender have so essentially changed his relation to his wealth as to have changed the logic applicable to his interest in that wealth? (Berle and Means 1932: 339; emphasis in original)

Berle and Means contended that to ignore the fact that the splitting of 'the atom of property' had changed the meaning of property and to apply the traditional logic of property to the modern corporation would mean that 'the bulk of American industry might soon be operated by trustees for the sole benefit of inactive and irresponsible security owners' (Berle and Means 1932: 354). They argued that these security owners did not merit such social support of their interests: 'the owners of passive property, by surrendering control and responsibility over the active property, have surrendered the right that the corporation should be operated in their sole inter-est—they have released the community from the obligation to protect them to the full extent implied in the doctrine of strict property rights' (Berle and Means 1932: 355).

The central message of *The Modern Corporation*, therefore, is the need to go beyond traditional legal and economic theory to develop a new concept of the corporation that can serve as a foundation for a theory of corporate governance. Only then, Berle and Means contended, could Americans come to terms with the emergence and sig-nificance of the corporate economy. Armed with such understanding, the community would then be in a position to demand that the modern corporation serve the inter-ests of all society:[6]

It remains only for the claims of the community to be put forward with clarity and force. Rigid enforcement of property rights as a temporary protection against plundering by control would not stand in the way of the modification of these rights in the interest of other groups. When a convincing system of community obligations is worked out and is generally accepted, in that moment the passive property right of today must yield before the larger interests of society. Should the corporate leaders, for example, set forth a program comprising fair wages, security to employees, reasonable service to their public, and stabi-lization of business, all of which would divert a portion of the profits from the owners of passive property, and should the community generally accept such a scheme as a logical and human solution of industrial difficulties, the interests of passive property owners would have to give way. Courts would almost of necessity be forced to recognise the result, justifying it by whatever of the many legal theories they might choose. It is conceivable,— indeed it seems almost essential if the corporate system is to survive,—that the 'control' of the great corporations should develop into a pure technocracy, balancing a variety of claims by various groups in the community and assigning to each a portion of the income stream on the basis of public policy rather than private cupidity. (Berle and Means 1932: 356)

---

[6] It was this conclusion that evoked most comment when the book was published in 1932. For Berle it represented a move to the left from the position that he had taken only one year prior to that in a debate with E. Merrick Dodd of Harvard Law School. In his exchange with Dodd, Berle had contended that if society intervened in the governance of corporations, 'The only thing that can come out of it, in any long view, is the massing of group after group to assert their private claims by force or threat—to take what each can get, just as corporate management do. The laborer is invited to organize and strike, the security holder is invited either to jettison his corporate securities and demand relief from the state, or to decline to save money at all under a system which grants to someone else power to take his savings at will. The consumer or patron is left nowhere, unless he learns the dubious art of boycott. This is an invitation not to law and orderly government but to a process of economic civil war' (Berle 1932: 1368–9).

The alternative approaches to corporate governance laid out in *The Modern Corporation* have been discussed here because they represented the three leading streams of mainstream thinking on corporate governance in the United States in the 1930s. But the discussion of corporate governance by Berle and Means also has a contemporary ring. Although the details of the arguments have changed to some extent, the three perspectives that they defined—the shareholder, the managerial, and the stakeholder theories of corporate governance—continue to capture the different points of view advanced in the discussion of corporate governance in the US until the present.

The contemporary shareholder and stakeholder theories of governance were discussed in Chapter 2. Their common weakness, I argued, was that they lack any concept of the corporation that explains how enterprises develop and utilize productive resources to generate corporate residuals that persist for sustained periods of time. In the absence of such a concept, these theories have no basis for understanding how corporate managers in the US became so powerful, how they allocated corporate resources to remain in control, and why they proved so resistant to attempts by outsiders to curb their power. Lacking any explicit recognition of the economic foundations of managerial control, these frameworks prove to be weak intellectual foundations for attempts to limit managerial discretion or to redirect it in the interests of one or other group in society. By failing to confront the economic logic of insider control these arguments maintain the pretence that outsiders could regulate corporate resource allocation and, more problematically, they provide no basis for contesting the identity of the corporate insiders, as managers have defined them, nor the types of investments that incumbent corporate strategists make.

The managerial perspective, represented in its contemporary form in the writings of US business school academics such as Michael Porter and Lester Thurow, is, at least in its recognition of the integral role of managerial insiders to corporate resource allocation, in much closer contact with the real world of corporate development than the shareholder or stakeholder arguments (Thurow 1988; Porter 1992). Yet, in focusing only on the managerial organization as the key generator of competitive advantage, the managerial perspective neglects the way in which the boundaries of corporate innovation processes are constructed. In particular, it neglects the fact that how control over corporate resources is vested in an economy, who the insiders are, and the identity of corporate strategists are shaped by the institutional evolution of the economy in which corporations are embedded. In ignoring the social foundations of incumbents' control over corporate resources, managerial theorists cede the basis on which systematic critiques of the existing distribution and exercise of corporate control could be made. Indeed, in the United States, their arguments have often served as tools in the rationalization and reproduction of the extant structure of managerial control in the economy.

None of the three leading perspectives on corporate governance provides a foundation on which managerial control over the allocation of corporate resources can be systematically challenged, at least on intellectual grounds. In practice, notwithstanding the concerns expressed, especially in the wake of the New Deal, about the emergence of a corporate oligarchy, corporate control in the US continued to be vested in the hands of corporate managers. Advocates of greater shareholder influence over the allocation of corporate resources were relatively quiescent until, as discussed in Chapter 5, structural changes in the financial sphere gave their arguments greater resonance with powerful interests in the US economy. In contrast, the closest the stakeholder view of corporate governance ever came to having a decisive effect on the governance of US corporations was with the establishment, or reform, of the Securities Exchange Commission (SEC), the Federal Trade Commission (FTC), and the National Labor Relations Board (NLRB), who can be thought of as 'stakeholder agencies' to protect the interests of consumers, security holders, and workers respectively (Kaufman *et al.* 1995: 47–8). These agencies operated from outside the corporation and none of them were empowered to interfere with the internal governance of the corporate enterprise. Managerial discretion over the allocation of corporate resources thus remained largely inviolate, a fact that is clearly seen in the evolution of the struggle by workers to improve their position in the US economy in the wake of the Depression.

3.4.2. A new deal for Workers

When, during the 1930s, even the most dominant industrial corporations failed to provide shop-floor workers with stable and remunerative jobs, many of these employees turned to industrial unionism to provide them with some control over their futures. As Sanford Jacoby put it:

Companies with massive layoffs and subsequent slow growth were not happy places in the 1930s. Those who lost their jobs underwent great hardship and found their careers permanently impaired. The experience created a lifelong preoccupation with security and stability. The same was true of workers who held on to their jobs. For them, the discrepancy between present and past, between the promise of the 1920s and the hardships of the 1930s, remained a bothersome reality. (Jacoby 1997: 51)

Backed by New Deal legislation that protected the rights of workers to organize unions and engage in collective bargaining, shop-floor employees in American manufacturing built powerful mass-production unions that would become a major force in ensuring them employment security and high wages in the post-World War II expansion. In 1933 11.3 per cent of the non-agricultural labour force was organized into trade unions; by 1955 the unionization rate had risen dramatically to 33.2 per cent (US Bureau of the Census 1976: 178).

Unions made particularly strong gains during the war years; their membership increased from 26.9 per cent in 1940 to 35.5 per cent in 1945 (US Bureau of the Census 1976: 178). Moreover, during this period, collective bargaining procedures were institutionalized in key sectors of the US economy including automobiles, steel, and rubber. With the end of the war in sight, unions began to concern themselves with the preservation and extension of their strength. Corporate managers, for their part, became increasingly concerned with rolling back, or at least controlling, union demands. Their divergent objectives soon brought organized labour and corporate executives into hostile conflict, which came to a head in the strikes of late 1945 and early 1946.

The scope for conflict was exacerbated by the desire of managers to re-establish their unilateral control over corporate activities, which they felt had been undermined by labour interests during the war (for an expression of this view, see Littler 1946). US managers were, in general, vehemently hostile to any attempt to interfere with their control over the production process. In attempting to explain the violent reaction by GM management to the UAW strike of 1936–7, Alfred Sloan later wrote that '[w]hat made the prospect [of unionism] seem especially grim in those early years was the persistent union attempt to invade basic management prerogatives. Our rights to determine production schedules, to set work standards and to discipline workers were all suddenly called into question' (Sloan 1964: 406). With the passage of the Wagner Act in 1935, and the affirmation of its constitutionality in 1937, corporate managers finally had to accept that they were required by law to bargain with labour unions in good faith. Nevertheless, they took pains to ensure that managerial prerogatives were recognized as beyond the scope of collective bargaining.

As James Atleson notes, however, even under conditions of wartime production these rights were not compromised to any significant degree:

The powerful wartime interest in labor peace could have led to a broad, inclusive reading of the scope of bargaining, especially given the unions' no-strike pledge. Yet, the interest in co-option, or in the institutionalization of dispute resolution, was apparently weaker than the War Labor Board's preference for unrestricted managerial freedom over certain matters. (Atleson 1993: 166)

In a number of decisions of the War Labor Board (WLB), it was explicitly stated that managerial rights fell outside the scope of collective bargaining. Atleson gives the example of the Montgomery Ward decision of 1943, in which it was deemed that arbitration did not extend to management activities related to

[c]hanges in business practice, the opening or closing of new units, the choice of personnel, the choice of merchandise to be sold, or other business questions of a like nature not having to do directly and primarily with the day-to-day life of the employees and their relations with their supervisors. (quoted in Atleson 1993: 164)

Yet, notwithstanding the precedent set by the WLB's insulation of managerial prerogatives from the collective bargaining process, when the war ended, managers seemed to believe that unions posed a serious challenge to their control over corporations. Harris describes the situation that managers perceived themselves to be confronted with:

The emerging American labour movement, stronger in many respects than it had been in 1939, talked in terms of a role for itself in politics, economic management, and workplace industrial relations which was larger than most businessmen were willing to allow. There was more talk than action, more ambition than achievement, but there was enough real growth in labor power to make even responsible unionism seem quite formidable.

What businessmen could see around them was bad enough; what they feared might be in prospect, if current trends were allowed to develop unchecked, might become intolerable. This explains the saliency of the 'management prerogatives' issue in 1944–47—the anxious, detailed discussion of how these prerogatives had been eroded, and how they could be defended and recovered. (Harris 1982: 88)

The threat to management control was seen as emanating from more than just the 'respectable' unions. A wildcat strike wave from 1942 to 1945 caused serious disruptions across a number of leading industrial sectors, reflecting a surge of shop-floor unrest aimed not only at managers, but also at union leaders. But the union leadership proved that it had not forgotten how to strike when, during the post-war bargaining rounds of 1946, 1947, and 1948, unions and management fought for advantage. For many, even most, unionists, their increased activism was designed to increase their leverage in negotiating wages and working conditions rather than a signal of their ambition to participate in corporate decisions about the allocation of corporate resources. But there were union leaders who wanted to go beyond the field of personnel policy in their negotiations with corporate management (Harris 1982: 67–74).

One of these was Walter Reuther of the UAW. He had taken over as head of the UAW General Motors Department in 1939 and had already aroused the suspicion and ire of GM management when in 1940 he announced his '500 Planes a Day' plan to produce military planes without disrupting civilian production. What became known as the Reuther Plan aroused interest and respect in many quarters but Charles Wilson, the president of GM, was less impressed by Reuther's experiment in 'counterplanning from the shop floor up' (quoted in Lichtenstein 1995: 162):

Everyone admits that Reuther is smart but this is none of his business . . . If Reuther wants to become part of management, GM will be happy to hire him. But so long as he remains Vice-President of the Union, he has no right to talk as if he were Vice-President of a company. (quoted in Lichtenstein 1995: 166)

When, in the first post-war bargaining round, Reuther attempted to link wage increases to GM's capacity to pay, calling on the company to open its books, so that all could see that they could afford higher wages without raising prices to consumers, GM management took it as further evidence of Reuther's desire to violate their rights to control the businesses they ran and they fought back with vehemence. The UAW struck to achieve their demands but

Reuther lost on all of the 'economic' issues of the strike. He had to move much further from his initial wage demand than GM did from its first wage offer, and he failed utterly in his attempt to introduce corporate pricing policy as a proper subject for bargaining or arbitration. The sovereign power of corporate management to make investment and pricing policy—'the very heart of management judgement and discretion in private industry'—was protected absolutely. GM did not even have to disclose any of the confidential information on which forecasts and decisions were based. (Harris 1982: 140)

GM was well satisfied with the settlement it won, not only for its implications for the economic performance of the company but also because of the agreement's broader significance:

The corporation had made its point, on behalf of the entire business community, that basic management rights were not negotiable. The scope of collective bargaining had been narrowly confined to wages, hours, and working conditions, and even there the corporation's power to take an initiative in instituting change was adequately broad. (Harris 1982: 143)

Most subsequent collective bargaining agreements followed the lead set by the 1945 UAW–GM contract in incorporating a 'right-to-manage' clause. From that time on, industrial unions did not, in general, challenge the principle of management's right to control the development and utilization of the enterprise's productive capabilities. An internal battle was fought over the appropriate agenda for organized labour but it ended in defeat for the left wing of the US labour movement. The conservative elements of the movement took control and pursued a bargaining strategy that was focused on winning job security, wage increases, and fringe benefits for their members (Lichtenstein 1982; Schatz 1983; Katz 1985). The contest for corporate control was thus lost before it had ever really begun.

The system negotiated between US mass-production unions and corporate management, which ensured that industrial corporations had to share the financial gains of the post-World War II prosperity with their shop-floor workers, has come to be described as 'job-control' unionism:

Each job is defined in very careful and elaborate detail. The union then imposes upon this detailed job structure a set of negotiated wages, actually specifying how much the employer must pay for each job or work task; a set of 'job security' provisions which determine how those jobs (and hence the wages attached to them) are to be distributed among the workers; and a set of disciplinary standards which limit, in the light of each worker's own particular work requirements, what obligations he or she has to the employer and how a failure to meet those obligations will be sanctioned. (Piore 1982: 8; see also Herding 1972; Kochan *et al.* 1986)

The system of job control did restrict the freedom of managers in the organization of shop-floor work, compared to what they had enjoyed before the war. In the mass-production industries, however, given the dominant managerial perspective on the role of workers in the production process, the post-war loss of flexibility in the allocation of blue-collar workers did not seem such a sacrifice, especially if it allowed managers to protect the internal governance of US corporations from more direct challenges to their control over the allocation of corporate resources.

3.4.3. Defending Corporate Managers' 'Right' to Manage

What justifications did corporate managers invoke, to themselves and to others, to legitimize their uncontested control over the allocation of corporate resources? Traditionally, managers had contended that their control over corporate resources was based on property rights and that their primary responsibility was to run corporate operations in the interests of shareholders. The ideology that corporations were run in the interests of shareholders lived on after World War II. The theme of 'people's capitalism'—the idea that US corporate enterprises were 'owned' and controlled in the interests of masses of small stockholders—was frequently expounded, especially by those, like the New York Stock Exchange, with a particular interest in promoting the illusion. Corporate managers themselves often found the perpetuation of the illusion of people's capitalism a useful one because, as Bayless Manning, the dean of Stanford Law School, put it in 1958, 'People's Capitalism and Corporate Democracy are slogans with an inverse relationship. Each expansion of the first undermines the second. Every sale of common stock to a new small investor adds to the fractionation of share-ownership which lies at the root of the impotence of shareholder voting as a check on management' (Manning 1965: 113).

The separation of ownership and control in many of the nation's leading corporations made it increasingly apparent that managers' characterization of themselves as shareholder-designates was unrealistic as well as coy. And those who spoke in favour of a people's capitalism—the 'corporate Jacksonians' as Manning labelled them—found themselves accused of participating with corporate management in the obfuscation of the central issues at stake with respect to the governance of corporations. As Manning observed,

Perhaps the most serious charge against the myth of shareholder democracy is that its slogans do much to create an impression in the public mind, and in the minds of the potential investors in a People's Capitalism, that a degree of shareholder supervision exists which in fact does not. It is quite arguable that the net effect of the corporate Jacksonians has been to impede their ultimate objective of responsible corporate management. The forms and mechanisms of shareholder democracy divert attention from the real problems of holding business managements to a desirable standard of responsibility. Modern international politics demonstrates that a centralized control group can do much behind a democratic panoply that could not otherwise be done. In actual effect, the paraphernalia of corporate democracy may operate as a first line of defense around management's high ground of control. (Manning 1965: 106)

Faced with such critiques from respectable and influential commentators, it is, therefore, not surprising that in the post-war era corporate managers sought other grounds for justifying the control that they exercised over the allocation of corporate resources. During the 1920s, as I noted above, an alternative to the view that corporate managers were the paid attorneys of capital had been propounded by the progressive executives of companies like GE. They had argued that, with the growing importance and socialization of corporate organization, corporate managers had become trustees for society as a whole. After the war, corporate managers increasingly represented themselves as 'socially responsible':

In managerial ideology, businessmen are held to be accountable to a variety of pressures and 'constituencies'—the state, the public interest, the consumer, the local community, the business community, employees, et al., variously ranked. But it is up to the management of any particular firm to decide what its obligations are, how to meet them, and when they have been met. Management is the 'trustee' or 'steward' of the various groups with an interest in the firm; it devotes itself to 'service' to them, and gains legitimacy thereby. Management claims that it is in the best position to reconcile and satisfy the numerous and conflicting demands made of it, and that its performance in doing so is adequate. There is no need for unions, the state, or others to impose specific, enforceable obligations upon it. (Harris 1982: 97)

The view of corporate management as trustees for society was by no means confined to the self-descriptions of corporate managers. It is already apparent in the faith expressed by Berle and Means that corporate management could develop into a 'purely neutral technocracy'. A similarly idealistic view of management is found among journalists, writers, and many leading scholars of the corporation in the postwar period. The broad acceptance of the managerial ideology of trusteeship seemed to be rooted in the technocratic consensus that prevailed in elite circles of US society after the war, and in the faith in professionalism that it spawned. In a view that resonated with the ideas of influential students of the corporation, the editors of *Fortune* declared in 1951 that '[t]he manager is becoming a professional in the sense that like all professional men he has a responsibility to society as a whole' (*Fortune* 1951; see also Drucker 1949: 35, 99, 102, 340, 342; Kaysen 1959; Sutton *et al.* 1956: 57–8, 65, 86–7, 155, 163, 165, 359; *Fortune* 1956).

Proponents of the 'managerialist' thesis of the corporation seemed content to let professionalism do the job of ensuring that the broader objectives which corporate managers espoused would be achieved. These social responsibilities were certainly not enshrined in corporate law. Although the burst of federal regulation in the 1930s, as well as later regulatory initiatives such as industrial safety and accident laws, created new legal requirements of which corporate managers had to take account in their allocation of corporate resources, the law did not attempt to interfere with the internal governance of the corporation in a way that would directly challenge managerial control. And, with the development of the 'business judgement rule', the courts became more and more reluctant to challenge corporate management on decisions that were deemed to be part of the normal process of running a business (Kaufman *et al.* 1995: 51).

But although the de facto legal treatment of the corporation ensured that corporate control remained firmly in the hands of managers, the acquiescence of corporation law and the courts to unilateral managerial control remained implicit. As Hurst noted, with the exception of laws authorizing the use of corporate funds for philanthropic purposes, 'the law added no definition of standards or rules to spell out for what purposes or by what means management might properly make decisions other than in the interests of shareholders' (Hurst 1970: 107). As Erber put it, 'The managers have not succeeded, either through legislation or adjudication, to resolve their ambivalent, contradictory status of power without property' (Erber 1986: 202).

The lack of formal legal recognition of the legal and economic obsolescence of the shareholder-designate concept of corporate management stemmed in part from the powerful emotional attachment in the United States to the idea that the shareholder 'owned' the corporation. Thus, notwithstanding the evidence that the development of the corporate economy had split the 'atom' of property, as Berle and Means had put it, 'the law's response to these facts', in Manning's judgement,

has been partially to ignore them, partially to try to exorcise them by mislabeling, and partially to decree that the clock of history shall run backward. Finding the shareholder a passing investor, we have insisted that he is an owner and a member of an electorate. Finding managements to be hirers of capital, we have tried to bury this disquieting fact by calling them hired of the shareholder-owners. Finding 'control' to have slid away from 'ownership,' we have sought to put the control back with the ownership where it 'belongs'. (Manning 1965: 107)

But the failure to recognize at law the reality of corporate control not only stemmed from an emotional commitment to the ideology of private property; it also reflected the vagueness of the most widely accepted alternative for justifying that control, the view of the manager as trustee for society. Edward Mason effectively highlighted its nebulosity in 1958 in an attack on what he called 'The Apologetics of Managerialism'. Mason contended that 'the institutional stability and opportunity for growth of an economic system are heavily dependent on the existence of a philosophy or ideology justifying the system in a manner generally acceptable to the leaders of thought in the community'. The power of classical economics, he argued, was that it had provided not only an analytical framework which could be used to explain economic behaviour, 'but also a defense—and a carefully reasoned defense— of the proposition that the economic behaviour promoted and constrained by the institutions of a free-enterprise system is, in the main, in the public interest' (Mason 1958: 118). Mason recognized that, towards the end of the nineteenth century, 'the growth of large firms and other institutional changes began to call into question the assumptions on which the system was built' to the extent that 'the attempted resuscitation by the National Association of Manufacturers, in 1946, of the "philosophy of natural liberty" is inevitably a somewhat moth-eaten patchwork' (Mason 1958: 199). The problem, from his point of view, was that the managerial literature, though it undermined the intellectual presuppositions of classical economics, did not provide 'an equally satisfying apologetic for big business' because it failed to provide answers to some critical questions:

Assume an economy composed of a few hundred large corporations, each enjoying substantial market power and all directed by managements with a 'conscience'. Each management wants to do the best it can for society consistent, of course, with doing the best it can for labor, customers, suppliers, and owners. How do prices get determined in such an economy? How are factors remunerated, and what relation is there between remuneration and performance? What is the mechanism, if any, that assures effective resource use, and how can corporate managements 'do right by' labor, suppliers, customers, and owners while simultaneously serving the public interests? The 'philosophy of natural liberty' had a reasoned answer to these questions, but I can find no reasoned answer in the managerial literature. (Mason 1958: 120)

To answer these questions would have required an economic analysis of the process through which corporate organizations allocate resources and returns. The contemporary bias among US economists towards neoclassical theory, however, at best diverted them from this task and, at worst, persuaded them to treat corporate activities as reducible to market forces (see Chapters 1 and 2). There were scholars who did make more serious attempts to understand corporate resource allocation. Yet, in taking the contours of corporate organization that they saw around them as inevitable, rather than the result of the particular social and economic evolution of the United States, much of this research fell prey to a different determinism (see, for example, Galbraith 1967; Chandler 1977).

When a serious challenge to unilateral managerial control over the allocation of corporate resources in US corporations did emerge, it did not come from scholars attempting to move beyond the limitations of the traditional logic of law and economics by studying the historical and comparative evidence on how corporate organizations actually worked. To the contrary, it came from scholars who were intent on reviving the philosophy of natural liberty in the analysis of corporate governance by proclaiming that corporations should be run for the sole benefit of their shareholders.[7] Notwithstanding the defects in its theoretical foundations, already discussed in Chapters 1 and 2 above, the shareholder theory of governance was to have important repercussions for the governance of US corporate enterprises, as will be illustrated in Chapters 5 and 6.

When the shareholder attack on managerial control came it was not, in its genesis, fuelled by an uprising of small shareholders, for, as Bayless Manning described them,

the usual shareholder's interest in the control factor is reflected in his unlimited boredom with the devices of corporate democracy, in his simple decision to depart when he objects to the way things are going, and in his eagerness to snap up Dodge stock in 1925 and Ford stock in 1956, ignoring the absence of voting control. It may be legitimately speculated that, but for the listing rules of the New York Stock Exchange, enormous blocks of pure nonvoting stock of major corporations would probably be outstanding in the hands of the public. In most situations, the control differences among publicly held corporations with fully nonvoting stock, the Ford pattern in which the common held by the public is substantially noncontrolling, and the General Motors pattern in which the publicly held common legally carries voting control, are primarily differences in words. (Manning 1965: 110)

The shareholder revolt did not rely on a volte-face by these passive shareholders. Rather, the shareholder theory that corporations should be run in the interests of shareholders was invoked by powerful interests to justify their attempts to take advantage of important structural changes in the productive and financial sectors of the US economy in ways that could advance their own economic and political positions *vis-à-vis* US corporate enterprises. To understand recent changes in the ideology of corporate control, and their implications for corporate performance, we have first to understand the nature of the changes that occurred in the productive and financial spheres. These changes are the subject of the next two chapters.

---

[7] For early and influential expressions of this view in the post-war period, see Manne (1962, 1965).

4

The Post-war Evolution of Managerial Control in the United States

4.1. Introduction

In the decades after World War II the US was indisputably the world's most productive economy. Although the effects of wartime devastation played an important role in retarding the relative performance of other leading industrial economies, even after these economies recovered, US enterprises retained a considerable lead in most industrial sectors (Nelson 1990: 121; Wright and Nelson 1995: 148). In the post-World War II decades, the United States not only held dominant positions in capital goods industries such as steel, machine tools, and chemicals but was also a leader in consumer goods industries such as automobiles, consumer electronics, and pharmaceuticals. The post-war leadership of US industry was not, however, confined to the mass-production industries. The country had also become dominant in high-technology industries. In the mid-1960s, as Table 4.1 shows, the United States had a strong market position in virtually all high-tech industries; in 1965, US enterprises controlled 50 per cent of world market share in aircraft and parts, 43 per cent in guided missiles and aerospace, 36 per cent in professional and scientific instruments, 36 per cent in office, computing, and accounting machinery, and 31 per cent in engines, turbines, and parts (Diwan and Chakraborty 1991: 43).

The leadership of US corporate enterprises in mass-production industries had been built up from the late nineteenth century, as described in the previous chapter, and the central elements of the system of governance that shaped the allocation of corporate resources in the post-war period bore a strong resemblance to their pre-war counterparts. In the quarter century after the war, however, the corporate control of many leading US mass producers evolved in ways that placed considerable internal pressures on the viability of the system of managerial control as the institutional foundation for industrial innovation. In particular, the ossification of the management–labour divide in these enterprises, as well as the growing distance that emerged between senior executives and the belly of the managerial organization, weakened the internal capacity of many US corporate enterprises to generate innovation.

In contrast to the mass-production industries, the post-war developmental strength of the US in high-technology industries was of a more recent vintage (Nelson 1990). Massive investments in R&D underwrote US pre-eminence in high-technology industries after the war. Into the late 1960s, in absolute terms, expenditure on R&D in the United States was more than double that of the United Kingdom, Germany, France, and Japan combined (Diwan and Chakraborty 1991:

TABLE 4.1 US Share of World High-technology Markets, 1965

Industry	SIC code	World market share, 1965 (%)
All high-technology industries		28.0
Industrial chemicals	281, 286	24.4
Plastics & synthetics	282	20.0
Other chemicals	284, 285, 287	16.7
Engines, turbines, & parts	351, 355	31.3
Office, computing, & accounting machinery	357	35.7
Electrical equipment	361–2, 365, 369	23.8
Communication equipment & electronic components	366, 367	20.4
Aircraft & parts	372	50.0
Guided missiles & space	376	43.1
Professional & scientific instruments	381–2, 386	35.7
Optical & medical instruments	383–85	20.6

Source: Diwan and Chakraborty (1991: 43).

150; Mowery and Rosenberg 1993). In 1965, the number of scientists and engineers engaged in R&D as a proportion of total employment was two and a half to three times as high in the United States as in Japan, Germany, or France (Nelson and Wright 1995: 151).

As in the mass-production industries, dominant corporate enterprises made critical commitments of resources to the development of industrial capabilities in the high-tech industries. The governance institutions that shaped resource allocation in US enterprises in the high-technology industries were similar in certain ways to those that governed, for example, the automobile and steel corporations. Yet, there were also important differences that stemmed from the extensive intervention by the federal government in the innovation process, the prevalence of startup firms, and distinctive employment practices in some of the dominant high-tech enterprises. The importance and timing of these differences varied considerably across the high-tech industries. In the discussion of high-tech governance that follows, I will focus on the electronics complex, which includes the microelectronics, computer hardware, and software industries, since, in the post-war period, its system of governance was the most distinctive of the high-tech sectors in comparison with that which shaped corporate resource allocation in the mass-production enterprises.

The electronics complex is also a useful vantage point from which to review the nature and implications of governance in the post-war high-tech industries because of its frequent characterization by academic and popular writers as the leading exemplar of the economic virtues of a system of corporate governance that supports market control. The historical evidence, as I shall show, supports a more complex interpretation of the relationship between corporate governance and economic performance. Indeed, I characterize the prevalent system of governance as a distinctly organizational phenomenon, albeit one which, largely because of the intervention of the federal government, looked somewhat different from that which prevailed in other dynamic industrial sectors. The differences in the nature of governance between the mass-production and high-tech industries ultimately had important performance implications when, as will be discussed in the following chapter, US industry was increasingly confronted by new competitive challenges from abroad. Competition proved most threatening in the mass-production industries. In general, the high-tech industries proved more resilient, although, in certain sectors, especially electronic components and computers, it was clear by the early 1980s that US enterprises faced serious competitive problems.

4.2. The Post-war Governance of Mass-production Enterprises

In most of the US industrial corporations that dominated the mass-production industries after World War II the organizational learning that was the basis for their competitive advantage continued to be concentrated among technical, administrative, and professional personnel within the managerial organization. The hierarchical segmentation of managerial employees from blue-collar workers and the development of skill-displacing technologies meant that the structures of organizational learning evolved in ways that systematically excluded shop-floor operatives. Nevertheless, the motivation of these production workers remained an issue; the corporations still relied on their steady work—high effort, low absenteeism—to obtain high levels of utilization of the installed mass-production technologies (Lazonick 1990).

In eliciting such effort, therefore, the mass-production corporations could gain economically by sharing some of the corporate surplus with their shop-floor operatives in the forms of more stable employment and greater wages and benefits than would otherwise be available to these workers. The combination of a growing economy and union-enforced seniority ladders in the post-war decades meant that blue-collar workers with the major corporations could realistically expect the corporation to provide them with long-term employment. Yet the corporate ideology persisted that shop-floor workers were merely 'hourly' employees, and hence easily interchangeable units of labour, whereas, as 'salaried' personnel, managerial employees were deemed to be members of the enterprise in whose skills the corporation had invested and in the retention of whose capabilities the corporation had an interest. The resultant organizational segmentation between managers and workers was thus a division between insiders and outsiders to the corporation's learning process—one that would make it difficult for these companies to respond effectively when from the 1960s they confronted international competitors who were generating higher-quality, lower-cost products through the integration of both managerial and shop-floor employees into processes of organizational learning. Even before international competition represented a major problem for the US mass producers, there were growing concerns about the internal limits of the US system of corporate governance for generating innovation.

4.2.1. The Internal Limits of Managerial Control?

With the slowdown in aggregate productivity from the mid-1960s, concerns were expressed that the US system of corporate governance, and more precisely the managerial control over the allocation of corporate resources that it supported, had reached its internal limits as a generator of economic development. Many commentators interpreted rising absenteeism, turnover, and strikes, as well as surveys of worker attitudes, as evidence that workers were increasingly discontent with their role in the production process. In its influential study of *Work in America*, the Department of Health, Education, and Welfare, for example, concluded that '[p]erhaps the most consistent complaint reported to our task force has been the failure of bosses to listen to workers who wish to propose better ways of doing their jobs' (HEW 1973: 37). There was considerable evidence that the social costs of worker alienation were high. Moreover, as Andrew Zimbalist put it, 'Alienated work also has economic costs. With the concurrent deskilling of jobs and the increasing level of educational attainment of the work force, the historically proven methods of Taylorism and work hierarchy seem to have exhausted their capacity to raise productivity' (Zimbalist 1975: 54; see also Marglin 1979; Weisskopf, Bowles, and Gordon 1983: 381–450).

Concerned that growing worker dissatisfaction was undercutting labour productivity and enterprise profits, some corporate managers began to take an interest in their employees' 'quality of working life'. The possibilities and challenges of job enlargement—the allocation of a range of tasks, rather than one single task, to a worker—and job enrichment—the delegation of control over the organization of work from managers to teams of workers—were widely discussed in management circles. Some corporations undertook unprecedented experiments with work reorganization in an attempt to improve corporate performance (Walton 1972).

Although many of these experiments proved successful in increasing productivity, most of them were discontinued by the corporations that initiated them. 'The paradox of successful failure' can be accounted for by a number of factors, including the loosening of labour markets in the wake of the oil-price shock of 1973 and the consequent increase in the costs to workers of expressing their dissatisfaction with their jobs (Marglin 1979: 478). But the loss of managerial commitment to work reorganization was also a defensive reaction to the challenge to unilateral managerial control over corporate resource allocation that successful experiments seemed to pose (Zimbalist 1975; Marglin 1979; Walton 1975: 21). As Stephen Marglin observed,

The basis of the social system of the capitalist factory is a strict hierarchy of command and status—and an ideology to match. Change the hierarchy of command and status, even on so trivial a matter as the speed of the line, and the entire consensual basis of the system may be disrupted. Workers who have been successfully socialized to accept their inferiority relative to supervisors and 'engineers' are emboldened by their mastery of control in one small area to reach out for more. Changes in organization change people's expectations, both of themselves and others; the experience of control enlarges not only the capacity for control, but the individual and group sense capacity. In short, changes in organization change people's heads. (Marglin 1979: 481)

For many managers, therefore, traditional methods of disciplining workers continued to prove more attractive than organizational innovations that had the potential, through their very success, to lead to a systematic challenge to 'managerial rights' (Lazonick 1990: 280–4).

Work reorganization was to resurface on the managerial agenda but only in the face of new competition that seriously threatened the dominant competitive position of US corporations in mass-production industries. The economic problems generated by the stark management–labour divide in US corporate enterprises were more difficult to ignore as US corporations proved vulnerable to international competition from the bottom up. In addition, from as early as the 1960s the system of managerial control in US industry evolved in a way that rendered many US industrial corporations vulnerable from the top down, as those who controlled the strategic allocation of corporate resources tended to become segmented from the organizations on which they depended to develop and utilize these resources—a form of organizational segmentation that I call 'strategic segmentation'.

4.2.2. The Trend towards Strategic Segmentation: Conglomeration

The leading US industrial corporations came out of World War II with their organizational capabilities extended by their wartime production experience. Major US corporations were already quite diversified by the end of the 1940s but until then they had tended to extend their product lines into related lines of business activity and to do so primarily through internal development rather than external acquisition. In the post-war decades, however, these corporations expanded not only through internal development but also on the basis of an unprecedented reliance on external growth, often into unrelated lines of business (Gort 1962: ch. 3; Rumelt 1974; Fligstein 1990: 261–73).

The emergence of the stock market in the first decades of this century had a profound effect on the development of industrial enterprise, through its facilitation of a separation of stock ownership from strategic control over internally generated corporate revenues. As the century unfolded it also became clear that, in making possible the financing of mergers and acquisitions through an exchange of corporate shares, the stock market also encouraged the continuous growth of corporate enterprise. As in the 1920s, so too in the 1950s, a booming economy provided many companies with internal resources for growth, while the booming stock market made acquisitions of other companies cheap and easy. The number of announcements to merge with or acquire another company grew from an annual average of 1,951 in 1963–7 to 3,736 in 1968–72, reaching a record peak of 5,306 in 1969 (see Table 4.2).

Using the Federal Trade Commission Line of Business data, David Ravenscraft and F. M. Scherer have shown that for the top 200 US manufacturing companies ranked

TABLE 4.2 Merger and Acquisition Announcements and Divestitures, US, 1963–1994
(Annual averages)

	1963–7	1968–72	1973–7	1978–82	1983–7	1988–92	1993	1994
Mergers & acquisitions (M&A)	1,951	3,736	1,474	1,384	1,666	1,277	1,529	1,863
Divestitures	207	1,290	1,266	789	1,023	953	1,134	1,134
As percentage of M&A	10.6	34.5	85.9	57.0	61.4	74.6	74.2	60.9

Note: In the 1960s and 1970s about 10% of all M&A and divestiture announcements were cancelled; in the 1980s about 7%; and in the 1990s about 4%.

Source: Merrill Lynch Advisory Services (1994: 2, 80, 120, 121).

by sales, the mean number of lines of business rose from 4.76 in 1950 to 10.89 in 1975. Of the 148 companies of the 200 largest in 1950 that survived until 1975, the mean number of lines of business was 5.22 in 1950 and 9.74 in 1975; the new-comers to the 1975 top 200 list were, on average, more diversified than the firms remaining on the list as well as the ones that dropped off it (Ravenscraft and Scherer 1987: 32; see also Rumelt 1974, 1982: 361; Fligstein 1990: 261–75).

As US corporations grew through expansion, extension, and diversification, they often reaped the advantages of building on existing capabilities to develop and utilize productive resources. But their growth also opened up possibilities for the onset of cumulation disadvantages of organizational segmentation (see Chapter 2). Such disadvantages are not inherent in rapid and large-scale enterprise growth, but are more likely to occur during such a process. The danger was that the very growth of the corporate enterprise, within markets, across vertical activities, and into new markets, would lead to the segmentation of those with strategic control of corporate resources from the organizations that would have to develop and utilize productive resources.

In his 1962 book Strategy and Structure, Alfred D. Chandler, Jr. documented the emergence and diffusion of the multidivisional structure within the American cor-poration from the 1920s through the 1950s. By means of administrative decentral-ization, the multidivisional structure was supposed to permit the enterprise to diversify into many new businesses without succumbing to strategic segmentation (Chandler 1962). But Chandler's conceptualization of the corporate head office as the realm of strategic decision-making and the corporate divisions as the realms of op-erational control already contemplated the segmentation between strategy and learning that by the 1950s was beginning to show itself in some of the largest, and previously most successful, US corporations that had grown rapidly through acquisition and even, in some cases, internal development.

General Electric is a case in point. Its expansion into consumer appliances in the interwar period had, by the 1940s and 1950s, brought to positions of strategic control managers who had acquired little understanding of the electrical engineering businesses, or of related technologies generated by GE Research Laboratories, which had been the foundations of the company's sustained competitive successes. Led by Ralph Cordiner, the company launched a major reorganization in the 1950s.[1]

Writing in 1962, Chandler thought that the organizational changes that had taken place at GE under Cordiner demonstrated 'future trends in the organization of the most technologically advanced type of American enterprise' (Chandler 1962: 369). Yet problems that GE faced in the 1960s and 1970s, manifested by its failure in a number of new businesses, including semiconductors, computers, and factory automation, reflected an organization that could no longer integrate strategy and learning. Although GE's top managers claimed to be decentralizing authority within the company, what they actually decentralized was responsibility for divisional or departmental performance, while keeping strategic authority and control in the head office. Managing by numbers, Cordiner and the men around him propounded the ideology that, equipped with the proper informational tools, a well-trained general manager could manage anything. By the 1960s this ideology of the 'general manager' had become conventional wisdom at the nation's business schools.

What happened to GE in the post-World War II decades happened as well to other US industrial enterprises. Whereas GE had entered the new businesses in which it competed after the war by relying to a considerable extent on internally developed capabilities, albeit with plenty of support from the US federal government, expansion through external acquisition proved the more common route to rapid corporate growth in post-war corporate America. In an analysis of the 200 largest corporations in the period from 1950 to 1975, Ravenscraft and Scherer found that entry by these corporations into new lines of business was predominantly accomplished through acquisition; only 14 per cent of these enterprises' new lines of business were entered through internal development (Scherer and Ravenscraft 1987: 13). Strategic segmentation proved to be even more of a problem for companies that relied heavily on external and unrelated growth for their expansion.

The example of RCA illustrates the point. RCA—the Radio Corporation of America—had grown, under David Sarnoff, into one of the leading electronics companies in the US from its origins as a vehicle for the control of the radio-related patents of GE, Westinghouse, AT&T and others. From the second half of the 1960s, largely under the influence of Robert Sarnoff, David's son and chosen successor, RCA committed enormous financial and organizational resources to the computer business in an attempt to compete with IBM, and to businesses entirely unrelated to its electronics capabilities such as records, books, carpets, car rental, and frozen food (Fisher, McKie, and Mancke 1983: 214; Graham 1986: 12–13). By 1975, only one-quarter of the company's revenues were earned in electronics (Chandler 1997: 90). In 1971 in a shareholder meeting that voted on the acquisition of Coronet Carpets, a woman stockholder challenged Robert Sarnoff: 'We have already gone from soup to nuts. Tell me, mister, where is it going to end? You are going to build an empire and look

---

[1] The following discussion of GE is based on O'Sullivan (1997).

TABLE 4.3 Distribution of Assets Obtained in Acquisitions of Large US Manufacturing and Mining Companies (pre-merger assets of $10 million or more), by FTC Merger Type Classification, 1948–1979 (%)

Type of merger	1948–55	1956–63	1964–71	1972–9
Horizontal	39.0	18.7	12.0	14.9
Vertical	12.7	20.0	6.6	8.3
Product extension	36.1	36.9	38.9	28.2
Market extension	2.1	6.7	7.7	3.0
Pure conglomerate	10.1	17.7	34.8	45.5

Source: Scherer and Ross (1990: 157).

what happened to all the empires' (*Wall Street Journal*, 22 Feb. 1971: 6; cited in Graham 1986: 13). The lady's remarks proved prescient. Later in 1971, after committing half a billion dollars in research money, as well as considerable management attention, to competing with IBM, RCA exited the computer industry a failure with the eventual loss of 13,000 jobs (Graham 1986: 13; Chandler 1998: 30; see also 202–28). In the longer term, failure reached right into the company's core as RCA failed to maintain its innovative capabilities even in its consumer electronics businesses. In 1987, RCA once more came under the control of GE and was subsequently dismantled.

The trend towards conglomeration—growth through unrelated diversification— extended into the US corporate economy far beyond RCA. According to Federal Trade Commission data and classifications, increasingly over the course of the post-World War II period, industrial mergers and acquisitions entailed not only diversification into new lines of business but conglomeration of lines of business that had no technological or market relations to one another. As can be seen in Table 4.3, in 1948–55 only 10.1 per cent of acquired assets were in the 'pure conglomerate' category, whereas in the period 1964–71 this figure was 34.8 per cent and in 1972–9 45.5 per cent. By 1972–9 horizontal or vertical acquisitions in the same line of business had fallen to 23.2 per cent of all assets acquired, down from 48.8 per cent in 1948–55. Among the most well-known conglomerates that emerged over this period were Beatrice Foods (290 acquisitions between 1950 and 1978), W. R. Grace (186), International Telephone and Telegraph (163), Gulf and Western Industries (155), Textron (115), Litton Industries (99), and LTV (58) (Ravenscraft and Scherer 1987: 30, 32, 38, 39). By 1973, 15 of the top 200 US manufacturing companies, as listed in Table 4.4, were classified as conglomerates.

Until the mid-1960s, most of the targets were small, closely held firms, often family firms, where the existing owner-managers wanted to liquidate their investment. These earlier acquisitions were generally financed by an exchange of equity, no doubt because this method of payment provided former owners with substantial tax advantages (Baskin and Miranti 1997: 274, 277). In the second half of the decade, however, cash and debt were the acquisition currencies of choice and conglomera-

TABLE 4.4 Conglomerates among the *Fortune* 200 Largest Firms, 1979

Rank	Company	Number of industries	
		Manufacturing	Non-manufacturing
8	ITT	14	24
15	Tenneco	13	15
42	Gulf & Western Industries	19	22
51	Litton Industries	11	8
66	LTV	8	10
73	Illinois Central Industries	11	15
103	Textron	14	2
104	Greyhound	7	12
128	Martin Marietta	8	6
131	Dart Industries	12	6
132	US Industries	17	7
143	Northwest Industries	11	7
173	Walter Kidde	12	10
180	Ogden Industries	5	8
188	Colt Industries	6	3

Source: Based on Chandler and Tedlow (1985: 772).

teurs began to target larger companies in, for example, oil, steel, banking, and insurance (Kaufman, Zacharias, and Karson 1995: 547–9).

During the 1960s, when the conglomerate merger movement was in full swing, the conglomerate promoters (and their academic admirers) touted the 'synergies' that were supposed to come from piling business upon business. 'Two plus two equals five' was a popular refrain of the conglomerateurs. According to one explanation that accurately reflects the ideology of the conglomerate era, after World War II a new generation of managers

were generally better educated and more familiar with the new scientific tools available to management such as computerized information systems, scientific decision making, and decentralized profit-center concepts. They put to the test the theory of the universality of financial management, that many businesses, no matter how diverse, can be successfully managed by relatively few executives contributing financial and planning expertise. More innovative than the predecessor generation of managers, they acted upon a new concept that under current economic conditions there was no problem in getting capital but that the real problem was putting the capital to work to satisfy the growth demands of their stockholders. (Hoffman 1972: 20).

By relying on the prevailing business ideology that a well-trained general manager could manage anything, the conglomerate movement glorified strategic segmentation. In acquiring companies and consolidating financial decision-making in the head office, the conglomerate stripped those who had been the strategic managers of the acquired businesses of strategic control. The conglomerates often retained these former top managers as divisional heads after the acquisition (maintaining former owners as managers was one IRS condition for the acquirer to be able to take advantage of tax offsets associated with the acquisition; these offsets were eventually curtailed in 1976 (Baskin and Miranti 1997: 277–8, 280)). But failure to meet financial performance targets could lead to their replacement by someone at the head office who, like the head office in general, generally had no idea of the processes of organizational learning or the strategies to shape them that the divisional businesses required to succeed.[2]

The number and total value of acquisitions increased dramatically as the 1960s unfolded. Conglomerate acquisitions peaked in 1968 and subsequently declined precipitously as the stock market declined. As the market turned bearish, conglomerates took a particularly hard beating; the Dow Jones industrial average fell from 985 at its peak in December 1968 to 631 (a decline of *c.* 36 per cent) at its nadir in May 1970 compared with an 86 per cent decline for an index consisting of ten conglomerate glamour stocks of the 1960s (Max Shapiro, *Dun's Review*, Jan. 1971: 30).

4.2.3. The Performance Impact of Conglomeration

In their statistical study of the results of merger and acquisition activity, Ravenscraft and Scherer concluded that 'on average, profitability declines and efficiency losses resulted from mergers of the 1960s and early 1970s', while their case studies revealed 'that synergies anticipated from acquisition frequently did not materialize' (Ravenscraft and Scherer 1987: 211–12). 'Much more important than their failure to achieve hoped-for synergies,' they argued,

was the failure to manage acquired companies as well as they were managed before acquisition. We have no reason to believe this was either intentional or fully anticipated. To the contrary, merger-makers of the 1960s and 1970s suffered from massive hubris. Successful in their mainline operations and perhaps in early diversification mergers, they overestimated their ability to manage a sizable portfolio of acquisitions, large and small, related and unrelated. By the time they learned that they had erred, they had already overextended themselves and were unable to cope with the problems emerging from accumulated acquisitions. Or alternatively, they recognized their limitations but pursued a damage-limiting strategy, continuing (like Beatrice Foods) to make mergers but ruthlessly selling off acquisitions that showed signs of persistent difficulty. (Ravenscraft and Scherer 1987: 212)

If, writing in 1962, Alfred Chandler had been optimistic about 'future trends in the organization of the most technologically advanced type of American enterprise', in his 1990 book, *Scale and Scope: The Dynamics of Industrial Enterprise*, he emphasized 'an overload for the decision-makers in top management' that arose during the 1960s. Citing the Ravenscraft and Scherer study, Chandler argued that such unprecedented diversification

---

[2] For a detailed case study of a failed conglomerate acquisition, see Holland (1989).

often led to a separation, that is, a breakdown of communications, between top management at the corporate office—the executives responsible for coordinating, managing, and planning and allocating resources for the enterprise as a whole—and the middle managers who were responsible for maintaining the competitive capabilities of the operating divisions in the battle for market share and profits. . . . These top managers in the corporate office no longer had, unlike their predecessors, the time to make and maintain personal contacts with the heads of the operating divisions. Nor did the senior executives have the product-specific experience needed to evaluate the proposals and to monitor the performance of the operating managers. Instead, in carrying out these critical tasks they had to rely on impersonal statistical data that had become far less relevant than the information systems devised and used in the 1920s and 1930s by corporate officers of diversified firms to carry out comparable functions. The over-load resulted, not from any lack of information but from its lack of quality and from the senior decision-makers' lack of ability to evaluate it. Top managers were beginning to lose the capabilities needed to maintain a unified enterprise whose whole was more than the sum of its parts. (Chandler 1990: 623–4)

In response to, and sometimes in anticipation of, problems stemming from strategic segmentation, many of the conglomerates began to restructure themselves in the 1970s. Ravenscraft and Scherer estimated that roughly one-third of all acquisitions (related and unrelated) made in the 1960s and early 1970s were sold off, typically when these businesses were experiencing 'poor and declining profitability' (Ravenscraft and Scherer 1987: 190). In 1975 and 1976, divestitures in the United States were actually greater than announced mergers and acquisitions (Merrill Lynch 1994: 120). Notwithstanding its striking results on the extent of the corporate sell-off, the Ravenscraft and Scherer study in fact ended before the biggest wave of divestitures. Using data on 33 major US corporate enterprises from 1950 to 1986, Porter found that more than half of the acquisitions made by these companies until 1980 had been divested by 1986; for unrelated acquisitions, the rate of divestment was even higher at 74 per cent (Porter 1987: 48, 51; see also Linn and Rozeff 1986: 428–36; Shleifer and Vishny 1991: 51–9).

The trend towards strategic segmentation had, however, more subtle and, in many ways, more enduring effects on US corporate enterprises than the measurable performance problems that have been identified. There is a difficulty in separating cause and effect but the close association between this emergent characteristic of many US corporate organizations, and the rise to prominence of a cult of professional management in these enterprises, is striking. Neil Jacoby, writing in 1969, in describing the trend towards, and perceived benefits of, managerial professionalization, captures well the spirit of US managerial culture in the post-war decades:

Radical changes occurred in the science of enterprise management after World War II. These changes had their roots in the wartime efforts of mathematicians to solve complex logistical and military problems by 'operations research'. Concepts and methods were then developed that were later found to be equally powerful in dealing with the management problems of a civilian economy. Intuitive judgement has been progressively superseded by rational decision-making processes. Such problems as evaluation of investment projects, choice of financing plans, locating facilities, scheduling production and controlling inventories are now solved by mathematical and statistical methods.

The concurrent phenomenal development of electronic computers has promoted and fa- cilitated the expansion of management science. The computer not only does routine account- ing with fantastic speed but performs the great volume of calculations involved in solving management problems. In 1950 only a few computers were operating in businesses; at the end of 1968 there were more than twenty thousand.

This fundamental development has created opportunities for profits through mergers that remove assets from the inefficient control of old-fashioned managers and place them under men schooled in the new management science. Managers are able to control effectively a larger set of activities. Being of general applicability to business operations, management science makes possible reductions in financial and managerial costs and risks through acquisitions of firms in *diverse* industries. These gains differ markedly from the familiar economies of scale in production, purchasing, or marketing that normally accrue from mergers of firms with *related* products. (Jacoby 1969: 45; emphasis in original)

Jacoby wrote these words in an article on 'The Conglomerate Corporation' and went on to contend that 'the new management science is the primary force behind con- glomeration' (Jacoby 1969: 45). But the ideology of the manager as professional was by no means confined to the conglomerates. Many of the nation's leading corporate enterprises were enthusiasts, perhaps the most famous example being the Ford Motor Company (FMC).

4.2.4. The Trend towards Strategic Segmentation: Core Corporate Enterprises

After the war, Henry Ford II, the founder's grandson, took control of his family company and hired an entirely new executive management team in an attempt to rescue FMC from the state of organizational and financial precariousness brought on by the tyrannical reign of his grandfather. Many of FMC's new executives came from General Motors and Henry Ford II's objective in hiring them was to have them repli- cate at FMC the managerial organization that was deemed to have worked so well at GM. But the young Ford also hired a group of young executives without any back- ground in the automobile industry. Known as the 'Whiz Kids', these men had worked together during the war at the Office of Statistical Control. Their objective in joining FMC as a group was to apply the quantitative techniques they had developed for the US military to business administration.

Their leader, and the man who had done much to build 'Stat Control' into the powerful organization that it became during the war, was Charles 'Tex' Thornton. In his book on *The Whiz Kids*, John Byrne summarizes the basis for the success of Thornton and his comrades in the following terms:

Stat Control's true source of power had little to do with the actual gathering of numbers. On their own, the numbers and facts did not tell you what to do. But Tex's officers would search for the trends and patterns revealed by the numbers. They would probe for the variations and the changes and consider what they meant. They could use the numbers to win compliance and submission, which was not all that different from holding up a totem before primitive people and announcing a new godhead. In the confusion and fear generated by war, people believed Thornton's numbers spoke the truth. Everyone wanted to believe someone had the answers, whatever those answers might be. (Byrne 1993: 44–5)

The mission of the Whiz Kids in joining FMC was to hold up a totem before a new primitive people, the men who made cars. Thornton himself soon left for Hughes Aircraft, disappointed in his ambitions to become the most powerful executive at FMC. Later he went on to apply his philosophy in building up Litton Industries, a company that in its heyday was perhaps the most celebrated of the conglomerates. But the remaining Whiz Kids stayed at FMC and steadily gained influence within the company.

Inspired not only by their experience during the war, but also by the ideas of management guru Peter Drucker, the Whiz Kids set about establishing an organization with well-defined lines of authority and responsibility. In particular, they preached the importance of 'decentralization', by which they meant breaking down the organization into operations that had full responsibility for 'the design, production, and sale of its product, having all the aspects of a separate business'. A critical advantage of such decentralization, they argued, was that realistic financial records could be prepared for these operations so that they could be evaluated on a profit-and-loss basis. Another advantage was that '[t]op management is relieved of the burden of routine operations and is left free to concentrate upon its fundamental jobs—planning, policy-making, and controlling' (from a report on 'Organizational Problems of the Ford Motor Co.', written by James Wright, one of the Whiz Kids, and quoted in Byrne 1993: 172–3). However, as Byrne perceptively notes,

Wright made decentralization sound so liberating. But it would actually imprison thousands in Ford. The practice of decentralization allowed professional managers to gain more clout and influence in large organizations. Yet, decentralization is business double-talk. Executives think of decentralization as a way to empower greater numbers of managers down the corporate ladder. In fact, under decentralization, managers often have less authority, because it makes the large corporation run itself, permitting central staffs to assume greater control. In the 1950s, staff-driven, over-populated corporate headquarters grew like topsy, allowing those removed from the making of products to drift still further away yet more effectively control operations. Decentralization was largely the invention of ambitious executives like Wright and his pals who lacked the nuts-and-bolts knowledge of business but sought control over it. (Byrne 1993: 173)

To concentrate their control, the Whiz Kids brought new, like-minded recruits into FMC, especially into the finance area. Robert McNamara, a former Harvard Business School professor, Ed Lundy, a former economics instructor at Princeton University, and Arjay Miller spearheaded the recruiting effort and ensured that FMC was a pioneer among US industrial enterprises in hiring MBAs. In the early years at Ford, they instituted controls that may well have saved the company from bankruptcy, but as they gained more ground in the corporate hierarchy, the darker side of the Whiz Kids' techniques became increasingly apparent. Eventually their influence took the company to a new extreme as destructive as that which had prevailed when the company lacked any serious financial controls whatsoever. By the late 1950s, the rule of finance seemed to be exacerbating the serious problems FMC was already experiencing as a result of its failed launch of the Edsel model in 1957 and its costly attempts to compete in the aerospace industry. As David Hounshell observed:

The Edsel debacle and the diversion of resources into aerospace pale in comparison to the managerial rigidities that began to set in at FMC by the mid-1950s, which were matched at the highest level of the company by the increasingly arbitrary, whimsical, and sometimes tyrannical decisionmaking exercised by Henry Ford II. The accounting, costing, and control system that the Whiz Kids and Treasurer Theodore O. Yntema, whom HFII had recruited from a tenured professorship at Michigan's business school, had developed and installed at FMC in the late 1940s was continually refined. With this system's refinement and the accretion of managerial authority in the company's accounting and control divisions, the system began to *drive* operational and mid-level strategic decisionmaking rather than *aiding* it. For example, the company began to judge the quality of its products not by some ideal standard of fitness, soundness, absence of defects, or customer satisfaction but by the costs that the company would incur by customers' filing claims against the company's warranties. FMC became notorious for what was called 'management by the numbers'—the opposite extreme from what had been the order of the day when Henry Ford ran the company. (Hounshell 1997: 30; emphasis in original)

The professionalization of management at Ford had repercussions that went far beyond the company itself. It influenced the rest of corporate America not only by example but also through the large numbers of Ford managers who left the company to work elsewhere. Nor was Ford an isolated case. Rather, the cult of the professional manager swept through US corporate enterprises like a wave. The other leading US corporation that stands out for its position at the crest of that wave, and deserves special mention for its central role in promoting the ideology of the manager as professional, was General Electric.

As noted above, the company undertook a major reorganization in the early 1950s. Virtually all of the existing management jobs within the company were redefined, a massive number of new managerial jobs were created by GE to staff the operating departments, divisions, and groups as well as the newly created service functions, and management turnover soared as the reorganization went into effect. To satisfy the enormous demand for new managers, a major investment programme, unprecedented in the history of GE or any other company in the United States, was undertaken to transform managers into 'professionals'.

In 1951, Ralph Cordiner assembled a team of GE executives, consultants, and professors to recommend ways to develop the management of GE. The team studied fifty other firms, pored over the personnel records of 2,000 GE employees, did time-motion studies of executives at work, and interviewed countless GE managers. Two years later the basic concepts and organizational building blocks had been developed and the team produced the 'blue books', a five-volume, 3,463-page management bible. In 1956 the company set up its own business school at Crotonville in New York to indoctrinate existing managers and new recruits in the principles contained in these books.

The official title of the 'blue books' was *Professional Management in General Electric* and the starting assumption for everything propounded in them, and the courses based upon them, was that management was a profession that relied on a set of general principles that could be taught in a classroom. From this perspective, when a man had become a good manager he could manage any business. In his address to the first class that attended Crotonville, Cordiner claimed:

when we become students of these principles and these disciplines of Professional Managing, it will be entirely possible to change people in areas as diverse as [from Steam Turbines to Construction Materials] or from electronic tubes to some other job, to illustrate another type of example, without in any sense losing the temper of the operation at either point. (Cordiner 1956: 4)

Managerial professionalism also had significance beyond the internal coordination of the corporations' business activities. As noted in Chapter 3, it was an attempt to build a platform on which US corporate executives could justify the enormous power that they wielded within the corporation and outside of it. As Ralph Cordiner put it: 'Enlightened capitalism recognises that it has stewardship responsibilities to everyone affected by the business: the share owners, customers, the public, employees, and suppliers. This business venture must be managed in the balanced best interest of all' (Cordiner 1952: 75). But how these interests were to be balanced was deemed to be entirely at the discretion of the managers. They were, after all, professionally qualified for the task.

GE recruited 1,000 college graduates every year as management trainees and they were immediately put on a training programme that lasted for two years. The main thrust of the programme was to indoctrinate the recruits in 'the managerial view'. In an article in 1953 William Whyte, the author of *The Organization Man*, described the position of the trainee managers at GE:

The very diversity of their training . . . underscores the jack-of-all-trades nature of the professional manager—and his superiority. GE officially encourages a man to be a specialist if he wants. The phraseology GE uses in describing the choice, however, is illuminating. It asks the trainee to ask himself 'Will I specialise in a particular field?' or 'Will I become broad gauge, capable of effort in many fields?' Trainees don't have to read too strenuously between the lines. (Whyte 1953: 153)

The task of a professional manager was not to work himself but to manage other people's work. Aspiring managers were taught that one of the most vital lessons that they must learn in order to become professionals was how to deal with interpersonal relations; among the important principles that they were taught was 'Never say anything controversial' and 'You can always get anybody to do what you wish' (Whyte 1953: 153).

Once they had finished the training programme and had secured a position in the managerial organization of General Electric—usually as an operating manager—the incentives of the aspiring professional manager were again made very clear. An operating manager, fresh from Crotonville, was accorded the status of, as William Whyte put it, a 'crown prince of business'; he was paid a relatively high starting salary, he was given responsibility for the profit performance of an entire department, and he was told that if he met his objectives he would be promoted to an even more lucrative position. A financial analyst who worked for the President's Office at the time described the explosion of financial opportunities for college graduates under decentralization:

a typical starting salary, in 1948, for a college graduate was $200 per month. GE's starting rate was $225. A salary of $8,000 or $9,000 would represent an ambitious lifetime goal for most college graduates of that year. The average pay of all company employees, at that time, was about $3,000. During the following fifteen years the *average* employee compensation was destined to pass the $8,000 mark, and the starting salary for a college graduate was to rise to $6,588. Enterprising executives were to be rewarded by salary levels of $30,000 and upwards in their rise through the vast new arena of middle management. (Greenwood 1974: 18; emphasis in original)

Faced with these incentives, what did the ambitious young college graduate care that the hoops he had to jump through were set from above, that he knew nothing about the technologies or the markets in the businesses he managed, or that his ignorance or short-term ambition might undermine the long-term competitive success of a business he would soon leave behind him? GE eventually had to care, as the company's belief in the concept of professional management, the idea that 'a manager is a manager is a manager', as Cordiner often put it, began to impede its performance. As George Wise observed:

Perhaps no belief has cost GE more money in the succeeding years. As it turned out, a marketing man could not run a computer business, a couple of appliance marketers could not run a nuclear power business, an aircraft engine manufacturing expert could not run a computer aided design business, and a couple of solid state physicists could not run a power systems business—to name just a few of the more egregious examples of Cordiner's creed as practised by him, and even by his successors long after the 'blue books' expressing Cordiner's management principles were gathering dust on a Crotonville library shelf. (Wise n.d.: 405)

It is hardly coincidental then that the only bright spot in GE's experience of new business development before 1970, aircraft engines, worked hard to break free of corporate resource allocation polices. Under the leadership of Gerhard Neumann, the aircraft engine division developed an organization that integrated the knowledge of its engineering workforce into a powerful learning process and worked hard to protect it from managerial professionalism. Writing in 1966, *Fortune* described Neumann's efforts to resist corporate policy:

Bucking corporate creeds, he vigorously resists attempts by headquarters to transfer his best people. In the days when Cordiner forbade staffs, Neumann tucked away a strategic planner on a departmental payroll. His team of top division managers is youthful but deep in experience in the industry, and has functioned together for many years. How long Neumann can keep this team together in the face of GE's philosophy of fast rotation remains to be seen. For Borch is still adamantly insistent that, however successful a division may be, the policy of switching executives must prevail. Says Borch, 'He's going to be surprised at how many people he's going to lose.' ('GE's Hard-driving Jockey in the Great Jet-engine Race', *Fortune*, July 1966)

The drive towards the professionalization of management both reflected and reinforced patterns of corporate organization and resource allocation that were distinctive to US corporate enterprises in the mass-production industries. As strategic segmentation became more exaggerated, as those with strategic control of corporate resources became increasingly distanced from the organizations that would have to develop and utilize productive resources, their resource allocation decisions increasingly relied on a process of decision-making that was abstracted from the businesses that these decisions affected. As Byrne put it:

In a way, the numbers became more important than judgement because many of the business professionals lacked the experience to bring wisdom to decision making. Like the Stat Control analyst in Washington, far removed from combat, the professional couldn't readily accept intuition because he had no experience to intuit from. The professional manager can manage anything, if it's from the abstract perspective of numbers on a sheet of paper or the screen of a computer. But it's a fool's paradise for sure. (Byrne 1993: 518)

The effects of strategic segmentation are clearly reflected in the capital budgeting and financial planning systems that were developed in major US corporations after World War II in parallel to the trend towards so-called 'decentralization' in many American corporate enterprises (Johnson and Kaplan 1987; Dulman 1989). As Baldwin and Clark point out, the essence of these capital-budgeting systems was the 'cash inflow–cash outflow view of investment' in which '[p]roject analysis was based on the concept of the time value of money, which permits analysts to compare the value of cash invested at one time with that of cash returned at another time by adjusting for interest' (Baldwin and Clark 1994: 80). By the end of the 1970s, nearly 90 per cent of major US corporations were employing discounted cash-flow techniques as a basis for resource allocation decisions, and those who were well versed in these techniques, among them many MBAs, rode to unprecedented power within corporate organizations on the wave of their growing popularity.

For certain investments, as Baldwin and Clark contend, these financial systems were highly problematic methods of resource allocation since '[n]ot all the compelling motives for making an investment could be translated into specific revenue and cost projections, even by those most adept in the methodology' (Baldwin and Clark 1994: 83). Senior corporate executives seemed to understand these deficiencies, tending to go around these financial systems when they made major strategic investments. Yet, as these executives became more and more segmented from those engaged in the development and utilization of resources, they increasingly lacked the understanding required to make the commitments of resources necessary to build and sustain innovative organizations. And, deeper in the organization, the financial systems skewed the incentives of those who might have better understood the relationship between resource allocation and the development of organizational capabilities: the 'combinations of human skills, procedures and routines, physical assets, and systems of information and incentives' that were necessary to achieve 'superior performance in speed, quality, flexibility, and innovation' (Baldwin and Clark 1994: 78). The problem with these financial systems was that they made apparent the costs of building organizational learning and gave responsibility for those costs to operating managers; '[b]y their nature, the investments necessary to build a capability were intertwined with the day-to-day operating procedures of the business. Thus the costs were all too visible to operating managers, whose first responsibility was to deliver profit to the organization as a whole' (Baldwin and Clark 1994: 106). The systems were not at all effective, however, in capturing the benefits of these resource commitments. Thus, 'profit-center managers had incentives to skimp on capabilities, and top managers had no way to discover that they were doing so' (Baldwin and Clark 1994: 107). In short, these systems seem to have fostered a distinct bias in the resource allocation practices of US corporate enterprises that relied on them. The problem was not, as some have argued, that US corporate enterprises were biased towards underinvestment across the board (Hayes and Abernathy 1980). Rather, they were biased towards investments whose costs and returns lent themselves to quantification and against investments, such as those in organizational capabilities, whose costs and returns did not (Baldwin and Clark 1994).

The source of this bias has remained obscure in the literature that has brought it to light. Theoretical attempts to explain it have been based on bounded rationality and asymmetric information (Sah and Stiglitz 1986; Bull and Ordover 1987; Thakor 1990). Yet, in light of the previous discussion in this chapter, the limitations of these 'explanations' is that they rely on models of atomistic individuals for understanding resource allocation. Thus they abstract from the growing social segmentation within corporate enterprises, and the struggle of corporate executives for legitimacy in the enterprises that they controlled, and the society around them, that made the professionalization of management and the employment of quantitative techniques so attractive to those who were struggling for control of the corporation.

The extent to which managerial professionalism and its effects on strategic resource allocation were creatures of the curiosities of US corporate governance came into sharp focus when unprecedented competitive challenges to US industry emerged from enterprises embedded in different social environments. In the German and Japanese systems of corporate governance sharp lines were also drawn between corporate insiders and outsiders. However, neither of these systems fostered the segmentation that was common in many US enterprises between those who strategically allocated resources and those who understood the organizational and technological challenges involved in particular businesses.

4.3. The Electronics Complex and the Governance of Innovation

There were crucial differences between the post-war electronics industry and other dynamic industries in the United States in the manner in which the social conditions that supported innovation were generated. Of particular importance in facilitating innovation in the electronics complex was the involvement of the federal government and the profusion of startups. That said, these conditions were by no means sufficient for generating the trajectory of sustained innovation that emerged in the electronics complex in the post-war decades. The commitment of dominant corporate enterprises to building and sustaining organizations that could develop and utilize productive resources remained vital to the dynamism of these industries.

4.3.1. The Role of the Federal Government

The extensive involvement of the federal government in the post-war electronics industries had an extremely important influence on the processes through which resources were developed and utilized. Although the timing and mix of policies pursued by the federal government varied considerably across the microelectronics, computer hardware, and software industries, in all three sectors of the electronics complex federal government policies had two crucial effects on the governance of innovation. First, in the early stages of these industries' development, the government, especially through its R&D funding and military procurement, took on some of the burden of the high levels of market and technological uncertainty inherent in the innovation process and, as a result, underwrote critical improvements in cost and quality that were to prove crucial to the commercial viability of these sectors. Secondly, the military procurement and antitrust policies of the federal government, as well as government funding of university research and education in electronics, combined to make it considerably easier for small firms to enter and survive in the electronics industries.

Bolstering Financial Commitment   The massive expansion of the federal government's role in industry during and after the Second World War made a critical difference to the institutional context that supported the financial commitment to innovation in the electronics industries. In some cases, the provision of government research funding had the effect of a direct subsidy to the dominant enterprises and reduced their exposure to the enormous uncertainty inherent in the innovation process in electronics. During the 1950s, IBM, for example, earned more than half of the revenues from its domestic electronic data processing business from government programmes (Flamm 1988: 87). In particular, IBM benefited enormously from its role in building computers for the military's Semi-Automatic Ground Environment (SAGE) air-defence system.

The SAGE concept was based on research, performed at MIT from 1945 to 1951 for the Air Force's Whirlwind project, to build a digital computer system that pioneered in the use of magnetic core memory. Jay Forrester, the MIT professor who had led the team that designed and built the Whirlwind, was given responsibility for the SAGE project at MIT's Lincoln Laboratory. To carry out the project, the challenge was to move from the Whirlwind prototype 'to a reliable, repeatable, practical design and to manufacture, install and maintain several dozens of the systems—systems of unprecedented complexity which employed heretofore unproved technologies' (Robert Crago, former manager of SAGE programme, quoted in Fisher, McKie, and Mancke 1983: 27). MIT recognized its need for assistance from industrial enterprises to undertake this challenge. In 1952, Forrester and three of his leading technical experts visited the facilities of contenders for the project, the favourites to win the contract being IBM, Remington Rand, and Raytheon. The four men voted unanimously for IBM and agreed that there was a wide gap between it and its closest contender, Remington Rand. IBM was chosen because, as Forrester put it, 'In the IBM organization we observed a much higher degree of purposefulness, integration, and esprit de corps than we found in the Remington Rand organization. Also, of considerable interest to us, was the evidence of much closer ties between research, factory, and field maintenance in IBM' (quoted in Pugh 1995: 208–9). The team also commented approvingly on the strong technical capabilities of IBM staff and the company's capabilities in manufacturing and maintaining computing equipment. As a result, Forrester felt confident that 'IBM could mass-produce a high-quality system' (quoted in Fisher, McKie, and Mancke 1983: 27).

In carrying out the SAGE contract, IBM made major strides in its organizational learning with respect to the design and manufacture of computers. Of particular importance was the knowledge it developed which allowed it to mass-produce high-quality core memory at low cost. SAGE was the first computer produced on an assembly line that relied on core memory and this kind of memory was at the heart of almost all computer systems produced from then until the 1970s. The innovations made at IBM during the SAGE project both contributed to the commercial success of core memory and gave the company an advantage in exploiting it (Fisher, McKie, and Mancke 1983: 26–30; for a general discussion of IBM and the US government, see Flamm 1988: 86–95).

The long-term benefits to IBM of the SAGE project were not, however, confined to the design and manufacturing expertise that the company acquired and developed in carrying it out. Just as important was SAGE's contribution to the development of IBM's organization. When it won the SAGE contract, IBM hired more than 7,000 engineers, programmers, and maintenance people, including some of the top electronics engineers in the United States, at a time when its total domestic employment was less than 40,000 people. The company managed to integrate many of these people into its organization and thus to retain and build on the learning that they had acquired in the course of the project. As Cuthbert Hurd, IBM's director of applied sciences in the early 1950s, put it: 'The several thousand engineering and programming and maintenance personnel who were hired to work on SAGE added greatly to the company's store of technical knowledge and expertise. These persons worked on developing and maintaining many of IBM's subsequent general purpose computer systems' (quoted in Fisher, McKie, and Mancke 1983: 30). IBM's success in retaining high-quality people, as compared with its leading competitors, was undoubtedly an important element in its ability to dominate the computer industry. As Flamm observed: 'IBM comes to mind as a firm widely known for excellent employee compensation and employment security, as well as low turnover. Rather than reflecting an uncommon measure of benevolence, this may well be a highly rational strategy in a business dependent on preserving the security of internal technical know-how' (Flamm 1988: 218, fn. 25).

Stretching the Space for Startups   The federal government's role in the development of semiconductors, computers, and software was not confined to its role as a financer of industrial R&D. The government also exerted an important influence on the governance of innovation in the computer, semiconductor, and software industries, through its military procurement and antitrust policies, as well as the funding of university research and curriculum development in technical subjects critical to the electronics complex. Perhaps the most important combined effect of these various policies was that they allowed startup firms to survive and prosper and thus contributed to the importance of new firms in the innovation processes that powered the development of the US electronics complex.

In the semiconductor industry, for example, the federal government exercised a decisive influence on the allocation of resources to innovation through its defence-related procurement. From 1955 to 1965 an average of 38 per cent of semiconductor production, for example, was for defence purposes and the military accounted for as much as 48 per cent of total production in 1960 (Mowery and Rosenberg 1998: 129). Military procurement was even more important in the early years of integrated-circuit (IC) production, averaging 69 per cent of total production from 1962 to 1968, a period that proved critical in achieving the enormous improvements in quality and reductions in cost that were crucial prerequisites for the commercial viability of the IC (Mowery and Rosenberg 1998: 132–3). Military procurement contracts typically included provision for upfront R&D allowances and the Pentagon also provided financial support to contract winners for the construction of production facilities.

The US military influenced the innovative activities of electronics firms not only because of the amount that it spent on the purchase of technologically complex products, but also because of the way in which it spent it. 'Buy American' provisions reserved the military market for indigenous producers. Moreover, the military was willing to purchase from fledgling producers in contrast to European governments, who allocated the majority of funds to tried and tested producers. In his analysis of the semiconductor industry, Tilton observed that

[t]he defense market has been particularly important for new firms . . . these firms often have started by introducing new products and concentrating in new semiconductor fields where the military has usually provided the major or only market. Fortunately for them, the armed forces have not hesitated to buy from new and untried firms. In early 1953, for example, before Transitron had made any significant sales, the military authorized the use of its gold-bonded diode. This approval has been called the real turning point for the new firms. During 1959, new firms accounted for 63 per cent of all semiconductor sales and 69 per cent of military sales.

Military demand has therefore stimulated the formation of new companies and encouraged them to develop new semiconductors by promising the successful ones a large market at high prices and good profits. Further, the military market, by activating learning economies, often serves as a stepping stone to eventual penetration into the commercial market. (Tilton 1971: 91–2)

The award of a military contract often made the difference to the viability of a startup, not only through the direct infusion of funds that it provided but also because banks and venture capitalists were generally willing to lend to the company on the strength of the contract. Increasingly, in awarding contracts, the military insisted on the availability of a second source of supply for the product, to ensure that it was not being overcharged by one supplier and that it would not be held hostage to the fate of one company. Demands for second-sourcing spread beyond military contractors as major corporate purchasers of electronics increasingly adopted the practice. To comply with demands for second-sourcing, suppliers had to share product designs and process expertise. The practice of second-sourcing thus encouraged considerable technology diffusion throughout the electronics complex, again creating space for startups (Saxenian 1994: 45; Jackson 1997: 86).

The opportunities for startup firms were also enhanced by the liberal cross-licensing practices pursued by dominant firms in the industry, largely in response to antitrust pressures from the US Department of Justice. In 1949, during the year in which the transistor was developed at Bell Labs, the US government filed an antitrust suit against AT&T. To deflect criticism of its dominant market position, AT&T adopted a liberal attitude towards the licensing of its critical semiconductor patents and it also diffused the production knowledge it had accumulated to other firms. The suit was settled in 1956 when AT&T signed a consent decree in which it agreed to license all of its existing patents to any domestic firm that was interested. AT&T was enjoined from seeking royalties on these licences, although it was permitted to demand cross-licences in exchange for access to its patents. Given that AT&T held the dominant patent position in semiconductor technology, and that all of the critical technological innovations in the industry were linked through cross-licences with AT&T, technical knowledge became widely diffused (Tilton 1971: 73–77). The government's strategy towards AT&T was of crucial importance for startups, as Mowery and Rosenberg note:

The 1956 settlement of the AT&T case significantly improved the environment for startup firms in microelectronics, because of the liberal patent licensing terms of the consent decree and because the decree prohibited AT&T from commercial activities outside of telecommunications. As a result, the firm with the greatest technological capabilities in microelectronics was effectively forestalled from entry into commercial production of microelectronic devices, creating substantial opportunities for entry by startup firms. (Mowery and Rosenberg 1993: 49)

The AT&T case also had an important effect on the computer industry, not only because computer companies were the largest commercial purchaser of semiconductors, but also because the telecommunications giant had a leading patent position in electronic data processing at the time (Fisher, McKie, and Mancke 1983: 67). Antitrust policies also enlarged the possibilities for entry in the computer hardware industry, through the suit that the US government filed against IBM in 1952. To conclude the suit, IBM, like AT&T, agreed to license its existing punched card and computer patents, as well as those it filed until 1961, at reasonable rates (Flamm 1988: 223).

The antitrust policies of the US government and the practice of second-sourcing combined to create a lax intellectual property regime. In the decades after the war there was little use of patents by governmental agencies or corporate enterprises to protect their returns from innovative investments in electronics, despite the research intensity of the sector (Bound *et al*. 1982). The story of Intel's startup was typical.

In its early years Intel relied on an innovative manufacturing process—the silicon gate process—as the critical foundation of its strategy to mass-produce memory devices at low unit costs. The process had actually been developed by an Italian scientist, Federico Faggin, who had worked at Fairchild Semiconductor with Intel's founders, Robert Noyce and Gordon Moore. When they left Fairchild to found Intel, Noyce and Moore brought the knowledge of the silicon gate process with them. It took considerable time, effort, and money for Intel to turn the technology into a viable high-volume manufacturing process. Nevertheless, the scientists who remained at Fairchild took umbrage at Intel's appropriation of an invention made in the Fairchild lab and posted a sign at Fairchild that said 'Silicon Gate was Invented Here' (Jackson 1997: 26–7, 115–16). Yet Fairchild did not sue Intel. Nor did it sue any of the others who left to set up their own 'Fairchildren', often, at least in the venture's early stages, on the basis of what they had learned at Fairchild. So great was the outflow of people and ideas that the majority of semiconductor firms formed in Silicon Valley in the 1960s could trace their origins back to Fairchild (Saxenian 1994: 26). But the phenomenon went far beyond Fairchild:

The large basic research establishments in universities, government and a number of private firms served as important 'incubators' for the development of innovations that 'walked out of the door' with individuals who established firms to commercialise them. This pattern was particularly significant in the biotechnology, microelectronics, and computer industries. Indeed, high levels of labour mobility within regional agglomerations of high-tech firms served both as an important channel for technology diffusion and as a magnet for other firms in related industries. (Mowery and Rosenberg 1998: 42)

As Tim Jackson observed in his recent history of Intel, 'the rules were different in the 1960s. The days had not yet arrived when technology companies would use patents, trade secrets, and other forms of intellectual property as commercial weapons' (Jackson 1997: 27). Ironically, given its own origins, Intel, in order to aid its efforts in pursuing 'renegade' employees, played a crucial role in ushering in the era of property rights 'where only the paranoid survive' that emerged in the US electronics industry from the early 1980s.

In addition to its military procurement and antitrust policies, the federal government also played a critical role in shaping the governance of innovation in electronics through the provision of unprecedented levels of funding for the expansion of research and education in universities that developed close links to industrial innovation processes (Nelson and Wright 1995: 150; Mowery and Rosenberg 1993, 1998: Rosenberg and Nelson 1994). These links varied by sector of the electronics complex but, in general, the federal funding of universities like Stanford and MIT enhanced the climate for startups because of the potential for new firms to spin off from

university research laboratories as well as the contribution that high-quality technical educational programmes made to the training of those who went to work for these
firms. Once again the government intervened in a way that disrupted the economic
logic which prevailed in other dynamic industries by showing itself willing to make
major investments in the development of learning in the economy without demanding control over the commercial returns from its exploitation. So long as the government was willing to underwrite investments in technological learning in this
manner, startups did not themselves have to make major commitments to the training of their people to secure a foothold in the industry, especially when they could
also minimize on marketing capabilities by supplying a niche, such as one of the
military markets for sophisticated components. There were, of course, other actors
besides the military who played critical roles in forging close links between universities and startup companies, Frederick Terman, the Dean of Engineering at Stanford
University, being the classic example (Saxenian 1994: 20–7; Leslie and Kargon 1996:
435–72), but the importance of the federal government's role is suggested by the
fact that the rate of startup of electronic companies was so high in Santa Clara County
and Massachusetts, regions that in the post-war decades were at once the homes of
the leading technological universities of the post-war period—Stanford and MIT—
and the major recipients of military procurement contracts (Saxenian 1996: Ch. 1).

In computers, university laboratories, especially at Harvard and MIT, received high
levels of financial support from the federal government and played a critical role in
the development of important technologies (Mowery and Rosenberg 1998: 136).
They also served as incubators for startup companies. The SAGE project, for example,
played an important role in promoting learning not only in IBM but throughout the
computer industry. In software, for example, a division of the Rand Corporation was
chosen by Lincoln Labs to undertake the enormous programming challenge for the
project. The task was assigned to a Rand division that subsequently spun off to
become System Development Corporation (SDC). SDC was to have an extremely
important effect on the emergent software industry. As Langlois and Mowery point
out,

One of the greatest contributions of SAGE was its training of a large cadre of educated systems
programmers. Indeed, because SDC was restricted by Air Force pay scales and because it sought
to play this training role, the company encouraged turnover, which ran to 20 percent per year.
As one SAGE veteran noted in the early 1980s, 'the chances are reasonably high that on a
large data processing job in the 1970s you would find at least one person who had worked
with the SAGE system'. (Benington 1983: 351; quoted in Langlois and Mowery 1996: 59)

SAGE also had an important influence on the early minicomputer industry. When
Jay Forrester, the head of the Lincoln Laboratory, sent one of his graduate students
to supervise IBM's work on SAGE, he chose Kenneth Olsen for the task. Olsen spent
two and a half years working at IBM's Poughkeepsie plant and, in the process, learned
much about the technologies and manufacturing processes being developed there, as
well as the strengths and weaknesses of IBM. Olsen then returned to the Lincoln
Lab, where he supervised the project to develop MIT's TX-0, the first high-speed

transistorized computer. In 1957 he left Lincoln Lab with Harlan Anderson, who had also worked on Whirlwind and SAGE, to establish a new company, Digital Equipment Corporation (DEC), which commercialized the minicomputer and became IBM's most important rival in the computer business. Olsen's first commercially successful minicomputer, PDP-1, was launched in 1960 and was modelled on the TX-0. Some of the company's later models were also based on technology developed at MIT (Flamm 1988: 127; Fisher, McKie, and Mancke 1983: 271–9). Although DEC was perhaps the most successful university spinoff in the computer industry, it was only one in a long list which spun off from universities like MIT and Harvard that were major recipients of federal government funds for computer development (Dorfman 1983: 299–316; Rosegrant and Lampe 1992: Saxenian 1996: 12–20).

In summary, the prevalence of startups in the US electronics industry can only be understood in light of the broader process of innovation of which they are a part, and the system of governance which shaped the allocation of resources to that dynamic process. From this point of view, the vibrancy of entrepreneurial companies in the electronics industry, which has so often been heralded by popular and academic writers as the great exemplar of market control—the triumph of the mobility of financial and labour resources in generating economic performance—stemmed, in fact, from an organizational process that was embedded in a complex system of institutions which largely emerged during and after the Second World War. As AnnaLee Saxenian put it, 'what appeared to both the actors and the outside world as an individual entrepreneurial process was in fact a social process' (Saxenian 1991: 44). Moreover, notwithstanding the ideology of market control, startups in the electronics industry in the post-war decades thrived not only because of the US entrepreneurial spirit that is so often emphasized, but also because the US government intervened in the process of innovation in a way that supported the viability of new firms to a degree not seen in other dynamic industries.

When the central economic actor in generating innovation was the corporate enterprise, to the extent that it allocated resources to developmental investments it was under considerable pressure to sell to mass markets in order to spread out the investment which it incurred over large numbers of units. In the decades after the war, however, the pressures to achieve mass distribution to cover the costs of development were substantially mitigated in the electronics complex. Innovation in the post-war electronics complex was collective, cumulative, and uncertain as it had been in other dynamic industries, arguably more so than ever before. Thus it demanded a process of resource allocation that was organizational, developmental, and strategic.

What made the electronics sector distinctive, especially in comparison with the dynamic sectors of the pre-war era, was that the burden of generating institutions which could support these features of the resource allocation process was no longer exclusively confined to the corporate economy. The 'developmental state' intervened to support innovation by providing some of the social conditions that supported financial commitment and insider control. In doing so the state not only shifted some of the burden of providing these conditions from the system of corporate governance.

It also changed the logic of corporate resource allocation so that companies that did not have a mass market could survive.

The pressures to sell to mass markets were reduced in the post-war period, and an umbrella for niche players created, in part by the government's willingness to provide financial commitment and to allow the private sector to exploit the commercial potential of research. But the government also limited the possibility of dominant firms attaining control of product markets by its encouragement of technology diffusion through second-sourcing and antitrust policies. Even where financial commitment had been provided by dominant corporate enterprises, as in the case of IBM and AT&T, the government weakened the link between financial commitment and commercial exploitation through its antitrust policies. In the case of AT&T, for example, the 1956 consent decree demanded not only the liberal cross-licensing of its patents but also enjoined AT&T and Western Electric 'from commencing [or] continuing, directly or indirectly, to manufacture for sale or lease any equipment which is of a type not sold or leased or intended to be sold or leased to Companies of the Bell System, for use in furnishing common carrier communications services' (quoted in Fisher, McKie, and Mancke 1983: 67). Thus AT&T was expressly prohibited from entering the semiconductor business that its research had essentially created, as well as the computer business, in which, as Fisher *et al.* put it, 'in the early and mid-1950s, AT&T had the potential to become one of the principal manufacturers and vendors of computer equipment' (Fisher, McKie, and Mancke 1983: 67). Startups in the electronics industry in the post-war decades did not thrive because of the strict enforcement of private property rights. To the contrary it was the lax intellectual property rights regime that created their opportunities.

If the vibrancy of startups can only be understood in light of their embeddedness in a complex social system that supported the allocation of resources to innovation, so too the role of other governance institutions that supported the development of new firms, such as the venture capital industry, can only be appreciated when studied as an element of that social context. As Richard Florida and Martin Kenney observe, in regions like California's Silicon Valley and Boston's Route 128, 'venture capital functions as an integral component of indigenous technology infrastructures—what we refer to as 'social structures of innovation'—which are characterized by significant concentrations of human capital, close proximity to major universities, and substantial public R&D expenditures. Venture capital plays a catalytic role in these infrastructures by encouraging entrepreneurs to form new companies and by providing the capital and contacts to facilitate such business formations' (Florida and Kenney 1988: 34–5).

4.3.2. *The Role of Venture Capital*

As in most industrial economies, there had long been individuals and families in the US who were willing to use their private fortunes to fund new ventures. In contrast, the history of venture capital as an industry in the US is usually reckoned to begin as recently as 1946, when American Research and Development (ARD) was established to specialize in the provision of funding for new ventures. ARD was founded in Boston by members of the local investment community and leading professors and administrators from MIT. It was run by Georges Doriot, a French brigadier general and a professor at Harvard Business School. One of ARD's founders, Karl Compton, the president of MIT, had thought of setting up a venture capital firm before the war, in order to promote the development of the regional economy, but his plans were stalled when the war began. Yet, with the expansion of federally funded research at MIT during and after the war, the opportunities for the private sector to capitalize on this research made his plan seem even more viable. Sure enough, the principal sources of ARD's deals were the federally funded laboratories at Harvard and MIT and by far its most successful deal was the $70,000 investment it made in Ken Olsen's spinoff from Lincoln Laboratory (Rosegrant and Lampe 1992: 72, 110–14).

The revealed success of ARD's investment in DEC when the latter went public in 1966—ARD's investment of $70,000 was then valued at $37 million—generated enormous interest in venture capital. Until that time, the numbers of venture-capital-financed startups had been fairly small. The financial community had initially been highly sceptical of the merits of the ARD concept:

AR&D had a novel and seemingly altruistic mission. Its goal was not only to make money, but to spur the creation of new companies in New England, and to bring important ideas into the marketplace. The innovative idea was not easy for the conservative Boston financial community to swallow, and the firm was just barely able to raise the $3 million it had to set as a minimum for its own start-up. (Rosegrant and Lampe 1992: 111)

Nor was the scepticism confined to the Bostonians. When Fairchild Semiconductor was established in 1957 by the 'Traitorous Eight', who quit Shockley Semiconductor because of differences with its famous founder,[3] it proved to be no easy task to secure the necessary financing. One of the eight contacted an investment bank in New York, Hayden Stone, which, in turn, got in touch with ARD. The venture capital firm was not interested and so, after a few other failed attempts to interest private investors, the bank turned to the corporate sector. Twenty-three companies later, it struck lucky: Fairchild Camera and Instrument Corporation said that it would finance the venture. Fairchild's president, John Carter, and its founder, Sherman Fairchild, were both technology buffs and were excited by the idea of financing their own semiconductor firm (Malone 1985: 70–1).

The basic problem that confronted the early venture capital industry was that to make decisions about the allocation of resources, it needed financiers who understood what was going on in high-tech industries and who could identify the people who were likely to be able to organize and operate an innovative enterprise. It was only when the electronics industry had developed sufficiently to generate these people, in sufficiently large numbers to staff more than a handful of firms, that an organized venture capital industry was developed. As Saxenian observes:

[3] William Shockley had directed the team at Bell Labs that invented the transistor. For an account of Shockley's business venture, see 'Shockley and the Pirates', ch. 2 in Malone (1985).

Contrary to popular belief, Silicon Valley's venture capital industry emerged out of the region's base of technology enterprises, not vice versa. As successful entrepreneurs like Fairchild's Eugene Kleiner and Don Valentine reinvested their capital in promising local start-ups, they created a new and different kind of financial institution.

Venture capitalists brought technical skill, operating experience, and networks of industry contacts—as well as cash—to the ventures they funded. Silicon Valley's venture capitalists became unusually involved with their ventures, advising entrepreneurs on business plans and strategies, helping find co-investors, recruiting key managers, and serving on boards of directors. (Saxenian 1994: 39; see also Bullock 1983; Florida and Kenney 1990).

The key point is that venture capital, like the allocation of resources to innovation more generally, is misunderstood when it is characterized as a 'purely' financial transaction. It bears little resemblance to exchange—the spot, anonymous, and predictable transaction—which is the bedrock of the theory of the market economy. Venture financing is more accurately characterized as a process that is developmental, organizational and strategic. As such it relies for its success on the financier's embeddedness in a network of relationships that keeps him continuously informed about the quality of the team he is funding and the products and processes they are developing. As Florida and Kenney describe it,

Venture capital investing is dependent upon tremendous information sharing between venture capitalists, entrepreneurs, consultants and a wide range of related actors who operate as networks to locate deals, organize companies, establish investment syndications and so on. Because of the intensive nature of this information flow, these venture capital networks tend to be personalized, informal and localized. Further, the relationship between venture capital firms located around concentrations of technology businesses and those in financial centres is to some extent symbiotic. (Florida and Kenney 1990: 34)

When it has been forgotten that venture financing is more than financial, as it has been in the venture capital industry on more than one occasion, the results have been disastrous. One example of the problem was the experience of small business investment companies (SBICs) in the 1960s. The Small Business Act of 1958 provided for the establishment of these companies to increase the availability of capital for small businesses. SBICs were permitted to borrow from the federal government, at low interest rates, up to four times the amount that they invested themselves. By the mid-1960s the number of these companies had exploded to 700 and they dominated the US supply of venture capital at that time. Excitement about the potential of these companies for reaping high returns on their investments was fuelled by the rising stock market and, in particular, by an initial public offerings market more lucrative than anything ever seen before. But hubris ended in disaster for the SBICs. As Bygrave and Timmons note: 'The very difficult, cash-consuming, hands-on challenges described by Doriot in working with smaller companies were greatly underestimated by these new entrants into the venture capital arena. The inevitable result was reminiscent of today's shakeouts in the savings and loan industry' (Bygrave and Timmons 1992: 21).

Already by the late 1960s, it was evident that about a third of the SBICs were in serious financial difficulty. When the stock market turned down in late 1969, their problems were further magnified. In the wake of these major setbacks, and with a quiescent market for new issues for much of the 1970s, the US venture capital industry contracted as the number of participants in the industry and the amount of capital committed fell dramatically:

Especially hard hit were startup and early-stage investing, which were nearly nonexistent through the mid-1970s. Institutional investors questioned the viability of long-term investing and the inevitable illiquidity associated with it. ARD watchers, once awed by its success, developed misgivings about the appropriateness of publicly owned entities carrying on such investing activities, because of the high visibility associated with being a public firm. (Bygrave and Timmons 1992: 23)

From 1978, however, the industry began to revive, largely because of a series of legislative initiatives that made venture capital a much more attractive investment option. Of particular importance was the reduction of the capital gains tax rate, initially from $49^1/_2$ per cent to 28 per cent, and then to 20 per cent, as well as legislation that made it much easier for pension funds to invest in venture capital partnerships. As Figure 4.1 shows, the 1980s witnessed an unprecedented flow of money into venture capital and provided the basis for the next crisis in the industry. Institutional investors, especially pension funds, were particularly important contributors to the upsurge. In 1978, pension funds provided 15 per cent of the $216 million committed; by 1988 they provided 46 per cent of a total of $2.95 billion (Venture Economics 1996).

As the money chasing venture capital deals ballooned, so too did the pressures for financial liquidity. Increasingly, funds were invested in expansions and leveraged buyouts rather than seed financing and startups because they were seen as surer bets.

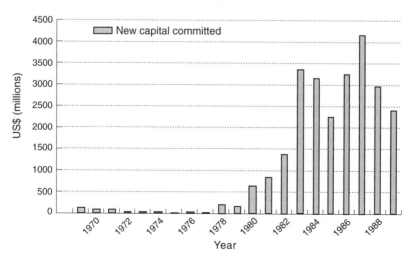

Source: Venture Economics (1996)

FIG. 4.1 Venture capital under management in the US, 1969–1989

In 1983 startups accounted for a peak of 43 per cent of the deals done; by 1989 they represented only 10 per cent of the companies receiving funds (Bygrave and Timmons 1992: 32). During the second half of the 1980s, the amount committed to startups actually fell from $526 million in 1986 to $288 million in 1989. In 1989, 69 per cent of total venture capital disbursements went to expansions and leveraged buyouts or acquisitions (Venture Economics 1996). Bygrave and Timmons contend that

newcomers to the industry may have been seduced by the prospect of relatively easy money in later-stage and LBO investments, a perception fueled by the junk bond euphoria of the mid- to late-1980s. Certainly, these had to look a lot more appealing than the time-intensive, painstaking, hands-on involvement so characteristic of classic venture-capital investing. Certainly, evaluating and investing in an established business with some track record and in-place management was more understandable than trying to figure out if a scientist, computer wizard, or engineering genius could turn an untried concept into a growth business. (Bygrave and Timmons 1992: 36–7)

Many industry observers were particularly critical of the contribution of institutional investors to growing demands for financial liquidity from venture investments. Their inexperience in venture capital financing and their unwillingness to learn about the organizations, technologies, and markets that determined the performance of the ventures they were financing led them, it was argued, to impose unreasonable pressures on entrepreneurs to deliver a return and to pull the plug when companies ran into problems. But the flood of money into the industry could also lead to overinvestment as uninformed investors followed each other *en masse* into 'hot' sectors.

When the returns on venture capital investments were tallied for the 1980s, the suspicions of these critics were confirmed. Although some funds had earned extremely high rates of returns, on average the decade was a dark one for venture capital investments: average returns reached a high point in 1983 but declined from then until the end of the decade and, in fact, fell below risk-adjusted returns from stock market investments during that period (Bygrave and Timmons 1992: 163). In some industries, the most notable example being the Winchester disk-drive industry, the result of overinvestment by venture capitalists was a bloodbath for competitors which ensured that none of them could make a return on their investment (Bygrave and Timmons 1992: 125–48; Sahlman and Stevenson 1987).

The experience of venture capital during the 1980s led some commentators to question the contribution of the industry to the generation of innovation in the US economy. Critics spoke of a transformation of the industry from venture to 'vulture' capitalism. They complained that venture capitalists were encouraging poaching and that as a result successful companies were being deprived of their most productive managers and engineers and their technologies. The ability of these companies to innovate and to compete on international markets was, as a result, being undermined (Wilson 1986: Ferguson 1988). Moreover, they argued that by funding excessive numbers of similar companies, many with less than outstanding leadership, they were wasting money and talent, adding little to the progress of technology, and artificially creating overcompetitive situations where no participant could make money. Some of the harshest criticisms of the venture capital industry during the 1980s emanated from luminaries within the electronics industry, especially semiconductors. The complaints were made by men like Andy Grove at Intel and Jerry Sanders at Advanced Micro Devices, companies that themselves had been one-time beneficiaries of venture capital financing. Their concerns reflected an awareness of the abiding importance of corporate commitment to building integrated organizations to develop and utilize productive resources in the electronics sector. Corporate enterprises that did build organizations capable of generating the learning required to sustain innovation did so in a manner that was, along some dimensions, different from the policies employed by their counterparts in other industries and, in others, variations on themes long pervasive in leading American corporations.

4.3.3. The Abiding Importance of the Innovative Corporation

Notwithstanding the importance of government intervention in the electronics complex in altering the economic logic of governance, as well as other post-war institutions such as the venture capital industry that could, at least under certain conditions, facilitate innovation in the electronics complex, it would be a mistake to believe that these institutions substituted for the support of the innovation process by the system of corporate governance. The comparative experiences of IBM, Remington Rand, and General Electric in the computer industry illustrate the importance of a corporate commitment to innovation if full advantage was to be taken of one facilitating condition, the government funding of research.

IBM, Remington Rand, and General Electric   There was much dissent within IBM about the wisdom of making such a commitment because of the risks that the SAGE project entailed for the company, described by one participant in the following terms:

Many of the concepts had been tried only in a laboratory. There was no guarantee IBM could hire the numbers of people that would be needed to carry out its responsibilities. Failure to deliver the computers successfully, because the project was so massive, could have led to adverse financial repercussions and damage to IBM's reputation . . . All of us were concerned in 1953 about the diversion of key engineering and systems persons and Applied Science persons who were barely completing the design of the 650, 701, and 702. Moreover, IBM would need to construct a completely new factory to build the SAGE computers and all of us in the highest management group wondered what would happen if the contract were cancelled in midstream. (quoted in Fisher, McKie, and Mancke 1983: 28)

Yet IBM decided to make the commitment to the project because it recognized the potential competitive advantage that it could reap on the basis of the learning it would acquire on the project. Thus, although government financing could play an important role in supporting the innovative activities of corporate enterprises, it was only a facilitating condition. Corporations themselves had to be willing to make major resource commitments to developmental investments, they had to build integrated corporate organizations that had the incentives and abilities to develop and utilize resources, and they had to ensure that strategic decision-makers were sufficiently integrated with these organizations to understand how resources had to be allocated to promote innovation.

It was IBM's willingness and ability to commit itself to building an innovative organization that allowed it to successfully exploit the opportunities that government funding held out. In contrast, the example of Remington Rand illustrates the problems that most competing companies encountered in meeting IBM's challenge in the computer industry. Remington Rand was originally, like IBM, a producer of punch-card equipment, typewriters, and other office equipment. The company had begun building in-house computer development capabilities. In the early 1950s it acquired Eckert-Mauchly Computer Corporation and Engineering Research Associates (ERA), two companies on the cutting edge of the development of electronic computer systems. Thus, it propelled itself into the leading position in the US computer industry. Both Eckert-Mauchly and ERA had made their critical breakthroughs on government-funded projects but they had both run into serious financial difficulties. A strong parent company like Remington Rand seemed to offer a solution to their problems.

Notwithstanding Remington Rand's early lead, and the view among well-informed observers that the company was set to dominate the industry, the company instead 'snatched defeat from the jaws of victory' (*Business Week*, 22 Nov. 1969). Although Remington Rand received considerable support from the government for the development projects it undertook, it was much less willing than IBM to commit its own resources, to develop the learning of its employees as members of an integrated organization, and to devolve strategic control over the allocation of corporate resources to those who understood the computer business. Fisher *et al.* summarized the central problem as follows:

Led by James Rand, described by John Lacey as an aging 'autocratic, iron-willed manager' who 'never really understood the [computer] business,' Remington Rand was unable to recognise the extent of the commitment that was necessary to the computer systems business to make it successful. Norris testified that the firm failed to make the 'financial commitment that was necessary' and failed to 'commit the time of the senior management of the Corporation in order to solve the problems that were involved in designing and manufacturing and marketing computer systems at that time.' In addition, Remington Rand was handicapped further by an unwillingness to take risks in its EDP business, a course that caused it to be too late in the marketplace with new products. (Fisher, McKie, and Mancke 1983: 39)

One symptom of Remington Rand's lack of commitment, and perhaps the most important source of the company's weakness in competition with IBM, was its failure to develop and retain people as part of an integrated organization. As a result, in all parts of the organization, from managers to salespeople, the organizational learning of Remington Rand's employees lagged far behind that of their counterparts at IBM. Employees became frustrated with the lack of opportunities within the company, as well as the infighting that dominated the segmented Remington Rand organization, and many key people left (Fisher, McKie, and Mancke 1983: 38–46).

The problems at Remington Rand were uncannily similar to those encountered by GE's computer division. Again strategic segmentation proved to be a major barrier to commercial success, but in the case of GE, as I have already discussed, it stemmed from the internal dynamics of organizational control rather than the unwillingness of an owner-manager to cede control to those who understood the computer business. GE emerged from the war with considerable strengths in electronics that looked as if they could form the basis for a successful computer business. In 1955 a company task force clearly recognized the opportunity:

> We are seeing the birth of a new industry . . . GE has the electronics now needed . . . it is the type of product which will slip easily into manufacture in our present electronic factories. IBM's 702 and Remington Rand's Univac are not machines which meet the real needs of users . . . We therefore conclude that the timing for entering the field is right. (quoted in Wise n.d.: 33)

By the end of the year GE had signed a contract to supply cheque-reading and book-keeping computers to the nation's largest bank, Bank of America (*Fortune*, Aug. 1960: 190). The newly established GE computer division had its own headquarters and plant and employed more than 1,000 employees in 1959 (Wise n.d.: 33). Despite its early lead, however, by the end of the 1960s GE, with less than 10 per cent of IBM's market share, ranked only as one of the 'Seven Dwarves' in the industry. GE's computer business sustained considerable after-tax losses from the 1950s until it was sold to Honeywell in 1970 (Fruhan 1979: 158).

The company failed to make a sufficient commitment of resources to building the business (Fisher, McKie, and Mancke 1983: 76–9), an interpretation accepted even by the chief executives who presided over GE during the critical period in which IBM established its market leadership. Ralph Cordiner, for example, considered that 'General Electric's mistake was that it failed to realize the opportunity and therefore made an inadequate allocation of resources, both human and physical, to the business' (Fisher, McKie, and Mancke 1983: 78). Fred Borch, Cordiner's successor, gave the following analysis of the problems:

> I think, first, in having the business, which was a very small one, of course, to begin with, at too low a level in the company to attract the level of managerial competence and technical competence that should have been brought into play in the business. That, I think, would be the most serious mistake. Had that been handled correctly to begin with, the resources would have been made available that were needed. But the real picture of what was needed to compete very aggressively and very successfully in the business never came up high enough in the organization to make a good business decision on it. That would be, I would say, the most significant mistake that we made. (*US* v. *IBM*, Deposition of Fred J. Borch, 20 June 1974: 20)

Finally, Reginald Jones, Borch's successor and GE's vice-president of finance in the 1960s, claimed that 'by the time that we caught up with the size of the opportunity it was truly a lost opportunity and it would have required inordinate investments to catch up and achieve a position of significance' (*US* v. *IBM*, Testimony of Reginald H. Jones, Transcript: 8869–70).

The main problem with these conclusions, however, is that they assume that knowledge should have flowed up the organization to facilitate an integration of strategy and learning. Yet, the complexity of GE's organization, designed and overseen by these men, meant that it would have been impossible for them to keep up sufficiently with what was going on in the various divisions of the corporation to intelligently exercise control over the allocation of resources. In fact, that they could not keep up was a symptom of the fundamental flaw in GE's organization, which concentrated strategic control in a small group of senior executives. Rather than figuring out how to move learning up the hierarchy, decisions about the allocation of resources should have been made by those lower down the organization who were integrated with the learning process that was going on in the computer division.[4]

Yet, even if senior executives at GE had recognized the need to devolve strategic control, they had created an additional barrier to integrating strategy and learning further down the organization. In line with the philosophy of professional management that was religiously expounded throughout the organization, GE was working hard to ensure that even the operating managers were segmented from the organizational learning processes on which the computer business relied. According to one former senior employee, the computer business suffered greatly from the belief of GE's highest echelons in the ideology of professional management:

The philosophy of professional management . . . is that management is a profession and a good manager can manage any kind of business.

This in fact works quite well for a mature or gradually declining business, where a man put into a business can model his behavior upon that of his predecessor's [sic] and then make adjustments as he learns what's really going on. In a rapidly evolving business, however, his predecessor's behavior, especially if it was unsuccessful, is a very poor model. And since he knows nothing about the business, he is a professional manager and came from Toaster or Welding, or whatever it may be, elsewhere in the General Electric Company, he really could not understand what he was managing.

But if you have a series of these managers above each other they feel they are in trouble, they now must do something. What can they do? They do not understand the business well. So the only thing they can do is to replace the man working for them.

So the net result of this was, as we got into difficulties, especially in bringing the 600 to market thereafter, we had a sequence of people running General Electric's computer business, none of whom, except when we come to Dick Bloch and John Haanstra—and, again, they were not in charge of the computer business but were key people—none of whom were experts in the computer business. Furthermore, we had a new one every eighteen months or so.

So that General Electric never developed experienced management that understood the computer business, and I believe this was a major part of why General Electric never learned how to manage the business properly. (John Weil, vice-president and chief technical officer of Honeywell, quoted in Fisher, McKie, and Mancke 1983: 190–1; see also Dorn 1985)

The success of IBM, and the problems experienced by Remington Rand, General Electric, and others in the computer business, clearly demonstrate the continued

---

[4] For a comprehensive account of the development of GE's computer business by some of the people who worked there, see Oldfield 1998.

importance of corporate resource allocation to support innovation, notwithstanding the heavy involvement of the government as a funder of R&D.

Building Innovative Organizations in Electronics   In corporate enterprises that did build organizations capable of generating the learning required to sustain innovation, they did so in a manner that was, along some dimensions, variations on themes long pervasive in leading American corporations and, in others, different from the policies employed by their counterparts in other industries. With regard to the provision of financial commitment, for example, the dominant electronics firms, like other leading US corporate enterprises, relied heavily on internal sources of funds for their financing. Hewlett-Packard (HP), for example, explicitly pursued a policy of self-financing from an early stage and reinvested most of its profits in order to make itself independent of outside financiers. The founders were, in fact, consciously opposed to the use of equity financing or long-term borrowing to finance corporate development (Packard 1995: 84–5; for IBM, see Foy 1975: 11–13).

Nor was HP alone in its financial practices. Reliance on internal funding is pervasive among dominant electronics firms. When these companies have gone public they have not tended to do so for the purposes of financing investment. Like many of their counterparts in other industries, corporate enterprises in the electronics industries have gone to the equity markets for one or more of three reasons: to liquidate the investments of the founders or venture capitalists; to acquire a currency for the acquisition of other companies; to develop stock-based compensation schemes for their employees. When HP went public in 1957, for example, the main rationale for doing so was to facilitate the extension of employee ownership of the company. The company's stock purchase plan was initiated soon after to allow employees to purchase HP stock at a preferential price. In retrospect, David Packard claims that his only regret in promoting employee stock ownership was that the company did not require employees who bought HP stock at a subsidized price to hold on to it and thus to bolster financial commitment to HP (Packard 1995: 89, 85–6; see also Cringely 1996: 257–9).

In introducing broad-based employee share ownership plans, these companies distinguished themselves from the conventional approach in corporate America in the decades after the war. Although in many dominant US corporations stock options were awarded to employees, typically the recipients were concentrated in the executive suite. The clash between these compensation policies and those being pioneered in the electronics enterprises became starkly evident when Robert Noyce proposed broad-based stock options at Fairchild. What ultimately became Intel's approach to compensation, and its clash with the pervasive managerial culture in mainstream corporations, reflected real differences in the way in which these different enterprises were organized and in whom they identified as the critical insiders for generating innovation. At a time when in many of the mass-production corporate enterprises there was a marked tendency towards segmentation within the managerial organization with, in many cases, the operations men being the losers as the power balance shifted, in Intel, as in most successful electronics companies, the engineers were generally regarded as central to the organizational learning processes that generated innovation.

Moreover, although the practices which these companies adopted varied considerably, they had in common the integration of a broader group of employees into the learning processes that generated their competitive advantage than was common in many other industries. To extend organizational integration in this manner, enterprises like IBM, HP, Motorola, Texas Instruments, and TRW introduced a whole battery of practices to keep those employees whom they considered critical to their learning processes committed to the corporate organization. The particulars of these practices varied from company to company but they tended to include, among others, a corporate commitment to job security with the use of layoffs only as a last resort; compensation packages which ensured that employees were well paid by industry standards; company-wide policies for pay, including profit-sharing, and other benefits, generally combined with an absence of exclusive managerial perquisites and other status symbols; personnel departments that were innovative and influential with top management; and the extensive use of employee surveys and other feedback mechanisms (Foulkes 1980: Jacoby 1997: 236–62).

Critical to making these institutions effective in shaping the incentives of insiders to commit their effort and initiative to the organization was employee confidence that these practices would endure. In many of these companies, the corporate commitment to its insiders was supported by the strong views of the company's founders or charismatic top managers on the appropriate treatment of people within business organizations. The Watson father and son exercised a decisive influence on the personnel practices of IBM. Bill Hewlett and David Packard devised and supported what has come to be known as the 'HP way' in the post-war decades (Packard 1995) and Ken Olsen, DEC's founder, was the inspiration and supporter of many of the minicomputer company's innovative organizational practices. The strength of these leaders' commitment, and the longevity of their influence, provided an umbrella under which the companies that they ran could pursue practices that were distinctive from much of corporate America. There was, of course, a certain vulnerability associated with corporate dependence on these men in that management succession could potentially bring about a destruction of what was distinctive about the governance of these enterprises (Foulkes 1980: 45–57).

Challenges to the viability of these 'manorial systems' of governance (Jacoby 1997) also stemmed from the vagaries of the economic cycle, especially given the importance of employment stability as a symbol of the corporate commitment to employees. It is not surprising that companies like IBM which retained their non-union status during and after the Great Depression, despite the labour–management turmoil all around them, were able to do so because of unusually fortuitous circumstances; in the case of IBM the award of a major contract from the government allowed them to maintain employment throughout the Depression. In general, in times of economic downturn, companies like IBM, HP, DEC, and Motorola went to considerable lengths to keep people employed. For example, David Packard gave the following account of HP's reaction to serious economic problems in 1970:

Because of a downturn in the US economy, our incoming orders were running at a rate quite a bit less than our production capability. We were faced with the prospect of a 10 per cent layoff. Rather than a layoff, however, we tried a different tack. We went to a schedule of working nine days out of every two weeks—a 10 per cent cut in work schedule with a corresponding 10 per cent cut in pay. This applied to virtually all our US factories, as well as to all executives and corporate staff. At the end of a six-month period, the order rate was up again and everyone returned to a full work schedule. Some said they enjoyed the long weekends even though they had to tighten their belts a little. The net result of this program was that effectively all shared the burden of the recession, good people were not released into a very tough job market, and we had our highly qualified workforce in place when business improved. (Packard 1995: 133–4)

Packard went on to say that HP's commitment to employment stability did not ensure 'absolute tenure status for people' but when reductions were seen as necessary there were concerted attempts to accomplish them through attrition, early retirement, and voluntary severance programmes.

Packard's description captures the essence of the employment philosophy of other leading electronics companies like IBM and Motorola (for IBM, see Foy 1975: 136–8). Their commitment to employees was based not on charity but on their resolutely instrumental approach to employee relations. Major investments were made by these companies in integrating employees as members of an innovative organization in order to generate a process of collective, and, most importantly, cumulative, learning. To let these employees go, it was believed, would be to dissipate the foundations for the company's competitive advantage, and thus to forgo the potential for returns on the investments that had been made in the learning of corporate insiders. The success of these practices was reflected in lower employee turnover; as Table 4.5 shows, turnover tended to be much lower in the larger companies than in smaller ones. Companies like HP, however, did even better than the average for large

TABLE 4.5 Employee Turnover Rates in the US Electronics Industry, 1979

Category	Employees					
	1–100	101–250	251–500	501–1,000	Over 1,000	Total
All Employees	59.1%	56.7%	50.2%	41.6%	27.2%	35.4%
No. of Companies	280	175	102	89	89	735
Non-exempt	78.4%	72.4%	61.0%	49.2%	35.3%	44.7%
No. of Companies	244	162	85	71	83	645
Exempt	28.0%	27.2%	24.2%	25.5%	15.3%	18.9%
No. of Companies	213	161	85	71	83	613

Source: American Electronics Association Benchmark Survey, 1980; reproduced from Okimoto, Sugano, and Weinstein (1984: 61).

companies; in 1978 its turnover rate was 8 per cent compared with an average of 27.2 per cent for US electronics companies with more than 1,000 employees (Okimoto, Sugano, and Weinstein 1984: 60).

The importance of retaining key employees was recognized not only by the electronics companies that predate World War II but also by most of the startups which grew to be dominant enterprises, with DEC and Intel being leading examples. Intel, for example, made enormous efforts to develop and retain committed people, and to encourage organizational learning among them, although in its determination to lose as few good people as possible to established competitors and startups, the company took a much more aggressive attitude towards its people than a corporation like HP. Intel initiated lawsuits against former licensees, rivals, and mobile employees whose mobility, the company argued, led to the dissipation of its intellectual property (Harrison 1994: 111).

Whether by fair means or foul, there is no greater testament to Intel's success in building an integrated organization than Michael Malone's pejorative characterization of the company's corporate culture in his well-known book on Silicon Valley, *The Big Score*:

Intel was in many ways a camp for bright young people with unlimited energy and limited perspective. That's one of the reasons Intel recruited most of its new hires right out of college: they didn't want the kids polluted by corporate life. The more cynical suggested that, as in the Marines, only children would stand for this kind of horseshit because they didn't know any better. But there was more to it than that. There was also belief, the infinite, heartrending belief most often found in young people, that the organization to which they've attached themselves is the greatest of its kind in the world; the conviction they are part of a team of like-minded souls pushing back the powers of darkness in the name of all mankind. Corporate Moonieism, if you will, but with both feet planted firmly on the ground, and leavened with a bit of California soul. (Malone 1985: 152)

Malone goes on to argue that 'to become the shining example of what an American company can be, Intel has eschewed many of those traits that are synonymous with being American'. To beat the Japanese, he claimed, 'Intel has had to become almost the ultimate Japanese firm' (Malone 1985: 153). The irony of Malone's point of view, and the countless similar ones that have been aired on the subject, is suggested by the allusion to the Marines. How can one describe as un-American an organizational pattern that is reminiscent of so many of the continually successful electronics enterprises in the US in the post-war decades?

Moreover, in comparison with Japan, the type of organizational integration found in US electronics companies generally preserved a distinctly American quality, as is suggested by the difference in the turnover of exempt and non-exempt employees in Table 4.5. Notwithstanding the fact that electronics companies tended to extend integration deeper into the organization than was the case in corporate enterprises in many other industries, there were many outsiders to the learning processes of these companies and prominent among them, as in most of corporate America, were most production workers. As Jackson put it in his recent book on Intel, 'the people who worked in the fabs were not all engineers who had joined with the hope of making hundreds of thousands of dollars from stock options. Most of them were hourly paid people, often young women starting on little more than the minimum wage, whose principal skills were dexterity, attention to detail, reliability, and resistance to boredom' (Jackson 1997: 144). As a result, many electronics firms were character-ized by what economists call internal dual-labour markets, with an insider elite of managers and engineers counterposed to 'the generally lower wage, more expendable labor force made up predominantly of Latino and Asian immigrants performing the more mundane, standardized, sometimes dangerous tasks—dangerous because of the chemicals that have to be physically handled, or because of chronic eye strain result-ing from having to stare constantly into high-powered microscopes' (Harrison 1994: 117).

Many of the leading US electronics companies went to considerable lengths to ensure that these workers did not acquire a collective voice in their operations; common to most of these companies was a strategy to remain firmly outside the dominant patterns of management–labour relations in the US by remaining non-union. To remain union-free in an environment in which the basic rights of workers to orga-nize and bargain were legally protected demanded a more sophisticated approach than those which had proven effective in an earlier era when American unions were still fighting for legal recognition. Some non-union employers continued to use sticks to beat back organizing efforts but in the post-war era, especially in the electronics industries, the strategic use of carrots also became critical.[5] As I have already noted, in some companies, like IBM and HP, a whole range of institutionalized practices was introduced by the leading electronics companies to give employees confidence that their interests were aligned with those of the corporation and that, as a result, they did not need unions to defend their position *vis-à-vis* their employers.

Yet, even though these companies were often willing to make certain concessions to their workers to persuade them not to organize, in general there were few moves to strategically incorporate production workers in organizational learning processes. The segmentation between insiders and outsiders in their organizations became more and more of a burden, especially as the electronics industries moved towards volume production. With the turnover of production workers so high, it became extremely difficult to maintain quality, not to mention generate continuous process improvements.

Many semiconductor firms started moving some of their fabs outside Silicon Valley in the 1970s to reduce the costs of labour mobility. Intel, for example, opened its first fab outside Silicon Valley in Livermore in 1973, and later in the 1970s it set up operations in Oregon and Arizona. The advantage of geographical dispersion was that '[e]ach time it built a new fab outside the Valley, the company could feed off a fresh labor pool, with few competitors to lure its best people away'. The challenge of main-taining high levels of performance, especially quality levels, in all of these fabs,

---

[5] For Intel management's reaction to an attempt to unionize the company's Livermore fab, see Jackson 1997: ch. 16; for IBM, see Foy 1975: 167–76).

however, proved very difficult—so difficult, in fact, that Andy Grove felt the need to launch a 'McIntel' campaign to standardize production across all of Intel's fabs (Jackson 1997: 145).

Notwithstanding these and other efforts, the outsider status of production workers in many electronics firms made it difficult to achieve high levels of production performance. Those US electronics companies that did achieve impressive quality records, IBM and HP being most notable in this regard, did so on the basis of organizational practices that strategically integrated production workers in their organizational learning processes (Okimoto, Sugano, and Weinstein 1984: 53–62). For companies that failed to make these commitments to those lower down the corporate hierarchy, their deficiencies in achieving high-quality, low-cost production were to become a serious competitive handicap in the 1980s.

4.4. Conclusion

In this chapter I have analysed the evolution of the system of corporate governance in the United States in the post-war period. In the mass-production industries, there was considerable continuity between the pre-war and post-war governance systems, most notably in the persistence of managerial control over the process of corporate resource allocation. Yet, even in those industries, one can identify important evolutionary changes in the post-war governance system. First, workers and managers became more and more segmented from each other within US corporate enterprises, as the line between outsiders and insiders to organizational learning processes became more defined. Secondly, those who controlled strategic decision-making pulled further away from the rest of the enterprise, even from the managerial organization itself. Some of the negative consequences of these changes for corporate resource allocation and corporate performance were analysed.

When one compares the mass-production industries and the electronics complex which emerged in the US after the war, one finds important differences in the governance institutions that shaped resource allocation. Of particular importance in the post-war electronics industries was the multifaceted influence of the federal government on the economics of innovation, the prevalence of startup firms, and the extension of organizational integration within the dominant electronics firms to a broader insider group than was common in the leading mass-production enterprises. The importance and timing of these differences varied considerably across sectors of the electronics complex. Moreover, to the extent that these industries moved towards volume production, as was the case for the semiconductor industry and the computer business once the microprocessor revolution had taken hold, the governance of resource allocation evolved. In particular, government involvement and influence became less important to the economics of innovation and, within enterprises, hierarchical segmentation became more extreme. In terms of governance, these industries began to look much more like the typical US mass-production enterprise.

In the 1970s and 1980s, US corporate enterprises faced new competition in mass-production industries, as well as in some high-tech sectors, in which they previously had been unchallenged. The nature and extent of these competitive challenges will be analysed in the following chapter. Moreover, just as the ground shifted in the productive sphere, the commitment of financial resources to corporate strategies came under considerable pressure due to structural changes in the financial sector of the US economy that led to increased demands for financial liquidity. In the next chapter, I will also analyse the pressures on the US system of corporate governance which emanated from the financial sphere. In combination, these productive and financial pressures created a crisis for the post-war system of managerial control. How US corporate enterprises have responded to this crisis, and the implications of their responses for innovation and sustainable prosperity, will be dealt with in Chapter 6.

5

Challenges to Post-war Managerial Control in the United States

5.1. Introduction

Beginning in the 1970s, US corporate enterprises faced an intensification of competition in both the mass-production and high-tech industries, in which they had been dominant during the post-war period. The nature and gravity of the competitive threat varied, in part because of differences in the way in which resource allocation in these various industries was governed. Yet in both cases, fundamental challenges to the technological and economic supremacy of the United States were posed by enterprises based in different social environments that developed and utilized broader and deeper skill bases to generate higher-quality, lower-cost products. Especially in the case of the Japanese, the challenges came from enterprises that integrated into processes of organizational learning not only managerial employees, as the Americans had done, but also shop-floor employees and employees of subsidiary enterprises which functioned as suppliers and distributors.

These competitive challenges demanded a response from US corporate enterprises but as they struggled with what was going on in the productive sphere, as they attempted first to define the competitive problem and then to react to it, the ground had shifted in the financial sphere. In particular, with the rise of institutional investors, and the increasing pressures that they placed on corporate enterprises to deliver higher returns on their corporate stocks, the commitment of financial resources to corporate strategies came under considerable pressure. These pressures manifested themselves in a particularly aggressive form in the 1980s with the rise of a market for corporate control. When that market collapsed in the late 1980s, leading institutional investors sought other levers for influencing corporate resource allocation in a movement that has been characterized as the rise of institutional investor activism.

5.2. The Productive Challenges: The Rise of New Competition

In the 1970s and 1980s the Japanese successfully challenged the Americans in the mass production of durable goods such as passenger cars, televisions, audio equipment, video equipment, photocopiers, and computers, industries in which the United States had previously reigned supreme. Japanese competitive advantage in these industries built on their advances in vertically related capital-goods industries such as steel, machine tools, semiconductors, and ceramics which provided the materials, the equipment, and the components for generating high-quality, low-cost products.[1]

The Japanese challenge was devastating in consumer electronics, an industrial sector in which, in the decades after World War II, the United States had been the unrivalled world leader. Indeed, during the middle decades of the century, a number of US-based companies—General Electric, RCA, Motorola, and Zenith among others—collectively created the consumer electronics industry. Critical to US dominance in these industries were its pioneering efforts, first in vacuum tubes, then in transistors, and finally in semiconductors.

By the 1970s the market for electronics products was vast. Between 1977 and 1985, the US consumer electronics market alone increased by well over 300 per cent in real terms, with video recording sales increasing from only 2 per cent of the total in 1977 to about 25 per cent in 1985 (Staelin et al. 1989: 42). During the mid-1980s, the total consumer electronics market in the United States was estimated to be about $30 billion per year. Yet, by that time, it was a market that had been lost or abandoned by most of the American companies that had previously dominated the industry. It was the Japanese who, in consumer electronics, generated such formidable, and often unbeatable, competition to the Americans. Companies such as Sony, Hitachi, and Matsushita entered the consumer electronics industries in the 1950s in products such as radios and tape recorders, and then developed their capabilities in audio and video equipment. The United States went from almost complete control of the radio market in 1955 to virtually no market share twenty years later. In many other consumer electronics product markets, the story was much the same. For example, in the rapidly expanding video recording markets, in which US companies had been the technological pioneers, Japanese companies such as Sony and Matsushita emerged as overwhelmingly dominant in the late 1970s and early 1980s (Rosenbloom and Cusumano 1987). As a result, US imports increased from less than 6 per cent of the US consumer electronics market in 1960 to over 50 per cent in 1979 (Magaziner and Reich 1982: 33).

The demise of RCA, the leader in consumer electronics, was an important element in the failure of the US industry. RCA pioneered in radio in the 1920s, enjoyed enormous success in television in the 1950s and 1960s, and proved a complete failure in video equipment in the 1970s and 1980s (Graham 1986). During the mid-1960s as it dissipated its financial and human resources in competing head to head with IBM in the computer industry, as well as in businesses wholly unrelated to its consumer electronics core, Japanese enterprises were honing their abilities to generate higher-quality, lower-cost products. By the 1970s, many of RCA's US competitors had sold out to foreign competitors, primarily Japanese companies, or had otherwise exited the industry. In 1985 RCA still had $2.3 billion in consumer electronic sales (about 10 per cent of the entire US market) but the company survived, as did GE in consumer electronics, largely by putting its brand name on products produced by

---

[1] An important analysis of US loss of competitive advantage in a number of major industries can be found in Dertouzos et al. (1989).

Japanese enterprises. In 1987 RCA was bought by GE but shortly afterwards its new parent sold the consumer electronics operations of both companies to the French electronics concern Thomson (Staelin *et al.* 1989; Chandler 1998). By then the US consumer electronics industry was practically dead. Zenith, the lone US-based company to manufacture televisions in the late 1980s, ceased producing televisions in the United States in 1995.

So too in the automobile industry, the competitive challenge to a previously dominant US industry came from the Japanese. From the first decades of the twentieth century, the United States had taken the lead in the mass production of automobiles. In 1950, with Europe and Japan still struggling to recover from the industrial damage of World War II, the United States produced over 80 per cent of the world's automobiles (cars, trucks, and buses) (Altschuler *et al.* 1986: 13). Even in 1960, when Europe and Japan had substantially rebuilt their war-torn economies, the United States retained about 50 per cent of world production, while the Europeans contributed about 35 per cent and the Japanese only about 2 per cent. The Japanese increased production from less than half a million vehicles in 1960 to 5.3 million in 1970 and 11.0 million in 1980, a year in which they surpassed the Americans as the world's largest producers of automobiles, with about 29 per cent of world production (Cusumano 1985: 1–26).

The Japanese gained competitive advantage through a transformation of the way in which products were developed and utilized in a wide range of industries. This productive transformation permitted Japanese enterprises to generate products that, in particular market segments, were both higher in quality and lower in cost than those of their competitors. By 1965, as Table 5.1 shows, labour productivity at Toyota was already 50 per cent higher than the average for the US Big Three, even after adjusting for its lower level of vertical integration, higher capacity utilization, and longer working hours. By the early 1980s, Nissan and Toyota were both approximately twice as productive as their American counterparts.

As part of the International Motor Vehicle Program (IMVP), researchers at MIT amassed plant-level data for automobile assembly operations at 38 plants and standardized them to take account of differences in working hours, product options such

TABLE 5.1 Vehicles per Employee, adjusted for Vertical Integration, Capacity Utilization, and Labour-Hour Differences, 1965–1983

Fiscal year	US Big Three	Nissan	Toyota
1965	4.7	4.3	6.9
1970	4.6	8.8	10.9
1975	5.3	9.0	13.7
1979	5.5	11.1	15.0
1983	5.7	11.0	12.7

Source: Cusumano (1985: table 49, p. 199).

as the size of the car, and other variables. Their results showed that even in the late 1980s, notwithstanding attempts by the US auto producers to substantially reorganize their assembly operations to copy Japanese practices, substantial productivity differences persisted between US and Japanese producers: the average US plant in North America spent an average of 26.5 hours on a vehicle compared with 19.1 hours for Japanese plants in Japan. Japanese-owned plants in North America, on average, were also more productive than their US-owned counterparts, spending an average of 19.5 hours on a vehicle. Moreover, an analysis of plant productivity and quality levels showed that high levels of productivity by the Japanese plants were not being achieved at the expense of quality; indeed, all of the Japanese-parented plants in Japan and North America registered above-average productivity and quality; US companies were much less effective at combining high quality and high productivity (Krafcik 1988: 41–52).

Central to the export success of the Japanese was their ability to penetrate the huge US automobile market. In 1965 US imports accounted for just 13 per cent of Japanese automobile exports. By 1970 this figure had risen to 38 per cent, and it peaked at 55 per cent during the second oil crisis of 1979. In 15 years—from 1964 to 1979—the number of Japanese automobiles imported into the United States increased from less than 20,000 to over 2.5 million. From the early 1980s, first in response to US government political pressure and then in response to rising Japanese wages and the strengthening yen, Japanese automobile companies began to build plants in the United States to produce cars for the US market, bringing their innovative production practices directly to the United States. Between 1982 and 1992, the Japanese invested almost $9 billion to set up 9 major assembly plants in the United States, employing more than 30,000 workers and with a capacity to produce 2.4 million automobiles per year, some 20 per cent of total US production (Kenney and Florida 1993: 95–6).

It was not only in the automobile industry that Japanese companies brought their productive capabilities, developed in Japan for domestic and foreign markets, to compete for markets by producing in the United States. From the early 1970s, for example, the Japanese consumer electronics companies were busy setting up production facilities in the United States, at first using some of the plants that had been abandoned by US producers. By 1989 Japanese industrial companies had set up 1,275 plants in the United States, employing over 300,000 people directly, in steel, computers, industrial machinery, rubber, and plastics as well as automobiles and consumer electronics (Kenney and Florida 1993: 219–21, 89).

The challenge of international competition proved especially visible in the mass-production industries but it was not confined to them. During the 1980s, although the US remained the leading world producer of high-tech products, its share of world production fell steadily from 36.6 per cent in 1980 to 29.5 per cent in 1990 (NSF 1998: appendix table 6-5). Japanese producers, in contrast, gained four percentage points of world market share in high-tech industries. By 1991 Japan had passed the US as the world's leading producer of high-tech products. These figures on production shares, in fact, underestimate the loss of competitive position by US producers in certain high-tech sectors because, being based on shipment data, they conceal the growing reliance of US producers on foreign suppliers.

In the computer industry, for example, US market share fell from 70 per cent in 1980 to a lower, but still dominant, share of 60 per cent in 1990 (Ferguson and Morris 1994: 107). US producers were, however, becoming increasingly dependent on foreign producers for components, a fact that showed up in a worsening trade balance, especially with Japan. Imports of office and computing machinery increased from 8.4 per cent of production in 1980 to 15.6 per cent in 1990. In 1980 the US had a small computer trade surplus with Japan; by 1991 that had deteriorated to a $5 billion deficit. The total electronics deficit, including consumer electronics, was c. $10 billion (Ferguson and Morris 1994: 108). The competitive problems of the US electronics industry were also reflected in a dramatic decline in the domestic content of production for the office and computer machinery industry; during the 1980s an average of only 35.4 per cent of the final output of this industry was attributed to domestic value added as compared with 44.7 per cent for the 1970s, as US producers became increasingly dependent on their Japanese competitors for memory chips, flat panel screens, and a wide variety of other electronic components (NSF 1998: appendix table 6-4).

There were increasing concerns as the 1980s unfolded that the computer industry would repeat the saga of consumer electronics, in which dependence on foreign suppliers had presaged the exit from the industry of the leading US competitors. In 1990 Andrew Grove, the chairman of Intel Corporation, gloomily pronounced that '[c]omputers are just like cars, or machine tools, or consumer electronics. American market share is trending down and Japan's is going up. I call it the X-curve. It would depress a cow' (Ferguson and Morris 1994: 109–10). Grove was in a good position to appreciate the extent of the threat, since one of the most dramatic shifts in relative competitive position of the US and Japan occurred in semiconductors.

During the 1970s and 1980s, Japanese companies such as NEC, Toshiba, Hitachi, Fujitsu, Mitsubishi, and Matsushita became world leaders in semiconductor production, especially in dynamic random access memories (DRAMs). While the Japanese share of global semiconductor sales rose from 26 per cent to 49 per cent between 1980 and 1990, the US share fell from 58 per cent to 37 per cent. In 1990 the Japanese held over 70 per cent of the world DRAM market, up from 22 per cent a decade earlier (Clausing et al. 1989; Macher, Mowery, and Hodges 1998). As Ferguson and Morris described the trend,

Throughout the 1980s, with export earnings soaring, and the highest savings rate in the world, the Japanese invested massively in semiconductor capacity, building dozens of huge new factories with astonishingly high productivity and yields. In just a few years, the price of semiconductor memory dropped a thousandfold, from $10 per thousand bits to less than a penny—almost certainly the greatest single productivity improvement in industrial history. Smaller American companies lost billions of dollars trying to compete, until they either folded completely, or, like Intel, quit making DRAMs to concentrate on other chips. (Ferguson and Morris 1994: 109)

Notwithstanding the complaints from US producers about Japanese dumping and their calls to the US government for protection, there had been plenty of evidence since at least the beginning of the 1980s, that the competitive challenge posed by the Japanese enterprises was more deeply rooted. In a presentation at the Electronics Industries Association in Washington in 1980, for example, a Hewlett-Packard (HP) senior manager had shown a slide that ranked American and Japanese semiconductor producers in terms of product quality. The best US firm delivered parts to HP with six times as many faults as the worst Japanese firm (Jackson 1997: 247; see also Macher, Mowery, and Hodges 1998)! At least in DRAMs the Japanese had once again proven the strength of their innovative capabilities to simultaneously achieve higher quality and higher productivity. These capabilities proved difficult for the US producers to imitate. Jackson describes how

[i]n March 1991, after Intel had been promoting manufacturing quality and cost as one of its key corporate objectives for six years, the company participated in a 'benchmarking' exercise where it shared confidential data from its chip fabrication activities with other big semiconductor companies around the world. The results showed that on overall manufacturing costs, the top two tiers of participants consisted of Japanese companies, the Koreans came next, and Intel last, on a par with Taiwan.

Intel was also slower at building factories than average, and slower to ramp production of a new product up to the desired level. On each new process, Intel took more than two years to achieve or approach the same yields as the competition. And on indirect staffing—the number of people in the fab site who were not actually working on the lines—Intel's head count was 'dramatically higher' than all of the other vendors surveyed. (Jackson 1997: 301)

What needs to be explained is the ability of the Japanese to transform low wages into high wages on a sustained basis. Protection of the home market and unfair trade practices do not provide compelling explanations in view of the ultimate, and relatively rapid, success of the Japanese in transforming low wages into high wages and gaining dominant shares of world markets. At the beginning of the 1970s Japanese wages per hour for production workers in manufacturing were only about one-sixth of US hourly wages. By the end of the decade, however, Japanese wages were about five-sixths of the US level, and during the 1980s the differential vanished. Between 1982 and 1994 hourly manufacturing compensation, measured in current US dollars, increased by 55 per cent in the United States, 178 per cent in West Germany, and 296 per cent in Japan (US Congress 1996: 399). Yet Japanese manufacturers continued to exert formidable pressure on their American and German competitors.

What made the Japanese such powerful competitors was the extent of organizational integration that they achieved within and across business enterprises. All of the management practices—'JIT manufacturing, total quality control, focused factories, concurrent engineering, short product development cycles, and close relationships with suppliers, customers, and laboratories', to quote one knowledgeable observer (Funk 1992: 45)—that, by the 1980s, were being exported from Japan to the rest of the world entailed broader and deeper organizational integration (Lazonick 1998). This organizational integration in turn enabled the Japanese to become the world leaders in the development and utilization of machine technologies and advanced materials that further transformed the ability of enterprises to generate high-quality, low-cost products—even as these enterprises paid their employees higher and higher wages. That the Japanese transformed themselves into a high-wage economy while paying financial interests low rates of returns manifests the financial commitment that permitted investments in organization and technology. These investments in turn generated products that outcompeted the previous world leaders in terms of both quality and cost.

Competition from Japan, occurring as it did across a broad, and interrelated, set of industries in which the United States had previously been world-dominant posed a formidable challenge to US prosperity. On the shop floor and within managerial structures of major US industrial corporations, the sustainability of the stable and remunerative employment of millions of American workers could no longer be taken for granted as US companies lost product markets in industries in which they had been the world leaders. The competitive problem that faced US corporate enterprises in all of these industries stemmed from the fact that the innovation process, of which the organizational learning process is its social substance, increasingly relied on the integration of an ever-increasing array of specific productive capabilities. In a wide range of industries, an innovative investment strategy had become one that entailed investments in deeper and broader organizational skill bases so that learning could extend further down the organizational hierarchy and involve more functional specialities. In responding to these competitive challenges, US corporate enterprises faced some major obstacles that stemmed from the pattern of organizational integration which had grown out of the governance system that had historically shaped their innovation processes.

One major organizational problem that many US corporate enterprises confronted in responding to these challenges was the hierarchical segmentation between managers and workers and the related corporate strategy of relying predominantly on the managerial organization for the development of new productive capabilities. In many US corporate enterprises there was, as a result, a systematic bias of major US corporations against making innovative investments in deep skill bases that extended down the organizational hierarchy to the shop floor.

Moreover, compared with the integrated organizational structures of foreign competitors, organizational learning within the managerial structures of many US enterprises was limited by the functional segmentation of different groups of technical specialists from one another. Specialists in marketing, development, production, and purchasing may have been highly skilled in their particular functions, but relative to their Japanese counterparts in particular, they tended to respond to incentives that led them to learn in isolation from one another. Functional segmentation made it difficult for such isolated specialists to solve complex problems that required collective learning.

The overextension of US corporate enterprises into too many different lines of business had helped to foster the strategic segmentation of top managers from their organizations. Thus it was more difficult for them to understand what type of innovative strategies they should pursue or the capabilities of their organizations to implement these strategies. As a consequence, there was an identifiable trend in many US corporations toward a greater and greater disconnection between those who controlled resource allocation decisions and the processes through which resources could be developed and utilized. In many cases, therefore, those with the power to make investments, or to shape the criteria by which they should be made, knew little about what types of investments should be made, and those who had the necessary ability to make investments lacked the control of resources that they needed to make these commitments.

In certain industries—industries such as consumer electronics, automobiles, steel, machine tools, and commodity semiconductors—the patterns of organizational integration and segmentation that prevailed in US corporate enterprises in the 1970s and 1980s proved debilitating in the face of new competitive threats. Yet, to study the organizational foundations of the competitive challenges that confronted US corporate enterprises during this period is to recognize that the US corporate economy did not face a generalized problem of innovation as some suggested at the time. Only when competitors' strategies had succeeded in generating higher-quality and lower-cost products on the basis of the integration of broader and deeper skill bases were US corporate enterprises systematically and severely challenged.

In other business activities, however, the systematic bias of US corporate enterprises to compete for product markets by investing in narrow and concentrated skill bases did not prove to be a liability, at least during this period. To the contrary, in science-based industries like pharmaceuticals, in microprocessors, in software, and in service sectors like finance, strategies that relied on narrow and concentrated skill bases continued to prove extremely effective as the basis of innovation for US corporate enterprises. Japanese enterprises did not, as a result, pose the kind of competitive threat that they presented in other business activities. In drugs and medicines, for example, US corporate enterprises increased world market share during the 1980s from 24.2 per cent in 1980 to 28.9 per cent in 1990. The domestic content of this industry's production also increased during the same period from 48.1 per cent in 1980 to 55 per cent in 1990. The Japanese position increased only slightly during the 1980s, from 19.9 per cent of world production in 1980 to 20.8 per cent in 1990 (NSF 1998: appendix tables 6-4, 6-5).

Yet, notwithstanding the continued vibrancy of certain key sectors of the US corporate economy, there were good reasons to be concerned about the dramatic loss of competitive position in so many industries at once. The success of these industries had allowed the US to generate a large base of good jobs, that is jobs which paid well and were reasonably stable, during the post-war decades. Moreover, through linkages with other sectors of the economy, they had supported the creation and distribution of wealth beyond the boundaries of their own immediate activities. Moreover, by developing and producing so many of the products that its citizens wanted to buy at prices they were willing to pay the US had maintained a healthy external balance of trade. Finally, and perhaps most importantly, it was feared that if US companies did not learn how to respond competitively to the Japanese challenge in these industries, this would encourage Japanese companies to devote their resources to learning how to outcompete US corporate enterprises even in sectors in which the Americans remained dominant.

The innovative capabilities of international competitors made it harder for US corporations to sustain the employment and wages of their labour forces, as well as all of the other favourable economic outcomes to which they had contributed in the past, unless the productive capabilities of many if not most of these employees could be radically transformed. There were, however, enormous institutional barriers to confronting the competitive challenge in automobiles, steel, and other industries. As noted in Chapter 2, once a company conforms to a certain type of integration it will be difficult to change it. To the market and technological uncertainty of innovation was added a behavioural dimension associated with organizational, and even institutional, transformation. There was an alternative strategy—to exit rather than confronting the challenge—which was potentially attractive given the strength of the competitive challenge and the major organizational barriers to change. Under these conditions, US corporate managers faced a strategic crossroads: they could find new ways to generate productivity gains on the basis of 'retain and reinvest', or they could capitulate to the new competitive environment through corporate downsizing. Much depended on the abilities and incentives of those who exercised control over corporate resources.

5.3. The Growing Pressures for Financial Liquidity

To develop and utilize productive resources on the basis of organizational learning requires financial commitment. Social institutions must support the ongoing access of business organizations to the financial resources required to sustain the innovation process. Financial commitment was central to the rise of the United States to its position of industrial leadership during the first half of the twentieth century and retained earnings formed the foundation of enterprise access to committed finance. From 1970 to 1989, for example, retained earnings accounted for 91 per cent of the net sources of finance for US non-financial corporations, while debt finance accounted for 34 per cent, with new equity and other sources of finance being negative (Corbett and Jenkinson 1996).

During the 1980s and 1990s, however, there was a marked shift in US governance institutions towards support for financial liquidity at the expense of commitment. Encouraging this shift in the governance system was a transformation in the way in which US households save. From the 1960s to the 1980s, fundamental changes occurred in US financial institutions which encouraged and abetted wealth-holding US households in their growing reliance on returns from investments in publicly traded common stocks. By depending increasingly on the stock market to augment their incomes and savings, these relatively privileged Americans developed a major stake in maintaining high returns on corporate stock.

Unlike the days when stockholding in any one company was fragmented among hundreds of thousands of household investors, the collective power of institutional investing now gives these wealth-holding households greater opportunities to reap high returns. Over the past three decades, institutional investors have become increasingly central to the American saving system. With their ever-increasing holdings of corporate stocks, institutional investors can now put pressure on US corporations to 'create shareholder value'. In the 1980s and 1990s, so successful have they been in their use of carrots and sticks to further the interests of their constituency that the 'maximization of shareholder value' has become a veritable mantra on Main Street as well as on Wall Street.

5.3.1. The Evolution of Household Savings

A transformation of the structure of US financial institutions and their interaction with the real sector of the US economy began in the late 1960s and early 1970s. Whilst the causes of this structural transformation are complex and various, the growing financial wealth of US households, as well as changes in the way that they allocated that wealth among different financial instruments, are a critical element of the story. An analysis of household financial assets reveals a dramatic shift in their allocation in recent decades; in particular, pension and mutual funds have registered enormous gains in their share of household financial assets at the expense of intermediaries such as banks and thrifts. Moreover, the trend towards the growing reliance of households on pension and mutual funds has increased at an accelerating pace; from 1982 to 1994 pension and mutual funds alone accounted for approximately 67 per cent of the net growth of households' total financial assets (Edwards 1996: 16–27).

Reflecting their growing importance in managing the savings of US households, pension and mutual funds' shares of corporate equities have increased dramatically. As Table 5.2 shows, pension funds held 24 per cent of US corporate stock in 1997, with private pensions accounting for 13.8 per cent and public pensions for 10.2 per cent, compared with 0.3 per cent in 1945. Over the same period, mutual funds increased their share of US corporate stock from 1.5 per cent to 16.2 per cent. In contrast to the growing importance of institutional investors, the share of corporate stocks held directly by individuals has fallen from 93 per cent in 1945 to 42.7 per cent in 1997. Institutional share ownership is even higher in the largest US corporations than in the population of corporate enterprises as a whole: in 1987, the institutional share of the equity of the top 1,000 US corporations was 46.6 per cent and, by 1995, it had increased to 57.2 per cent (Brancato 1997: 21).

The shift of stockholdings to institutional investors had by no means exhausted itself by the mid-1990s. During the last half of the 1980s, the net new cash flow into equity mutual funds ranged from a high of about $21.9 billion in 1986 to a low of −$16.2 billion in 1988. During the early 1990s, however, the flow of new money into mutual funds picked up speed, and during 1993–5 net additions to mutual funds averaged about $125 billion per year. In 1996 and 1997 net additions

TABLE 5.2 US Corporate Stock Held by Households and Institutions, 1952–1997 (%, except for total value)

Year	Total value (billions of dollars)	Household	Foreign	Insurers	Private pension	Public pension	Mutual funds	All financials[a]
1945	118	93.0	2.3	2.4	0.3	0.0	1.5	4.3
1950	143	90.2	2.0	3.3	0.8	0.0	3.2	7.4
1955	282	88.1	2.3	3.2	2.2	0.1	3.4	9.2
1960	420	85.6	2.2	3.0	3.9	0.1	4.7	12.1
1965	735	83.8	2.0	2.9	5.6	0.3	5.0	14.0
1970	841	68.0	3.2	3.3	8.0	1.2	5.2	28.5
1975	846	59.0	3.9	4.9	12.8	2.9	4.7	36.7
1980	1,514	59.6	4.9	5.2	14.8	2.9	3.1	35.2
1985	2,319	48.6	5.9	5.6	21.3	5.2	5.1	44.9
1990	3,537	51.2	6.9	4.6	15.9	8.3	7.1	41.5
1995	8,331	48.6	6.3	5.4	14.2	9.0	12.8	44.3
1996	10,062	45.7	6.5	5.5	14.1	9.5	15.0	46.9
1997	12,776	42.7	7.2	5.7	13.8	10.2	16.2	49.3

[a] Insurers, pensions, mutual funds, bank personal trusts, and other.

Source: US Board of Governors of the Federal Reserve System (various years).

to equity mutual funds rose to the unprecedented levels of $217 billion and $227 billion respectively. In the first seven months of 1998, the pace of inflows remained vigorous. However, in conjunction with the downturn in the US stock market in August 1998, the inflow of cash slowed down sufficiently to bring the net inflow for the year to $159 billion, which represented a 30 per cent fall compared with 1997. Yet, as the market regained its vigour, in late 1998 and especially in early 1999, inflows revived again (Investment Company Institute: http://www.ici.org).

5.3.2. *Dealing with Growing Intergenerational Dependence*

The importance of pension funds as a repository of financial wealth is related to the process of population ageing under way in the US. A substantial proportion of the recent upsurge in the share of mutual funds, moreover, is attributable to their growing popularity for pension provision; at the end of 1996, retirement plan assets represented 35 per cent of all mutual fund assets (Investment Company Institute). The number of individuals in the US aged 65 or over per 100 working-age individuals increased from 15.4 in 1960 to an estimated 19.8 in 1995 and is projected to rise to 32.2 in 2030. Although the US trend towards population ageing is less pronounced than in other advanced industrial countries, especially Italy, Japan, and Germany, it represents, nevertheless, a substantial growth in intergenerational dependence (UN 1995).

That the phenomenon of population ageing has had such a dramatic effect on financial institutions in the US reflects not only demographic trends but also the particular form that social provisions for retirement have taken in that country. Of particular importance is the fact that the government pension scheme is much less significant as a source of pension income in the United States than, for example, in a country like Germany; social security accounts for about 40 per cent of the retirement income of US pensioners compared with nearly 70 per cent for German pensioners (Turner and Watanabe 1995: 136). For the more fortunate Americans, private pensions have stepped into the breach, and the US government has encouraged their development through tax incentives.

Of particular importance in making pensions available to more than an elite of the wealthiest Americans, albeit still to an elite of the working population, has been the development of employer-based pensions. The structure of these pension plans in the United States has been influenced in critical ways by the evolution of the corporate economy. Pension plans were first introduced by US corporate employers on a significant scale in the early decades of the twentieth century; there were 13 plans in existence in 1899 but by 1919 the number had risen to 300 plans covering 15 per cent of the US workforce (Sass 1997: 54). The plans were concentrated among the leading enterprises and they were designed to serve the needs of employers to control their workforces by reducing labour mobility and warding off unionization. Workers had little security in terms of their pension claims (Sass 1997: 38–55).

The Great Depression threw the private pension system into turmoil. It also prompted the direct intervention of the federal government in the pension arrangements of the population with the passage of the Social Security Act of 1935. With lower-paid workers partly taken care of by the federal government, corporate plans increasingly focused on catering for executives. In particular, when the New Dealers raised income taxes on high-income earners, corporate pensions looked attractive as a tax-efficient vehicle for compensating those employees whom corporations regarded as critical to their operations. As a result, the percentage of the workforce covered by pension plans established in the 1930s was only 41 per cent, as compared with 78 per cent for those established before 1930 (Sass 1997: 115).

From 1926 the US government had promoted employer pensions through favourable tax treatment. With the passage of the Revenue Act of 1942, the government increased the tax advantages for pension plans but also strengthened the requirement for broad employee participation as a condition for favourable tax treatment of corporate pension plans (Sass 1997: 151–2). In casting the income tax net ever broader, and in pursuing its wage-stabilization programme during the war, the government further encouraged the use of pensions as a way of compensating employees. By 1945, private pensions covered 6.5 million employees compared with 2 million in 1938. After the war, even with the reduction of income tax rates and the restoration of wage flexibility, the institution of the private pension remained in place because, as Sass put it, 'executives now understood firsthand the value of the pension in retaining key personnel' (Sass 1997: 119; see also 88–112).

Despite the intention behind the Revenue Act of 1942, private pension plans remained biased towards managerial employees, and some expressly excluded blue-collar workers. Moreover, the real value of these workers' Social Security benefits fell dramatically in the inflationary forties; the average benefit replaced only 19 per cent of the average wage in 1950 compared with 30 per cent in 1940. As a result, some US unions, especially those affiliated with the growing Congress of Industrial Organizations (CIO), became increasingly interested in protecting and enhancing their members' claims to pension benefits. They applied political pressure to increase Social Security benefits. They also fought successfully to put pensions on the agenda in collective bargaining with employers (Ghilarducci 1992: 29–51; Sass 1997: 113–44).

The CIO initially defended its claims for higher pension benefits by drawing an analogy between pensions for workers and the depreciation of physical capital. A similar logic was used by the Steel Industry Board (SIB), established in July 1949 by President Truman in an attempt to break a deadlock in labour–management relations in the steel industry. The SIB resisted the United Steelworkers' demands for wage increases, on the grounds that they were inflationary, but instead recommended the institution by the steel companies of non-contributory pensions for their employees. The steel companies initially rejected the SIB's conclusion that employers should be required to provide workers with a non-contributory pension. In September 1949, the United Steelworkers went on strike to pressure the steel companies to implement the SIB's pension recommendations (Sass 1997: 132–35).

In the meantime, the UAW and Ford Motor Company (FMC) had negotiated a non-contributory employer pension plan. The plan had originally been proposed by Ford in 1945 and had been accepted by the leadership of the UAW. The rank and file had previously rejected the plan in favour of a wage increase but in 1949 Walter Reuther's campaign to marshall support for employer pension plans within the UAW proved successful and the plan was instituted at the end of September 1949. The UAW–FMC plan set the pattern for pensions in much of the manufacturing sector. It also increased the pressure on the steel companies to conclude an agreement on pensions with the United Steelworkers. In November 1949, Bethlehem Steel agreed to a non-contributory pension plan similar to the UAW–FMC plan. The other major steel companies soon followed its lead (Sass 1997: 135–6).

By the early 1950s, pension plans had become a commonplace element of CIO labour contracts. These plans assumed a standard form: 'They were funded, noncontributory defined-benefit plans, paying modest benefits and granting full credit for past service. They made retirement from blue-collar employment a relatively smooth transition and a reasonably comfortable prospect' (Sass 1997: 137). Most of the CIO-negotiated plans were single-employer plans. Some CIO unions, most notably the UAW, made attempts to institute joint management–union control of single-employer plans in the late 1940s and 1950s. These efforts were, however, strenuously resisted and, as a result, single-employer plans have remained largely under the control of the sponsoring employer. Increasingly, unions focused their pension initiatives on ensuring high contributions to these plans. In justifying their efforts in this regard, they moved away from the argument that employers had a social responsibility to provide for the 'depreciation' of their human resources and increasingly treated pensions as deferred wages that they bargained over as they did other forms of wage compensation (Ghilarducci 1992: 34).

Given the CIO's success in negotiating plans, the American Federation of Labor (AFL) unions, although they had until then shown less interest in pensions, felt obliged to follow where the CIO had led. Many AFL union members worked for small and medium-sized enterprises and the unions' favoured form of pension plan was, as a result, a multi-employer plan. The Labor–Management Relations Act of 1947 (often called the 'Taft–Hartley' Act) prohibited unions from exercising sole control over these plans, notwithstanding the fact that employers were permitted to do so for single-employer plans. Multi-employer or 'Taft–Hartley' plans had to be administered by a board of trustees, one half to be appointed by management and the other by labour (Ghilarducci 1992: 45; Sass 1997: 184).

By 1960, private pensions covered 41 per cent of the US workforce compared with 19 per cent in 1945. By 1979, coverage had risen to 45 per cent of the private sector workforce and half of those covered were union members. By then 83 per cent of union members participated in a pension plan compared with 39 per cent for non-union workers (OECD 1993: 10; Sass 1997: 179, 139; Freeman 1985). These figures suggest the vital role that the union movement played in extending coverage of employer pension plans after World War II. Unions promoted that extension, not only through the direct effect of their negotiations on unionized employers, but also because they raised the benefit hurdle for non-union workers. As a result, as Sass observes,

[u]sing its right to bargain collectively, labor had created a private social welfare system comparable in coverage to that of corporate employers. Without union pressure, post-war business might never have provided production workers with significant pension benefits. Social Security alone may have satisfied management's basic need for blue-collar pensioning. The federal program had legitimated 65 as the national retirement age, and it guaranteed that all ex-workers, separated voluntarily or otherwise, would not go penniless. Management had little interest in expensive pension programs to develop career commitments among its production workers. (Sass 1997: 140)

As pension funds grew in scale, they increasingly invested their accumulated funds in corporate securities; from 1960 onwards about two-thirds of private pension fund assets were invested in corporate stocks and bonds. Already in 1960, corporate equities had outrun corporate bonds as the corporate securities of choice for private pension plans. As a result, there was an upsurge in the flow of funds from pension plans into the equity markets, and since then this flow has maintained a fairly steady trend upwards. In the current bull market, there has been a particularly striking shift into equities. In 1985, 41.2 per cent of the assets of defined benefit pension portfolios and 38.1 per cent of those of defined contribution portfolios were invested in equities; by the first quarter of 1998 those shares had increased to 53.7 per cent and 47.6 per cent respectively (EBRI, *Quarterly Pension Report*, Sept. 1998).

In allocating the resources under their control, pension trustees, be they corporate executives, joint labour–management boards, or investment managers, were legally

bound to act as 'prudent men': they were to allocate funds 'with the care, skill, prudence, and diligence under the circumstances then prevailing that a prudent man
acting in a like capacity and familiar with such matters would use in conducting an
enterprise of like character and with like aims' (Sass 1997: 182). In the late 1960s,
however, a number of apparent violations of the prudent-man standard caused considerable concern about the efficacy of the existing regulation of employer pensions;
the most notable examples were the alleged self-dealing of Jimmy Hoffa and the
Teamsters in the management of the Central and Southern States Pension Fund
(CSPF) and the underfunding of the Studebaker pension plan in the wake of the
company's exit from the US auto industry. These events set the ball of pension reform
rolling, although it was helped along the way by other external events such as the
economic downturn in 1973 and the concurrent stock market crash.

The Employee Retirement Income Security Act (ERISA) was introduced in 1974
with the objective of securing the benefits of participants in private pension plans
through the introduction of a comprehensive framework for the regulation of
funding, vesting, insurance, and disclosure. If pension plans were to be eligible for
tax benefits, the vesting period had to be shortened to reduce the risk of employees
being left without any pension. The Act tightened funding requirements and the
Pension Benefit Guaranty Corporation (PBGC) was established to insure pension
promises in the event that an employer with an underfunded pension plan went bank-
rupt. Of particular importance were the guidelines that ERISA introduced for the
operation of pension plans. Whereas in the past, the prudent-man standard was to
be applied to each investment made by a plan trustee, the architects of ERISA, reflecting the emerging conventional wisdom on Wall Street, interpreted prudence with
reference not to individual investments but to the investment portfolio as a whole.
As Sass observed, 'Diversification and the performance of the portfolio as a whole
were the key ideas. Investments "imprudent" by themselves thus could increase the
"prudence" of the entire fund. Put and call options, for example, could hedge a stock
portfolio; a portfolio with volatile investments and low-risk securities could yield
a standard investment-grade return at a lower overall risk' (Sass 1997: 206). It is,
however, important to note that what made diversification so central to the interpretation of prudence as put forward by ERISA was not any statutory definition of
prudence contained in the Act, because it contained none. Rather it stemmed from
the Act's exhortation to institutional investors to go along with the conventional
wisdom among financial investors on what constituted 'prudent investment' through
its requirement for 'diligence . . . that [would be used] in conduct of an enterprise
of a like character and with like aims' (s. 404(a)(1)(B), 29 USC, s. 1104(a)(1)(B),
1988). There were important implications of these standards of behaviour for institutional investors' influence on corporate resource allocation, as I shall discuss in the
next section.

5.3.3. *The Economic and Political Importance of the Stock Market*

As a result of trends in the accumulation and allocation of financial assets, a large
and growing minority of US households is now heavily dependent on corporate equi-

ties for financial returns in general, and retirement incomes in particular. To the extent that institutional investors have significance in US corporate governance today, it is largely because they have ridden a wave of structural change in the United States that has created a large constituency of Americans who, with longer life-spans, earlier retirements, and accumulated financial assets, find it in their interests to favour arguments for financial liquidity. By relying increasingly on the stock market to augment their incomes and savings, these relatively privileged Americans have developed a major stake in maintaining high returns on corporate stock.

In 1995, 40.3 per cent of US households had direct or indirect stock holdings compared with 31.6 per cent as recently as 1989. These holdings accounted for, on average, 41.5 per cent of the financial assets of all US households in 1995, up from 28.6 per cent in 1989 (US Department of Commerce 1998: 532). Moreover, during this period, financial assets were themselves becoming increasingly important as a basis for household wealth, having risen from 27.9 per cent of total household assets in 1989 to 34.1 per cent in 1995 (Kennickell, Starr-McCluer, and Sundén 1997: 12, 6). Notwithstanding the increased reliance on the stock market by US households, equity participation is very unevenly distributed across the population. In 1992 the 0.5 per cent of stock owners with the largest equity portfolios, including both direct and indirect holdings, owned 36.8 per cent of all equity; the top 10 per cent owned 89.4 per cent and the bottom 80 per cent a paltry 1.8 per cent. Since more than one-third of the gains or losses on corporate stock accrued to the roughly half a million households with the largest equity holdings, and almost 90 per cent of the gains to the richest 10 per cent of households (Poterba and Samwick 1995: 328), the US is a far cry from the picture of a shareholder democracy that some pundits have painted.

If the distribution of equity holdings is highly unequal it is nevertheless true that all US households, including poorer ones, have become much more dependent on the stock market in recent decades. As Figure 5.1 shows, stockholdings have become more important as a share of financial assets for all income groups. From the perspective of corporate control, the most important general repercussion of the increased reliance of US households on the stock market, and the growing importance of institutional investors, has been the greatly increased pressure for higher returns on corporate securities that it has engendered. Demands for higher yields for shareholders have in turn created growing systematic pressures for financial liquidity on US corporations.

5.3.4. The Deal Decade

The potential effects of these pressures manifested themselves in a spectacular fashion during the 1980s when corporate America was caught up in a wave of restructuring induced by the emergence of a vigorous 'market for corporate control'. In historical perspective, the 'Deal Decade' was distinctive in a variety of ways. Perhaps its most notable characteristics were the emergence of hostile transactions, the large size of the average target, and the unprecedented reliance on aggressive financial techniques to conclude transfers of corporate control.

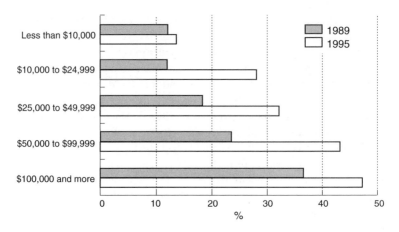

Source: US Department of Commerce (1998: 532)

FIG. 5.1 Stockholdings' share of financial assets by family income group, US, 1989 and 1995
(family income in constant US dollars)

Until the mid-1970s, hostile takeovers were regarded as beyond the bounds of reputable business practice for established corporations and were largely the preserve of speculators. Leading investment banks generally refused to finance these transactions. In 1974, the International Nickel Company of Canada (INCO) broke with tradition when it launched a hostile bid for the Electric Storage Battery Company (ESB) (Brooks 1987: 1–5). In 1975, United Technologies followed INCO's lead with its hostile takeover of Otis Elevator, and Colt Industries followed suit with an attack on Garlock Industries. As Figure 5.2 shows, from then until the end of the 1980s, hostile bids became commonplace.

To look at numbers of hostile bids compared with all tender offers is to underestimate their importance. Many of the target companies of hostile bids were very large and thus their share of transaction value was larger than their proportion of bid numbers. Moreover, some friendly bids were reportedly concluded by management in response to the fear of an unfriendly bid. Nevertheless, it is important to recognize that notwithstanding the emotion whipped up in managerial circles during the 1980s about the attacks by raiders on US corporations, the majority of deals concluded were agreed by incumbent boards of directors of target companies.

What is striking in historical perspective, whether for hostile or friendly deals, was the scale of targets. For the first time in US corporate history, major enterprises were put into play and some of the largest corporate enterprises in the US, including RJR Nabisco, RCA, Gulf Oil, and Kraft, became takeover targets. The average target price reached a high of $215.1 million in 1988; the largest acquisition of the decade was concluded in that year when Kohlberg Kravis Roberts (KKR) paid $25.1 billion for RJR Nabisco.

The explosion of the market for corporate control, and in particular the fact that it could cast its net wide enough to capture major US corporations, was facilitated

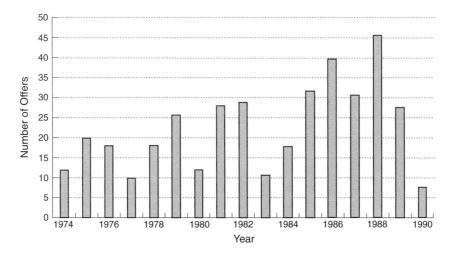

Source: Merrill Lynch Advisory Services (1994)
FIG. 5.2 Number of contested tender offers, US, 1974–1990

by major changes in the structure of the US financial sector. From the late 1960s, a number of important regulatory changes led to intensified competition among US financial enterprises. For investment banks, in particular, the margins in their traditional businesses, especially underwriting, decreased substantially. These banks were, as a result, induced to search for new sources of profits. By the 1980s trading had displaced underwriting as the investment banks' key profit centre but trading had its own shortcomings, not least the large amounts of capital that banks had to put at risk to compete. In this climate the mergers and acquisitions (M&A) business looked increasingly attractive to investment bankers; they did not have to put their own money at risk to compete in the business yet the fees they could earn were enormous. It is hardly surprising, therefore, that they worked hard to create as much momentum as they could for the market for corporate control; as John Brooks put it, 'many corporate takeovers originate in the minds of investment bankers, and are fomented by them for the purpose of collecting huge advisory fees—that is, the process is driven by the bankers (and lawyers) and their fees' (Brooks 1987: 243–4).

In their efforts to fuel the market for corporate control, US investment banks pioneered an unprecedented range of new and, more importantly, profitable techniques for financing transfers of corporate control. The widespread deployment of these techniques did not happen automatically. Rather, it depended on the development of a network of relationships that could harness the growing pressures for financial liquidity in the US economy. Nowhere was the process of building this substructure more important, and its role in facilitating the market for corporate control more evident, than in the development of the leveraged buyout (LBO).

An LBO is a deal in which a small group of investors, which often includes some of the incumbent managers of the target firm, purchases the equity of a company with finance raised by borrowing against the assets of the target company. Once the

business has been bought out, the cash flow that it generates, through ongoing operations or asset sales, is used to pay off the debt. LBOs made their initial appearance
in the 1970s and at that time their targets were, for the most part, business units of
major companies that were being restructured in the wake of failed conglomeration
strategies or family-owned businesses in which owners were seeking lucrative ways
to cash out. In the early stages of the LBO movement, the targets were relatively
small and the deals were generally friendly.

During the 1980s the number of LBOs rapidly increased and the average value of
the transactions rose dramatically. Indeed, from 1983 until 1991, the average value
of LBO transactions was substantially higher than that of M&A transactions in
general, notwithstanding the fact that the latter were at historically high levels
(Baker and Smith 1998: 24). As a result, although LBO transactions always represented a small minority of the number of M&A transactions, they were much more
important as a share of transaction value. The largest buyouts of the decade all
occurred in the second half of the 1980s (Baskin and Miranti 1997: 290), and as the
1980s unfolded, LBO transactions showed an increasing propensity to be hostile
transactions; the biggest deal of the decade was the infamous hostile LBO of RJR
Nabisco by KKR.

Critical to the expansion of the LBO market was the capacity of key players to
rapidly raise huge amounts of capital to finance transactions. After the takeover, the
common stock of the target company was generally controlled by the general partners of LBO firms and the corporate executives who participated in the buyout. These
players were responsible for concluding the deal and making it pay off afterwards.
Although the general partners usually put up some of their own funds, most equity
finance came from investors who bought into these deals as limited partners in LBO
funds. In the early days of the LBO movement, these limited partners tended to be
wealthy individuals and, to some extent, commercial banks. However, the shrewd
LBO firms soon recognized that they could transform the LBO business, and their
position in it, if they could gain access to bigger pools of money. Public pension
funds, in particular, proved helpful in furthering the ambitions of these firms.

Managers of these pension funds had previously been prohibited from making
equity investments because they were deemed to be too risky. Increasingly, however,
state legislatures responded to complaints that returns on public pension funds were
too low to allow them to meet their obligations by removing constraints on equity
investments. KKR was particularly successful in winning the trust of public pension
fund trustees and managers. In gaining preferential access to the funds that they controlled, KKR propelled itself into the position of 'the leveraged buyout kingpin'
(Kaufman and Englander 1993: 75; see 72–75).

From the point of view of the LBO firms and participating management, one
attraction of the LBO deal was that they had to put down a minority of the equity
finance to acquire control of the target company. The real sweetener in the LBO deal,
however, was the fact that equity finance accounted for only a small proportion,
between 1 and 20 per cent, of the total financing of the takeover. The majority of
the purchase price of targets in LBO deals was financed by debt; in the three biggest

LBOs of the decade, 6 per cent or less of the total financing package—6 per cent for RJR Nabisco, 5.1 per cent for Beatrice, and 3 per cent for Safeway—was accepted as full consideration for the entire common stock (Baker and Smith 1998: 109; Baker 1992: 1105; Kaufman and Englander 1993: 83).

Given LBOs' high levels of debt financing, critical to the operation of the whole LBO movement was the willingness of investors to hold debt instruments. In this regard, senior debt, secured on the assets of the target company, proved least problematic and was generally provided by commercial banks. Persuading investors to hold subordinated debt was the real challenge for LBO firms. In the early stages of the LBO movement, insurance companies and commercial banks were the main focus of LBO firms' overtures. However, these investors' concerns about risk, and especially in the case of insurance companies the pressure that they exerted for a greater piece of the action in LBO deals, limited the fundraising ability of the LBO firms. However, the rise of the junk bond market removed these constraints and facilitated the rise of LBO activity to new heights.

Junk bonds were not invented for the Deal Decade. They had been around for decades but were generally described as low-grade or high-yield bonds. There had been an active new-issues market for these bonds before World War II but it declined thereafter. By the beginning of the 1970s, only 4 per cent of all corporate bonds were low-grade. Moreover, many of these bonds were 'fallen angels', once highly rated investment-grade bonds that had fallen from grace when the issuing companies experienced difficulties. A resurgence of the low-grade bond market began in the late 1970s. Drexel Burnham Lambert, the investment bank whose name has since become synonymous with junk bonds, did not lead the charge; Lehman Brothers pipped it to the post when it underwrote a series of new issues of these low-grade bonds. Yet, as Gaughan observes, 'Drexel Burnham Lambert's role was the key to the growth of the low-grade/high-yield bond market. It served as a market maker for junk bonds, as they had begun to be called, which was crucial to the dramatic growth of the market' (Gaughan 1996: 303).

Led by Michael Milken, the head of its junk bond business, Drexel provided liquidity for junk bonds by developing a network of investors who could be called on to buy new issues. Mutual funds, insurance companies, pension funds, especially state and local government pension funds, and savings and loans banks were the most important members of Milken's network. All of these financial enterprises were under growing pressures to deliver high returns on their investments to their ultimate beneficiaries. The attraction of being members of Milken's network was that it appeared that they could make high yields and maintain access to a liquid market for the securities which they held. As Benjamin Stein observed,

This was a vital inducement to the insurance company portfolio managers, pension fund managers, or any other investors whom Milken approached. Buyers of bonds don't want to get fired for having excessive, illiquid, low-credit-rated issues in their portfolios at an inopportune moment. Milken promised them that he would 'take them out' of the bonds at a moment's notice. This not only made the bonds a better buy, but also made their buyers more secure in their jobs. (Stein 1992: 75)

With the junk bond market booming and Drexel firmly in control of it, it looked as if Milken could deliver on his promises. By 1982 junk bond issuance had grown to $2.4 billion a year; in 1985 it had soared to $14.1 billion, and then went even higher to $31.9 billion in 1986. Drexel dominated the market with 57 per cent of the total market share of new public issues of junk bonds in 1983, falling to between 40 and 50 per cent from 1984 to 1987 as more investment bankers made serious attempts to compete for junk bond business (Gaughan 1996: 306).

Although junk bonds represented only a small fraction of total acquisition financing, half of all the junk bonds issued were used to finance or refinance acquisitions. Over the course of the 1980s, that share increased from 35 per cent in 1985 to 65 per cent in 1989 (Blair 1993: 9). The dramatic expansion of the junk bond market thus had an important effect on the level and nature of merger and acquisition activity. As Gaughan describes it,

The junk bond market and the use of junk bonds as a financing tool for mergers and acquisitions and leveraged buyouts represent one of the most influential innovations in the field. The availability of very large amounts of capital through the junk bond market made possible the participation of many who would never have considered participating otherwise. The access to such large amounts of capital also made even the largest and most established firms potentially vulnerable to a takeover by much smaller suitors. (Gaughan 1996: 302)

In the hubris surrounding junk bonds, the fact that they were extremely risky was often overlooked and indeed the sellers of junk took considerable pains to obscure that fact. The risks associated with junk bonds increased dramatically as the 1980s unfolded. In a study of junk bonds issued between 1977 and 1986, Paul Asquith, David Mullins, and Eric Wolff showed that the cumulative default rates on junk bonds were considerably higher than previous studies had shown and than underwriters of junk bonds were wont to admit; by 1986 the default rate on junk bonds issued in 1977 and 1978, for example, was almost 35 per cent (Asquith, Mullins, and Wolff 1989). Moreover, as Barrie Wigmore showed in his study of junk bond issues from 1980 to 1988, the average quality of junk bonds, as measured by interest coverage, debt as a percentage of net tangible assets, and cash flow as a percentage of debt, deteriorated substantially as the market for junk bonds exploded (Wigmore 1989).[2] The economics of LBO transactions also deteriorated as the decade unfolded; buyout prices to cash flow ratios increased, especially in deals financed by junk bonds, ratios of cash flow to total debt obligations fell, and management teams and dealmakers took out higher rewards at earlier stages of the deal (Kaplan and Stein 1993).

By the end of the 1980s the Deal Decade came to an abrupt end partly because, in the wake of the 1987 stock market crash, investors became increasingly concerned about the risk that they were bearing on junk bonds. Other factors that contributed to the decline included the crisis in the savings and loan industry, which had played

---

[2] Earnings before interest and tax coverage of interest charges declined from 1.99 in 1980 to 0.71 in 1988; debt as a percentage of net tangible assets increased from 60% in 1980 to 202% in 1988; cash flow as a percentage of debt fell from 17% in 1980 to 3% in 1988.

a critical role in the junk bond market, the jailing of several key players in the market for corporate control, and the general slowdown of the US economy. The junk bond market began its collapse in late 1988. The LBO market also went into a dramatic decline; the total value of LBOs of public companies plummeted from more than $60 billion in 1988 to less than $4 billion in 1990 (W. T. Grimm, *Mergerstat Review*, 1991). The enactment by most states of anti-takeover statutes that permitted corporations to adopt mechanisms to fend off hostile bids, and the adoption of a range of anti-takeover defences by a large number of public corporations, also played a role in bringing the Deal Decade to a close. More than half the states of the US (38 as of mid-1994) passed 'stakeholder' laws which permitted, and in some cases mandated, the consideration by directors of the impact of their actions on constituencies other than shareholders, including employees, suppliers, and local communities.

To proponents of shareholder value, the demise of the market for corporate control represented a major setback for the US system of corporate governance. That institutional investors who had reaped major rewards from it should feel this way was hardly surprising. Pension and mutual funds had reaped huge profits in the market for corporate control not only through their holdings of junk bonds, investments in LBO funds, and the like, but also as buyers and sellers of corporate stock in mergers and acquisitions (Useem 1996: 25–6). As we shall see in the next section, with the demise of the market for corporate control, the foreclosure of their opportunities for easy profit induced some institutional investors to adopt a much more activist stance towards corporate governance.

Distress was, however, not confined to players in the market for corporate control. Influential financial economists weighed in with intellectual support. From their point of view, hostile takeovers and LBOs had played a critical disciplinary role in the US corporate economy in the 1980s. Michael Jensen and Richard Ruback, for example, described the market for corporate control as 'a market in which alternative managerial teams compete for the rights to manage corporate resources' and argued that it played an important role in promoting corporate performance: 'competition among managerial teams for the rights to manage resources limits divergence from shareholder wealth maximisation by managers and provides the mechanism through which economies of scale or other synergies available from combining or reorganizing control and management of corporate resources are realized' (Jensen and Ruback 1983: 6). At the height of the Deal Decade, Jensen's advocacy reached almost hysterical proportions when he claimed that the 'organisational transformation' then under way—by which he meant the 'takeovers, breakups, divisional spinoffs, leveraged buyouts, and going-private transactions' of the 1980s—were facilitating 'remarkable gains in operating efficiency, employee productivity, and shareholder value' in the US economy (Jensen 1989: 61–2). For academics like Jensen—and many financial economists agreed with his general views on corporate governance, albeit in less vociferous terms—the heroes of the 1980s were the LBO firms and the takeover specialists.

Yet despite the vigour with which the shareholder theory was propounded in the US in the 1980s, there is a striking dearth of unambiguous evidence to support it, even when the arguments are taken on their own terms. Studies that purport to measure the effects of the market for corporate control on corporate performance have largely focused on the effects of takeovers and LBOs on shareholder wealth. Most of this research consists of 'event studies' in which the 'abnormal' changes in stock prices of bidder and target companies around the time of the public announcement of these transactions are used as a proxy for their economic effects; abnormal returns represent the difference between actual and expected stock returns as calculated using an asset pricing model such as the Capital Asset Pricing Model (CAPM). Yet, even if we accept the questionable assumption that corporate performance can be adequately proxied by abnormal returns to shareholders, the empirical findings based on the event-study methodology fall short of providing clear-cut support for the alleged benefits of the market for corporate control.

Advocates of the economic merits of the market for corporate control rely heavily on one empirical finding that is unambiguous: that shareholders in target firms earn sizeable positive returns around the time of takeover announcements. In merger and acquisition transactions during the period from 1976 to 1990, the shareholders of target companies received an average premium over market value of 41 per cent (Jensen 1993: 837). Estimates of the total abnormal returns from the announcement of a bid through to its conclusion vary from 15.5 per cent to 33.9 per cent (Dodd 1980; Asquith 1983; see also Asquith *et al.* 1983; Malatesta 1983; Dodd and Ruback 1977).

In contrast to the gains of target company shareholders, however, the wealth of acquiring company shareholders showed little change or even decreased around the time of the transaction (Bhagat, Shleifer, and Vishny 1990). Since the bidder firms were, on average, much larger than the targets, the enormous premia paid to target firms did not always imply a positive change in the wealth of the target and acquirer shareholders combined. Most event studies focus only on the weeks surrounding the takeover bid but if we extend the period of analysis the returns to bidder shareholders become negative. Jensen and Ruback reviewed six studies that calculated these returns one year after the takeover was concluded. These studies found abnormal negative returns, averaging −6.56 per cent, with the exception of one study which showed a slightly positive abnormal return of 0.6 per cent. As Jensen and Ruback concluded: 'These post-outcome negative abnormal returns are unsettling because they are inconsistent with market efficiency and suggest that changes in stock price during takeovers overestimate the future efficiency gains from mergers' (Jensen and Ruback 1983: 21). Magenheim and Mueller (1989) and Agrawal *et al.* (1992) claim that abnormal returns to bidders were negative over a three-year period (−16 per cent) and a five-year period (−10 per cent) respectively.

The unimpressive returns to acquirer shareholders, as well as concerns about the time consistency of shareholder returns on takeovers, cast doubt on the contention by proponents of shareholder theory that the market for corporate control is a mechanism for disciplining corporate management. To question the reliance on changes in shareholder wealth as proxies for corporate performance is to cast even more doubt on the shareholder theory of corporate governance. With regard to the market for corporate control, for example, studies based on accounting data suggest that the returns to target shareholders overestimate the economic gains that occur through disciplinary action.

To the extent that takeovers act as antidotes to managerial deficiencies in the allocation of corporate resources, one would expect the returns to target shareholders to be abnormally low prior to the bid and to improve once the bid is completed. Some studies have found that targets of hostile bids do exhibit abnormally poor performance (Ravenscraft and Scherer 1987; Morck *et al.* 1988) but others find no significant difference in the pre-bid performance of the targets of hostile and friendly transactions (Franks and Mayer 1996). Nor is there persuasive evidence from empirical analyses of post-acquisition performance that the market for corporate control improves corporate performance. Ravenscraft and Scherer (1987) found that profitability actually declined after acquisitions. Herman and Lowenstein (1988) concluded that during the 1980s there was a noticeable decrease in the post-acquisition return relative to the pre-acquisition period. With a few exceptions, most empirical studies of post-acquisition performance have failed to provide strong evidence of the disciplinary role of takeovers and some have even suggested that the market for corporate control reduces economic performance.

Notwithstanding the vigour with which the efficacy of the market for corporate control is asserted by proponents of shareholder theory, therefore, the balance of empirical evidence can hardly be interpreted as unequivocal support for their theoretical claims. Scepticism about the claims of financial economists is warranted even on the basis of their own preferred empirical methodology, but especially when one challenges their central assumption that shareholder wealth is an adequate proxy for corporate performance. And there are good reasons to raise questions about the wisdom of interpreting gains in stock valuations as indicators of real improvements in the performance of the corporate economy.

One direct challenge to that assumption has come from financial economists who have attempted to analyse the source of the enormous abnormal gains to target-company shareholders in the market for corporate control. They have suggested that these gains are evidence not of efficiency improvements but of transfers of value away from other claimants on enterprises' cash flows. One argument which has been made is that shareholders gain at the expense of lower wages and pensions for employees and fewer employment opportunities. A frequently invoked example of this phenomenon is Carl Icahn's takeover of TWA in 1985, when the reduction of $200 million in total wages was larger than the entire takeover premium (Shleifer and Summers 1988). On the basis of their analysis of a sample of 62 hostile takeover bids launched between 1984 and 1986, Sanjay Bhagat, Andrei Shleifer, and Robert Vishny concluded that layoffs after takeovers are common and can explain 10–20 per cent of the premium (Bhagat, Shleifer, and Vishny 1990). Other studies have suggested that decreased tax liabilities of target firms can in part account for takeover premia; in these cases there is a transfer of value from the government to the shareholders (Kaplan 1989; Bhagat, Shleifer, and Vishny 1990). It has, however, proven difficult to account for most of the shareholder gains from takeover activity in terms of transfers from other stakeholders. Yet the quest for the sources of these gains only makes sense to those who believe that they can be accounted for predominantly in terms of changes in the real economy, whether those changes be associated with the creation or the redistribution of value.

Conventional financial economists have traditionally ruled out the possibility of significant dislocations between financial market valuations and corporate performance by invoking the assumption that financial markets are informationally efficient, that is, the efficient markets hypothesis (EMH). The EMH holds that a capital market is efficient if, as Burton Malkiel put it, 'it fully and correctly reflects all relevant information in determining security prices. Formally, the market is said to be efficient with respect to some information set, ϕ if security prices would be unaffected by revealing that information' (Malkiel 1987: 120). When financial economists use the concept of market efficiency in the sense of the EMH, what they are referring to is the capacity of a market to impound information.[3] The importance of the EMH to financial economics, and especially to the shareholder theory of corporate governance, can hardly be overstated. In the words of Terry Marsh and Robert Merton, 'To reject the Efficient Market Hypothesis for the whole stock market . . . implies broadly that production decisions based on stock prices will lead to inefficient capital allocations' (Marsh and Merton 1986). Yet, despite the centrality of the EMH to financial economics, its empirical status is highly questionable.

The hypothesis cannot, in fact, be empirically tested in isolation from assumptions about the way in which economic actors price securities. In other words, one cannot assess whether a financial market 'fully and correctly reflects all relevant information in determining security prices' without knowing what 'correctly' and 'relevant' mean. One must, therefore, rely on some assumptions about the 'appropriate' or 'rational' way to price securities. As Fama put it, 'Market efficiency per se is not testable. It must be tested jointly with some model of equilibrium, an asset pricing model' (Fama 1970: 384).' Basically the problem is 'that we can only test whether information is properly reflected in prices in the context of a pricing model that defines the meaning of 'properly'. As a result, when we find anomalous evidence on the behavior of returns, the way it should be split between market efficiency or a bad model of market equilibrium is ambiguous' (Fama 1991: 1576).

In fact, 'anomalous' evidence on the behaviour of returns is rife. All of the models of asset pricing on which financial economists rely posit some relationship between risk and return. The CAPM, for example, is based on the proposition that asset prices are determined by risk that cannot be reduced by holding a diversified portfolio of stocks. Yet, as I discussed in Chapter 2, the relationship between risk and return that

---

[3] A distinction is often drawn between three different types of informational efficiency. Markets are said to be weak-form efficient when security prices reflect all information available in past prices. Semistrong-form efficiency implies that security prices reflect all publicly available information. Finally, the strong form of the EMH means that security prices reflect all information available, be it publicly or privately held.

financial economists commonly assume is an article of faith rather than a proven fact. As Richard Roll, a leading financial economist, commented:

Perhaps the most important unresolved problem in finance, because it influences so many other problems, is the relation between risk and return. Almost everyone agrees that there should be some relation, but its precise quantification has proven to be a conundrum that has haunted us for years, embarrassed us in print, and caused business practitioners to look askance at our scientific squabbling and question our relevance. Without a risk/return model that allows one to quantify the required rate of return for an investment project, how can it be valued? (Roll 1994: 7)

What then is the basis for the widespread reliance of financial economists on the EMH? The methodological difficulties of performing empirical tests of the EMH mean, as Brenda Spotton and Robin Rowley noted, that

the commitment to EMH often stems from a prior conviction that efficiency is clearly desirable and must emerge from some evolutionary process which removes inefficient market participants, rather than from a clear evidential basis. Data, from this perspective, merely confirms the obvious presence (apart from some irritating, hopefully ephemeral, anomalies) and convenience of market efficiency. (Spotton and Rowley 1998: 671)

When financial economists make claims, such as that of Burton Malkiel, that 'the empirical evidence in favour of EMH is extremely strong. Probably no other hypothesis in either economics or finance has been more extensively tested' (Malkiel 1987: 122), what they are referring to is indirect evidence that is *consistent* with the EMH. The leading examples of empirical analyses of this type are studies which suggest that stock prices follow a random walk and that they respond quickly to announcements which convey new information about fundamentals. All of these analyses suffer from serious methodological limitations but perhaps their most problematic deficiency is that their findings are also consistent with theories of the behaviour of stock markets which compete with the EMH, most notably a variety of theories which contend that stock markets are subject to fads and bubbles (see, for example, Summers 1986; Davidson 1978; Glickman 1994; Raines and Leathers 1996).

To challenge the EMH is to threaten the 'efficiency' interpretation of the Deal Decade put forward by advocates of shareholder governance. Yet, to many commentators, the momentum behind the market for corporate control seems to be more accurately characterized as resulting from a set of institutional contingencies than as a Darwinian process through which inefficiencies in the corporate economy were weeded out. From this point of view, there is no reason to expect that financial variables will be closely associated with real variables or, more specifically, that stock valuations can be taken as evidence of productive changes in the real economy. Similar observations have led many of those who have studied the institutional transformation that supported the market for corporate control, and practitioners who lived through it, to be sceptical of financial economists' interpretations of the Deal Decade.

In the first volume of his recent book on *Securities Markets in the 1980s* Barrie Wigmore, for example, underlined the difference. In one corner, Wigmore noted, were the academics who 'have argued whether takeovers promoted efficiency or were simply wealth transfers that reduced income taxes or victimized poorly protected parties such as workers, suppliers, and host communities. On the one hand, raiders and leveraged buyout firms have been lionized as the new wave of entrepreneurs, and on the other hand corporate chief executives have been accused of simply wanting to create larger companies to further their compensation and prestige' (Wigmore 1997: 374). In contrast, Wigmore claims, practitioners saw the merger market in the 1980s as the product of a series of institutional changes, important among them being the relaxation of antitrust rules to allow combinations between, or asset sales to, firms in the same industry as well as 'the unprecedented leverage provided by the banks and the junk bond market' (Wigmore 1997: 374). Some other commentators who have interpreted the Deal Decade in a similar vein have taken a harsher view of the role of financial economists in supporting its legitimacy. For example, Benjamin Stein, a journalist with the financial weekly *Barron's*, drew an analogy between doctors willing to perform studies that 'proved' that deadly drugs were safe and the support by leading professors of finance for the Deal Decade (Stein 1992: 128). And even within financial economics, there has been at least a partial recognition that the market for corporate control 'overheated'. For instance, Steven Kaplan and Jeremy Stein, in their study of 'The Evolution of Buyout Pricing and Financial Structure in the 1980s', recognize that although such a conclusion 'does not fit comfortably with traditional notions of efficient markets' the evidence 'fits well with a specific version of the overheated buyout market hypothesis. According to this version, the 'demand push' from the public junk bond market that began around 1985 caused the buyouts of the late 1980s to be both more aggressively priced and more susceptible to costly financial distress than earlier deals' (Kaplan and Stein 1993: 316).

That the overall evidence suggests that the market for corporate control was driven by institutional changes which were distinct from what was happening in the productive economy is not to say that in certain cases it did not contribute to the improvement of the value-generating capabilities of particular corporate enterprises. In some cases, especially in the early years of the LBO movement, when the device was used primarily as a means for selling a division to management, or selling a privately held company, it may have served a useful function. For divisional selloffs, in particular, it may have helped to remedy the problems of strategic segmentation by undoing the mistakes of the conglomerate era. By placing in positions of strategic control 'middle managers' who understood their lines of business far better than senior conglomerate executives, these divisional buyouts created the possibility for the reintegration of strategy and learning—a type of organizational integration that conglomeration had typically destroyed.

It should not be forgotten, however, that to the extent that these transactions responded to deficiencies in corporate organizations' ability to generate innovation, these problems had, in many cases, been created by the previous conglomeration era in which the stock market had played a central and facilitating role. It is, therefore, inappropriate to elevate the market for corporate control to the status of corporate governance solution, as many financial economists have been wont to do. Rather, it served as a willing and important accomplice to a management fad that led corporations into what two leading financial economists claim was 'a thirty year detour for US business' (Shleifer and Vishny 1991).

Moreover, even when deals were motivated by the identification of competitive problems in the companies or divisions that they targeted, they could not solve them. At best, they provided the possibility for their solution by putting in place strategists who knew what needed to be done. The critical question was whether these strategists would have the autonomy and the motivation to make the resource commitments required to rebuild innovative organizations. One obvious danger was that the debt-service requirements of LBOs would limit the ability to invest in new learning processes. The debt that financed buyouts did not fund investments in new productive assets but merely transferred claims over the returns to existing assets. By leveraging up the existing asset base, LBOs demanded that companies trim the fat of day-to-day operations. The question was whether it also required them to cut out the bone of developmental investment.

The evidence available on the effects of LBOs suggests that although, on average, these transactions may have contributed to an improvement in the performance of target firms immediately after the LBO, they did not lead to improvements in the productive capabilities of these firms in the long term and may well have endangered them. In the most extensive study of post-LBO results to date, Long and Ravenscraft found that LBOs substantially increased operating performance over a period of three years. These gains were not, however, sustained after that period; in the fourth and fifth years operating performance fell back to levels close to where they were before the LBO. Besides medium-term gains in operating efficiency, post-LBO firms in the Long and Ravenscraft sample also displayed a significant fall in their income tax to sales ratios. Although these income tax savings persisted into the fourth and fifth year after the buyout, they declined rapidly over time (Long and Ravenscraft 1993).

In the initial years after the buyout, interest payments on the debt burden created by the transaction outweighed the operating performance improvements and tax savings. Moreover, given that the debt to asset ratios remained high even five years after the buyout, net profits were increasingly squeezed as the medium-term gains faded away over time. As a result, these firms were, at least on average, hardly in a strong position to make major financial commitments. It is therefore not surprising that LBOs led to cuts in R&D (Long and Ravenscraft 1993) (although many targets were performing only low levels of R&D) and capital expenditures (Kaplan 1989). No empirical study has yet managed to relate these reductions to performance of the post-LBO firms although a number of scholars have hypothesized that there is a relationship.

Proponents of shareholder theory have tended to dismiss the significance of these cuts and to argue that the LBO movement imparted a new discipline to corporate resource allocation. George Baker and George David Smith, for example, in their recent book, *The New Financial Capitalists: Kohlberg Kravis Roberts and the Creation of Corporate Value*, contend that

[i]f scholars made public policy, the debate would have been settled in favor of letting the market work. As more data accumulated, more positive academic findings on the buyout restructurings of the 1980s would be reinforced and extended. The cumulative evidence confirmed that leveraged buyouts generally had resulted in improvements in the post-buyout performance of the assets that remained in the buyout partnerships' control. (Baker and Smith 1998: 39)

Given the at best mixed results on the effects of LBOs it is difficult to see what evidential basis they have for their interpretation of the implications of LBOs on productive efficiency, although there is a subtle qualification in their reference to assets that 'remained in the buyout partnerships' control'. Their statement also reflects their dismissal of concerns about the long-term impact of LBO transactions on investment. Baker and Smith are content to make the following statement on the subject: 'The evidence on capital spending was mixed, but it was likely that many companies had been overspending before their buyouts' (Baker and Smith 1998: 219). No supporting evidence is provided for their assertion. Given that, as Long and Ravenscraft observe, post-LBO firms were particularly vulnerable to the recession that began in the US in the 1990s, only true believers would be inclined to accept their assertion on faith alone.

From the perspective of the innovative enterprise, the issue of the relevant investment strategies goes beyond the impact of pressures for financial liquidity on the levels of R&D and investment in plant and equipment. In many industries, R&D activities are critical learning processes but these industries were to a large extent excluded from the LBO movement. Even in R&D-intensive industries, and certainly in other sectors, there is much more to organizational learning processes than R&D. Indeed, if learning derived from R&D activities is not integrated with learning derived from production and marketing activities, investments in R&D may well be investments that do not pay off. Yet, in corporate law and in accounting practice, the human capabilities on which organizational learning depends are not treated as corporate assets. The conventional concept of property on which this law and practice is based ignores the collective assets and collective returns that are the essential realities of the innovative enterprise.

It may be that some post-LBO companies reduced their investments in R&D and capital investment, but made major commitments to transforming their organizations to generate innovation. The only way to get at the effects on the innovative capabilities of LBOs, and the Deal Decade in general, is to track target companies over long periods of time relative to appropriate benchmarks. That task is a challenging one since many of these companies, or parts of them, were subsequently sold off to other companies and integrated as part of their operations. It is, therefore, not that surprising that so few case studies of the long-term evolution of LBO targets have been undertaken. The handful of examples which do exist have been written by proponents of shareholder value. Since they tend to begin from the premise that the appropriate way to measure the 'creation of value' is to focus on stockholder wealth, they provide limited resources for those with more critical questions about trends in the innovative capabilities of these firms (see, for example, Baker 1992).

Yet, in reaching a conclusion on the Deal Decade, from the perspective of the US system of corporate governance one issue remains of paramount importance: the Deal Decade was driven by a dynamic that was, in its origins and its momentum, distinct from the real economy. Thus it was unlikely, except by chance, to provide the requisite antidote to the real productive problems in the US corporate economy that have been outlined in section 5.2. And, as the forces that drove the Deal Decade gained momentum, the challenge of developing and utilizing productive resources paled into insignificance beside the hubris of making deals. As levels of debt rose to facilitate more and bigger transactions it was clear that what was mooted as the cure for the ills of US corporations was likely to do more harm than the disease. Ultimately the weakness of the LBO mechanism, and the market for corporate control in general, was that it was responsive not to the needs of companies to improve their productive capabilities but to the demands of financial interests to reap high returns. The evidence on the productive gains that resulted from letting those demands have priority in the 1980s, in a way that they had never had before in the US during the twentieth century, would seem to be a long way from justifying the costs of the 1980s mania, including the highest rates of corporate bankruptcy since the Great Depression and the US government's bailout of the savings and loans institutions.

The real import of the Deal Decade, however, goes beyond these events. Its true significance to the evolution of the US system of corporate governance was that it transformed the notion of what was legitimate for one person or a small group of people to extract from US corporate enterprises to the extent that they were willing to become the ostensible servants of financial interests. Until that time the rewards of corporate executives had been many times those of the people they managed but they had nevertheless been structured by the logic of building and sustaining an organization. During the 1980s, however, corporate executives began to realize that they could break free of the long-term logic of the organizations which they controlled to the extent that they were willing to exploit, as individuals, the positions which they had won through their success within the organization.

5.3.5. The Rise of Institutional Investor Activism

With the demise of the market for corporate control, institutional investors turned to different means to enforce their demands for financial liquidity on corporate enterprises. In particular, from the mid-1980s, a number of major institutional investors began to take a more aggressive stance *vis-à-vis* incumbent corporate managers in the proxy process. The California State Public Employees Retirement System (CalPERS), a defined-benefit pension fund for California's public employees, played a critical role in the trend towards increased institutional investor activism.

Traditionally, CalPERS, like most institutional investors, had voted its proxies with corporate management. In the mid-1980s, at the urging of Jesse Unruh, the California State Treasurer and a member of the board of CalPERS, that practice was challenged. An attempted takeover of Texaco by the Bass brothers in 1984, and the company's subsequent buyout of the raiders at a substantial premium to the market price, prompted Unruh to action. California's state pension funds had substantial holdings of Texaco stock and Unruh was distressed that they had no say in Texaco management's decision to compensate one class of shareholders differently from another (Monks and Minow 1991: 212–13). To remedy what he considered an untenable situation, Unruh promoted a new style of activism by CalPERS and founded the Council of Institutional Investors (CII) to encourage other institutional investors to adopt an activist stance. Most of Unruh's co-founding members of the CII had responsibility for public pension funds and it was these funds, rather than the private pension funds or mutual funds, which were most prominent in the trend towards institutional investor activism.

The early efforts of the CII focused on knocking down barriers to the market for corporate control through the sponsorship of shareholder resolutions to reduce poison pills, greenmail, and golden parachutes, and through the application of pressure on corporations to opt out of states' anti-takeover statutes. Public pension funds reaped rich rewards from their active participation in the Deal Decade. As a result, these fiduciaries were hostile to the anti-takeover devices that were gaining popularity among corporate managers and state legislatures in the late 1980s. Prior to 1987, there were no shareholder proposals about poison pills; from 1987 to 1993, in contrast, 190 proposals to rescind poison pills were tabled by shareholders. In the late 1980s, public pension funds, including CalPERS, the California State Teachers' Retirement System (CalSTRS), the New York City Employees' Retirement Fund, and the State of Wisconsin Investment Board (SWIB), accounted for the vast majority of these proposals. Shareholder support for pill rescission proposals increased from 29.5 per cent in 1987 to nearly 48 per cent in 1989 before dropping off somewhat in the early 1990s. These levels of support made rescission proposals by far the most successful of shareholder proposals voted on at annual shareholder meetings during that period.[4]

Notwithstanding their relative success, CalPERS and other institutional investor activists recognized that, by focusing narrowly on anti-takeover provisions, they left corporate managers considerable latitude to fight back. In the late 1980s, therefore, the focus of institutional investor activism widened from anti-takeover devices in particular to the structure of the shareholder–management relationship in general. CalPERS began publishing, on an annual basis, a list of companies that it would target in its campaigns for 'corporate governance' reform. In the early 1990s, CalPERS played a central role in the unprecedented removal of the CEOs of some of these target companies, including GM, IBM, Westinghouse, and American Express.

Despite the fact that the ousting by institutional investors of the CEO of a major corporation was unprecedented in the history of the US corporate economy, the ambitions of most activist institutional investors for transforming the US system of corporate governance were far from radical. Indeed, their very definition of corporate

---

[4] The voting results for other shareholder proposals filed by CalPERS can be found at www.calpers-governance.org/alert/facts/.

governance was extremely limited. CalPERS, for example, focused primarily on the board of directors and its relationship with corporate management. Specifically, the fund put pressure on companies to make board members independent of corporate insiders and to increase their oversight of senior management. It recommended, among other initiatives, the appointment of independent chairmen and directors, the 'de-staggering' of boards (allowing the entire board to be changed in one year), and the institution of committees to determine executive compensation. Moreover, in choosing corporations on which to focus their efforts, CalPERS went for safer targets as time passed. Whereas in the early years of its activist efforts, the fund had targeted companies, be they strong or weak performers, that violated its standards of appropriate behaviour, it increasingly focused its attentions on corporate enterprises who had, on the basis of the previous five years of financial results, widely recognized performance problems; in the words of Dale Hanson, CEO of CalPERS from 1987: 'You're not going to see me trying to stick my nose into a Merck or a GE or a Home Depot, because these people have done very well. Who gives a damn if they have confidential voting?' (quoted in *Fortune*, 15 June 1992: 92)

Notwithstanding its relative conservatism, or perhaps because of it, institutional activism captured the imagination of a number of prominent public policy and legal scholars who were seeking to reform the US system of corporate governance (see, for example, Coffee 1991; Gilson and Kraakman 1991; Black 1992; Pound 1992). John Pound, for example, regarded the rise of institutional investor activism as heralding the emergence of a new political model of corporate governance in which active investors seek to change corporate strategies by winning the votes of dispersed shareholders through persuasion, rather than by using their financial resources to buy voting power. Pound argued that the major economic advantage of the political model was that it could address specific problems in the corporation without imposing changes in control, changes in management, and the enormous transactions costs attendant on them. Thus, he claimed, activist institutional investors were effective substitutes for the market for corporate control as a means of generating shareholder value (Pound 1992). Academic proponents of institutional investor activism highlighted the regulatory barriers that allegedly stood in the way of its greater effectiveness in maximizing shareholder value (Black and Coffee 1994; Roe 1994) and, in many cases, added their voices to those of institutional investors who were pressuring the Securities and Exchange Commission (SEC) to remove them.

There has, for example, been an ongoing debate in recent years about reform of the proxy process. In October 1992 the SEC responded to some of the concerns of activist institutional investors by making it easier for shareholders to communicate with each other about proxy proposals; prior to that reform, any communication among a group of more than ten shareholders necessitated an extensive approval process by the SEC. More recently, activist shareholders have been putting pressure on the SEC to widen the scope of issues deemed appropriate for a proxy vote. Shareholders generally submit proxy proposals under SEC Rule 14a-8. If a proposal is accepted, the shareholder has the right to have it included, together with a 500-word supporting statement, in the proxy statement distributed by the corporation to its shareholders in advance of the annual shareholder meeting. The corporation can exclude a shareholder's proposal from its proxy statements if it violates certain procedural and substantive requirements of the SEC. Procedural eligibility rests on four main issues: ownership of shares, notice and attendance at shareholder meetings, timeliness of proposal submission, and number of proposals. Rule 14a-8 also lays out 13 circumstances under which a company can omit proposals from its proxy statement on substantive grounds.

Perhaps the most important basis for the exclusion of proposals from a corporation's proxy materials is SEC Rule 14a-8(c)(7). The rule permits omission of a proposal that 'deals with a matter relating to the conduct of the ordinary business operations of the registrant'. The 'ordinary business rule' was adopted by the SEC in the early 1950s 'to confine the solution of ordinary business problems to the board of directors and place such problems beyond the competence and direction of the shareholders', as the then SEC chairman explained. He considered that 'it is manifestly impracticable in most cases for stockholders to decide management problems at corporate meetings' (Statement of J. Sinclair Armstrong to the Subcommittee on Banking and Currency, 1957, quoted in Whitman 1997: 28). The ordinary business of a corporation is therefore considered to be the domain of corporate executives rather than shareholders. There is, however, an exception to this rule. When the ordinary business of the company involves significant issues of social policy, shareholders' proxy proposals may not be rejected on the basis of Rule 14a-8(c)(7).

With regard to what constitutes an issue of social policy concern, the SEC has, in response to pressure from shareholders, changed its opinion on a number of matters. For example, it originally held that executive compensation was excludable under the 'ordinary business' rule. In February 1992, however, the SEC required that companies include non-binding shareholder resolutions about CEO pay in their proxy statements. Moreover, to facilitate informed shareholder discussion of issues pertaining to executive compensation, the Commission imposed new requirements on corporations for disclosure of top executive compensation ('Shareholder Groups Cheer SEC's Moves on Disclosure of Executive Compensation', *Wall Street Journal*, 14 Feb. 1992). The SEC has also reversed decisions that had previously excluded proposals on golden parachutes, tobacco products, and plant closings (Transamerica Corp., 10 Jan. 1990; Philip Morris Companies, Inc., 13 Feb. 1990; Pacific Telesis Group, 2 Feb. 1989).

In recent years the SEC has been subject to growing pressures from some institutional investors and religious groups to include resolutions on employment practices on their shareholder proxy ballots. These shareholder activists have argued that adverse publicity or litigation on, for example, sweatshop or discriminatory employment practices can damage a company's reputation and therefore adversely affect the bottom line. The SEC came under strong fire from these groups when, in 1992, it permitted Cracker Barrel, a restaurant chain, to exclude shareholder proposals dealing with its hiring policies that discriminate on the basis of sexual orientation. Through its Cracker Barrel decision, the SEC effectively established a rule that would allow corporations to exclude all proxy proposals related to employment practices on the grounds that they were 'ordinary business' issues. In the 'no-action' letter that the SEC issued to Cracker Barrel in 1992, it stated:

the fact that a shareholder proposal concerning a company's employment policies and practices for the general workforce is tied to a social issue will no longer be viewed as removing the proposal from the realm of ordinary business operations of the registrant. Rather, determinations with respect to any such proposals are properly governed by the employment-based nature of the proposal. (Cracker Barrel Old Country Stores, Inc., SEC No-action Letter, 1992, WL 289095 (SEC), 13 Oct. 1992; cited in SEC, *Amendments to Rules on Shareholder Proposals*, 17 C.F.R. Part 240, Release No. 34-40018)

A number of institutional investors, led by the New York City Employees' Retirement System, took the SEC to court over its Cracker Barrel decision. They won the first round but the decision was later overturned when the SEC appealed it (Brossman and Tatman 1998). In May 1998 the SEC introduced several amendments to the rules related to shareholder proposals, including one which reversed the Cracker Barrel decision. Shareholder proposals concerning employment-related practices that raise significant social policy issues will not, therefore, be automatically excluded. The SEC will now evaluate whether a proposal relates to 'ordinary business' on a case-by-case basis.

Debates over what constitutes a legitimate shareholder proposal will undoubtedly continue. The SEC recognized that it has to respond to 'changing societal views' (by which it means the views of shareholders) on these matters. But, although the SEC's mandate may be to protect the interests of investors, it seeks to balance their demands with those of corporate executives. Thus, to the extent that there is a broadening of issues that shareholders are allowed to discuss, the process will undoubtedly be a lengthy and embattled one.

Yet, the opposition of corporate management to these initiatives is not the only constraint on investor activism. In fact, most institutional investors have little interest in exercising themselves about governance issues. For all the attention that the likes of CalPERS have garnered, they are in a minority when it comes to actively voting the shares that they hold and 'jawboning' management and boards of directors about reforming their corporate governance practices. As Table 5.3 suggests,

TABLE 5.3 Average Stock Turnover Rates by Type of Institutional Investor, US, 1993 and 1995 (%)

Type of Funds	1993	1995
Corporate pension	33.2	24.8
Public pension	13.3	20.7
Mutual funds	48.2	42.3
Money managers	56.7	59.2
Insurance companies	53.6	46.4
Banks	24.3	25.3

Source: Based on Brancato (1997: 27).

many institutional investors have focused their energies on churning their portfolios of shares and thus seem unlikely to have strong incentives to make the commitment required to push for changes in corporate resource allocation. With the growing popularity of indexation as a portfolio strategy for institutional investors, moreover, these incentives would seem likely to be reduced rather than enhanced.

Perhaps the most important reason why institutional investor activism remains a minority pursuit is that activism is costly and there is considerable controversy about its effectiveness as a means to enhance shareholder value. As Barry Rehfeld put it in a recent article on 'Low-cal CalPERS' in *Institutional Investor*,

There is actually scant evidence that CalPERS—or, for that matter, any shareholder activist— has produced significant stock gains in targeted companies through standard governance actions. Conventional governance tactics—proposals to eliminate poison pills, destagger board elections, institute confidential voting, forbid the same individual from serving as both chairman and CEO, link executive compensation to performance and require independent directors—can only have a direct impact on the structure of corporate boards. But because these efforts fail to address the underlying problems depressing share prices, CalPERS's brand of shareholder activism often has the quality of rearranging the deck chairs on the Titanic. (Rehfeld 1997: 107–8)

The evidence on institutional activism in general suggests that a similar conclusion is warranted. Bernard Black, himself an advocate of the 'promise of institutional investor voice' in the early 1990s, recently reached the following conclusion:

It's hard to be against institutional investor activism, even the on-the-cheap activism prac- ticed by American institutions. But does this muted activism really matter—does it affect the bottom line performance? Studies of this question are beginning to accumulate. On the whole, they offer no convincing evidence that shareholder activism affects bottom line performance. To be sure, discerning an effect of activism on performance is not easy. Institutional activism could have a positive effect that is economically significant, yet still buried in the noise of other factors that affect performance. Still, the absence of convincing evidence of a relation- ship between activism and firm performance suggests that activism does not have a major impact on firm performance. (Black 1998: 462)

Given these rather desultory empirical results on the effects of institutional investor activism in promoting shareholder value, it is not surprising that the latest arrival on the shareholder activist front is pushing an agenda that, to a greater or lesser extent, goes beyond stock valuation. In the 1990s, the most active institutional investors in the US have been unions. Their goal in entering the corporate gover- nance arena is to take advantage of the fact that their members represent an impor- tant proportion of the ultimate beneficiaries of much of the institutional money in the US capital markets. They hope to leverage what has been described as 'labour's capital' or 'working capital' to better promote the interests of their constituency.

The funds with which unions have been predominantly concerned thus far are the Taft–Hartley funds. Although they are not strictly speaking union pension funds, as their trustees are appointed in equal numbers by management and the union, in effect unions have often managed to control these funds (Schwab and Thomas 1998: 25).

Unions have much less influence over corporate pension plans where the trustees are appointed exclusively by corporate management; unions are generally involved in bargaining with employers over corporate contributions to these plans or benefits paid to retirees but they have traditionally had no direct involvement in managing the plan assets. Recently, however, there have been moves within the union movement to develop bargaining strategies to influence the allocation of these funds too.

The efforts of unions to influence US corporations through pension fund activism have met with much hostility from corporate executives, who have gone so far as to request that the SEC limit unions' capacity to submit shareholder proposals (*Business Week*, 23 Oct. 1995). But to date the proposals put forward by unions have in fact been difficult to distinguish from those of institutional investors like CalPERS. As Schwab and Thomas put it:

The amazing thing about these union-sponsored shareholder proposals is how ordinary they are, from the perspective of any institutional investor. They involve standard corporate-governance issues designed to maximise the value of the corporation by improving the efficiency of the market for corporate control and aligning manager incentives with shareholder interests. (Schwab and Thomas 1998: 13)

In fact the pattern of union-sponsored proposals is not really amazing at all. Even if unions wanted to focus on issues that are directly related to their agenda as the representatives of US workers, their ability to do so is extremely limited. They are, to a great degree, hemmed in to the concerns of the pro-shareholder-value brigade by the fiduciary duties of pension trustees and SEC rules on shareholder proposals.

The fiduciary obligations of the trustees of Taft–Hartley funds, and especially those imposed by the Employee Retirement Income Security Act (ERISA), mean that the benchmark for the allocation decisions of these trustees are the standards set by the US investment industry as a whole. To the extent that trustees of union pension funds can be shown to be trading off the financial goals pursued by typical investment managers for other goals, even goals that may be acceptable to union members, they can be held personally liable for what is considered to be a breach of their fiduciary duty (Schwab and Thomas 1998: 25–6).

Union pension fund activism is also subject to the restrictions imposed by the SEC on the content of shareholder proposals through the provisions of Rule 14a-8(*c*). One provision that is particularly important is Rule 14a-8(c)(4), which allows companies to exclude from their proxy statements shareholder proposals that are deemed to promote the shareholder's personal interests rather than the interests of shareholders in general. The ordinary business provision is also an important barrier to unions' attempts to use 'labour's capital' as a weapon to force corporate management to discuss issues that pertain to the welfare of US workers. Just how powerful is the ordinary business rule in excluding virtually all of these concerns is evident from the SEC's recent recapitulation of the policy underlying the standards to be applied in making determinations about substantive eligibility under the ordinary business rule:

The policy underlying the ordinary business exclusion rests on two central considerations. The first relates to the subject matter of the proposal. Certain tasks are so fundamental to management's ability to run a company on a day-to-day basis that they could not, as a practical matter, be subject to direct shareholder oversight. Examples include the management of the workforce, such as the hiring, promotion, and termination of employees, decisions on production quality and quantity, and the retention of suppliers. However, proposals relating to such matters but focussing on sufficiently significant social policy issues (e.g. significant discrimination matters) generally would not be considered to be excludable, because the proposals would transcend the day-to-day business matters and raise policy issues so significant that it would be appropriate for a shareholder vote.

The second consideration relates to the degree to which the proposal seeks to 'micro-manage' the company by probing too deeply into matters of a complex nature upon which shareholders, as a group, would not be in a position to make an informed judgment. This consideration may come into play in a number of circumstances, such as where the proposal involves intricate detail, or seeks to impose specific time-frames or methods for implementing complex policies. (SEC, *Amendments to Rules on Shareholder Proposals*, 17 C.F.R. Part 240, Release No. 34-40018)

Notwithstanding these barriers, there are signs that unions are getting more ambitious in their role as institutional investor activists. In 1997, the AFL-CIO set up a new Center for Working Capital to promote and coordinate union pension fund activism and Richard Trumka, the secretary-treasurer of the AFL-CIO, described its agenda in the following terms: 'Our goal is to make worker capital serve workers, not just when they retire, but on a day-to-day basis' (*Business Week*, 29 Sept. 1997). Some unions have shown considerable creativity in getting around some of the regulatory obstacles that they face to pursue issues that affect union members as workers by leveraging the combined strength of their pension assets; for example, during a strike at Wheeling-Pittsburgh Steel Co. in 1996 the Teamsters and other unions persuaded Dewey Square Investors Corp. (the largest shareholder in WHX, the holding company that controlled Wheeling-Pittsburgh), the manager of a substantial sum of union pension money, to put pressure on the management to end the strike. The main stick that the unions used was the fact that the strike had caused the share price of WHX to plummet. Trumka warned Dewey that '[i]f this is your philosophy, you shouldn't be managing worker money' (*Business Week*, 29 Sept. 1997).

It is, however, certain that unions will face major hurdles if they make more concerted efforts to use their influence over pension money to pressure corporations to pursue goals that go beyond, let alone against, shareholder value. Ironically, many of the restrictions that unions have run up against in their attempts to influence the governance of US corporations also reflect the gap between the rhetoric and reality of shareholder capitalism in the United States today. What the SEC 'clarification' amounts to is a restatement of the fact that, notwithstanding the recent resurgence of the ideology of shareholder democracy in the US, the US corporate governance system still enshrines the view that managers have a 'right to manage'. Without any access to information on 'ordinary business', other than to the limited degree to which it is provided in the annual reports and 10-Ks of corporations, institutional investors, whatever their interests, can have little serious influence over the way in which corporations allocate resources.

The only way for institutional investors to get access to such information seems to be to take major stakes in particular companies and use the voting power that goes with them as a means to persuade managers to be more forthcoming about their strategic decisions. Perhaps the most infamous example of a money manager of this type is Michael Price, who formerly headed the Mutual Series funds, and was duly described by *Fortune* magazine as 'the scariest SOB on Wall Street'. Money managers like Price, as well as other activist mutual funds such as Fidelity Investments, maintain a much stronger focus on the stock market performance of corporations than public pension funds like CalPERS. As Robert Pozen, general counsel and a managing director of Fidelity Investments, put it:

The clearest cases for activism are those where we think the price of a company in a merger, acquisition, or tender offer is too low. If we can get the price increased, that goes directly to our clients' bottom line. At the other end of the continuum, we have things like whether we should have a chairman who is also CEO, or part-time chairman, or outside chairman. In our view that's a procedural frill that doesn't systematically go to providing value to the shareholders, though in a particular case it might be important. (*Fortune*, 8 Mar. 1993; see also Pozen 1994)

Yet, disparaging though he is about the efforts of public pension funds, Pozen's words hardly suggest that what Fidelity Investments and other activists of their sort have in mind is any closer to the business of developing and utilizing productive resources. Rather, their efforts seem similar to the efforts of investment banks in the 1980s when they fuelled the merger market.

It is, of course, doubtful that institutional investors have the competence to do more than concern themselves with 'procedural frills' or grease the wheels of the merger market given that they are complete outsiders to the process through which enterprises develop and utilize resources. Corporate executives have been quick to highlight deficiencies in their understanding of what does and should go on in corporate America. For example, Charles Wohlstetter, a former CEO of Contel, described what he considered to be the undesirable implications of growing institutional activism in a discussion in the *Harvard Business Review* of 'The Fight for Good Governance':

In sum, we have a group of people with increasing control of the Fortune '500' who have no proven skills in management, no experience at selecting directors, no believable judgment in how much should be spent for research or marketing—in fact, no experience except that which they have accumulated controlling other people's money. (Wohlstetter 1993: 78)

Wohlstetter's intended targets were the public pension funds, but money managers like Price are not immune from similar criticisms if the recent debacle with Al Dunlap and Sunbeam is anything to go on. In 1996, Price, Sunbeam's biggest shareholder with 17 per cent of its stock, recruited the infamous 'Chainsaw Al' to run the housewares company. Sunbeam's stock soared over the next two years as Dunlap proceeded to reduce employment by 12,000 through layoffs and divestitures as he closed or sold 80 of the company's original 114 operations ('Dangerous Games', *Barron's*, 8 June 1999). Yet, Dunlap's ambitions, at least in this instance, went beyond cost cutting; he promised to turn Sunbeam into a growth company with a wave of new product development notwithstanding the low margins and intense competition that prevailed in the industry. By the middle of 1998, however, Dunlap's strategy was in tatters and, accused of massaging the numbers to maximize shareholder value, he was forced out. Price supported him until close to the end, apparently unaware of, or unconcerned about, the negative repercussions on product quality of Dunlap's cost cutting, the failure of his much-vaunted new product development strategy, and the extent of accounting gimmickry in Sunbeam ('How Al Dunlap Self-destructed', *Business Week*, 6 July 1998; 'The Sunbeam Soap Opera', *Forbes*, 6 July 1998).

Yet the fact that institutional investors have limited incentives and abilities to guide corporate resource allocation does not necessarily imply that incumbent senior managers have the incentives and abilities to do so either, at least in ways which ensure that corporations contribute to the sustainable development of the US economy. That Wohlstetter pays no attention to the capacities of the corporate executives who currently control resource allocation, even to defend them, makes it doubtful that his agenda is really 'the fight for good governance'. It may be that he assumes that senior executives are the ones who, in the modern corporation, know more than everyone else about 'how much should be spent for research or marketing' and the like. But that would seem to be a point of view which requires some empirical support in light of the rather unimpressive strategic decisions made in US corporations in recent decades.

5.4. Conclusion

For obvious reasons, few corporate managers express great interest in questioning the existing structure of corporate control. For those who are less constrained by their vested interests or faith in the virtues of the status quo, it seems reasonable to conclude that institutional investors are a long way from transforming the system of US governance from managerial capitalism to investor capitalism. Nor is it clear that such a change would be for the better. Indeed, it is only from a theoretical perspective which regards the corporation as essentially reducible to the CEO, and the central challenge of corporate governance as the minimization of agency costs in the relationship between shareholders and managers, that the prospect of institutional investor activism seems a realistic route to improving economic performance.

The only prospect of fundamental change in the US system of corporate governance emanating from this source would seem to be labour's capital initiative. US unions, long excluded from any role in the governance of US corporations in their role as the representatives of workers, may yet exercise some influence on the allocation of corporate resources as representatives of their pension interests. In principle, unions are much better positioned than any other group of activist investors to develop an informed perspective on corporate resource allocation which is substantially different from that of incumbent corporate managers. In practice, however, they face enormous barriers to doing so both within their own organizations and, more importantly, in the institutional environment in which they are attempting to operate.

From an organizational control perspective, the challenge of governing corporations to enhance economic performance must of necessity grapple with the more fundamental issues surrounding the appropriate system of institutions, from the perspective of generating economic performance, for shaping who exercises control over corporate resources, what kinds of investment decisions they make, and how the returns on these investments are distributed. None of these issues has been a serious element of the discussion of 'corporate governance' stirred up in the US by institutional investor activism. As a consequence, senior managers, it would seem, remain in the driving seat in the US corporate economy. What has changed, as we shall see in the next chapter, are their incentives. The growing pressure for financial liquidity in the US economy has provided them with the opportunity to enrich themselves under the mantra of 'creating value for shareholders'. Although they may be singing the song of the resurgent ideology of shareholder democracy it would seem that they also control the music to a considerable degree.

6

US Corporate Responses to New Challenges

6.1. Introduction

The growing demands for financial liquidity, combined with the productive challenges discussed in the previous chapter, created significant pressures on the stability of the post-war system of managerial control in the US. In the 1980s and 1990s, the US corporate economy reacted to these combined pressures in what, in historical perspective, were dramatic ways. The most striking dimension of the general corporate response was the growing propensity of US corporations in the 1980s and 1990s to downsize their workforces and to distribute corporate revenues to stockholders. The strategy to 'downsize and distribute' stands in contrast to the historical norm for these corporations of favouring the retention of corporate revenues for reinvestment in plant, equipment, and personnel.

What underlies the prevalence and persistence of strategies to downsize and distribute among US corporate enterprises? The interpretation that dominates popular and academic writing on the subject of corporate control in the United States in the late 1990s is that these trends in US corporate behaviour reflect a resurgence of market control over corporate resources that has regenerated the foundations for prosperity in the US. From this point of view, changes in competition and technology—often collectively described as 'the modern industrial revolution'—have necessitated 'downsize and distribute' strategies by most major US corporations. Should these corporations try to maintain existing levels of operations, so the argument goes, the long-term viability of these enterprises, and indeed that of the US corporate economy as a whole, could be in jeopardy.

Financial markets, in generating pressures on US corporations to 'maximize shareholder value', have, in recent decades, pushed corporate restructuring to heights that, it is claimed, it would never have reached if left to the discretion of corporate managers. It is to the greater corporate focus on shareholder value, and the institutional changes that have brought it about, that we owe the 'new' economy of the 1990s. Those willing to undertake radical corporate restructuring, from this perspective, are regarded as the heroes of the new economy and they deserve to be richly rewarded for their efforts to improve corporate efficiency, especially given political opposition from entrenched interests who seek to preserve the status quo (for examples of the academic literature in this vein, see Jensen 1993; Dial and Murphy 1995; Murphy 1997). Evidence of the dramatic increase in the stock market valuation of US corporations, and the resurgence in the profitability of these enterprises in recent years, is often invoked, by those who subscribe to this view of the US corporate economy, as persuasive evidence in support of their view of the salutary economic effects of recent changes in US corporate governance.

There are, however, those who are highly sceptical of the claim that recent trends in stock market valuation and corporate profitability are, in themselves, sufficient evidence of the improved performance of US corporate enterprises. Critics argue that talk of a new era of prosperity for the United States is grossly exaggerated. They point out that the evidence available on indicators of productivity and investment are unspectacular in historical perspective. What has been going on in recent decades, they contend, has mainly been a massive redistribution of resources from labour to capital. Where you stand on the so-called new economy, therefore, depends on where you sit; financial interests and corporate executives have done incredibly well from these trends but the vast majority of the US working population has suffered a decline in its relative living standards.

Besides concerns about redistribution as the driver of the new economy, other questions have been raised about the extent to which trends in corporate profitability and stock valuations are reliable indicators of real activity in the US corporate economy. A number of influential commentators, including the chairman of the Securities and Exchange Commission, Arthur Levitt, have expressed disquiet about current accounting practices in corporate America. These critics have argued that corporations are accounting for stock options, mergers and acquisitions, and corporate restructuring in ways that allow them to report inflated and steady earnings to keep Wall Street analysts happy. With regard to stock market valuations, moreover, there are additional concerns that the sheer volume of new money flowing into the equity markets, the changing nature of the demand for equities, and other forces affecting the balance between the demand and supply for stocks, have induced price inflation in the stock market that has little to do with the way in which US corporations develop and utilize productive resources.

Concerns about the redistributive component of recent corporate resource allocation, as well as the relationship between corporate profitability, stock valuations, and the real corporate economy, certainly point to the need for a more complex analysis of corporate governance and corporate performance than the shareholder value advocates provide. Yet, those who, in recent years, have emphasized the shortcomings of shareholder theory have not provided a framework for a rigorous analysis of the relationship between corporate resource allocation and corporate performance. Lacking a framework within which to carry out such an analysis, they stand accused of implicitly favouring a return to the past and ignoring the very real competitive problems experienced in the 1970s and 1980s by many US corporations that continued to favour strategies of 'retain and reinvest'.

I attempt to overcome some of the deficiencies of current critiques of the shareholder theory of governance by using the organizational control perspective, developed in Chapters 1 and 2, as a framework for analysing what has been going on in the US corporate economy in recent years. Viewed through this lens, the available evidence on recent trends in the allocation of corporate resources in the United States suggests considerable variation within the US corporate economy in terms of the willingness and ability of corporate strategists to rebuild corporate organizations to generate innovation. Notwithstanding the limitations of existing evidence, one can identify a general proclivity among US corporations towards a strategy of innovating on the basis of investments in skill bases that are narrower and more concentrated than before. To the extent that US corporations have remained innovative, they have done so by focusing on generating products that can make use of skill bases that integrate a relatively small number of highly educated personnel focused on a narrow range of highly specialized activities.

There are ongoing debates in different industries about the long-term sustainability of these strategies and in many industries, such as semiconductors and aircraft engines, it is, as yet, far too early to be sure that US corporations can maintain their competitive advantage in the long run. Of more importance, however, is the social sustainability of these corporate strategies. The strategic proclivity to engage in activities that make use of narrow and concentrated skill bases has meant that a significant proportion of the US labour force who had previously had access to stable and remunerative corporate employment has found that a new 'market economy' neither values their skills nor offers them the education and training required for gaining better access to improved employment opportunities.

6.2. The Responses of Major US Corporations

In the 1980s and 1990s US corporate strategists responded to productive and financial challenges by altering their decisions about the allocation of corporate resources and returns. One unambiguous trend in the past two decades is the emphasis in US corporate resource allocation on distributing both people and money from the company to labour and capital markets. That trend is striking in historical perspective given the propensity of US corporations in the past to retain both people and money within the corporation.

6.2.1. The Corporate Propensity towards Downsizing

Since around 1980, most major US corporations have been engaged in a process of restructuring their labour forces in ways that have eroded the quantity of jobs that offer stable employment and good pay in the US economy. Hundreds of thousands of previously stable and well-paid blue-collar jobs that were lost in the recession of 1980–2 have never been subsequently restored. Between 1979 and 1983, the number of people employed in the economy as a whole increased by 377,000 or 0.4 per cent, while employment in durable goods manufacturing—which has supplied most of the good blue-collar jobs—declined by 2,023,000 or 15.9 per cent. Indeed, the 'boom' years of the mid-1980s saw hundreds of major plant closings. Between 1983 and 1987, 4.6 million workers lost their jobs, of which 40 per cent were from the manufacturing sector (Herz 1990; more generally, see Staudohar and Brown 1987; Patch 1995). The elimination of these well paid and stable blue-collar jobs is reflected in the decline of the proportion of the manufacturing labour force that is unionized from 47.4 per cent in 1970 to 27.8 per cent in 1983 to 18.2 per cent in 1994.

Throughout the 1980s US corporations displayed a mounting predilection toward downsizing. It was not only blue-collar workers who were affected. Professional, administrative, and technical personnel—so-called 'white-collar' employees—also began to lose out. In the 'white-collar' recession of the early 1990s tens of thousands of managerial positions were eliminated. Even in this recession, blue-collar workers bore the brunt of displacement, but the dismissal of professional, administrative, and technical employees became more prevalent.

Overall, the incidence of job loss in the first half of the 1990s was even higher than in the 1980s; during the first half of the 1990s, rates of job loss increased to about 14 per cent, higher than even the quite substantial rates of about 10 per cent in the 1980s. On the basis of his analysis of the Displaced Workers Surveys, Henry Farber estimates that the rate of job loss for 1981–3, a period with a slack labour market, was c. 13 per cent. As the labour market tightened during the mid-1980s, the job loss rate fell. When the economy went into recession from 1989, the job loss rate increased again to a level similar to the recession of the early 1980s notwithstanding the fact that the recession of the late 1980s was much milder. Moreover, even as the economy moved into a recovery from 1991, the job loss rate rose to ever higher levels, a trend that continued through 1995, despite the continued acceleration of economic expansion (Farber 1997: 55–142).

Leading the downsizing of the 1980s and 1990s were many of America's largest corporations. In the decades after World War II, the foundations of US economic development were the willingness and ability of the nation's major industrial corporations to allocate their considerable financial resources to investment strategies that created the good jobs that many Americans began to take for granted. In 1969, the 50 largest US industrial corporations by sales directly employed 6.4 million people, equivalent to 7.5 per cent of the civilian labour force. In 1991, these companies directly employed 5.2 million people, equivalent to 4.2 per cent of the labour force (Lazonick and O'Sullivan 1997a: 3). And since 1991 the downsizing of these companies has gone forward at a steady pace. By the early 1990s even US firms known for their no-layoff commitments—IBM, DEC, Delta—had undergone significant downsizing and layoffs of blue- and white-collar workers (Weinstein and Kochan 1995: 16).

The American Management Association (AMA) conducts a survey every year of layoffs by major US companies.[1] As Table 6.1 shows, one striking finding of this survey is that job elimination has continued to be pervasive among US corporate enterprises, and to result in substantial reductions in their workforces, notwithstanding the considerable improvement in the business cycle that has occurred as the 1990s have unfolded. Moreover, notwithstanding the downward trend since 1994–5

---

[1] The AMA survey is sent to human resources managers in AMA member companies every year. AMA's corporate membership consists of 9,500 organizations which together employ 25% of the American workforce. Over 85% of surveyed firms gross more than $10 million annually, which puts them among the top 5% of US corporations.

TABLE 6.1 Trends in layoffs by major US corporations, 1990–1997

	1990–1	1991–2	1992–3	1993–4	1994–5	1995–6	1996–7
Percentage reporting job elimination	55.5	46.1	46.6	47.3	50.0	48.9	41.1
Average percentage of Workforce Affected	9.6	9.3	10.4	9.2	7.7	7.1	6.2

Source: American Management Association (various years).

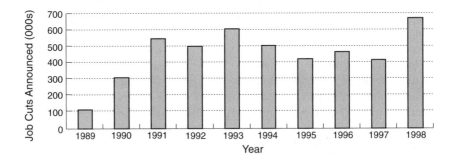

Source: Challenger, Gray, and Christmas

FIG. 6.1 Announced staff cuts by major US corporations, 1990–1998

in the proportion of companies reporting job elimination, the recent Challenger, Gray, and Christmas estimates of announced staff cuts by major US corporations suggest that another upsurge in layoffs by US corporations is in the offing (see Figure 6.1).

As Table 6.2 shows, the AMA survey also demonstrates that job cutting is much more prevalent among larger employers than smaller ones. Almost 60 per cent of companies employing more than 10,000 people, for example, laid off some of their workforce in 1996–7.

The costs of job loss to displaced workers have been substantial. They have a large probability—*c*. 35 per cent on average—of not being employed on the survey date after displacement. On average, displaced workers, when re-employed, receive real weekly earnings that are some 13 per cent less than before they lost their original jobs (*c*. 9 per cent for workers displaced from full-time jobs who are re-employed on full-time jobs) (Farber 1997). And these are estimates only of the wage effects of losing a job.

There are, of course, other costs to workers of downsizing. Prominent among them is growing worker insecurity at the prospect of losing a job and the anxiety that these expectations breed. A commonly used, although imperfect, proxy for such effects is job tenure. From 1983 to 1998 there was a slight decline in the median years of

TABLE 6.2 Trends in job cutting by company size, US, 1990–1997

No. of employees	1990–1	1991–2	1992–3	1993–4	1994–5	1995–6	1996–7
Less than 100	47.2	39.3	36.5	36.6	34.3	40.5	31.5
100 to 499	53.4	46.0	42.6	35.2	41.7	42.8	35.6
500 to 2,499	54.9	42.0	46.7	46.4	47.6	49.4	42.4
5,000 to 9,999	58.0	49.0	56.0	57.2	60.5	66.5	53.7
10,000 or more	71.8	57.0	54.0	65.4	55.5	65.8	59.1

Source: American Management Association (various years).

TABLE 6.3 Median years of tenure with current employer, US,
1983–1998

Age	1983	1991	1998
Men			
35–44 years	7.3	6.5	5.5
45–54 years	12.8	11.2	9.4
55–64 years	15.3	13.4	11.2
Women			
35–44 years	4.1	4.5	4.5
45–54 years	6.3	6.7	7.2
55–64 years	9.8	9.9	9.6

Source: US Bureau of Labor Statistics (1998).

tenure of employed wage and salary workers with their current employer from 5 years to 4.7 years. However, the average for male and female workers masks significant differences by gender. For male workers, the decline in tenure is striking. For male workers aged 25 years and more, median tenure fell from 5.9 years to 4.9 years from 1983 to 1998. As Table 6.3 illustrates, a decline in tenure was common to all subgroups within this age bracket, but it was particularly pronounced for men aged 55 to 64, whose median tenure fell from 15.3 years to 11.2 years between 1983 and 1998. That these overall declines were registered, notwithstanding the general trend towards an ageing of the male workforce, is especially striking. In all age groups, the fall in tenure was sufficiently great to outweigh the positive impact of ageing on tenure. Women aged 25 years and over enjoyed an increase in median tenure from 4.2 years to 4.4 years, although some of this effect was a result of the ageing of the female workforce. Most age groups within the female working population experienced an increase in median tenure. A notable exception was women aged 55 to 64 years, whose median tenure fell from 9.8 years in 1983 to 9.6 years in 1998.

Job tenure figures must be used with caution as proxies for job security. With layoffs occurring on a large scale, the proportion of workers with long tenure could rise, not because workers as a group are enjoying greater security, but because workers with lower seniority are being laid off. In the aircraft and parts industry, for example, the fact that median tenure rose sharply from 6.3 years in 1991 to 9.6 years in 1998 at a time of widespread layoffs seems to be at least partly attributable to this effect.

Changes in the employment performance of major US industrial corporations appear to be related to changes in the ways in which those who control these corporations have been choosing to allocate corporate revenues. The rhetoric used to support widespread layoffs proclaims that the prime, if not only, corporate responsibility is to 'create value for shareholders'. And under the slogan of maximizing shareholder value, US corporate enterprises seem to have become obsessed in the 1980s and 1990s with boosting profits and distributing revenues to their shareholders.

6.2.2. The Rise in Dividend Payouts and Stock Repurchases

During the 1950s, 1960s, and 1970s, payout ratios—the ratio of dividends to after-tax adjusted corporate profits—varied from a low of 37.2 per cent in 1966 (when increases in dividends lagged increased profits) to a high of 53 per cent in 1974 (when profits fell by 19 per cent while dividends went up by 8 per cent). But averaged over any five-year period during these three decades, the payout ratio stayed remarkably stable, never going above 45.9 per cent (1970–4) and never falling below 38.8 per cent (1975–9). The stability is even greater over ten-year periods—47.9 per cent for the 1950s, 42.4 per cent for the 1960s, and 42.3 per cent for the 1970s. These payout ratios were high by international standards, manifesting the extent to which US corporations returned value to stockholders even before the rise of the institutional investor.

TABLE 6.4 US Corporate Payout Ratios, Stock Yields, and Bond Yields, 1950–1997 (%, annual averages)

	1950–9	1960–9	1970–9	1980–9	1990–7
Payout ratio[a]	47.9	42.4	42.3	49.3	49.9
Total stock yield[b]	17.7	8.3	−1.7	11.7	13.0
Stock price yield[c]	14.8	7.5	1.4	12.9	13.6
Dividend yield[d]	4.9	3.2	4.1	4.3	2.8
Change in CPI	2.1	2.4	7.1	5.6	3.3
Real bond yield[e]	1.3	2.7	1.2	5.8	4.7

[a] Corporate dividends as a percentage of corporate profits after tax with inventory valuation and capital consumption adjustments.
[b] Stock price yield plus dividend yield adjusted by the change in the year-to-year change in the consumer price index (CPI).
[c] Annual percent increase in Standard & Poor's composite index of 500 stocks.
[d] Dividend–price ratio for the 500 stocks in the Standard & Poor's composite index, based on annual averages of monthly data.
[e] Yield on Moody's Aaa-rated corporate bonds.
Sources: US Congress (1992: 366, 378, 397, 403; 1999: 431).

A shift in payout ratios seems to have occurred in the 1980s and 1990s. In 1980, when profits went down by 17 per cent (the largest profits decline since the 1930s), dividends rose by 13 per cent, and the payout ratio shot up 15 points to 57 per cent. Thereafter, from 1980 through 1995, the payout ratio only descended below 45 per cent twice, in 1984 and 1985—not, however, because dividends fell but because the increase in dividends did not keep up with the increase in profits. There was no five-year period within the period 1980 to 1997 during which the payout ratio did not average at least 47 per cent, and over the entire period of 18 years it averaged 50 per cent.

Since the mid-1980s, moreover, increases in corporate dividends have not been the only way in which corporations have distributed earnings to stockholders. Prior to the 1980s, during a stock market boom companies would often sell shares on the market at inflated prices to pay off debt or to bolster the corporate treasury. In general, although equity issues have never been an important source of funds for investment in the development and utilization of the productive capabilities of US corporate enterprises, they tended to issue more equities than they repurchased. But during the 1980s, the net equity issues for US corporations were negative in many years, largely as a result of stock repurchases.

In 1985, when total corporate dividends were $84 billion, stock repurchases were $20 billion, boosting the effective payout ratio from under 40.4 per cent, based on dividends only, to 50 per cent with the addition of stock repurchases. In the quarter following the stock market crash of 1987, there were 777 announcements by US corporations of new or increased buybacks ('The Buyback Monster', *Forbes*, 17, Nov. 1997). In 1989, when dividends had risen to $134.4 billion, stock repurchases had increased to over $60 billion, increasing the effective payout ratio to over 81.4 per cent. With close to $70 billion in stock repurchases in 1994, the effective payout ratio was about 66 per cent ('Firms Ponder How Best to Use their Cash', *Wall Street Journal*, 16 Oct. 1995: A1 and A9). In 1996, stock repurchases were $116 billion, for an effective payout ratio of 72 per cent ('The Hidden Meaning of Stock Buybacks', *Fortune*, 8 Sept. 1997). Although for any one year, the announced buyback plans tend to be lower than actual repurchases, the continued high levels of announced buyback plans since 1996 suggest that US corporate enterprises continue to favour buybacks as a respectable use for their cash; US corporations announced plans to buy back $177 billion of stock in 1996, $181 billion in 1997, and $207 billion in 1998 (Securities Data Corporation).

For major corporations stock repurchases have now become a systematic feature of the way in which they allocate revenues and a critically important one in terms of the amount of money involved. General Electric is a leading example. From 1994 to 1998, for example, its cumulative dividend growth was 84 per cent compared with 29 per cent for the S&P 500 firms as a whole. Moreover, during the same period, the cumulative amount of cash that GE spent on share repurchases, at $14.6 billion, rivalled the $15.6 billion paid out in cumulative dividends. Together these two outflows of cash amounted to an extraordinary 74.4 per cent of GE's cumulative cash from operations from 1994 to 1998. Notwithstanding the enormous amounts that the company has already spent on repurchases, in December 1997 GE's board of directors increased the authorization to repurchase company stock to a massive $17 billion (GE 10K, 1998).

6.3. Assessing the Implications of 'Downsize and Distribute'

To proponents of shareholder value, recent shifts in the behaviour of US corporate enterprises represent a necessary and efficient response to the 'new' economic reality that corporations confront. This view has been put forward by Michael Jensen, for example, in his influential presidential address to the American Finance Association in 1993. He contended that since 1973 the world has been in the throes of a 'modern industrial revolution' in which technological, political, regulatory, and economic forces have been changing the global economy in a fundamental way: 'As in the nineteenth century, we are experiencing declining costs, increasing average (but decreasing marginal) productivity of labor, reduced growth rates of labor income, excess capacity, and the requirement for downsizing and exit' (Jensen 1993: 831).

Jensen argued that, with a handful of exceptions, US corporations have not been adequately responsive to what he considers the widespread need for them to shrink themselves. And even when corporate executives voluntarily undertake massive restructuring, he claims that the process takes too long. In short, 'It appears that internal control systems have two faults. They react too late, and they take too long to effect major change.' In contrast, 'Changes motivated by the capital market are generally accomplished quickly—within one and a half to three years' (Jensen 1993: 854). And it is as a result of these pressures, exercised directly in the 1980s through the market for corporate control, and more indirectly in the 1990s with the demise of that market, that there have been major changes in the way that US corporate executives think about what they do and for whom they do it.

Writing in 1998, George Baker (Jensen's colleague at Harvard Business School) and George Smith summarized these changes and their allegedly favourable implications for the performance of the US corporate economy:

Today, managers are generally more concerned with maintaining 'core competencies' than expanding lines of business, with maximising economic values than with building corporate empires, with promoting entrepreneurial behavior than with reinforcing corporate compliance. Corporate budgeting has become more rigorous, organizations less fat, and restructuring more routine throughout the corporate economy. All this has occurred as managers have relearned the virtue of hitching their personal fortunes to those of their shareholders. The use of stock options as a significant part of executive pay packages has increased dramatically. In 1997, the Business Roundtable's new 'Statement on Corporate Governance' reflected a profound change in the collective thinking of the nation's more prominent senior executives: 'the principal objective of a business enterprise is to generate economic returns to its owners . . . if the CEO and the directors are not focused on shareholder value, it may be less likely the corporation will realize that value.' That corporate profits and productivity have been rising for the first time in decades is due in part to these changing attitudes and behavior among owners and managers alike. (Baker and Smith 1998: 205–6)

For leading proponents of shareholder value, therefore, 'the marvellous economy of the 1990s'—'a new era of sustained economic growth, vibrant securities markets, and at this writing, nearly full levels of employment' (Baker and Smith 1998: 206)—testifies to the validity of their analyses of the relationship between corporate governance and economic performance.

6.3.1. The Lean, Mean, Corporate Machine?

There is no denying the dramatic increase in the stock market valuation of US corporations in recent years. The Dow Jones Industrial Average (DJIA) increased by an enormous 186 per cent from 1985 to 1994 compared with 88 per cent from 1955 to 1964, −17 per cent from 1965 to 1974, and 47 per cent from 1975 to 1984. Since 1994 the stock market has continued to surge; in 1995 the annual DJIA increased by 18.5 per cent, in 1996 by 27.8 per cent, and in 1997 by 29.6 per cent (US Congress 1998: 390). In 1998, notwithstanding a major decline in the third quarter, the index rebounded dramatically in the closing months of the year to net an annual increase of 16.1 per cent. By July 1999, the DJIA was already 16.1 per cent higher than on 31 December 1998 (http://www.hyse.org).

By 1995, the ratio of the market value of corporate equities to GDP reached a post-war high of 1.13. Since then, it has risen still further to 1.28 in 1996, 1.55 in 1997, and a phenomenal 1.8 in 1998. Price–earnings (P–E) ratios have, since the mid-1990s, also reached higher levels than at any time in the post-war period. In 1997, the P–E ratio for the S&P 500 broke annual records when it reached 21.9. In 1998, that record was smashed again when the P–E ratio rose to 27.9. When P–E ratios are averaged over five-year periods, the exceptionalism of stock market behaviour in recent years is also clear: the average P–E ratio from 1993 to 1998 was 20.48, compared with previous five-year highs of 18.74 from 1960–5 and 16.42 from 1966–70. What makes the high P–E ratios of recent years especially notable is that they have broken post-war records during a period in which corporate earnings themselves have surged (Poterba and Samwick 1995; US Department of Commerce 1999: 524).

The corporate pre-tax profit rate, having fallen steadily since the late 1960s, has displayed a marked upward trend since 1982. The trend flattened out in the recession of the early 1990s, but it did not decline substantially as it had in previous recessions (Baker 1995; Poterba and Samwick 1995: 304). Since 1992, corporate profits have risen at an extremely rapid rate; in 1992–3, corporate profits rose by 15.1 per cent, in 1993–4 by 15.8 per cent, in 1995–6 by 11.6 per cent, and in 1996–7 by 9.0 per cent (US Congress 1999: 431). As a result, for the period from 1992–7 as a whole, corporate profits grew at a higher rate than for any other five-year period in the post-war era. There was a noticeable slowdown in profit growth in 1998. Nevertheless, the growth sustained so far in the 1990s has pushed pre-tax profit rates to levels not seen in the US economy since the 1960s (Baker 1995; Poterba and Samwick 1995: 304–5).

Besides rising stock market valuations and corporate profitability, it is also true that, as Baker and Smith put it, 'managers have relearned the virtue of hitching their personal fortunes to those of their shareholders'. From 1980 to 1994 the direct compensation (salary, bonus, and stock option grants) of the average CEO in a sample of the largest US corporations increased by 209 per cent in real terms. Although the average CEO's salary and bonus increased in real terms by a substantial 97.3 per cent, the real boost to CEO direct compensation came from stock option grants; the mean value of stock option grants to CEOs increased, in real terms, by a massive 682.5 per cent during the period. By 1994, salaries and bonuses represented 51.6 per cent of direct compensation compared with 80.9 per cent in 1980; in 1994, nearly 70 per cent of CEOs were awarded stock options compared with 30 per cent in 1980 (Hall and Liebman 1997: table IIa; fig. 1). And CEO direct compensation has continued to rise in recent years (*Business Week*, 21 Apr. 1997, 20 Apr. 1998, 19 Apr. 1999).

Direct compensation is, moreover, only one element of CEO remuneration. An important additional source of indirect compensation is the increase in the value of CEOs' stockholdings, many of which have been accumulated through option grants. From 1980 to 1994, the annual mean wealth increases for CEOs totalled 119 million 1994 dollars, representing nearly 5.5 times the comparable total for annual mean direct compensation. As the stock market has surged in the 1990s, these wealth increases have gained apace; from 1991 to 1994 alone, the mean total wealth increase for CEOs amounted to 54.3 million 1994 dollars (Hall and Liebman 1997: Table IIa).

If there is little dispute about the trends in stock market valuation, corporate profitability, and executive pay that shareholder value advocates highlight, what remains controversial are the links between these trends and the capacity of US corporations to generate wealth through the development and utilization of productive resources. To subscribe to a theory of financial market behaviour which holds that stock market valuation is an unbiased measure of the value-creating potential of a corporate enterprise, as most financial economists do, is to believe that the creation of shareholder wealth is synonymous with the creation of economic value. For those who rely on analysis rather than faith, however, the link between stock market performance, corporate profitability, executive pay, and corporate performance is much less clear than shareholder value proponents admit.

6.3.2. Does Where You Stand Depend on Where You Sit?

The leading alternative interpretation of the trends seen as so favourable by shareholder value advocates is that corporate executives have been boosting profitability and financial returns to themselves and to shareholders on the backs of the current and future welfare of other groups in the economy, especially workers. From this perspective, that corporate profitability has grown in recent years, and that the stock market has gained apace, cannot in themselves be taken as evidence of improvements in the value-creating capabilities of the US corporate economy. To the contrary, from this point of view, what has been happening in the US corporate economy is largely a redistribution of existing corporate resources. That the academic proponents of

shareholder value have commanded so much attention is a symptom of their political adroitness in hitching their wagons to the right interest group rather than the
analytical soundness of their arguments about the generation of economic value.

Academics who emphasize the importance of resource redistribution in accounting for recent economic trends contend, for example, that the trend towards higher
corporate profitability and stock market valuations does not seem to be accounted
for by sustained improvements in productivity. Overall, productivity growth in the
current business cycle and recovery have not been particularly strong in historical
perspective (Mishel, Bernstein, and Schmitt 1999: 26). Productivity trends in the
manufacturing sector have been more impressive. Although from 1979 to 1997 the
average annual growth rate in output per hour in US manufacturing was 3.1 per cent
compared with 3.8 per cent in the UK, 3.7 per cent in Italy and Belgium, and
3.6 per cent in Japan, in the 1990s there has been an improvement in the relative
performance of US manufacturing: from 1990 to 1997 output per hour grew at an
average annual rate of 3.7 per cent, higher than the comparable figures of 3.5 per
cent for France, 3.4 per cent for Italy, 3.2 per cent for Germany, and 3.2 per cent for
Japan, although lower than the 5 per cent recorded in Sweden. Yet the long-term
significance of the recent trend in productivity figures remains unclear; much of the
improvement was registered in 1994 and 1995 with annual gains in output per hour
of 5.9 per cent in 1994 and 6.5 per cent in 1995. In 1997, by contrast, productivity growth declined to 4.6 per cent, which was considerably lower than the rate of
6.8 per cent achieved in France, 6.5 per cent in Sweden, 6.1 per cent in Japan, and
5.9 per cent in Germany (Bureau of Labor Statistics 1998; see also Sparks and Greiner
1997). As Stephen Roach, chief economist of Morgan Stanley, and formerly one of
the most ardent advocates of corporate strategies to downsize and distribute, put it
recently:

Only one of these explanations, however, is consistent with a true economic renaissance—the
sustained improvement in trend productivity growth, which would lead to a meaningful
improvement in the standard of living. By contrast, the other possibility is tantamount to a
very different model of restructuring—essentially a slash-and-burn approach that would generate only temporary productivity gains from a steady stream of one-off efficiencies; in this
latter scenario, however, the only encore is the proverbial 'next' cut. As a result, the slash-and-
burn model ultimately leads to increasingly hollow companies that are unable to maintain
market share in an ever-expanding global economy. Two models. Two similar short-term outcomes. But two very different endgames—one highly beneficial and the other ultimately
destructive. At this point in time, the jury is still out on which approach has been driving
the great Anglo-Saxon restructuring experience. It all boils down to which verdict endures
the ultimate test of time. (Roach 1998: 15–16)

Critics of the 'marvellous economy of the 1990s' add to the ambiguity of the productivity statistics for understanding economic performance evidence of a substantial
redistribution of resources from labour to capital in the US economy to support their
claim that US corporate enterprises have been effective in improving their competitive position through the restraint of wages rather than on the basis of long-term

improvements in labour productivity. Even to the extent that productivity has improved, few of the benefits have been passed on to the large majority of the US labour force. Productivity grew by 9 per cent from 1989 to 1997 but compensation fell, in real terms, by 4.2 per cent for all workers and by 7.8 per cent for male workers (Mishel, Bernstein, and Schmitt 1999: 18). Over the same period real hourly wages stagnated or fell for the bottom 60 per cent of workers except for low-wage workers, whose wages rose 1.4 per cent during that time; wages for the bottom 80 per cent of men were lower in 1997 than in 1989 (Mishel, Bernstein, and Schmitt 1999: 5).

Indeed, broad-based wage stagnation or decline has been a feature of the US economy for more than a quarter of a century. From 1979 until 1988 the average hourly earnings of production and non-supervisory workers fell 5.7 per cent in real terms. They continued on their downward trend from 1989 to 1996, when they fell 3.3 per cent in real terms. It was only in 1997 and 1998, five years after the longest boom in US history began, that real wages began to register noticeable real increases; in 1997 and 1998, real average hourly earnings of production and non-supervisory workers increased by 1.5 per cent and 2.4 per cent respectively (Bureau of Labor Statistics; Economic Policy Institute). In the first quarter of 1999, however, there was a marked slowdown in wage growth.

Only a small minority of US citizens at the peak of the income distribution have enjoyed the fruits of economic prosperity in recent decades. Their relative success is reflected in the striking growth in income inequality in the United States over the last 25 years: in 1979, the income of an American at the 95th percentile of the income distribution was 3 times the median income and 13 times the income of an American at the 5th percentile; in 1996, the comparable ratios had increased to 4 times and 23 times respectively (Burtless 1999: 32). The richest 5 per cent of US families increased their share of aggregate income received by all US families from 15.3 per cent in 1979 to 20.7 per cent in 1997 (Economic Policy Institute).

A number of economists have argued that these and similar trends lend credence to the view that the profitability of US corporate enterprises has come, at least partly, at the expense of the majority of US workers. As Dean Baker and Lawrence Mishel put it in an article entitled 'Profits Up, Wages Down: Worker Losses Yield Big Gains for Business':

The ability of firms to restructure costs so as to obtain historically high profitability reflects the dominant power of employers in labor markets. Wage increases among both white-collar and blue-collar workers and among both union and nonunion workers have been very weak, and below the inflation rate, for several years, despite an unemployment rate so low that the Federal Reserve Board felt it necessary to slow the economy. This high profitability is simply the reflection of the dominance of employers in the shaping of wages and working conditions in today's labor market. (Baker and Mishel 1995: 5)

That current high profit rates reflect a shift of resources from labour to capital has been hotly disputed by some economists on the grounds that capital's share of economic output, although it has increased since the late 1980s, remains lower than in the decades prior to that. However, as Baker pointed out, the fact that capital has sustained its share of income, despite the dramatic decline in the size of the capital stock relative to economic output during the 1980s and 1990s (from a peak of 2.14 in 1982 to 1.43 in 1994—a post-war low), means that those with claims to capital returns are in the lucky position of 'getting more for less' (Baker 1995). Moreover, as Baker observes, it is difficult to justify these profit rates on the grounds that they will induce higher levels of investment now and ultimately higher productivity in the future given the relatively weak investment performance of the US economy as a whole during the period of rising profitability. As Figure 6.2 shows, there was a marked decline in gross investment as a proportion of GDP from 1984. The trend shifted upward with the beginning of the current recovery but levels of investment are still nowhere near where they were in the post-war decades.

To critics of the US economy of the 1990s, that corporate profitability and stock market valuations have increased so much in recent years largely reflects the growing power of one interest group over another. Given that the majority of US citizens hold no shares at all, directly or indirectly, and that the distribution of shares is so skewed towards the wealthiest shareholders, there is little merit to the argument that, through stock ownership, the fruits of the prosperity of the 1990s are distributed more broadly than the wage distribution suggests. Those benefits have, in fact, been reserved for a small elite of Americans.

One group that has gone to considerable ends to secure a place in the winner's circle is corporate senior management. So successful have senior corporate executives been in lining their own pockets, under the guise of creating value for shareholders, that, to a greater extent than has ever been the case since the rise of the corporate economy, they have separated their fate from that of the rest of the working population. They have achieved real rates of growth in their compensation that leave the

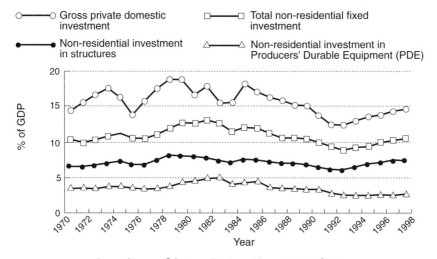

Source: Survey of Current Business (Aug. 1998: 147–8)

FIG. 6.2 Gross investment in the US relative to GDP, 1970–1998

rest of the US labour force in the shade. On the basis of a sample of large US public corporations, *Business Week* reported that, in 1965, CEOs made 44 times the average factory worker's wages, already a substantial multiple, but by 1997 that ratio had risen to 326 times, and in 1998 it increased again to 419 times (*Business Week*, 20 Apr. 1998, 19 Apr. 1999). Much of these gains have come, as I have already observed, through stock option grants. Although in some companies, especially in high-tech sectors, stock option plans extend beyond the executive suite, CEOs and top executives have been the main beneficiaries of such corporate largesse.

To critics of the shareholder perspective, that CEOs have been compensated so handsomely in the 1980s and 1990s is proof, not of their adeptness in managing corporate resource allocation to generate economic value, but rather their willingness to align themselves with the growing power of financial capital in the US economy. And if shareholder value advocates give legitimacy to corporate executives' efforts to turn their success as organization men into substantial holdings of corporate stock, these executives have retained enough control over corporate decision-making to structure the so-called 'pay-for-performance' relationship on their own terms. For all the pious talk of the importance of bearing risk commensurate with returns, for example, most stock options awarded to executives have constant exercise prices. If the stock price rises significantly above that exercise price, the executives are rewarded even though the rising price may have nothing to do with CEO actions and may simply reflect a strong bull market (as has been the case in recent years) and/or a sectoral boom. As *Fortune* magazine put it in a recent article on 'pork in executive compensation': 'that old cliché about "bull market genius" explains a lot of what is going on—Wall Streeters who are being in the right place at the right time, corporate executives who are pocketing above-average salaries while their companies underperform their peers' (*Fortune*, 7 Sept. 1998: 63). There have been calls for relative performance evaluation for executives to ensure they are compensated only for the performance of companies they manage. For example, it has been suggested that the exercise price be tied to indexes such as the S&P 500 and/or to a price index for similar companies. Yet, it is generally academics who get most exercised about these 'subtleties'. Institutional investors, with a few notable exceptions like the State of Wisconsin Investment Board, have expressed only muted interest in whether or not there is any economic justification for CEO pay packages. While the party continues for them, it seems that they have little interest in crossing swords with the other revellers.

The issue of whether there is a relationship between CEO pay and the relative performance of corporate stock is, of course, only the tip of the iceberg of concerns about the extent to which CEOs are in fact being paid for *their* performance. One obvious concern is that senior executives are making hay while it is the rest of the corporate organization that toils to pay the bills. As Henry Mintzberg put it,

Next time you hear a chief executive go on about teamwork, about how 'we' do it all by pulling together, ask who among the 'we' is getting what kind of bonuses. When you hear more about the chief having to take the long view, ask how these bonuses are calculated. If cooperation and foresight are so important, why are these few cashing in on today's stock price? Isn't it time we recognized this scandal for what it is: sheer corruption of the very essence, not only of our institutions, but of our societies as democratic systems? (Mintzberg 1998: 3)

Any analysis of the level and composition of senior executive pay should be informed by an understanding of the relationship between value distribution and value creation. Most academics who have been calling for 'pay for performance' at the top of US corporations do so from a theoretical framework—shareholder theory—that lacks anything approximating a serious analysis of the relationship between distribution and innovation in corporate enterprises. Indeed, how far the literature on corporate governance in financial economics is from understanding that relationship is evident from the call in a recent article in the *Journal of Economic Perspectives* for an integration of the mainstream literatures on corporate governance and the theory of the firm on the grounds that

[a] complete understanding of the corporate ownership and control issues discussed by Berle and Means requires some notion of what a firm is; in other words, an answer to Coase. This literature, unlike the theory of the firm, recognises that at least one actor in the firm, the chief executive officer (CEO), is the agent of shareholders. But it ignores the other agents in the firm and, as a result, it delivers little in the way of a theory of organizations. Can we better understand the conflict between shareholders and management, if we recognize that there is more to management than the CEO? (Bolton and Scharfstein 1998: 96)

That such a statement of the obvious should merit publication in a leading economics journal would be hard to credit if it were not for the gross deficiencies in the current theoretical state of the art on corporate governance. It is cheering that there has been a public recognition of some of these shortcomings. But there are also serious limitations evident in what the above statement contemplates as a remedy: the central focus of the governance literature, it is assumed, will remain as before—the relationship between shareholders and management. No scope is reserved for the possibility that understanding how organizations generate value will lead to a fundamental revision of questions about how corporations should be governed.

In my discussion of arguments that suggest the need for scepticism about the merits of the shareholder value mantra as a guide to recreating the foundations for economic prosperity, and the evidence invoked to support its beneficial effects, I have focused primarily on academic analyses. But one does not have to look to the ivory towers to find sceptics. A small minority of corporate executives have also had harsh words for the prevalent ideology in corporate America. A leading example is Ken Iverson, chairman of Nucor, the market leader in the minimill steel sector and a darling of Wall Street. He has lambasted 'corporate fatcats' who buy into today's fashion 'to compensate top management with huge sums that increase every year and bear no relation to how well or poorly the company and its workers are doing' and treat their employees as disposable:

Most don't get job security. Workers' short-term interests tend to run a distant third behind those of shareholders and executives. When those short-term interests conflict, people lose their jobs, no matter how hard they've worked—and no matter how much the company may need them down the line. That is why, through the longest expansion in history, many people remain haunted by the specter of recession and by memories of massive, dispassionate 'reductions in force.' And that is why so many workers remain deeply distrustful of management, even when managers try to rebuild the bridges of trust. After all, it was managers who tore down those bridges in the first place. (Iverson 1998: 45)

Nor does Iverson have much time for what he describes as 'junkie analysts':

Managing with a long-term perspective is just common sense to us. But, I'll admit, not everybody sees things as we do. And, like managers in most large businesses, we must sometimes answer to those who froth at the mouth, pound on tables, and yell at us to do whatever it takes to maximise earnings *right now*! I'm referring, of course, to stock analysts.

Some of our officers recently met with a group of stock analysts in New York City. Here is the gist of my opening remarks to them:

'Many of you, with your short-term view of corporations, remind me of a guy on drugs. You want that quick fix, that high you get from a big spike in earnings. So you push us to take on more debt, capitalize startup costs and interest, and slow down depreciation and write-offs. All you're thinking about is the short term. You don't want to think about the pain of withdrawal that our company will face later on if we do what you want. Well, Nucor isn't going to respond to that kind of thinking. We never have, and we never will.'

These days, you can't swing a dead cat without hitting some corporate executive whining that Wall Street won't let him run the company for long-term growth. But I say complaining is a waste of time. In the end, you have to choose your master—the investor or the speculator. (Iverson 1998: 52)

Henry Schacht, former head of Lucent Technologies and Cummins Engine, has also been a strong, albeit more guarded, critic of the current trends in US corporate governance. In an interview for a recent PBS documentary on 'Surviving the Bottom Line' Schacht described what he believed was going on in the US corporate economy:

We're emptying the middle. A very few people used to be in the middle yet are amongst those very few of us who are doing extremely well. An awful lot of other folks, their wives have gone to work, they no longer can take their vacations, they are having troubles getting their kids through school.

And they're saying 'hey, what's this all about?' And, this is not going to last. You cannot have the very few of us making these enormous amounts of money, and a larger and larger number of folks feeling that the system of which they are the majority is treating them less fairly than they feel is equitable, and I think they are right. This isn't going to last. (full text of interview at http://www.pbs.org/bottomline/html/schacht.html)

To the extent that what has been going on in the US economy has been largely a redistribution of existing resources, upward trends in stock market valuations, corporate profitability, and CEO pay based on these indicators tell us little about the present and future value-creating capabilities of the US economy. Besides the issue of redistribution, moreover, there are other reasons why there is considerable and growing scepticism that the upsurge in corporate profitability and stock market valuations is a reflection of improvements in the real corporate economy.

6.3.3. Oh, What a Complex Web We Weave . . .

In recent years questions have been raised by equity investors about the usefulness of reported profitability for evaluating the health of US corporations due to concerns about the reliability of underlying accounting procedures. Warren Buffett recently commented that although 'it was once relatively easy to tell the good guys in accounting from the bad', in recent years, 'probity has eroded':

Many major corporations still play things straight, but a significant and growing number of otherwise high-grade managers—CEOs you would be happy to have as spouses for your children or as trustees under your will—have come to the view that it's okay to manipulate earnings to satisfy what they believe are Wall Street's desires. Indeed, many CEOs think this kind of manipulation is not only okay, but actually their *duty*.

These managers start with the assumption, all too common, that their job at all times is to encourage the highest stock price possible (a premise with which we adamantly disagree). To pump the price, they strive, admirably, for operational excellence. But when operations don't produce the result hoped for, these CEOs resort to unadmirable accounting strategems. These either manufacture the desired 'earnings' or set the stage for them in the future.

Rationalizing this behavior, these managers often say that their shareholders will be hurt if their currency for doing deals—that is, their stock—is not fully-priced, and they also argue that in using accounting shenanigans to get the figures they want, they are only doing what everybody else does. Once such an everybody's-doing-it attitude takes hold, ethical misgivings vanish . . . Bad accounting drives out good. (Chairman's Letter, Annual Report, Berkshire Hathaway, Inc., 1998: 14–15; emphasis in original)

The Securities and Exchange Commission has also expressed considerable concern about the extent of 'earnings management' in corporate America. In a speech in March 1999 at Stanford Law School, Arthur Levitt, chairman of the SEC, noted that 'in recent months I have expressed concern that the motivation to satisfy Wall Street earnings expectations may be overriding common sense business practices. In the process, I fear we are witnessing a gradual, but noticeable erosion in the quality of financial reporting.' He went on to say:

It's difficult to hold the line on good practices when competitors operate in the gray area between legitimacy and outright fraud. A gray area where sound accounting practices are perverted; where managers cut corners; and, where earnings reports reflect the desires of management rather than the underlying performance of the company. While the problem of earnings management is not new, it has risen in a market unforgiving of companies that miss Wall Street's consensus estimates. For many, this pressure has become all too hard to resist. (speech by Arthur Levitt to Directors' College, Stanford Law School, 22 Mar. 1999)

Among the leading US corporations considered to be at the cutting edge of 'best practice' in earnings management are some of the giants who have led the recent stock market surge—often described as the 'Nifty Fifty'—including America Online (trading in March 1999 at a P–E ratio of 353.0), Microsoft (70.2), Coca-Cola (45.1), General Electric (37.8), and IBM (27.6).[2] Three areas where there is major concern

---

[2] See 'Learn to Play The Earnings Game (and Wall Street will Love You)' and 'How the Pros do it', *Fortune*, 31 Mar. 1997; 'Sipping the Fizz in Coca-Cola's Profit', *Wall Street Journal*, 1 May 1997: C1;

with respect to the relationship of contemporary accounting procedures to economic reality are stock options, mergers, and restructuring.[3]

With respect to stock options, for example, under current accounting rules these options do not have to be listed as a cost on the income statement. Thus, some analysts argue, companies that rely heavily on options to compensate their employees are understating their labour costs and overstating their profits. Shares allocated to stock option plans have now reached unprecedented levels. To account for them as a compensation expense would, therefore, have a material effect on corporate earnings. According to Pearl, Meyer and Partners, shares allocated for management and employee equity incentive plans at the 200 largest US corporations rose to 13.2 per cent of shares outstanding in 1997 compared with 6.9 per cent in 1989; 14 of these companies now have options allocations that amount to more than 25 per cent of their shares outstanding (*Forbes*, 18 May 1998: 215).

The Financial Accounting Standards Board (FASB) tried to introduce a new accounting standard that would require companies to run option costs through their income statements. But the major accounting firms and many corporate executives lobbied heavily against it and FASB eventually dropped its proposal in 1995. As Dennis Beresford, chairman of FASB from January 1987 to June 1997, put it: 'The argument was: reduced earnings would translate to reduced stock prices. People said to me, 'If we have to record a reduction in income by 40%, our stock will go down by 40%, our options will be worthless, we won't be able to keep our employees. It would destroy American business and Western civilization' ('Stock Options are Not a Free Lunch', *Forbes*, 18 May 1998: 216). FASB did succeed in introducing a standard that requires companies to report the effect of stock options on their earnings (in their 10Ks) but it leaves a lot of discretion about the nature of this reporting in the hands of corporate executives and their accountants.

6.3.4. *The Supply and Demand for Corporate Equities*

There are also concerns about the relationship between stock market valuation and what is happening in the real economy that go beyond issues of profitability and its reporting. One analyst recently estimated that only 20 per cent of the increase in the S&P 500 could be attributed to improvements in reported profitability; the remainder of the increase reflected an inflation in the price at which these earnings were valued by the market. A variety of stories about the real economy have been told to 'explain' why investors have become so bullish, many of them tales about technology, especially information technology, and its likely future effects on productivity. Such tales have, of course, always abounded in bull markets and there are those who discount them, believing that the bull market has much more to do with forces

'Mickey Mouse, CPA', *Forbes*, 10 Mar. 1997; 'How General Electric Damps Fluctuations in its Annual Earnings', *Wall Street Journal*, 2 Nov. 1994: A1. P–E ratios are based on prior 12 months' earnings; see Bary (1999).

[3] For the controversy over accounting for mergers, see 'Will FASB Derail the M&A Express?', *Global Finance*, Dec. 1998; for concern over accounting for corporate restructuring, see 'How General Electric Damps Fluctuations in its Annual Earnings'.

affecting the demand and supply for corporate equities than with changes in the real economy.

Many commentators on the US stock market, writing in financial and business weeklies, have argue that the sheer volume of new money flowing into that market has caused price inflation there. In a paper entitled 'Index Funds and Stock Market Growth', Goetzmann and Massa have provided strong support for that argument; they claim that the upsurge in flows into index mutual funds has led to material and sustained increases in stock prices (Goetzmann and Massa 1998). Moreover, it seems that it is not just the level of demand for corporate equities that is affecting stock prices but also the nature of that demand. In a recent article on 'Institutional Investors and Equity Prices', for example, Paul Gompers and Andrew Metrick contend that changing patterns of share ownership have led to stock price appreciation for certain types of stocks that appeal to increasingly dominant players on the demand side of the equity markets. Specifically, they argue that large institutional investors, those with at least $100 million under management, when compared with other investors, seem to prefer stocks that have greater market capitalizations, are more liquid, and have higher book-to-market ratios and lower returns for the previous year. They contend that the growing importance of these investors in the stock market—their share of publicly traded stocks rose from 26.8 per cent in March 1980 to 51.5 per cent in December 1996—may have been partly responsible for the rise in the price and return on large stocks relative to those on small stocks (Gompers and Metrick 1999). In a similar vein, concerns have been voiced about the influence of day-traders—traders who use the Internet to buy and sell stocks—on stock prices, especially the prices of Internet company stocks.

In addition to changes on the demand side of the market, there has also been a reduction of the supply of corporate equities, including the stocks most favoured by large institutional investors and those that make up leading indices, which may also have added to price inflation in the stock market. Companies have been net purchasers of stock in the 1980s and 1990s as they invest massive amounts of money to buy back their own stock, notwithstanding the fact that share prices are at unprecedented levels by any valuation method and can thus hardly be considered a bargain. Like buybacks, merger and acquisition transactions initially add to the upward pressure on the demand for a particular stock and then, if they are completed, remove the stock from the market altogether. Domestic US merger and acquisition activity reached an all-time high in 1994 and since then has risen to staggering levels. As Figure 6.3 shows, the value of transactions since 1994 has made the 1980s fade into relative insignificance. And foreign acquirers have been adding to this momentum, Daimler-Benz and Deutsche Bank being notable examples with their respective bids for Chrysler and Bankers Trust.

Where all of these considerations leave the relationship between corporate profitability, stock valuations, and the productive capabilities of corporate America is, at this stage, anyone's guess. There are some signs of a more critical approach to stock market valuation as more and more evidence of what look like 'anomalies' from the perspective of the efficient market hypothesis (EMH) has accumulated. Of particular importance has been empirical research on market volatility which sug-

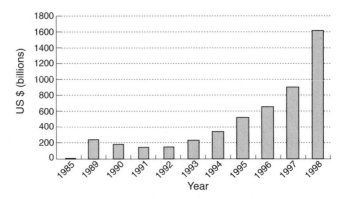

Source: Securities Data Company, Newark, NJ, press releases based on Merger & Corporate Transactions Database

FIG. 6.3 US domestic merger and acquisition transactions, 1985–1998

gests that price changes occur even in the absence of any new information. Robert Shiller's analysis of the relationship between dividends and stock prices is the classic paper on the subject (Shiller 1981). It is generally assumed in financial economics that stock prices represent an estimate of the present value of future dividends. Shiller pointed out, however, that variations in the present value of actual dividends paid out over the century are too small to explain volatility in stock valuations. In his more recent work, Shiller contends that stock markets are, as a general rule, influenced by fads and fashions and invokes evidence on popular models used by investors to analyse the 1987 US stock market crash (Shiller 1990). Indeed, the crash, given the apparent absence of any major news that might justify it, raised serious questions in the minds of a number of leading economists about the validity of their assumption of a close correlation between stock valuations and the economic fundamentals. In a paper entitled 'What Moves Stock Prices?' David Cutler, James Poterba, and Lawrence Summers, for example, highlighted 'the difficulty of explaining as much as half of the variance in aggregate stock prices on the basis of publicly available news bearing on fundamental values' (Cutler, Poterba, and Summers 1989: 9). Various other lines of empirical research have also fostered critiques of the EMH. For example, considerable evidence has been collected over recent decades which suggests that information on the size of firms, their price–earnings ratios, and their market-to-book ratios predict future returns, facts which are inconsistent with the hypothesis that stock prices reflect all publicly available information.

A number of financial theorists, who describe themselves as behavioural financial economists, have argued that to understand the anomalies that have already been uncovered, and indeed stock market behaviour more generally, there is a need to overhaul the theoretical foundations of financial economics. Whereas conventional finance theorists assume that only 'rational' behaviour affects equity prices,[4] behavioural

---

[4] Even if some, indeed most, traders are irrational, it is argued that rational traders will ultimately drive the irrational traders out of the market by trading to drive stock prices back to fundamental values.

finance theorists argue that how people actually behave makes a difference to stock prices. Specifically, behavioural finance is based on the observation (based on cognitive psychology and decision theory) that in some circumstances humans make systematic 'errors' in judgement and that these behavioural biases affect equity prices. Behavioural theorists have focused on various different types of non-rational behaviour. They have argued, for example, that under certain circumstances individuals may be prone to non-wealth-maximizing behaviour such as excessive trading of stocks due to overconfidence. Individuals may also make cognitive errors, usually because of their reliance on heuristics, rules adopted by economic actors to simplify their decision-making processes, which may lead to biases in certain situations. Notwithstanding its relatively recent vintage, behavioural finance has already generated a considerable body of empirical evidence to support its various claims with respect to the manner in which behavioural biases influence stock prices.[5]

There has, however, been far from a general acceptance within financial economics of the implications for the credibility of the EMH of the empirical findings on anomalies and the theoretical and empirical research in behavioural finance. Indeed, orthodox financial economists have tended to respond in a defensive way. Fama, for example, although he recognized in his 1991 update of his original article on the EMH that 'the task is thornier than it was 20 years ago', remains firmly committed to the hypothesis on the rather dubious grounds that

the alternative hypothesis is vague, market inefficiency. This is unacceptable. Like all models, market efficiency (the hypothesis that prices fully reflect available information) is a faulty description of price formation. Following the standard scientific rule, however, market efficiency can only be replaced by a better specific model of price formation, itself potentially rejectable by empirical tests. (Fama 1998: 284)

Fama is by no means alone among financial economists in his views. Indeed, there seems to be quite a consensus around the merits of, to paraphrase Keynes, being precisely wrong rather than vaguely right, as revealed by a sympathetic explanation of the resistance to behavioural finance among most financial economists:

A general criticism often raised by economists against psychological theories is that, in a given economic setting, the universe of conceivable irrational behavior patterns is essentially unrestricted. Thus, it is sometimes claimed that allowing for irrationality opens a Pandora's box of *ad hoc* stories which will have little out-of-sample predictive power. (Daniel, Hirshleifer, and Subrahmanyam 1998: 1840–1)

That the proponents of the shareholder theory of corporate governance include among their party some of the most orthodox of all financial economists in part explains their unwillingness to countenance the critiques of the EMH. Michael Jensen once famously stated, for example, that he believed 'that there is no other proposition in economics which has more solid empirical evidence supporting it than the Efficient Market Hypothesis' (Jensen 1978: 95).' But their reticence is also

---

[5] For reviews of the behavioural finance literature, see Thaler 1993; Heisler 1994; see also Daniel, Hirshleifer, and Subrahmanyam 1998.

explicable by the devastating consequences that any concession on their part would have for their arguments about corporate governance.

Undoubtedly a theory that purports to explain the relationship between corporate governance and corporate performance must rely on a more complex analysis of the relationship between the stock market and corporate performance than shareholder value proponents would allow. The value of behavioural research in finance to this endeavour should not be overstated. Behavioural theorists have proven to be effective critics of their more orthodox brethren. Mavericks though they are among financial economists, however, they remain wedded to some of the most restrictive elements of the conventional framework in their field for understanding financial markets, most notably, the assumption of quasi-stationarity and equilibration (Spotton and Rowley 1998). Arguably other economists, such as Veblen, Schumpeter, and Keynes, as well as contemporary economists working along similar lines, have delved much further into understanding the evolution and behaviour of financial markets and their relationship with the real economy. All of them have emphasized the possibility, and indeed the likelihood, that there will be long periods of dislocation between the financial and the real sectors of the economy because they considered that the stock market evolves through a path-dependent process which is historically specific and subject to a different dynamic than that which affects the real economy. Their conclusions are thus even more threatening to the theory of shareholder governance than the arguments made by behavioural finance theorists. Certainly, the assumption which is central to the shareholder theory of corporate governance, that shareholder returns are a reasonable, objective arbiter of real corporate performance, seems untenable.

Notwithstanding the importance of concerns about the plausibility of financial economists' assumptions concerning the relationship between the stock market and the real economy, the central problem with the shareholder theory for understanding the relationship between corporate governance and economic performance lies elsewhere. Arguably its real weakness is not so much its assumption of efficient stock markets as the more general definition of economic efficiency on which it relies. Specifically, the concept of resource allocation on which the shareholder theory of corporate governance is based precludes any understanding of the dynamic process of innovation through which productive resources are developed and utilized to generate higher-quality and/or lower-cost products.

From this point of view, the arguments that I have considered which focus on the redistribution of resources in the economy, as well as the stakeholder theories of corporate governance that are implicitly or explicitly part of their microeconomic foundations, are also subject to serious limitations. In focusing primarily on the distribution of resources, they do not provide a theoretical framework for understanding exactly what is going on in the US corporate economy and its long-term implications for sustainable prosperity. Ultimately, if the foundations are being laid for a more productive corporate economy in the United States, the fact that a significant redistribution of resources occurred in the process of getting there will fade into insignificance, perhaps even for many of those who have suffered from it.

It is critical, therefore, that we get at the question of whether resources are being developed as well as redistributed in the US corporate sector. To do so, however, we need a methodology to study the extent to which, and the way in which, corporate enterprises are innovating in the United States. The stakeholder perspective does not, however, provide such a framework, either in its macroeconomic or microeconomic guise. To the extent that its proponents attempt to get at the dynamic relationship between the development and utilization of resources in the corporate economy, they are therefore forced to rely—and always long after the fact—on measures of productivity and investment that are far too blunt as instruments for getting at the relationship between corporate resource allocation and sustainable prosperity. Moreover, the benchmark employed in these analyses is the past history of the US corporate economy. As a result, the proponents of these arguments are often criticized for their nostalgia for an idealized past and their implicit failure to come to terms with the serious competitive problems that showed up in the US corporate economy in the 1970s and 1980s.

In previous chapters I emphasized the importance of these problems and, from the organizational control perspective, I have sought to understand their origins. One source of competitive difficulties, brought on predominantly by corporate conglomeration and the ideology of management that it legitimated, was what I have described as the 'strategic segmentation' of top managers from the organizations in which they had to reinvest. Out of touch with the capabilities of the organizations over which they presided, and with the types of organizational learning required to develop new capabilities, top managers ceased to have the incentives and abilities to engage in 'retain and reinvest' strategies. These problems of reinvestment also arose from a source external to the corporation, namely the rise of new international competitors who built business organizations that could generate higher-quality, lower-cost products than once-dominant US corporations were capable of producing. In general, the effective challenges to US corporations came from international competitors who had made investments in broader and deeper skill bases that integrated the efforts of people with different levels of hierarchical responsibility and functional capability into powerful organizations for developing and utilizing technology.

Strategic segmentation and international competition undoubtedly created the need for the restructuring of many US corporations. From the perspective of organizational control, that restructuring process was an inherently political one, as stakeholder advocates have claimed, in that it inevitably involved the downgrading of the claims of some participants in the economy. Given its political nature, a critical question is whether the process of destroying elements of an extant system of organizational control set the stage for the renewal of the foundations for sustainable prosperity. For this to be the case, however, innovative investments had to be made. Such investments would mean committing resources to the development of integrated skill bases, and whether these investment strategies would require the employment of more or fewer people is an open question. It is possible that, in implementing their strategies to 'downsize and distribute', US corporate executives have also been able to rebuild innovative organizations. It is also possible, however, that top managers have focused so much on job cutting and disgorging the free cash flow their enterprises generate that they have fallen short of meeting the challenges of allocating corporate resources to innovative investment strategies.

6.4. Innovation and Prosperity in the 'New' Economy

In the post-World War II era that extended through the 1970s—decades when US corporate governance favoured strategies of 'retain and reinvest'—US blue-collar or 'hourly' workers were well paid and provided with stable employment, even though by world standards they were poorly educated and trained. During this period there was a general improvement in the distribution of income that contrasts with the worsening of the income distribution since that time. The corporations that employed these workers had achieved market dominance by developing managerial organization and fostering managerial learning, and shared some of the gains of this dominance with production workers, whose cooperation in the utilization of mass-production technologies was required on the shop floor. But in the 1970s and 1980s, the lack of investment in shop-floor skills proved to be the Achilles heel of US corporations in international competition, and especially in competition with Japanese companies that had innovated by investing in broader and deeper skill bases than US companies (Lazonick 1990; Lazonick and O'Sullivan 1996, 1997a).

Given the long-standing bias of the US system of corporate governance that had fostered a neglect of investment in shop-floor skills, in response to competitive challenges from abroad US strategists had the option of strategically targeting corporate resources on regenerating the organizations which they controlled to overcome their historical legacy of segmentation. Some US enterprises certainly showed a marked tendency towards breaking down organizational barriers to innovation and reinvesting in upgrading the skills of their workforce to allow broader-based participation in the processes of learning that generated innovation and competitive advantage. By the 1990s the result of such efforts in a number of manufacturing industries and activities in which US corporations chose to compete rather than exit was improved productivity, product development, quality, profitability, and trade performance.

Perhaps the greatest commitment to respond creatively to competitive challenges was found in the US automobile industry. Consistent with the skill-base hypothesis, US automakers attempted to respond innovatively in the 1980s and 1990s by instituting reforms aimed at promoting higher degrees of hierarchical and functional integration within their organizations than had been the case in the post-war decades. The traditional organization of work in the automobile companies had confined production workers to narrowly defined and repetitive tasks as elements in an overall system of production based on optimizing the flow of production of standardized products. To the extent that these workers had any scope to exercise their initiative and creativity in ways that raised productivity and quality they did so because they possessed long-standing craft skills in the maintenance and adjustment of machinery that had not yet been automated away. These skills had been formed through the persistence of traditions of craft learning rather than the strategic allocation of corporate resources to organizational learning. At the beginning of the 1980s, when it became apparent that the Japanese automobile companies could continue to compete on the basis of quality and cost even as wages rose, the Big Three of the US automobile industry began to learn and adopt Japanese management practices. A common characteristic of such practices was the integration of production workers into the processes of organizational learning. At the same time, during the 1980s, the leading Japanese automobile companies were making substantial investments in manufacturing capacity in the United States, in which the organizational integration of non-union shop-floor workers into learning processes was the rule.

But, with the notable exception of GM's Saturn experiment, there was little if any attempt to change the *institutions* of labour–management relations at Chrysler, Ford, and General Motors. Even as, under competitive pressure from the Japanese, there were plant-level changes in work practices designed to integrate shop-floor workers into processes of organizational learning, production workers still remained 'hourly' workers, while, apart from the presence of the head of the United Automobile Workers (UAW) on the Chrysler board of directors (a result of the government bail-out of Chrysler in the late 1970s), unions exercised no influence on the strategic processes that allocated corporate resources and returns. The case of Saturn—General Motors' multi-billion dollar investment in a new organization to develop, manufacture, and market an American-made small car—demonstrates the potential but also the high cost and fragility of the involvement of shop-floor labour in enterprise governance in a national environment that is hostile to such institutional arrangements.

The Saturn project had its origins in the ambitions of Roger Smith, GM's chairman and CEO since January 1981, to prove that GM was capable of making world-class small cars. From the late 1950s small-car imports challenged US automobile producers in their own home market. At first these cars came from Europe, but in the mid-1970s, following the Arab oil embargo, more and more American consumers turned to more fuel-efficient Japanese cars. In an effort to counteract this trend toward small-car imports, the US auto manufacturers included an increasing number of domestically manufactured small cars in their product ranges. But as the US producers attempted to shoehorn large-car designs into smaller packages and to lower costs by speeding up production, US-made small cars of the 1960s and 1970s developed a deserved reputation for being defective products.

Such was especially the case for General Motors, the world's leading car manufacturer, whose Corvair of the early 1960s was made infamous by Ralph Nader in his book *Unsafe at Any Speed*, and whose Vega of the late 1960s received wide publicity because of the absenteeism and alienation of the blue-collar labour force that assembled it at the GM plant in Lordstown, Ohio (Nader 1965). During the 1970s, especially after the Japanese import invasion took hold, GM took some steps to correct these problems. But with big cars much more profitable than small cars and under the illusion that the prime source of the Japanese challenge was cheap labour, these efforts were half-hearted.

In January 1981, when Roger Smith took over as chairman and CEO of GM, he launched a concerted effort to overcome the mediocre standing of GM in the small-car market. His first manoeuvre included the rejection of the S-car project, which had been heralded as a successor to the Chevette. Instead, Smith initiated an out-sourcing arrangement with the Japanese car company Isuzu, in which GM had owned a large stake since 1971. The result of this venture—the GEO Prizm—did not, however, enjoy any great success (HBS 1994: 7–8).

Meanwhile by the early 1980s American producers became increasingly aware that the central source of Japan's sustained competitive advantage in the automobile industry was innovative organization, not cheap labour. GM therefore entered a joint venture with Japan's foremost automobile producer, the Toyota Motor Corporation, called New United Motors Manufacturing Incorporated (NUMMI), to gain access to state-of-the-art management practices. Toyota supplied management and $100 million to launch NUMMI. GM put up a smaller amount of cash and also provided an unused factory. The blue-collar labour force was made up of re-employed union-ized workers—members of the UAW—most of whom had been laid off when the old GM factory shut its doors. GM also sent a management team to NUMMI with the specific intention of learning Japanese management practices, which could then be diffused throughout the GM organization.

Increasingly, informed GM managers came to recognize that the key to Japanese success in the automobile industry was a more cooperative and integrated relation-ship between management and labour in the development and utilization of tech-nology. In the early 1970s, even before the full brunt of the Japanese challenge had been felt, some GM managers and UAW leaders had sought to deal with sagging worker morale as manifested in the 'blue-collar blues' at Lordstown. But joint GM–UAW initiatives in Quality of Work Life and Employee Participation Group Intervention programmes had failed to take hold (see Chapter 4). Yet by the early 1980s there was ample evidence, not only from the Japanese but also from, for example, Volvo's innovative Uddevalla manufacturing plant in Sweden, of the benefits to be gained by teamwork that integrated shop-floor workers in processes of organizational learning.

That view was reinforced by the Saturn project. GM had come under increasing fire from a number of sources for its strategy of maintaining a position in the small-car market by putting its brand on cars made outside of the company. The company was accused of giving up on US workers and their capacity to build world-class cars. In 1982 GM, with the approval of Smith, funded an internal study to redress the company's problems in competing in the small-car market. The study showed that GM possessed the technological capability to produce a small car in the United States. Yet to do so in a way that could match the Japanese in quality and cost would require a transformation of GM's traditional mode of work organization. Instead of devel-oping technologies that could take skill and initiative off the shop floor, the company had to develop shop-floor skills and encourage shop-floor initiative as an integral part of a process of making full use of advanced technologies and improving the quality of the products. Indeed, one of the people involved in the study which resulted in Saturn said that, when the study team 'looked at all the disciplines to find out what we needed to do differently to become competitive . . . the bottom line was that it wasn't just design, engineering and manufacturing that needed to change but the entire business of running the business' (Keller 1989: 94). The mandate of the team was subsequently broadened 'from studying technological issues to evaluating all the decision-making processes related to building and selling cars—particularly those involving labor and management' (HBS 1994: 8).

At the end of 1983, in an unprecedented move for a US automobile corporation, GM management invited the UAW to join it in planning the Saturn project. In December 1983, Donald Ephlin, vice-president of the UAW, and Alfred Warren, GM's vice-president of industrial relations, announced the establishment of the Saturn Study Center, its mission to 'identify and recommend the best approaches to integrate people and technology to competitively manufacture small cars in the United States'. In early 1984 that centre spawned a 'group of 99', made up of GM and UAW people, to undertake a major benchmarking study that would help them to understand how best to proceed with their project of building a world-class car with US managers and workers.

One year later, in January 1985, Roger Smith announced the launch of Saturn as 'a wholly-owned subsidiary of GM, and the first new nameplate added to the GM fine line of automobiles since Chevrolet was added in 1918' (O'Toole 1996: 39). The Saturn Corporation would occupy a greenfield site in Spring Hill, Tennessee. Its mission was twofold: '1. To market vehicles developed and manufactured in the United States that are world leaders in quality, cost, and customer satisfaction by integrating people, technology, and business systems; and 2. To transfer knowledge, technology, and experience throughout General Motors' (Rehder 1994a: 8).

GM management and the UAW worked out a 1,600-word agreement in July 1985 that represented a radical departure from the traditional union–management relations that underlay the GM–UAW boilerplate employment agreement used through-out the company. As Robert Rehder observed, the agreement

required a working partnership of Saturn management and UAW officers and members at all levels of decision making during Saturn's development and all throughout its operation. This state-of-the-art management collaboration extends from the office of the CEO to workers on the assembly line. It is based on joint decision making from strategic planning to shop-floor problem solving. The agreement clearly sets new standards for industrial democracy in the US auto industry, like those in Northern Europe. (Rehder 1994a: 8)

Saturn's organization can be thought of as a set of concentric circles. In the centre was the basic work unit, a self-directed work team consisting of six to fifteen people that took responsibility for a variety of tasks ranging from production, maintenance, and inventory control to scheduling, work allocation, recruitment, and training. Work units were coordinated by a charter team member, appointed by members of each work unit, with responsibility for conducting weekly meetings and overseeing the implementation of group decisions. Other decision circles, including the work unit module, the business unit, and three action committees for manufacturing, tech-nical development, and customer relations, took responsibility for the coordination of activities at higher levels of the organization. These decision circles were composed of Saturn and UAW representatives. So too the highest-ranking management team at Saturn, the Strategic Action Council, included the Saturn president and the president of the local UAW, as well as representatives of the other decision circles within the organization (Rehder 1994*a*; HBS 1994: 14; White 1997; Shaiken, Lopez, and Mankita 1997).

That the Saturn experiment is seen as pathbreaking, at least in the context of the US corporate economy, is attributable not only to its pioneering governance structure but also to its deviations from traditional agreements on matters of job classification, training, and compensation. The standard system of extensive job classifications found throughout the industry was abandoned in favour of broad job descriptions to facilitate flexibility in the rotation of workers from one task to another. Saturn also stipulated an annual minimum of training hours for each individual and workers were given full access to information on manufacturing, product engineering, sales, and all other aspects of Saturn's operations. The division also made a much stronger commitment to the protection of workers' job security (at least for 80 per cent of its workforce) than is typical of the US automobile industry, although it did not guarantee that there would be no layoffs in the event of a major downturn in the industry. Saturn's approach to compensation also broke with tradition in the industry. Workers were no longer compensated on an 'hourly' basis. Rather they were put on salaries at a rate of nearly 90 per cent of the average wage paid to workers in the rest of the automobile industry. In addition, part of their compensation—beginning with 5 per cent in 1992 with an increase to 12 per cent by 1997—was made contingent on certain performance criteria. The basis for the 'at-risk' portion of pay has evolved over time depending on the particular challenges that Saturn has confronted. In 1992, for example, the 5 per cent contingency pay was tied to training; each worker was required to perform 92 hours of training that year to develop new skills. By 1997, the formula had become more complex and workers received the full 12 per cent only if they met three types of performance criteria related to training (5 per cent), quality (5 per cent), and team skills (2 per cent). Finally, workers could receive an additional 'reward' allowance that was originally wholly dependent on profitability but was later based on productivity and also on quality; in 1992 that portion amounted to $1,800 but in 1995 and 1996 it rose to $10,000. To the extent that they received this reward pay, Saturn workers could earn a higher level of compensation than the average worker in the automobile industry (Bohl 1997: 52).

As a working experiment in organizational change, Saturn is widely viewed to have been a *technological* and *market* success. But to be an *economic* success on a sustainable basis the company needed both to increase its capacity to produce small cars and to move from the production of smaller cars into mid-sized-car markets. From the outset, the governance of relations among 'stakeholders' within Saturn Corporation was kept separate from the structures that governed these relations in the rest of General Motors. But, as a wholly-owned subsidiary of GM, strategic decisions concerning the building of new plant and the entry into new market segments, not to mention costly items such as advertising budgets, have rested with the parent company. GM launched Saturn as a $5 billion project, but then halved the investment, and, on the grounds of global overcapacity, built only one assembly line rather than the two that had originally been planned (*Fortune*, 15 Feb. 1988: 18). In the 1990s, GM headquarters has been unwilling to permit Saturn to build new capacity, and at times has forced Saturn to delay product improvements. For example, in 1994, plans for a new interior including passenger air bags had to be put off for a year, as was also the case in 1995 with a plan for a wholesale facelift that included an entirely new exterior styling, a quieter engine, and an improved chassis. Meanwhile, Chrysler used these two years to hone the production of its small car, the Neon, and gained market share from Saturn (*Business Week*, 28 Feb. 1994).

In 1989 a former high-ranking GM executive remarked: 'If Roger Smith died tomorrow, the headline would read GM CHAIRMAN DEAD. The following day the headline would be, GM CANCELS SATURN PROJECT' (*Fortune*, 13 Mar. 1989: 35). Smith stepped down as CEO in August 1990, to be replaced by another Saturn supporter, Robert Stempel (O'Toole 1996: 177). But a boardroom coup in December 1992 which replaced Stempel with Jack Smith meant that Saturn lost its support at the top. The GM subsidiary was now too established to be simply cancelled, but allocation of resources to Saturn has increasingly been subject to GM's globalization strategy. All of Saturn's models must utilize more GM-made parts than had previously been the case. A brand-name Saturn was permitted to enter the mid-sized-car market, but the car had to be based on a model developed by GM at Europe's Adam Opel AG division. In August of 1996, GM approved a $927 million budget for the conversion of Opel's Vectra into the Saturn Innovate, with production, not at Spring Hill, Tennessee, but in a fifty-year-old Wilmington, Delaware plant that had been scheduled for closure. Of particular significance, the labour contract at the Wilmington plant is one negotiated under the main GM–UAW agreement, and therefore largely different from that for the Spring Hill complex.

Whatever Saturn's initial accomplishments in 'integrating people, technology, and business systems' in the development and production of cars in the United States, its ultimate dependence on the GM governance structure has prevented it from 'transferring knowledge, technology, and experience' not only 'throughout General Motors', but even throughout the Saturn subsidiary itself. Yet with the exception of its Saturn subsidiary, GM has been the slowest of the Big Three US automobile producers to innovate by building broader and deeper skill bases to develop and utilize technology, and throughout the 1980s and 1990s, GM has been losing market share.

In 1994, faced by the control over resource allocation exercised by GM, Michael Bennett, the local president of the UAW at Saturn, examined the idea of employee stock ownership plans (ESOPs) as a way of securing funding independent of the parent company. But the proposal was defeated at the monthly meeting of the Saturn local, in part because GM's top managers had responded to the proposal by promising money for new models and capacity expansion (O'Toole 1996: 192). Increasingly, however, GM's ambivalence towards Saturn became a major problem for the local union as it struggled to maintain the spirit of its cooperative relationship with the automaker.

In addition to its problems in dealing with GM management, the local union leadership also faced significant challenges from within its own organization, the UAW, both from union members working in the Saturn plant and from senior union officials in the International Union. The traditional local union structure had been substantially modified at Saturn. Of particular importance was the allocation of responsibility for the resolution of interpersonal conflicts and other grievances within the framework of the cooperative structures that were specific to the Saturn organization. Formal union representation was only to be utilized as a last resort in the event that team efforts as well as joint management–union efforts to resolve the problem failed. Mike Bennett, the local president, claimed that a greater resort to formal union grievance procedures 'would politicise the partnership, diminishing the ability of individuals in these positions to equally balance the needs of people with the needs of the business' (Rubinstein, Bennett, and Kochan 1993: 361). There was, however, opposition to Bennett's view within the local, who argued that there was a serious risk that individual worker rights would be sacrificed to the demands of the business. In particular, some workers expressed concern that their local union leaders were too close to management to be adequate representatives of workers' interests. As Robert Rehder put it:

While union officials and representatives at Saturn are heavily involved in decisions affecting the operation of the plant, there does remain a question as to how many of the team members on the line believe they have a significant voice and measure of control over their work environments. Has Saturn created a parallel hierarchy of union/management co-managers neither of which truly represents the workers? (Rehder 1994b: 27)

In 1993, a group of dissidents within the local ran against the incumbent leadership on a platform that had as a central element a restoration of traditional grievance procedures and a renewed emphasis on seniority to protect workers from victimization by the business leaders of Saturn. They were defeated but only narrowly (Shaiken, Lopez, and Mankita 1997: 41–3). There was to be little respite, however, for Bennett and his sympathizers. The pressure on them heated up shortly afterwards when the International UAW became involved in the dispute. Tensions between the local and the International UAW had been increasing behind the scenes for some time. In 1989 Don Ephlin, who had played a central role on the UAW side in the formation of Saturn, announced that he would retire from his position as director of the GM department in the International Union. He was replaced by Steve Yokich, the former head of the UAW Ford department, who was not a strong supporter of the Saturn project.

In May 1993, in an initiative spearheaded by Yokich, the International Union stated its intention to modify the Memorandum of Agreement between the UAW and GM that regulated labour–management relations at Saturn. The International claimed it was taking action in response to complaints it had received of civil rights violations by Saturn's local union. The latter denied the International's right to change the agreement but in March 1994 the president of the UAW, Owen Bieber, overturned their appeal and claimed that Yokich was empowered to re-negotiate the agreement on behalf of the UAW.

The local was invited to join the bargaining over the Saturn agreement, but the leadership refused to be involved on the grounds that it considered the changes proposed by the International to be unnecessary. Eventually, at the end of 1994, after two agreements had been turned down by the local, changes to the memorandum were ratified by a narrow majority of the local membership. Of particular importance was the fact that much greater emphasis was to be placed on seniority rather than ability and experience in transfer and layoff decisions, teams were no longer allowed to hire their own members, and union representation on the shop floor was increased (Shaiken, Lopez, and Mankita 1997: 41–3).

The International, under Yokich's direction, also supported the decision to undertake the production of the new Saturn line of cars in a plant with a traditional structure of labour–management relations. When, from the middle of the 1990s, relations between GM management and the local union at the Spring Hill plant deteriorated, increasing numbers of union members questioned the merits of the distinctive structure of labour–management relations at the Saturn plant and echoed the International's calls for more traditional forms of contractual protections for labour interests. The downturn in the small-car market that the Spring Hill plant served played an important role in bringing these issues to a head.

In 1997 sales of Saturn's Spring Hill production fell 10 per cent as consumers increasingly favoured bigger sedans and sports utility vehicles. In January 1998, sales were down 20 per cent compared with the previous year and in February 1998 the year-on-year decline was 21 per cent. One effect of the sales decline was that Saturn workers received no bonuses; as a result they made $4,000 less for the year than their counterparts in the rest of GM. Saturn cut back production and workers spent their spare time training and tidying up the plant. But increasingly fears were expressed that in the event the sales trend worsened the no-layoff policy would be revoked. As one worker put it, 'Saturn says there's a no-layoff policy and that's a crock. GM is GM. They'll do whatever they want' (*Atlanta Journal*, 8 Mar. 1998). Support increased within the local for the introduction of a traditional union–management contract with Saturn and the guaranteed wage conditions and security provisions that it would bring.

The leaders of the local union worked hard to persuade their members to maintain the distinctive agreement. But they also publicly attacked GM management for what they saw as its weakening commitment to Saturn. They claimed that GM was deliberately undermining Saturn's autonomy. First, the company had refused to give Spring Hill a new model that would allow it to reduce its dependence on the small-car market even though Saturn had requested that a mid-sized car and a mini sports utility vehicle be built at Spring Hill. Secondly, GM's corporate strategy to move towards common manufacturing platforms for different types of cars, and its increasing emphasis on outsourcing parts production as one element of this strategy, threatened Saturn's highly integrated production system. Bennett complained that 'GM is like a big black hole. Saturn's been trying to move off in another orbit, but it looks like we're getting pulled back in' (*Atlanta Journal*, 8 Mar. 1998). That Bennett and other union leaders levelled such public criticism at GM's strategy was to some extent a product of the Saturn experiment. In the words of David Weil, an industrial relations expert at Boston University, 'There's an inevitable thing that happens when you involve people more in their work—everyone's expectations increase. People start to question strategic decisions, like, "Why the hell haven't you introduced sport-utility vehicles?"' (*Atlanta Journal*, 8 Mar. 1998).

Nor were the leaders of the local alone in their criticism of GM management. An article entitled 'Why didn't GM do More for Saturn?' in *Business Week* conveys the tone of a more general reaction:

Give the No. 1 auto maker credit for accomplishing the hard part—launching from scratch a division that has been Detroit's one smashing, cross-generational victory in the war to win back import buyers. But rather than doing everything possible to build on that success, GM is now letting Saturn wither on the vine. It has allowed sibling rivalry to smother Saturn, delaying and denying additions to its lineup while favoring fading brands with new products. (*Business Week*, 16 Mar. 1998)

The local membership saw some grounds for optimism that these criticisms might have an effect on GM. In March 1998 there was a vote on whether to keep the existing labour agreement or replace it with a conventional UAW contract. Although support for labour's distinctive arrangement with management was lower than the previous time a vote had been taken, it was retained by a majority of two to one.

Shortly afterwards it seemed that workers' optimism had been warranted when Jack Smith, the chairman of GM, gave his approval for a study to be undertaken to broaden Saturn's mission and expand the division. It was expected that Saturn's new mission would entail the expansion of its product line to include a sports utility vehicle. The pill from GM was not, however, entirely sweet. Some GM executives reportedly said that most of the parts for such a vehicle would be built in modules by outside suppliers. There were also fears that the company would take a similar approach to the next generation of small cars.

Tensions within Saturn continued to mount and in July 1998, in sympathy with strike action being undertaken by the International in other parts of GM, the vast majority of Saturn workers voted to authorize union leaders to call their first strike against the company. Saturn workers were reported to be increasingly concerned about loss of production due to outsourcing of work to other plants and their waning role in strategic decisions that affected Saturn's performance and future, as well as their dwindling pay. Again, as an excerpt from *Barron's*, the financial weekly, suggests, criticism of GM management abounded:

the company's one winner, its best chance of learning to do business better, is withering on the vine. UAW members at the Saturn assembly plant in Spring Hill, Tennessee, have voted for a local strike. There are many reasons for their unhappiness, but a big one is the hostility GM's bureaucracy in Detroit has shown to the cooperative management system at Saturn. Real

GM managers would rather fight and lose than have a profitably civil relationship with workers. (*Barron's*, 10 Aug. 1998)

Yet, by this stage, workers in the local union had lost faith in GM's commitment to Saturn's being 'a different kind of car company'. In February 1999, they voted out of office all of the union leaders who had led the local through the Saturn experiment and replaced them with new officials who advocated a more traditional structure for labour–management relations in Saturn.

Given the barriers to restructuring the organizational foundations for sustainable prosperity in the US economy that the Saturn case reveals, it is perhaps not surprising that in a wide range of industrial activities the efforts of enterprises to overcome their historical legacy of organizational segmentation have been much more halting than has been the case in the automobile industry. Many enterprises have relied to a greater extent on other types of strategies to survive. In particular, they have favoured outsourcing and downsizing strategies and, in some cases, wholesale exit from business activities in which their patterns of organizational segmentation have, in the face of intensified competition, proven to be a barrier to generating competitive success.

Commitment to downsizing and outsourcing alone cannot, however, form the foundation of the competitive advantage of an enterprise for any extended period of time. These strategies have thus tended to be combined with innovative efforts. Yet, increasingly these efforts have been concentrated in activities in which enterprises innovate and compete by investing in the capabilities of narrower and more concentrated skill bases. Such skill bases integrate the productive activities of a relatively small number of highly educated personnel focused on a narrow range of highly specialized activities. The examples of the semiconductor and aircraft engine industries illustrate what seems to be a more general trend in US industry.

The US semiconductor industry has played the role of 'a "poster child" for US competitive decline during the 1980s and resurgence during the 1990s' (Macher, Mowery, and Hodges 1998: 107). As I noted in the previous chapter, the relative competitive decline of US producers in the 1980s was dramatic: US chipmakers' global market share plummeted from nearly 62 per cent in 1980 to 37 per cent in 1989 with Japanese producers making up much of the difference. By the middle of the 1980s, the Japanese dominated the global supply of semiconductor memory devices, and there were growing concerns in the late 1980s that Japanese producers would repeat their success in the DRAM market and ultimately dominate the entire market for chips. In fact, predictions of the demise of US chip producers proved wrong. The US industry experienced a resurgence in its international competitive position beginning in 1990, and by 1997 its share of the world semiconductor market had increased to 50 per cent compared with 29 per cent for Japanese firms (Macher, Mowery, and Hodges 1998: 111).

To some extent the relative improvement in the competitive position of US producers reflects their renewed commitment to remedying problems in their internal organizations that had acted as obstacles to effective competition with the Japanese in the 1980s. They have certainly reorganized their manufacturing operations to improve quality, increase productivity, and speed up the introduction of new process technologies. Notwithstanding these improvements, however, the manufacturing capabilities of the American semiconductor firms still lag behind their best Japanese competitors, as well as other cutting-edge Asian firms. For US producers, given the historic exclusion of production workers from organizational learning, the more effective strategic response was to concentrate less on revamping their manufacturing operations and more on innovating in design-intensive activities, the segment of the value chain in which the existing organizational structures of these companies gave them the most competitive strength. In the semiconductor industry US firms exited from DRAMs, which were relatively manufacturing-intensive, towards microcomponents, which were much more design-intensive. Moreover, within microcomponents some US semiconductor firms decoupled design from production, outsourcing the latter to 'silicon foundries', many of which are located outside the US, especially in Taiwan and other Asian countries. In the extreme version of the decoupling model, semiconductor firms were 'fabless' and, as a result, completely dependent for their production needs on foundries. Reflecting the decoupling of different elements of the value chain, although North American firms accounted for 32 per cent of world semiconductor trade in 1994, only 18 per cent of world exports originated in North America. As one report on *The Globalization of the Semiconductor Industry* put it,

the story being told here is that the US firms have been more aggressive than other semiconductor companies in moving production facilities offshore in search of lower labor and facility costs, mainly at the finishing stages of production. While this contributes to job creation and economic growth in the offshore region, it may not necessarily affect the job creation or economic growth prospects of the country where the owner companies are located. (DRI/McGraw-Hill 1996: 6)

Recent trends in the aircraft engine industry also raise questions about the relationship between corporate strategies of US producers and the benefits accruing to the US economy. Three producers—Pratt and Whitney (owned by United Technologies Corporation) and General Electric Aircraft Engines, both US corporations, and Rolls-Royce, a British company—have dominated the world market for aircraft engines since World War II. As recently as 1997 they accounted for more than 90 per cent of the order backlog for the large turbofan engines that drive aircraft used for commercial travel. The stability in the market share figures for final aircraft engines, however, obscures the growing reliance by the Big Three on suppliers in other countries for production and increasingly for product development as well. Beth Almeida describes the general trend in the industry in the following terms:

Since the 1970's, there has been a steady growth in long-term supply arrangements that encompass not only manufacturing activities, but product development activities as well. Such arrangements are commonly referred to as 'risk-and-revenue-sharing partnerships' or RRSPs. Supplier firms that enlist as RRSP members 'buy a stake' in an engine program at the time of its launch, committing to finance some fixed share of the project (risk) in exchange for a defined work-share (revenue), hence the term. . . . These RRSPs reflect a 'modular' design and production strategy on the part of the systems integrators where each firm in the partnership takes on the responsibility for the design and manufacture of a particular engine 'module' over the life of the program, with the systems integrator responsible for specifying the 'interfaces' between modules and for final assembly. While it would be a stretch to label systems integrators as 'virtual manufacturers' (they still retain in-house design and manufacture of a number of 'core' components), it is true that the growing importance of RRSPs lessens the extent to which we may still view the industry as an American/Anglo-dominated oligopoly. (Almeida 1998: 6)

To illustrate her point, Almeida has recalculated the adjusted market shares of the Big Three once the extent of their reliance on suppliers is taken into account. As Table 6.5 shows, the difference is striking, especially for GE, whose share falls from an unadjusted figure of 61 per cent to just over half of that at 33 per cent.

There are ongoing debates with respect to different industries about whether the strategic proclivity of US corporations to engage in activities that make use of narrow and concentrated skill bases can form the basis for sustained competitive advantage. Some commentators believe that US firms can outsource production and still maintain control over the value chain by investing heavily in design-intensive activities where they currently have, and can maintain, world-class capabilities. With respect to the electronics industry, for example, Michael Borrus and John Zysman have argued that US firms have pioneered a new form of competition, which they describe as 'Wintelism'. They claim that

the terms of competition have shifted away from final assemblers and the strategy of hierarchical (i.e. vertical) control of technologies and manufacturing. The character of the shift in market power is popularly suggested in the advertisements of PC producers like IBM, Toshiba, Compaq or Siemens-Nixdorf whose systems are nearly identical and who emphasize components of software that have become de facto market standards—'Intel Inside,' or 'Microsoft Windows installed'—rather than unique features of their own brands. 'Wintelism' is the code word that best captures the character of the new global electronics era because Intel and Microsoft pioneered many of its dominant industrial and business practices and are now

TABLE 6.5 Order backlog for large engines for major civil aircraft, August 1997

Company	Unadjusted Share (%)	Share Adjusted for RRSP[a] (%)
GE	61.0	32.8
Pratt and Whitney	19.6	13.5
Rolls-Royce	15.0	11.2
RRSP		38.0
Undecided	4.5	4.5
Total	100	100

[a] Risk-and-revenue-sharing partnership.

Source: Almeida (1998).

leveraging their market dominance to alter the terms of competition in other informatics markets. (Borrus and Zysman 1997: 4)

In Wintelist competition the '"core assets" are the intellectual property and know-how associated with setting, maintaining, and continuously evolving a de facto market standard—a process that requires perpetual improvements in product features, functionality, performance, costs, and quality' (Borrus and Zysman 1997: 15). In the new environment, contracting out production to their suppliers 'permits system firms to concentrate on Wintelist product definition and market strategies while conserving capital and gaining production flexibility' (Borrus and Zysman 1997: 12). Thus, they regard cross-national production networks (CPNs) as the production organization counterpart to Wintelism.

From this perspective, it is American electronics producers' success in shifting the terms of competition towards Wintelism that accounts for their continued competitive success. In the late 1980s as US electronics firms became increasingly reliant on Asian producers, especially Japanese enterprises, for underlying technologies, influential commentators predicted that they would go the way of their consumer electronics counterparts. But, as Borrus observed,

A decade later things look decidedly different. The new generation of US firms was almost everywhere ascendant and the Japanese were on the defensive and seeking alliances with the new market leaders. This breathtaking reversal of industrial fortunes was not the result of careful planning. Built in equal parts of serendipity, entrepreneurial innovation, desperate experimentation, inter-firm cooperation, and policy intervention, the competitive strategies pioneered largely by American firms were rather surprising. US firms constructed an alternative supplier base in Asia to the Japanese for components, processes and manufacturing know-how, in effect commodifying their areas of greatest dependence. Simultaneously, they reasserted control over new product development by de-coupling the key technical standards that defined new products from commodity technology inputs, and then aggressively protecting those standards through strengthened intellectual property protection. (Borrus 1998: 2)

From this point of view, given that US firms have pioneered Wintelist competition, and the relative strength of the US industry in design-intensive activities, their control over the strategic sources of value in the electronics industry is unlikely to fade in the foreseeable future.

There are, however, those who are less convinced by predictions of continued US dominance. One concern that has been raised is the extent to which enterprises to which US electronics are outsourcing have the capabilities to upgrade what they know to allow them to undertake the activities in which US companies are currently dominant. Indeed, Borrus himself, in a book on the global electronics industry written in collaboration with Dieter Ernst and Stephen Haggard, underlines the possibility of such a learning process taking place. They are, as a result, cautious in making predictions about continued US dominance of the industry. They state that 'despite the current triumphalism in US pronouncements on Asia and on Japan, we are quite hesitant to accord long-term competitive preference to the US CPN form' and go on to argue that much depends on the types of learning processes that evolve to generate innovation in different sectors of the electronics industry. Their research on the capabilities in the Japanese, Taiwanese, and Korean electronics sectors suggests that it is not at all clear today that those learning trajectories will be such that US firms can maintain the type of innovative dominance they have enjoyed in recent years (Borrus, Ernst, and Haggard, forthcoming).

Moreover, some challenge the extent to which one can generalize the logic of Wintelism, on the grounds that the confluence of factors that led to the dominance of Intel and Microsoft was historically specific and unlikely to be repeated. Of particular importance to the emergence of Microsoft and Intel as industry standards-setters was their relation to IBM. In August 1980, when Microsoft signed a contract with IBM to develop an operating system for IBM's first personal computer, Microsoft did not even possess a suitable operating system, but had to deftly purchase one from another small Seattle software company. As Martin Campbell-Kelly and William Aspray argue, had it not been for the income stream that Microsoft derived from its IBM connection through the first half of the 1980s, its other product failures would have put it out of business, as was the case with thousands of other software startups (Campbell-Kelly and Aspray 1996: 263). Moreover, it was IBM's success in setting the industry standard for what later became known as 'PCs'—a standard that was assured when Compaq reverse-engineered IBM's Basic Input–Output System as a basis for its 1986 introduction of its 'IBM clone' (Jackson 1997: 277–8)—that subsequently created the foundation for Microsoft's worldwide dominance of PC operating software. So too, with Intel. IBM's adoption of its microprocessors for the personal computer when it was being developed in its skunkworks in Boca Raton provided Intel with revenues that enabled it to avoid bankruptcy in the mid-1980s as it lost its DRAM market to the Japanese (Jackson 1997: ch. 27), while the ability of IBM to set the hardware and software standards for the new PC industry gave Intel the platform to dominate the world market for PC microprocessors.

But the larger question is why IBM itself had such power to shape the standards for a new industry. When, in response to the success of the Apple computer in 1979, IBM quickly developed its personal computer, it was a company that dominated the world's computer markets. Like the computer industry more generally before the personal computer revolution of the 1980s, as I observed in Chapter 4, the hardware and software capabilities which IBM developed in becoming the world's dominant computer company had as their technological foundation major government programmes to fund computer research and as their market foundation the demand of the government for computers. Of particular importance for funding these government research and procurement programmes was the US military, and of particular importance for government funding of the military was the Cold War. In the words of Thomas Watson, Jr., the CEO of IBM who oversaw its rise to dominance in the computer industry from the 1950s through the 1970s, 'it was the Cold War that helped IBM make itself the king of the computer business' (quoted in Campbell-Kelly and Aspray 1996: 168–9). Through the IBM connection, therefore, 'Wintelism' is a product of this national effort to develop computer technology. Whether, with the globalization of the PC industry and in the absence of a renewed national effort, US dominance of the standards, and of the high-value-added design work, can be maintained must therefore be seen as an open question.

Similar combinations of bullish and bearish commentaries can be found about other industries in which US strategic responses are evolving in ways that are similar to what is happening in the electronics sector. Borrus and Zysman claim that the logic of Wintelism is not confined to the electronics industry, although it has gone farther in that industry than in any other, but may also be used to understand the evolving competitive dynamics in industries like telecommunications and automobiles. Other scholars have made similar arguments, based on the concept of modularity, to explain the evolving competitive dynamics in a variety of industries, including the aero-engine industry.

As Brusano and Prencipe describe it: 'Modularity is a design strategy aimed at defining a standardised set of interfaces among components. Each component (module) is allocated a specific task to be performed respecting the given interfaces. These, in turn, are not allowed to change during an intended period of time' (Brusoni and Prencipe 1999: 1). The aero-engine industry has been characterized by an increasing trend towards product modularity. The leading systems integrators in the aero-engine industry—GE Aircraft Engines, Pratt and Whitney, and Rolls-Royce—have, to an increasing extent, externalized certain activities, especially manufacturing but also, more recently, detailed design work, to suppliers of aero-engine components. On the basis of detailed empirical research on the industry, Brusoni and Prencipe described the trend as follows:

Thanks to accumulated knowledge of components' behaviour as well as of the entire system behaviour, systems integrators can decompose the engine system more effectively and focus more on a few 'soft' capabilities, such as software codes, rather than 'hard' ones, such as manufacturing. Our interviewees have, in fact, confirmed that manufacturing is no longer deemed critical for the integration of the engine system, whereas design and development play a much more prominent role. Within the design activities, however, engine manufacturers focus more on 'concept design', leaving 'detailed design' to suppliers or better RRSPs. (Brusoni and Prencipe 1999: 14)

Thus, in outsourcing various activities involved in designing and building aero-engines, what the systems integrators are relying on is their ability to maintain control over the integration process through their dominance in advanced design. To be effective in that process may require these integrators to maintain some capabilities in manufacturing, engineering, and detailed design, but these skills and knowledge may be retained not by undertaking these activities but rather through research projects (internal and external) and training programmes (Brusoni and Prencipe 1999: 16).

The confidence of the incumbent systems integrators in their ability to maintain their competitive positions even as they rely on more concentrated skill bases as the foundation for their innovative strategies may, however, be misplaced. Some companies have been developing capabilities as suppliers of aero-engines that may provide the basis on which they can expand their knowledge base to allow them to become systems integrators. Of particular interest in this regard are the activities of three Japanese companies that are members of the Japan Aero Engines consortium, which has played an important role as a supplier of aero-engines components. The three 'Heavies', as they are described, are Ishikawajima-Harima Heavy Industries (IHI), Kawasaki Heavy Industries (KHI), and Mitsubishi Heavy Industries (MHI), and they are all century-old shipbuilders with long experience in turbine engine technologies. In the post-World War II decades these companies, along with a number of others in Japan, both cooperated and competed in the development of capabilities. IHI was the most aggressive in pursuing gas turbine research (its president was a turbine engineer and the company had a relationship with Toshiba, which in turn had a long-standing relationship with General Electric), and its J3 turbojet, developed for military use in the 1950s, was Japan's first indigenous jet aircraft engine. In 1993, under licence from GE, IHI produced more than half of the F-110-129 engine for the F-2 fighter support plane, co-developed by the United States and Japan. IHI remains Japan's leading aircraft engine manufacturer, with, for example, its excellence in the precision engineering of composite materials enabling it to be the prime subcontractor in the production of carbon fibre blades for GE's commercial jet engines (Samuels 1994: Ch. 7).

Thus far no Japanese company has been the systems integrator for an aero-engine that has entered commercial use. But the Japanese companies have played an increasingly important role in the international production networks, and have developed superior capabilities that could enable them to be serious competitors for the incumbent systems integrators in the development of new engines. For example, in 1997, the *Wall Street Journal* reported,

The West has largely stopped worrying that Japan will become a big force in aerospace, but one company is beginning to look like a contender. Japan's biggest maker of jet engines, Ishikawajima-Harima Heavy Industries Co., has quietly become a force that the world's aerospace giants must reckon with, Western aerospace experts say. The company, known as IHI, has helped the world's largest jet-engine makers on projects, including the power plants on Boeing Co.'s newest commercial jet. IHI's strength in technologies such as composite materials make it an increasingly crucial partner in new engine projects. And it is believed to have plans to design and build large-scale engines of its own. (*Wall Street Journal*, 17 June 1997)

The report quoted a Boeing official (who was not to be identified) as saying: 'IHI could very well surpass General Electric and Rolls-Royce in next-generation technology.' Indeed, more recently, IHI, in collaboration with WHI and MHI and with the promise of a 15 billion yen subsidy from MITI, has launched a project to develop a supersonic transport jet engine that will dramatically reduce noise levels and nitrogen oxide discharges compared with conventional supersonic engines, and which could go into commercial use around 2005. According to a report in *Nihon Keizai Shimbun*, 'the Japanese team is currently ahead of other countries in developing such engines', and GE, Pratt and Whitney, Rolls-Royce, and Snecma are set to join in the Japanese-led project (*Nihon Keizai Shimbun*, 17 Apr. 1999).

It seems, as yet, far too early to be sure about the long-run sustainability of US corporations' competitive advantage in electronics, aero-engines, and other industries. What is beyond question, however, is that the skill-base bias of US corporate investment means that a significant proportion of the US labour force who previously had access to stable and remunerative corporate employment has found that increasingly in the 1980s and 1990s their scope to make a productive contribution to the US economy and to earn a reasonable wage from doing so has narrowed dramatically. One clear symptom of these problems in the US economy is the worsening of the income distribution. That US labour economists have failed to provide an adequate explanation of growing income inequality seems, at least in part, to be attributable to their neglect of the influence of corporate strategies, and indeed the whole system of corporate governance, on technology, work organization, and, as a consequence, the employment options available to the US workforce.

Proponents of the 'new market economy' would argue, however, that it is not through the reinvestment strategies of existing corporations that one should expect better employment opportunities to emerge. The argument can be summarized as follows. The release of labour and capital from major corporations has provided the basis for the flourishing of new ventures in industrial districts such as Silicon Valley based on the highly dynamic and internationally competitive US information technologies sector. In effect, the dismantling of corporate control over the allocation of resources and returns in the economy has enabled labour and capital markets to reallocate those resources to start-up companies that are fast, flexible, and innovative and that are driving the current boom in the US economy. In cross-national comparative perspective, it is claimed, such dynamic new ventures are precisely what are missing in Japan and many of the advanced economies of Europe. Nothing could do more to jump-start these economies than to import American-style institutional investing and corporate restructuring so that the mechanisms of the market can redirect the allocation of labour and capital.

The current boom conditions in the US economy, and the undoubted success of Silicon Valley in the information technology sector, would seem to provide powerful support to those who argue that the pursuit of shareholder value is the path to sustainable prosperity. Yet, for those concerned with promoting equity and stability in the global economy there are a number of reasons why, even for the United States, let alone for other nations, the American-style new venture model may not be the superior alternative to corporate resource allocation that it is purported to be. Moreover, it may very well exacerbate existing problems related to resource allocation by major US corporations.

First, in the 1980s and 1990s employment in successful new ventures in the United States has consisted of relatively narrow and concentrated skill bases that bring lasting benefits mainly to the most highly educated segments of the population. Indeed, these new ventures have been able to draw on an international pool of highly educated labour, thus making it less necessary for the United States, as a society, to invest in upgrading the overall quality of education available to the American labour force. Almost a third of scientists and engineers in Silicon Valley, for example, are Asian-born, and many others originate in Israel and Europe. Thus, employers from the region are applying considerable pressure on the US government to loosen immigration restrictions so that they can have access to an even greater pool of foreign labour who come to work (often after studying) in the United States with high-quality primary and secondary educations from their native countries.

Within the US economy, therefore, the success of the new venture model may well exacerbate the problem of the distribution of income as it rewards the most highly educated segment of the labour force extremely well without applying pressure for the upgrading of the training and education, especially at the primary and secondary levels, for many, if not most, Americans. In Silicon Valley, for example, households in the bottom 20 per cent of the income distribution experienced an 8 per cent decline in their real income from 1991 to 1997 compared with a 19 per cent increase for the top 20 per cent. As the *Economist* put it in an article entitled 'The Digital Divide',

The canneries and defence companies that used to provide immigrants with well-paid jobs have disappeared. High-tech giants such as Hewlett-Packard once prided themselves on their ability to promote talented shop-floor workers. Now they have contracted out their manufacturing to specialists, many of them abroad. The tone of the Valley is being set by smaller companies that value speed and flexibility above all else: a marvelous development for educated job-hoppers, but a dismal one for people who start at the bottom. (*Economist*, 17 Apr. 1999: 63–4)

To some extent, as the *Economist* suggests, ladders that used to allow people to climb from lower-quality to higher-quality jobs have been broken because fewer lower-quality jobs are being created in high-tech regions. But, as the article also suggests, there is also a growing tendency by centre firms to treat certain groups of workers as members of a contingent workforce in a way that they have not done in the past. The phenomenon of 'permatemps' has now become an increasingly important feature on the employment landscape in Silicon Valley and in high-tech firms more generally. In many cases these workers not only lack prospects of advancement towards the core of these companies, but also lack basic health insurance and pension provision.

Secondly, remuneration in the information technologies sector has increasingly relied on stock-based rewards. The sustained boom in the stock market has made stock options extremely important for attracting and retaining employees both in new information-technology companies and in established enterprises that have to compete with new ventures for personnel. These remuneration schemes meant, for example, that in 1998 both Microsoft and Intel spent more on stock repurchases than they did on research and development. Many smaller companies are in effect financing themselves by the willingness of employees to accept stock options in lieu of immediate remuneration.

Just how important stock options are in substituting for wages and salaries is suggested by the material effect on the earnings of a number of leading high-tech firms of accounting for these options as a current expense. According to a recent study by

Smithers and Co., a consulting firm, if reported earnings in 1996 were adjusted to take account of the costs of stock options, Intel, Microsoft, Cisco Systems, Dell Computer, Hewlett-Packard, and Texas Instruments would have reported losses; the earnings of a number of other companies, such as Computer Associates International, Oracle, and Sun Microsystems would have shown a more than 300 per cent drop in their earnings (*Forbes*, 18 May 1998: 216). The angry reaction from high-tech executives to proposals by the Financial Accounting Standards Board (FASB) that would require companies to account for options as operating expenses is also suggestive of their materiality. Thus, to the extent that the stock market turns down, and with it the expectations for gains on stock options, it seems likely that many new ventures will find that the financial commitments required to develop and utilize productive resources are beyond their means or those of the venture capitalists who support them.

Thirdly, as already discussed in Chapter 4, the historical foundations of the technologies that are currently being developed and utilized by US new ventures lie in the successful growth of a wide variety of established US corporations—IBM, Hewlett-Packard, Lucent Technologies (formerly part of AT&T), Motorola, Xerox, Texas Instruments, Intel, and Microsoft, to mention only some of the more prominent ones—whose own development relied, directly or indirectly, on massive government procurement contracts and research initiatives over the past decades. The current reallocation of labour and capital to new ventures in the United States is just the most visible tip of the developmental iceberg, once known as the 'military-industrial complex', that took the American economy decades to put in place. There are questions about whether, in taking advantage of the profitable opportunities made possible by this accumulated investment in technological infrastructure, the American economy is currently regenerating the new technological infrastructure that can provide foundations for equity and stability in the twenty-first century.

An article in *Electronic Business* in November 1998 reported that executives at a number of leading high-tech firms such as Applied Materials Inc., Intel, TI, Cisco, and HP had acknowledged that most of their R&D is aimed at products scheduled for sale within five years or less. Increasingly, they rely on external R&D, including consortia with other firms, ties with universities, licensing agreements, and venture funds to finance start-ups, for access to long-term research. That trend is worrying many in the industry. Mark Weiser, chief technologist at Xerox's Palo Alto Research Center, expresses concern that the electronics industry is not committing adequate resources to basic long-term research and contends that '[t]he electronics industry is doing well now because of research investments made 20 years ago' ('The New R&D', *Electronic Business*, Nov. 1998: 4).

Finally, those new ventures that do become successful—and they are only a very small minority of all startups—must pursue a 'retain and reinvest' strategy if they are to become generators of remunerative and stable employment opportunities. From this point of view, one major problem in the current institutional environment in which these ventures are being formed is that the enormous pool of venture-capital money chasing deals in high-tech industries may well be making it more difficult for new ventures to become successful over the long term. That potential problem is in turn related to the financial revolution of the 1980s and 1990s, which has led to a persistent search for higher and higher yields by institutional investors.

The annual flow of money into the venture capital industry steadily declined from 1987 to reach a low point of less than $2 billion in 1991. Since then there has been a substantial revival in the fortunes of the industry, with new commitments to venture capital funds rising especially fast from 1993 to a record of $6 billion in 1996. The increased inflows are related to improvements in returns achieved by the venture capital industry, after the decade of extremely poor results discussed in Chapter 4.

As the experience of the 1980s showed, however, being awash with money is not necessarily a good thing for the venture capital business. Thus, the surge in fundraising from the middle of 1990s has led to concerns among some students of the industry that the venture market is overheating. For example, in a recent article entitled 'Venture Capital Growing Pains: Should The Market Diet?', Paul Gompers expressed concern that the pace of inflows had fostered an environment in which venture capitalists could operate with few controls:

In the current fundraising environment, established venture capital organizations have the luxury of raising new funds with little effort. In fact, their most difficult job is often determining how to ration the intended investment of potential investors. In these situations, the venture capitalist can raise money on his own terms. Funds raised over the last several years are witnessing large increases in fees with a concomitant reduction in the number and restrictiveness of covenants. Institutional investors have little recourse if they want to continue investing in private equity. If they refuse to invest, many others will step in to take their place. The importance of this shift in the balance of power is critical in the future health of the industry. (Gompers 1998: 1099)

The specific symptoms of the laxity of the environment that Gompers highlights include upward pressure on the prices of venture deals, a reduction in the relative amount of money invested in early-stage companies by venture capitalists, an increase in the compensation of venture capitalists, much of it in the form of stock distributions as opposed to cash payments, and a reduction in the restrictiveness of limited partnership agreements that govern their investment behaviour (Gompers 1998: 1095).

Contributing to the problem of overheating in venture capital are trends in the market for initial public offerings (IPOs). Rising returns to venture capitalists have been fuelled by the strength of the IPO market, which is a crucial determinant of returns on venture capital funds (Gompers 1998: 1093). It seems true, therefore, as Bernard Black and Ronald Gilson contend, that 'a well-developed stock market that permits venture capitalists to exit through an initial public offering (IPO) is critical to the existence of a vibrant venture capital market' (Black and Gilson 1998: 245). What Black and Gilson do not mention, however, is that the IPO market which generates incentives for venture capitalists to make commitments to companies that they can later take public is, as a highly speculative market, a far cry from the efficient market of orthodox financial economics. This fact was recently captured in an article in *Fortune* called 'The Ugly Truth about IPOs', which pointed out that of the 3,500 companies who had gone public since 1993, more than half of them were trading below their offering price and a third of them were more than 50 per cent below that price. The article goes on to say that 'the typical IPO of the last decade proved to be at best a mediocre investment—and at worst an outright wealth destroyer' (*Fortune*, 23 Nov. 1998). More generally, the IPO market has been shown by a number of academic studies to be particularly prone to bubbles and fads (Heisler 1994: 88–9). Arguably one of the most striking examples of such a phenomenon is the recent hubris surrounding the IPOs of Internet companies ('Anything.com Likely to be Hottest Issue in Class of '99', *New York Times*, 18 Jan. 1999).

To the extent that the stock valuations of startup companies deviate substantially from their real economic value, it is questionable whether the reliance on stock option rewards is a healthy foundation for the incentives of participants in these ventures. Employees of these companies may face the perverse incentive of leaving good companies to work for less viable ones to the extent that the stocks of the latter are more overvalued than those of the former. In the limit, bad companies could drive out good companies by acting as a barrier to their retention of staff.

These various trends raise serious questions about the likely economic effect of the current process of venture creation on the long-term process of development and utilization of productive resources in the US economy. In fact, notwithstanding the conventional wisdom on the subject in popular and academic circles, we know very little about the efficacy of American-style venture capital for generating innovation as compared with alternatives. In Gompers' words,

while recent work has examined international patterns of venture fundraising, no work has yet undertaken a study of the relative efficiency of the technological innovation process in different financial systems. Is the US venture capital model really superior to the Japanese model of innovation within a large company? (Gompers 1998: 1102)

In the current climate there is good reason to question the common assumption that the vibrancy of venture capital fundraising necessarily promotes the development of the economy, given that it seems to be encouraging somewhat disturbing trends in the behaviour of those involved in the startup and buildup of new ventures.

6.5. Conclusion

The promotion of equity and stability in any economy requires an understanding of the kinds of organizations, institutions, and policies that will enable these new enterprises to 'retain and reinvest' in ways which enable them to prosper and grow. Even if the current technological and market environment calls for the downsizing of established corporations and the spawning of new enterprises, equity and stability in the US economy will only be possible when the quantity of good jobs lost through corporate restructuring is more than replaced by better jobs created through enterprise growth. Moreover, unless major business enterprises have an interest in investing in a larger quantity of superior employment opportunities than is now the case, they will have little interest in supporting governmental efforts to upgrade the nation's education, training, and research capabilities.

If there are questions about the foundations and future of productive investment in the United States, there are also questions about the sources and availability of American savings. Corporate policies of 'downsize and distribute' have provided the underlying impetus to the stock market boom of the 1990s, but the sustained and rapid rate of increase in stock prices is the result of a massive flow of funds into the stock market through equity-based mutual funds. Since the 1960s US households have been increasing the proportion of their financial assets that are invested in pension and mutual funds. Reflecting their growing importance in managing the savings of US households, pension and mutual funds' shares of corporate equities have increased dramatically. In the late 1990s, the dramatic trend towards the institutionalization of share ownership may well slow down as individual investors rush into the booming market, in some cases even giving up their jobs to become day traders. Yet, the persistence of the momentum behind the extended stock market boom, or more precisely of the massive inflows to the equity markets and the rising expectations of portfolio investors that are central to supporting that momentum, is open to question.

The savings rate of US households, already low by international standards in the 1980s, has plunged further in the 1990s. Today, an older generation of Americans— the ones who were able to accumulate significant savings, pensions, and other assets during the era of 'retain and reinvest'—may be reallocating their financial resources to capture the returns of the booming stock market. But what if, as appears to be the case, the younger generations, living in an era where corporations are not willing to make the commitment to their workforces that they have in the past, will not have the same opportunities as the older generations for the accumulation of financial assets? And, indeed, what if the returns to the financial assets of older generations, who have become increasingly reliant on the stock market for returns on their savings to fund their consumption expenditures, cannot be sustained?

7

From Managerial to Contested Control in Germany

7.1. Introduction

Corporate governance has, in recent years, become a highly charged political issue in Germany. Since 1993, when Germany entered its worst recession in post-war history, there has been an escalation of the perennial debate about *Industriestandort Deutschland* or 'Germany as an industrial location'. Many German employers claim that the high wages, short working hours, tight labour market regulations, and high taxes that prevail in Germany have undermined the international competitive position of German industry. They warn that German companies will be forced to relocate production abroad if drastic reforms of corporate structures, and, indeed, the foundations of the social market economy, are not undertaken to ensure closer attention to the bottom line.

In parallel to their expression of concern about conditions in their external environment, some prominent German corporate managers have been calling for an increased focus in corporate resource allocation on 'shareholder value', even if it comes at the expense of social cohesion. In emphasizing the need to 'create value for shareholders' these German managers are now expounding the view that has dominated the US discussion of corporate governance for more than a decade. It is more than a little ironic that a perspective which stresses the importance of financial mobility as a route to optimal economic outcomes is gaining ground among influential German corporate managers, bankers, and academics. Only a short time ago the availability of 'patient capital' on the basis of close bank–industry relations was regarded as a critical strength of the German post-war system of governance, in comparison with its US and British counterparts (see, for example, Albert 1991; Porter 1992; Streeck 1995). Yet, in the 1990s, companies like Daimler-Benz and Deutsche Bank, previously seen as synonymous with the German system of corporate governance, have been in the forefront of the shareholder value movement in Germany.

The rhetoric of shareholder value, as invoked by German managers, has not gone unchallenged. German labour representatives have had a significant voice in the governance of German corporate enterprises in the post-war period and some of them have publicly expressed their disquiet with talk of shareholder value and the ideology of casino capitalism of which, they allege, it is a harbinger. Moreover, from a very different quarter, among serious proponents of shareholder value, there is a certain scepticism that German managers know what they mean, and mean what they say, when they speak of the merits of shareholder value for enhancing corporate performance. As an article in *Euroweek* put it: 'Some [bankers] speak glowingly about the changes which are now being brought about in German boardrooms with respect to shareholder value; others can scarcely prevent themselves from laughing at the notion that, with a very few exceptions, corporate Germany has made any progress at all towards realising shareholder value' (*Euroweek*, April 1998).

What then is at stake in contemporary discussions of corporate control in Germany? Has the battle been joined that will determine the future of the German system of corporate governance? Or do contemporary discussions of the subject reflect rhetorical sparring among various interest groups to secure tactical advantage? To understand why the German system of corporate governance has recently become such a controversial subject, as well as the likely significance of contemporary discussions of the subject in Germany, we have first to understand the political and economic foundations of the post-war system of corporate governance, a task that I undertake in this chapter. Secondly, we must analyse the extent to which recent political and economic trends are confronting these foundations, a subject that I will take up in Chapter 8.

Like its US counterpart, the characteristic features of the post-war system of corporate governance in West Germany have deep roots in the region's history. In section 7.2, I analyse the evolution of managerial control in pre-war Germany and identify its central institutional foundations as inter-company shareholding and bank–industry relations. These institutions persisted in the Federal Republic of Germany (FRG) after the war. Through the institution of codetermination, however, the post-war system of corporate governance was transformed beyond its narrow pre-war confines into a contested form of organizational control, as described in section 7.3. In shaping control over corporate resource allocation, these social conditions were complemented by institutions—especially the dual system of apprenticeship—that supported the organizational integration of resources in German business enterprises. In section 7.3 I discuss how, on the basis of the system of governance that supported organizational control, German companies achieved considerable success in industrial sectors in which high quality was more important than low cost as a basis for competitive advantage. I also analyse how the type of organizational control that emerged in the post-war period influenced the distribution of wealth in the economy.

7.2. The Pre-war Foundations of Managerial Control

From the late nineteenth and early twentieth century, the competitive success of major German enterprises was built on a system of institutions that supported the integration of managers in organizational learning processes. Supporting investments in the incentives and abilities of managers was the evolution of a governance system that created the social conditions on which managerial insiders gained control over the allocation of resources and returns in the German corporate economy. Although the institutions of worker apprenticeship and codetermination have roots that date back to the medieval guilds and the Bismarck era respectively, they were not systematically integrated into the pre-war German system of corporate governance, notwithstanding attempts to do so during the Weimar period. Thus, organizational control in Germany before the war was essentially managerial control.

7.2.1. The Organizational Integration of Managers

The competitive success of the German enterprises that emerged to dominate their markets from the late nineteenth century was originally built on the basis of institutions which supported the integration of managers into the organizational learning processes undertaken by these enterprises. During the same period, the US, as I have already noted, also experienced a transformation of the social organization of enterprise that involved the long-term employment of professional managers by business organizations. What was distinctive about the German enterprises, in comparison with their US counterparts, was the depth of technical learning among managerial insiders and the close links that were forged between science and industry.

During the nineteenth century Germany put in place the world's most sophisticated system of higher education, which would ultimately make the nation a leader in the science-based chemical and electrical industries. State-building ambitions, particularly those of Prussia in the wake of its ignominious defeat by Napoleon, provided the initial incentive for the promotion of technical education. To develop and disseminate technical knowledge in the Prussian economy, the Berliner-Gewerbe Institute was established in 1821, followed by a number of other technical institutes (originally *Polytechnische Schulen*, renamed as *technische Hochschulen*), and a network of trade schools in the provinces (Gispen 1989; Konig 1993).

From the middle of the nineteenth century, these schools became important in supplying the emerging German industrial sector with technically trained managers. Industrial enterprises also forged long-term research links with these educational establishments, often sending their employees to work on joint projects with academics (Landes 1969; see also Keck 1993). Complaints abounded in the latter half of the century, however, that the increasing emphasis on theoretical knowledge in the education of engineers was undermining German industrial performance, particularly in industries such as light machinery in which the US held the advantage through mass production based on interchangeable parts (Gispen 1989). In the 1890s the German government introduced a new type of engineering education, a network of *Ingenieurschulen*—designed to supplement the existing system of higher technical institutes—that was consciously modelled on the practical skills and shop training of US engineers (even as 'shop culture' was making way for 'school culture' in the US) (Gispen 1990; Calvert 1967).

The continued conflict for professional status between an academic group of engineers and a more practice-oriented faction ultimately led to the concentration of power in the engineering profession in the hands of a third group—the managerial and entrepreneurial engineers—who had an interest in integrating theory and practice and had the ability to cement the links between German industry and technical education (Gispen 1989). The resulting relations between industry and institutes of higher education played a critical role in supporting the nation's competitive advantage in chemicals, metals, electrical machinery, and heavy machinery. In the first few years of this century, the balance of German exports shifted from textiles and consumer goods to these technically based industries (Chandler 1990).

The more important that technical knowledge became for the activities of a business enterprise the more likely it was that technically trained recruits would take over managerial functions (Kocka 1980: 95). By 1900 many German companies had built hierarchies of salaried managers and many of these managers were engineers. Some of these technically trained administrators succeeded in climbing high enough within these companies to participate in strategic decision-making. Although family control remained more pervasive in Germany than in the US at this time many well-known German entrepreneurs and their family members were talented engineers in their own right.

German companies initially acquired international competitive advantage from the late nineteenth century primarily by developing and integrating skills within the managerial structure rather than on the shop floor. An apprenticeship system in *Handwerk* existed that had its roots in the guild system of craft apprenticeship in the Middle Ages. It provided many workers to the burgeoning industrial sector but was not specifically designed to serve the needs of industry (Sorge and Warner 1986). Many of the larger employers thus invested in their own facilities and programmes to modify and supplement the traditional training structures. However, these schools provided only minimal instruction in industrial work for traditionally trained craftsmen. German employers controlled the workplace, and dominated the process of shop-floor skill formation, but generally proved unwilling to extend organizational integration to their shop-floor work forces.

7.2.2. *The Institutional Support for Financial Commitment*

Supporting investments by managerial insiders in the development and utilization of corporate resources was a set of institutions that evolved to furnish financial commitment to German industry. In comparative perspective, the relationship between the Berlin credit banks or 'Great Banks' (*Grossbanken*) and major German industrial enterprises is one of the most distinctive features of the country's industrialization process during the last decades of the nineteenth century. Especially after German unification in 1871, these banks, the A. Schaafhausen'scher Bankverein, the Disconto-Gesellschaft, the Darmstädter Bank, and the Berliner Handelsgesellschaft, which were established prior to unification, and the Deutsche Bank, the Commerz- und Disconto-Bank, the Dresdner Bank, and the Nationalbank für Deutschland, which were set up in the decade after it, acted as venture capitalists by providing financial commitment to developmental investments. In servicing the demands of industry, the banks advanced capital through current account arrangements that operated like a combined deposit account and line of credit (Riesser 1931: 266; Whale 1930: 37–8). In 1883, credit advanced by these banks through current accounts comprised 51 per cent of credit extended by the *Grossbanken*; in 1913, 73 per cent (Eistert and Ringel 1971: 156).

The *Grossbanken* initially set up technical departments, and, later, trustee

(*Treuhand*) societies, to help them evaluate the organizational and technological capabilities of the companies that they financed. To remain close to strategic decision-making, they secured seats on the *Aufsichtsräte* (supervisory boards) of their client companies. The *Grossbanken* that came to dominate German industrial finance in the 1880s and 1890s were those that played this venture capital role for the mining, machinery, and electrical industries.

When these ventures became going concerns, the banks floated shares to the public to enable these companies to repay bank loans (Riesser 1931: 368; Whale 1930: 37–52; Pohl 1984: 80–1). These issues began the process through which equity ownership became separated from control in a number of leading German industrial enterprises. The banks first took the securities on their own books and then distributed them when they deemed conditions favourable (Whale 1930: 446–8; Feldenkirchen 1991: 131; Tilly 1992: 104). After a flotation, the banks maintained a continuing relationship with the joint-stock company (*Aktiengesellschaft* or AG) but generally ceased to finance its investments. Even for companies that had relied heavily on bank finance in their early stages and maintained current account links with the banks, retained earnings became the foundation of their continued growth as going concerns (Pohl 1984: 80; Feldenkirchen 1991: 129, 1983, 1985; Hoffmann *et al.* 1965: 273; Rettig 1978; Tilly 1986; Wellhöner 1989).

The *Grossbanken* also provided financial commitment to proprietary enterprises in which the founding families had already financed the transition from new venture to going concern. In some instances, bank financing became important when what had been a going concern found itself in financial distress (Wellhöner 1989: 97, 107, 121, 125–34, 155–7, 171–3, 217; Feldenkirchen 1991: 126–7). In such cases, the *Grossbanken* sometimes used their influence to insist that the enterprise be reorganized as an *Aktiengesellschaft* (Kocka 1971: 147–8; Gall *et al.* 1995: 37–45; Edwards and Ogilvie 1996: 439–40). To the extent that these 'bail-outs' proved successful, as in bank-financed ventures, the industrial enterprises in question came to rely increasingly on retained earnings as a source of investment finance (Feldenkirchen 1991: 128).

In providing financial services to industry, the *Grossbanken* had a strong interest in institutional arrangements that bolstered financial commitment to industrial enterprises. The *Grossbanken* derived their revenues not only from current account transactions but also from their securities businesses, which from 1885 to 1908 contributed almost 25 per cent of the gross profit of the credit banks, with the gross profit generated through commissions on securities issues increasing more than five-fold over the period. Industrial securities were an important component of this business; such shares accounted for 25 to 30 per cent, and industrial bonds 7 to 12 per cent, of the market value of securities issued in Germany during the early 1900s (Riesser 1931: 334–6, 359–63, 465).

The *Grossbanken* took pains to build their reputations as issuers of high-quality securities known as *Emissionskredit*. This reputation facilitated flotations of their own and their clients' securities. A bank's current account relationship with an industrial enterprise gave it access to information for evaluating the enterprise's strength and thus its potential attractiveness to portfolio investors. Their *Emissionskredit* was so valuable to the banks that they were inclined to repurchase shares they had issued if there was a subsequent decline in stock prices (Riesser 1931: 5–6, 247, 356, 368; Whale 1930: 121).

The *Grossbanken* placed securities with investors in their own deposit networks, and worked hard to ensure that their depositors were content with the quality of their portfolios. Their success in building a far-reaching network of deposit branches, a process in which Deutsche Bank took the lead, allowed the *Grossbanken* to greatly expand their capacity to float securities (Riesser 1931: 9–10, 608). Within these networks, the banks deliberately sought out those investors who would be stable stockholders. To attract them, the banks encouraged industrial companies to maintain stable dividends while recognizing the need of industrial managers to retain earnings for reinvestment (Hoffmann 1959; Pohl 1984: 81).

The proxy voting system, or *Depotstimmrecht*, gave the banks significant influence over the allocation of corporate resources. Then, as now, the predominance of bearer shares gave the banks the right to vote securities that they held on deposit, in trust for their customers (Riesser 1931: 608–11; Whale 1930: 54). An important inducement to the widespread deposit of shares was an exemption for shares held in trustee accounts from a stamp tax imposed by Bismarck on the transfer of shares (Riesser 1931: 324, 618–22). By encouraging stable shareholding and by coordinating the exchange of shares among their own customers, the *Grossbanken* largely usurped the business of the German stock exchanges. In 1907 the *Frankfurter Zeitung* contended: 'Considering the way in which affairs have developed on the stock exchange, one should speak today of the trend in banking rather than the trend of the stock exchange, because the big banks are increasingly turning the latter into a subservient instrument and directing its movements as they see fit' (*Frankfurter Zeitung*, 21 June 1907, quoted in Hilferding 1981: 149; see also 107–29, 130–50).

By creating a market in industrial shares and controlling the proxy votes as trustees of these shares, the *Grossbanken* contributed to the separation of ownership of stock from control over the allocation of corporate resources. As Germany's leading industrial enterprises evolved, the banks inevitably had to share control with salaried managers within industrial enterprises, on whose administrative and technical experience they had to rely for allocating corporate resources (Kocka 1980: 92, 1973; Whale 1930: 55–65). By 1900, in many of the most successful companies, the autonomy of industrial managers in strategic decision-making had increased as the practice of maintaining an exclusive relationship with one bank, or *Hausbank*, had lost ground to multi-bank links. Some of these multiple financial linkages developed through mergers; others reflected the deliberate attempts of financially strong companies to restrict the influence of any one bank. More generally, the high profitability of leading industrial enterprises led to enormous competition among banks to provide financial services to these companies (Whale 1930: 55–7; Edwards and Ogilvie 1996: 440; Feldenkirchen 1991: 133; Kocka 1980: 89–98; Pohl 1984: 82; Wellhöner 1989: 236–47).

In a number of leading German enterprises, families rather than the *Grossbanken* ensured financial commitment. At companies like Siemens, Krupp, Deutscher Kaiser (Thyssen), Rheinische Stahlwerke (Wolff), Hörder Verein and Stollwerk, the founders and owners continued to hold the majority of capital and laid down their firms' strategies (Brockstedt 1984: 237–67; Kocka 1971, 1973: 578–89; Pohl 1982: 439–71). In many of these family-controlled companies, the propensity to retain earnings would seem, in some cases, to have been heightened by the desire to avoid bank influence (Feldenkirchen 1991: 127). In all of these companies the key to the successful investment of retained earnings was the building of integrated organizations of salaried technical and administrative personnel (Kocka 1980; Chandler 1990: 393–587; Brockstedt 1984; Pohl 1982).

7.2.3. The Growing Autocracy of Managerial Control

The financial independence of leading industrial enterprises was strengthened further after the First World War. Expansion for war production, subsequent military defeat, the loss of international markets, and the victors' demands for reparation payments had a crippling effect on the German economy. Yet enterprises that before 1914 had invested in managerial organizations entered the Weimar Republic in relatively powerful positions. They had been accorded preferential treatment in the award of contracts by wartime military procurement offices. The large profits realized from those contracts, as well as their already substantial accumulated earnings, provided them with investment funds, or at least a capacity to borrow from abroad, at a time when the rest of industry was financially constrained (Turner 1985: 10–11; Pohl 1984: 85).

In the flight into fixed assets induced by the unprecedented inflation during the early Weimar years, many of these powerful enterprises converted their access to finance into an enormous expansion of their productive capacity. They also used these resources to take shares in other enterprises, thus creating industrial concerns (*Konzerne*). These were organizations in which a holding company held long-term shareholdings in a number of member firms that maintained their legal identities but combined some of their resources and coordinated certain dimensions of their activities. The holding office's task was to encourage an integration of the financial and investment strategies of these companies (Liefmann 1977: 225–32).

Many of the amalgamations were financially motivated and resulted in the creation of huge empires whose productive activities were unrelated or distantly related (Liefmann 1977: 249; Pohl 1984: 86–7). Some collapsed or ran into serious financial difficulties with the end of the inflation and the stabilization of the currency in 1924–5 (Liefmann 1977: 259–61; Feldenkirchen 1988: 126–7). Industrial combinations gained new justification in the aftermath of monetary stabilization as the *Rationalisierung* (literally, rationalization) of German industry, undertaken by major enterprises to control capacity and output, gained momentum (Levy 1935: 9, 10, 206–7). The process of building these structures created a dense web of interlocking shareholdings and directorates among companies. As a result, there was a substantial increase in the size of securities portfolios maintained by industrial corporations, from 10 per cent of net assets in 1913 to 30 per cent in the 1920s and 35–40 per cent in the 1930s (Tilly 1982: 160). By 1927 nearly all of the top 100 companies in Germany were *Konzerne* (Siegrist 1980: 87).

The post-war inflation and the profitability of financial transactions associated with conglomeration and rationalization, as well as increasing competition from the savings, cooperative, and foreign banks, shifted the *Grossbanken*'s business interests (Balderston 1991; Feldman 1992). Financial liquidity, which relies on the generation of high returns from existing assets, became relatively more attractive during the 1920s than financial commitment, the provision of services to promote industrial development. To cope with inflation, many of the *Grossbanken* turned from their traditional credit businesses to speculation in securities and foreign exchange. The *Grossbanken* made substantial paper profits during the inflation and increased their dividends to stockholders from between 7 and 12 per cent in 1919 to between 10 and 18 per cent in 1920 and between 13 and 24 per cent in 1921 (Whale 1930: 238). They also extended their business activities by buying up provincial banks at a relatively low cost, given the differential between the prices of their respective shares (Weber 1938: 147; Feldman 1992: 246–7).

The acceptance of the Dawes Plan and the return to gold restored international confidence in the German economy, with high interest rates attracting considerable capital imports, especially from the United States. The *Grossbanken*, meanwhile, had lost a substantial proportion of their deposits because of the inflation (Holtfrerich 1986: 271–8). Their securities business suffered as the domestic capital market languished following stabilization. Leading industrial enterprises increasingly bypassed the *Grossbanken* by raising money through foreign flotations underwritten by foreign banks (Balderston 1991: 572). The *Grossbanken* also faced increased competition from other domestic banks, in particular the deregulated savings banks (Feldman 1992: 563–5). From the late 1920s, in the face of falling profit margins, the *Grossbanken* financed riskier businesses, thus setting the stage for the 1931 German banking crisis.

Meanwhile, within industry, conglomeration and rationalization resulted in an overcentralization of strategic control (Levy 1935: 10, 227; Pohl 1982: 113–21). Increasingly, control was managerial rather than familial as dominant enterprises combined and bought out smaller companies. There has been, and remains, great controversy over the extent to which the industrialists who consolidated their power in the 1920s actively collaborated with the Nazis in the 1930s (Abraham 1981; Turner 1985). What is certainly clear is that when the Nazis rose to power, the highly concentrated industrial sector provided ready foundations for its coordination by the Third Reich to mobilize the economy for war.

Under the Nazi programme of militarization, financial commitment became paramount. The Nazis permitted profits to grow even as they controlled wages through a tight incomes policy; by 1938 profits were 105 per cent higher than they had been in 1928, whereas total wages were 3 per cent lower (Hoffmann *et al.* 1965: 506–9). To ensure that profits would be invested in productive capacity, the Nazis passed a Company Law in 1937 that formally recognized the separation of ownership and control which had already largely taken place in German industry. This act strength-ened the position of incumbent managers against what were described as 'the mass of irresponsible shareholders who largely lacked the necessary insight into the posi-tion of business' (Neumann 1944: 288). The Nazis also introduced a number of legal and taxation provisions that restricted dividend distributions and favoured the reten-tion of earnings (Pohl 1984: 91). From 1933 to 1938 retained profits on lucrative government contracts financed well over 60 per cent of the increase in industrial capital, with the rest coming from the issue of stock. New shares were not placed on the capital market but were absorbed by other industrial corporations. The Nazis also strengthened the linkages among companies through their policy of enforced cartelization followed by their system of main committees and industrial rings (Neumann 1944: 593; Pohl 1984: 91). Especially during the early 1940s, they trans-formed the economy's traditional sectors by forcing many smaller enterprises to inte-grate their industrial operations with those of the larger combines, which, through stockholdings, often assumed formal control (McKitrick 1994).

7.3. The Post-war System of Corporate Governance

Immediately after the war, in reaction to the abuse of concentrated power to which, as evidenced during the Nazi period, managerial control could lead, there was con-siderable political support for transforming the German system of corporate gover-nance. With Germany's defeat, the declared intention of the Allied Occupation forces, particularly the Americans, was to break up the concentration of economic power in German industry and banking and replace it with market control. But the onset of the Cold War, and the perceived importance of the West German economy as a bulwark against the power of the Soviets, led to a decline in the commitment to this path.

7.3.1. The Persistence of Financial Commitment

Despite the dissolution of industrial trusts, such as the I. G. Farben chemical combine, the constituent companies often re-emerged as dominant autonomous enterprises and established links with one another. Many of the major German industrial enterprises on which the post-World War II German economy relied were those that became dominant before World War II and prime vestiges of pre-World War II managerial control—namely, inter-company shareholding networks and bank–industry relations (as shareholders, as supervisory board members, and, most importantly, as trustees for their depositors' shares)—remained strong in the post-war decades. These institutions played an important role in insulating German enterprises from market control. Yet in Germany, as in many other advanced industrial economies, the most important source of financial commitment for the corporate sector in the post-war era was the access of the major industrial enterprises to internally generated funds which rendered most of them relatively independent of external sources of finance (Dyson 1986; Esser 1990: 17–32; Edwards and Fischer 1994: 228–40).

In general, inter-company links remained extremely tight in the post-war West German economy; in 1960 non-financial enterprises accounted for 35.7 per cent of total assets held in West Germany in the form of shares, making them by far the largest stockholder group (Edwards and Fischer 1994: 182). Although strictly comparable figures are not available, the level of inter-company stockholding would seem to have at least remained steady since then; in 1984 non-financial enterprises held 36.1 per cent of shares issued by German enterprises (Edwards and Fischer 1994: 180). Quantitatively much less important as a stockholding group than non-financial enterprises, banks and insurance companies nevertheless held significant equity participations in German corporations in the post-war period; banks accounted for between 7.6 per cent and 10.3 per cent in 1984 (depending on whether one includes investment funds which are, to a large extent, owned by the banks) of the total nominal value of shares issued by German companies (Edwards and Fischer 1994: 180).

A study of bank holdings in 74 large West German enterprises in 1974–5 showed that the 'Big Three'—Deutsche Bank, Dresdner Bank, and Commerzbank—together accounted for two-thirds of bank participations, and were thus among the most influential stockholders in the West German economy (Gessler Commission 1979: 467). The single most important stockholder in Germany was not, however, a bank but the country's largest insurance company, Allianz AG. Insurance companies as a group accounted for a relatively small proportion of the shares of German enterprises, but Allianz appeared in many of the inter-company shareholding networks that span German industry and for this reason was often referred to as 'the spider in the web' (Owen Smith 1994: 338).

The importance of inter-company shareholding explains the substantial difference between patterns of direct and ultimate shareholding in the German corporate economy. In 1973 more than 70 per cent of the market value of the equity capital of listed AGs was accounted for by companies in which the share of the largest shareholder was at least 25 per cent (Iber 1985: 1111). A study of the 300 largest German industrial enterprises in 1972 showed that, classified in terms of direct ownership, 'owner-controlled' companies accounted for 75.1 per cent of the sample's aggregate turnover; in contrast, when categorized in terms of ultimate ownership, manager-controlled firms accounted for the majority of total turnover (64.6 per cent) and owner-controlled firms for 35.4 per cent (Schreyogg and Steinmann 1981: 533–56).

The gap between direct and ultimate ownership largely stemmed from the fact that the companies which represented the most important nodes in inter-company shareholding networks are among the most diffusely held in Germany. But even these companies have been insulated from market control in the post-war period. More than 75 per cent of the value of domestic shares in Germany were held on deposit by the private banking sector, and the vast majority of these shares were deposited with the Big Three (Owen Smith 1994: 359). They exercised proxy voting rights for these shares, subject to certain requirements for stockholder approval. The Monopolkommission concluded from an analysis of the equity votes represented at general meetings of stockholders in 1974 that banks controlled an average of 56.7

per cent of the total votes. Only 7 per cent came from the banks' own stockholdings and an enormous 49.5 per cent was based on the proxy votes that they exercised on behalf of their depositors (Monopolkommission 1978: 199). The importance of proxies was greater for the largest AGs; in the ten largest AGs by turnover the banks controlled a total of 67 per cent of the votes compared with 42.6 per cent in the AGs ranked from 51 to 100 (Monopolkommission 1978: 199).

It was their role as depositories of the shares of diffusely held companies that was the greatest source of potential influence by the banks on the German corporate economy. It gave them a significant voice at shareholder meetings and, since shareholders' representatives on supervisory boards were elected at the annual general meeting, on the composition of supervisory boards. In a study of supervisory board representation, the Monopolkommission found that banks were directly represented on the supervisory boards of 75 of the largest 100 AGs in 1974, with 179 seats in total being occupied by the banks, 102 by the *Grossbanken*, and 55 by Deutsche Bank alone (Monopolkommission 1978).

Notwithstanding the extent of bank representation on supervisory boards, Gerum, Steinmann, and Fees concluded, on the basis of their analysis of AGs with more than 2,000 employees in 1979, that banks could not control decision-making on the supervisory board, even if they acted in concert, because they only occupied 16.4 per cent of shareholder seats on average and 8.2 per cent of the total number of supervisory board seats. They also found, on the basis of their study of these companies' articles of incorporation, that in only 20 per cent of these cases was supervisory board consent required for the enterprise's general product or market strategy, and in only 10 per cent of companies was such consent needed for general business plans or investment finance plans (Gerum, Steinmann, and Fees 1988: 74). Members of the supervisory board tended to meet infrequently; for 86 per cent of the AGs surveyed their supervisory boards met only twice a year (Gerum, Steinmann, and Fees 1988: 108). Members of the supervisory boards—bankers or otherwise—were thus highly dependent on insiders for their understanding of the business. With some exceptions, the *Vorstand* (management board) rather than the *Aufsichtsrat* (supervisory board) is the main decision-making body of the German AG and its members are salaried managers who, in the post-war decades, generally have been promoted up through the enterprise (Lawrence 1984: 36).

The relationship of the *Grossbanken* to the allocation of corporate resources in the FRG has been the subject of ongoing controversy, as it was prior to and during World War II. Although these banks have often been portrayed as controllers of West German industry, the available evidence instead suggests that the banks have acquiesced in a post-war system of governance that bolstered insider control. In the highly regulated financial system that was put in place in the FRG and in which, through the regulation of banking competition, the *Grossbanken* were accorded the scope to develop strong positions in a number of attractive market segments, they had stronger incentives to support organizational control in the corporate economy than to confront it. They had a significant interest in the continued success of the Federal Republic of Germany's leading industrial enterprises since these companies represented a lucrative source of revenues for their short-term lending, export financing, and corporate financial services businesses (Gall *et al.* 1995: 610–56).

Bank control over corporate resource allocation, and certainly its uncontested exercise, seems implausible because of the banks' limited ability to exercise it. As I have already observed, there were real limitations to the exercise of bank power through direct shareholding, proxy votes, and supervisory board seats. Moreover, the access of the major industrial enterprises to internally generated funds rendered most of them relatively independent of bank finance (Dyson 1986; Esser 1990: 17–32; Edwards and Fischer 1994: 228–40). It should be pointed out, however, that in contrast to the relative financial autonomy of the large non-financial enterprises in Germany, the banking sector has played an important role in providing finance for small and medium-sized enterprises. The banks most actively involved in long-term financing activities for these companies were the savings and cooperative banks, rather than the commercial banks (Deeg 1995, 1996; Vitols 1995).

As had been the case before the war, so in its aftermath; internal funds soon became the predominant source of investment finance for major German industrial enterprises (Wallich 1955: 166). Indeed, the importance of retained earnings in financing German industrial reconstruction created considerable concern about the concentration of power in the hands of the propertied classes (Roskamp 1965). As early as the 1950s internally generated funds were by far the most important source of finance for German enterprises, funding more than 75 per cent of net investment. The banks, focused on the reconstruction of their own organizations and asset bases, had only limited funds to lend, and these tended to be provided in the form of short-term loans. Sometimes these funds were used by companies for long-term purposes but the banks attempted to limit this behaviour to control their maturity risk. To the extent that long-term funds were provided by the banking system, they were ultimately funded from the Marshall Counterpart Fund and channelled to the banks by the Kreditanstalt für Wiederaufbau (Reconstruction Loan Corporation) (Shonfield 1965: 276). The banks bore the credit risks of the loans that they made out of these monies—loans that were primarily directed toward bottleneck investments in the economy (Shonfield 1965: 279; Abelshauser 1982: 34–53).

As Table 7.1 shows, the importance of internal sources of investment finance persisted throughout the entire period from 1950 to 1989. Even after the reopening of capital markets in 1956, to the extent that large German companies have sought access to external finance, bank loans have been the preferred source rather than equity or bond issues; long-term debt accounted for 12.1 per cent of the net sources of investment finance and equity issues for a tiny 1.5 per cent (for an extended discussion, see Edwards and Fischer 1994: 49–70). In major industrial enterprises, internally generated funds were even more important as a source of finance for investment than for producing enterprises in general; internal funds accounted for 88.1 per cent of the net sources of finance for investment by large manufacturing AGs compared with 72.7 per cent for producing enterprises for the period from 1971 to 1985 and long-term loans accounted for 1.7 per cent and 14.4 per cent respectively (Edwards and Fischer 1994: 127). In international comparison German enterprises—large firms

TABLE 7.1 Net sources of investment for German producing enterprises, 1950–1989 (%)

	1950–89	1950–9	1960–9	1970–9	1980–9
Internally generated funds	75.4	75.4	74.1	71.3	80.1
Provisions for pensions by enterprises	3.7	3.2	2.0	4.3	4.9
Capital transfers from government	5.5	1.2	4.0	7.9	9.0
Bank borrowing	11.7	11.8	13.4	12.0	10.2
Long-term	12.1	9.0	11.5	15.6	12.6
Short-term	−0.4	2.8	1.9	−3.7	−0.4
Funds from insurance enterprises	0.5	1.2	0.9	0.5	−0.4
Bonds	0.5	2.3	0.7	−0.4	−0.7
Shares	1.5	1.9	2.4	0.6	1.1
Other	1.2	3.0	2.6	3.9	−4.1
Foreign trade credit	−1.2	0.0	−1.1	−1.5	−2.2
Total	100.0	100.0	100.0	100.0	100.0

Source: Edwards and Fischer (1994: 54).

as well as the producing sector as a whole—are as reliant, and if anything more reliant, on internal funds as a source of investment finance than their counterparts in other advanced industrial economies (Mayer and Alexander 1990: 450–75; Hall 1994: 110–43; Corbett and Jenkinson 1996: 71–96).

7.3.2. *Contesting Managerial Control: The Institution of Codetermination*

The legal framework introduced in the FRG after World War II preserved the main features of company law that ensured the subservience of the individual shareholder to the business organization. As Thomas Raiser put it:

Under German law, in the public company the power of the managing board is rather strong, because Article 76 rules directors to guide the company under their own responsibility, free from any binding instructions of either shareholders or supervisory board. Only fundamental changes require approval of the shareholder meeting, and the supervisory board may exercise a veto in certain cases where the by-laws provide such a veto. This widely discretionary power of the managing board favors a bias towards managerial 'absolutism' which sometimes hardly can be stopped. (Raiser 1988: 37)

A critical difference between the German system of corporate governance before and after the war, however, was that the institution of codetermination shifted pre-war managerial control toward a contested form of organizational control.

The onset of the Cold War led the US military government, with the cooperation of the newly installed FRG government, to block the more ambitious plans for integrating workers into the governance of industrial enterprises. The West German movement for industrial democracy thus fell short of its ambitions. Nevertheless, the post-war institution of codetermination (*Mitbestimmung*) did extend to workers some direct influence over the allocation of corporate resources, giving the FRG the most extensive formal system of employee representation in the world.

Codetermination is composed of two key elements: employee representation on the supervisory boards of corporate enterprises and on works councils that operate at plant level. Passed only under the threat of a major strike, the Codetermination Act of 1951 mandated parity worker representation on the supervisory boards of enterprises in the coal, iron, and steel industries (*Montanmitbestimmung*). It also provided that the labour director in these companies—a member of the management board—could not be appointed against the wishes of the worker representatives. In other industries, workers were denied equal representation; enterprises with more than 500 employees were obligated by the Works Constitution Act of 1952 (Betriebsverfassungsgesetz) to reserve only one-third of the supervisory board seats for employee representatives. The Codetermination Act of 1976, however, mandated that all companies with more than 2,000 employees increase employee representation on their supervisory boards from one-third to one-half of the seats. The position of chairman of the board was required by law to be filled by a shareholder representative. In the event of a tied vote he was granted a double vote. Thus the law firmly tilted the balance of control of the supervisory board against employees. Companies with more than 500 and less than 2,000 employees continued to allocate one-third of their supervisory board seats to worker representatives (Streeck 1984: 391–422; Raiser 1988: 111–29).

The control over resources that labour representatives exercise through their participation on supervisory boards is limited by the restricted role that the board as a whole plays in corporate decision-making. Indeed, there have been suggestions that employers have limited the powers of the *Aufsichtsrat* as a whole with a view to further controlling the influence of employees (Gerum, Steinmann, and Fees 1988). Certainly, many German employers were hostile to the Codetermination Act of 1976 and they challenged it in the Federal Constitutional Court on the grounds that it violated private property rights (Raiser 1988; Thimm 1981: 13–22). The employers' case was, however, dismissed.

The formation of works councils (*Betriebsräte*)—the second instrument of employee influence over corporate decision-making—was mandated by the Works Constitution Act of 1952. These councils are elected by all blue-collar and white-collar workers in a plant and are designed to give labour the right to participate in and receive information about the management of the shop floor. Under the 1952 Act, works councils have important codetermination rights over issues such as working hours, piecework rates and bonuses, and working conditions, as well as transfers and dismissals. The Act also gives works councils rights to information about personnel planning, financial matters, and major strategic changes. Works councils' codetermination rights are thus strong with respect to social and personnel matters but weak in relation to financial and strategic issues (Müller-Jentsch 1986, 1995).

In contrast to the codetermination of supervisory boards, the works councils were a conservative initiative. In being granted exclusive domain over labour representation at the plant level, works councils were made formally independent of the unions. Intended to serve as a counterweight to the political power of the unions, the role of works councils was to cooperate with management for 'the benefit of the employees and of the establishment'. Fearing that they would transform labour representation in the FRG into a system of 'yellow' or enterprise unions that would ultimately undermine labour's political power, German unions stridently opposed the introduction of works councils (Markovits 1986; Müller-Jentsch 1995). What transpired in fact was that, notwithstanding their initial objections, the unions established close links to works councils so that by the early 1970s more than 80 per cent of works councillors in the FRG were union representatives (Thelen 1991: 80; Müller-Jentsch 1995).

Through works councils, worker representatives arguably exercise more influence over the allocation of enterprise resources and returns than they do through their seats on codetermined supervisory boards (Markovits 1986; Müller-Jentsch 1995). Even in areas where it does not have formal codetermination rights, a works council can delay management decisions by strategically using its rights in other areas (Müller-Jentsch 1995). The power of the works councils is, however, proscribed by the statutory ban on strikes to enforce workplace demands. Moreover, in exercising their influence through the mechanism of the works council, labour representatives, union members or otherwise, are legally bound to act in a manner that promotes the overall health of the enterprise (Müller-Jentsch 1986, 1995).

Besides the formal institutions of codetermination, the role of labour unions in collective bargaining is an important indirect channel through which workers, or more precisely worker representatives, can influence the allocation of corporate resources. The unions are organized along industrial lines and come together under an umbrella organization, the DGB (German Federation of Unions). Most employers are members of employers' organizations that bargain with unions over wages and other matters (Markovits 1986; Baethge and Wolf 1995).

The substance of employee representation in German corporate governance depends on the manner in which the various channels of worker influence—supervisory board representation, works councils, and union bargaining—interact with each other. Notwithstanding the substantial challenges for the labour movement in coordinating these channels, as well as the restrictions on the influence on corporate resource allocation that is possible through each of them, in historical and comparative perspective the institutions that support employee representation have certainly extended organizational control in German industry beyond pre-World War II managerial control.

7.3.3. Organizational Integration in Post-war Germany

The conditions of financial commitment and insider control that emerged in post-war Germany were complemented by institutions that supported the organizational integration of resources in German business enterprises. Of particular importance in the post-World War II era was the West German system of apprenticeship—the dual system—which provided the institutional support for the integration of workers with managers as insiders to the processes of organizational learning that generated the innovative capabilities and competitive advantages of German enterprises. The German experience is thus starkly contrasted with that of the US, where, to a large extent, workers have been excluded from organizational learning in the post-war decades.

The apprenticeship training structures in handicraft, industry, and services remained independent of each other until the Nazi period (Sorge and Warner 1986). During the last half of the 1930s and the early 1940s, the Nazis mobilized and reorganized the productive capabilities of the German economy for war. The authoritarian hand of the state intervened to shape the skill formation process in a critical way by integrating the *Handwerk* sector into German industry. The training system was standardized and regulated, thus laying the foundation for the modern German system of apprenticeship (McKitrick 1994). After World War II the government of the FRG retained training structures in much the same form as the Nazis had shaped them. The regulation and administration of apprenticeship training changed, however, to reflect changes in the social order.

The post-war German system of apprenticeship is a 'dual system' that combines formal vocational education and on-the-job training. Specifically, a full apprenticeship in this dual system entails practical training in a company for three or four days per week and attendance at a vocational school (*Berufsschule*) for the remainder of the work week. The practical workplace training provides systematic exposure to the whole range of work situations and problem-solving tasks in a legally defined and regulated occupation. At the end of three years the apprentice is examined on both theoretical and practical competence, and receives his skilled worker's certificate (*Facharbeiterbrief*) (Münch, various years).

Employers and workers, through their respective associations, exerted substantial influence on the structure of the apprenticeship system. Trade unions, employers' associations, and a number of government ministries participated in the joint regulation of the training system at the industrial and national levels. Employer and worker representatives influenced regional training policy through their participation on the vocational training committees of local chambers of commerce. The unions exerted only an informal influence on training at the enterprise level, but workers had some influence over the structure of in-firm training programmes and their implementation in the workplace through the works council (Münch, various years; Streeck *et al.* 1987). The costs of the apprenticeship system were borne in part by governments at the national and *Lander* levels, in part by employers through voluntary participation, and in part by apprentices themselves in the form of the relatively low wages that they received during their training period (Münch, various years; Casey 1986: 65).

The training structures that supported worker learning ensured that German production workers were highly skilled, thus permitting functions such as maintenance and quality control to be kept to a large extent on the shop floor (Sorge and Warner 1986: 124). A German worker's skilled status was not inextricably tied to his current job, and German unions were organized on an industrial rather than a craft basis. Technological change, therefore, did not threaten his conditions of employment to the same extent as it did a British craftsman, for whom the demarcation of his realm of work was a critical foundation of his bargaining power and reward structure. Hence the virtual absence of demarcation disputes in German companies (Lawrence 1980: 134; Sorge and Warner 1986: 101, 125; Lane 1989). Because workers were versatile in the tasks that they could perform, they could be redeployed in response to day-to-day variations in staffing requirements (Maurice, Sellier, and Silvestre 1986: 69). The standard term in German companies for this redeployment capability is *Einsatzbreite*, which was used both formally and informally in evaluating individual workers for promotion (Lawrence 1980: 134). The German worker's understanding of the systemic nature of production enhanced his capacity for technical problem-solving (Maurice *et al.* 1986: 70; Sorge and Warner 1993).

Central to the post-war success of German industry was the integration of worker skills with the technical skills of managers. German managers were notable for the high level of formal qualifications that they held (Lawrence 1980: 76). The vast majority of managers engaged on the technical side of German companies had engineering qualifications. Although less prevalent on the commercial side, engineering nevertheless boasted a stronger showing than any other discipline (Lawrence 1980: 80; Lane 1989).

Their strong technical backgrounds gave managers a detailed knowledge of the production process, with a particular emphasis on how to build high-quality products. The formal structures of skill formation on the commercial side of German enterprises have historically been less well developed than those on the technical side. German universities provided courses in business economics (*Betriebswirtschaftslehre*), but this distinctively German approach to business education emphasized operational management techniques rather than management as a discipline in its own right. Business education was also available through the vocational system in the form of commercial apprenticeships (*kaufmanische Lehre*). Like the study of business economics, however, these apprenticeships had a strong production focus (Lawrence 1980: 65, Locke 1984, 1989).

The high level of formal qualifications in German companies did not reflect an exclusive reliance on university campuses as a source of future managerial talent. German companies did recruit for their management structures from universities, in particular favouring those graduates with engineering degrees (*Diplom Ingenieur*) (Lawrence 1980: 76). However, these graduates were rarely admitted to senior levels immediately and were expected first to gain experience on the factory floor or in other operational areas (Smyser 1992: 70). Those who were recruited by the company without a university degree could also climb up the company hierarchy, in some cases from the shop floor to the boardroom. At the upper management levels, about one-quarter started their careers as workers (Maurice *et al.* 1986: 118).

To travel this path, an aspiring manager had to accumulate formal qualifications in addition to displaying practical capability within the firm. A network of vocational schools facilitated access to the formal education that allowed the student to build on his basic apprenticeship training. Before 1970 the standard route to admission to an engineering course, at what was then called an *Ingenieurschule*, was a three-and-a-half-year apprenticeship (Münch 1982). The engineering qualification offered by these schools, the *Ing Grad.*, was thus evidence of a student's extensive academic and practical training. The possibility for German engineers to position themselves for managerial careers through apprenticeship and vocational school provided an alternative to the academic route through a university. The *Ing. Grad.* degree proved very popular among German companies, and was particularly common at the middle-management level (Lawrence 1980: 66; Münch 1982).

The importance of additional formal education in improving promotion prospects in German companies was manifest in the close relationship between hierarchical position and formal qualification in German industry. The ability of apprenticed workers to become engineer-managers promoted hierarchical cooperation with a strong technological foundation. Many engineers, and the *Ing. Grad.* in particular, held the *Facharbeiterbrief*, and thus shared a common theoretical and practical knowledge base with the skilled worker and the foreman (*Meister*). The organizational integration of technical skills in the managerial and blue-collar structures of German companies led to a focus on quality in product and process, and many German companies competed on the basis of the excellence of their goods and services (Streeck 1992: 341). This common commitment of managers and workers to the strategy of producing high-quality products also complemented the extensive decentralization of production decision-making within enterprises.

The increase in the importance of technical skills in building competitive advantage rendered functional expertise, rather than a more general entrepreneurial capability, important as a basis for top managerial authority in German companies (Lawrence 1980: 183). Although functional expertise may not have been sufficient for a candidate to be promoted to the ranks of top management, the promotional policies of most German companies meant that it was a necessary condition of being considered for a senior corporate position. German managers have traditionally been rather sceptical of the notion that the qualities required in top managers could be effectively taught in the systematic manner used in American business education programmes. As a result, German post-experience management education programmes placed more emphasis on building relationships among top managers than on academic instruction. In 1979, on the basis of his study of fifteen large West German firms, Heinz Thanheiser observed:

The managers at the highest level, even on the board, were extremely sceptical about the idea of professionalism in management. They did not, then, share the confidence that their American colleagues had in the transfer of 'management know-how,' confidence which gave them the courage to create the 'conglomerates'. The German leaders [*dirigeants*] view diversification from a different angle: 'we have seriously studied the potential of Sector X (close to us from a technological standpoint) into which we could have easily entered. But nobody on the Board of Directors knows the market, the competitors, the clients . . . Consequently we don't touch it' (Thanheiser 1979, quoted in Locke 1989: 273).

As Thanheiser pointed out, such a view differed greatly from the dominant perspective in American business in the post-war decades, which has already been discussed in Chapter 4 (see also Dyas and Thanheiser 1976).

7.4. Corporate Governance and Performance

The institutionalization of organizational control in post-war Germany played a crucial role in the competitive strategies of those West German companies that competed on the basis of quality, and allowed them to develop a competitive advantage in markets such as luxury automobiles, precision machine tools, and electrical machinery—industries that until recently qualified as stable technology. The prevalence and success of high-quality, niche-market strategies in the German economy, and more fundamentally the social foundations of innovation and development in Germany that supported these competitive strategies, are readily seen in the structure of West German foreign trade. In 1979 the leading German exports were electrical and non-electrical machinery, which together amounted to DM78.2 billion, chemicals and pharmaceuticals (DM58.8 billion), and road vehicles (DM50.3 billion). These industries together accounted for 62.3 per cent of manufacturing exports but other product groups were also significant net exporters (OECD 1995: 146–7).

From the late 1960s and 1970s new industrial competitors, and in particular the Japanese, mounted competitive challenges to German industry as they had to the Americans. However, many German producers whose competitive advantage was based on their capacity to produce high-quality products managed to avoid confrontation with Japanese competitors. In the automobile industry, for example, luxury car producers such as Daimler-Benz, BMW, Porsche, and Audi were not directly hit by Japanese competition and they expanded production and employment through the 1970s. In the German car industry as a whole, however, import penetration increased from 30 per cent of the German market in 1970 to 41 per cent in 1980 (Jürgens et al. 1993: 36). In 1980, a quarter of the imported cars were produced in Japan; the share of Japanese brands in total registrations in Germany increased from 0.1 per cent in 1970 to 1.7 per cent in 1975 and then to 10.4 per cent in 1980 (AAMA 1983: 33–4, 1986: 36–7, 1990: 28–9).

These changes largely confronted Germany's high-volume car producers—VW, Opel, and Ford. All of these companies experienced a sharp fall in output and employment in 1974–5; VW, for example, cut back employment by 26 per cent or nearly 33,000 workers in 1974–5 (Streeck 1984: 56 ff.). These companies experienced a rapid recovery after the oil price crisis, although it was somewhat more muted at VW than at Opel and Ford (Jürgens et al. 1993: 36). But in the face of growing import penetration by the Japanese, all of the German car producers began to reorganize their production processes to move upmarket to higher-value-added strategies. They improved their product designs, quality, and product ranges and focused to an increasing extent on the European market, to which the Japanese producers had restricted access. With the domestic mass producers, especially Volkswagen, biting at their heels, the German luxury producers also pursued upgrading strategies during this period (Jürgens *et al.* 1993, 59–62; Streeck 1989).

An important exception to the sustained competitive success of the high-quality strategies of German producers was the binocular and camera industry. The Germans had achieved an apparently impenetrable market position but the Japanese managed to outcompete them through process innovation. By the early 1970s, German companies like Rollei, Voigtlander, and Zeiss, who had previously dominated the world market for expensive amateur photographic equipment, were reeling in the face of competition from Japanese products of comparable quality but much lower in price (Vogl 1973: 131–2).

The relative strength of Japanese producers in process innovation was also at the root of their success in competition with German producers in industries in which cost competition prevailed and in which the Germans had failed to develop distinctive bases of competitive advantage. In both Germany and Japan, organizational integration is prevalent, but differences in the nature of organizational learning, and in the social institutions that support it, are reflected in important variations in the innovative capabilities of enterprises. In Germany the internal organization of the enterprise derives from an industry-wide strategy to set high-quality product standards, whereas in Japan the organizational structure derives from an enterprise strategy to engage in continuous problem-solving to cut costs. In industries such as steel and consumer electronics, for example, the relative strength of Japanese companies in process innovation was to prove formidable.

The German steel industry expanded rapidly in the 1950s; from 1950 to 1960 German output of crude steel more than doubled, from 14 million tonnes to more than 34 million tonnes (Esser and Väth 1987: 632). Production increased from 1960 to 1974 but the industry was then already in the throes of rationalization; the number employed in the industry was reduced from 418,000 in 1960 to 346,000 in 1974 (Esser and Väth 1987: 634). With the intensification of competition in the 1970s, the German steel industry moved into crisis. Japanese capabilities posed a serious competitive challenge by this time; in 1975 a Japanese worker required 6.2 hours to produce a ton of raw steel, a German worker 8.9, an American worker 10.5, a French worker 12.1, and a British worker 17.4 (Esser and Fach 1989: 240). As Esser and Fach described the competitive position of the German steel industry, 'In technology and organisation Japan's steel industry was its superior, and the Japanese advantage held with respect to product quality as well as production technology' (Esser and Fach 1989: 240). Production, exports, and profits in the German steel industry all experienced major declines from the mid-1970s; employment fell by 60,000 in the period from 1974 to 1980 (Esser and Väth 1987: 635). By 1977 the European Community had introduced protectionist measures for the steel industry (Tsoukalis and Strauss 1987) and, although the German steel producers were generally hostile towards these measures, they gave the West German steel industry the space to restructure itself without sparking major social conflict (Esser and Fach 1989: 241).

The German consumer electronics industry was also severely affected by rising foreign competition. The industry had grown rapidly after the war; in 1950 it employed about 20,000 people and by 1970 employment had risen to 127,000 (Bosch 1990: 54). By 1983 40 per cent of the jobs in existence in 1970 had been lost and the industry was predominantly in foreign hands. Once again the main challenge came from the Japanese, who had developed superior capabilities in improving product reliability. But leading Japanese enterprises were also strikingly more productive; in the 1970s the number of man-hours per television set in Japan was 1.9 compared with 3.9 in Germany. The productivity difference has been attributed to the integrated approach to automation technology and the intensive training of personnel at all levels in Japanese firms (Scibberas 1977, 1981; Wengenroth 1997: 168).

It was not only in the integration of electronics in consumer goods that German companies encountered competitive problems during this period. Where the post-World War II system of governance was least successful as a basis for the competitive advantage of German enterprises was in computers, semiconductors, and telecommunications, industries that came into existence or were completely transformed after World War II through the development of electronics technology. Some German companies competed in these industries—for example, Siemens and Bosch in telecommunications—but in general the Germans failed to establish a national competitive advantage in these sectors in the post-war decades (see Malerba 1985; Van Tulder and Junne 1988; Sachwald 1994).

However, one German high-technology industry—the pharmaceuticals industry—performed extremely well. Indeed, German enterprises have a long history of competitive success in the pharmaceuticals and chemicals industry. One important explanation for the success of German companies in pharmaceuticals relative to other high-technology sectors seems to be rooted in the structure of the post-war educational system and, in particular, its shortcomings as the basis for the organizational integration of scientists into enterprise learning processes; in 1965 Japan had 8 per cent more scientists and engineers employed in non-academic jobs than West Germany; by the mid-1980s the gap had grown to 27 per cent (Keck 1993: 141). The German pharmaceuticals companies had benefited from such an integration, but in a much earlier era when the educational system had been structured along different lines; in the late nineteenth century, 'technological innovation, based on the country's educational and research systems, was the key factor that enabled the [dyestuffs, synthetic fertilizers, and pharmaceuticals] industry to establish itself as leader on the world export market' (Keck 1993: 127).

The system of organizational control had an important influence not only on the patterns of wealth generation in the German economy but also on the manner in which that wealth was distributed. It allowed West German employees to participate in the fruits of industrial success and, as a result, contributed to relatively low income inequality in West Germany as the country grew wealthier (Streeck 1995; Abraham and Houseman 1993). The system of organizational control also facilitated the spreading of the costs of industrial rationalization. Social plans, which provided for the protection of workers in the event of mass redundancies, were pioneered in the coal industry in 1957 and in the steel industry in 1963. There were major layoffs in other sectors of German industry in the 1950s and 1960s but it was only in the coal, iron, and steel industries, where parity representation had been established and unions were strong, that these plans were implemented (Bosch 1990: 31). In 1972, however, the Works Constitution Act made it compulsory for all firms with more than twenty employees to negotiate a social plan with the works council in the event of major changes in the firm.

The early social plans relied primarily on financial compensation to sustain redundant employees while they looked for new jobs (Bosch 1990: 31). From the mid-1970s, as the opportunities for redundant workers to find alternative jobs diminished, these plans relied more heavily on early retirement schemes to ease the burden of downsizing. Social plans therefore allowed employers to substantially reduce their labour forces without massive labour strife at a cost that was heavily subsidized by government early retirement schemes. Particularly important was the early retirement programme for unemployed workers. If an employee was made redundant at the age of 59 he could draw unemployment benefits for a year and then qualify for a pension from the federal government at age 60. Employers made extensive use of this scheme by 'firing' workers at 59 and supplementing the unemployment and pension benefits that they received from the government (Bosch 1990: 34; Abraham and Houseman 1993: 26–7).

Figures for the steel industry in North Rhine-Westphalia during the period 1976 to 1986, as shown in Table 7.2, illustrate the importance of early retirement schemes in the process of rationalization. In the steel industry alone approximately 130,000 jobs, or nearly 40 per cent of the industry's employment, were eliminated from the

TABLE 7.2 Rationalization of the steel industry in North Rhine-Westphalia, 1976–1986 (number of employees)

Adjustment measures	Hoesch	Krupp	Krupp Klöckner	Mannes-mann	Thyssen	Total
Transferred to other group companies	809	2,969	96	6,400	5,200	15,474
Placement in other firms	98	—	—	—	—	98
Early retirement	11,864	10,700	850[a]	7,630	19,783	50,827
Other cuts in manning levels						
Dismissals for operational reasons	—	—	—	—	—	—
Severance agreements and/or redundancy payment schemes	1,500	—	118	—	4,849[b]	6,467

[a] Since 30 Sept. 1983.
[b] Including foreign workers who departed under the terms of legislation introduced on 28 Nov. 1983.

Source: Bosch (1990: 33).

mid-1970s to the mid-1980s. Many of these job losses were regionally concentrated or located in economically depressed parts of Germany. Nevertheless, West Germany was alone among the European steel-producing countries in contracting production and employment whilst preserving social peace (Esser and Fach 1989: 223). Early retirement was also used extensively in the automobile industry. In the wake of the oil price crisis, for example, VW reduced employment by 33,000 or 26 per cent of its workforce (Streeck 1984: 56 ff.). Notwithstanding the pressures to reduce employment at VW, as Jürgens, Malsch, and Dohse noted, 'it was possible to achieve the reduction of personnel by means of so-called "bloodless" measures: voluntary pay-offs, early retirements, "natural fluctuation," and a hiring freeze' (Jürgens, Malsch, and Dohse 1993: 116).

The burden of rationalization was also distributed through the use of the state's short-time working programme. If employers reduced the work hours of their employees, they were permitted to pay them only for the hours that they worked if the works council approved; the Federal Labour Office then paid them a prorated amount of the statutory unemployment benefits for the hours that they did not work. The scheme was made increasingly generous in a number of ways during the 1970s. For example, before 1969 short-time benefits were available for a maximum duration of six months; by 1975 the limit had been extended to 24 months. Thus, as Abraham and Houseman pointed out, 'Companies engaged in long-term restructuring have been able to minimize layoffs by using short-time work schemes while their work force was being reduced through attrition and, in many cases, through early retirement' (Abraham and Houseman 1993: 25).

Notwithstanding the common perception that measures to protect job security and to spread the burden of downsizing inhibit the process of rationalization, a comparative analysis of restructuring in Germany and the US concluded that '[o]n the whole, the evidence that we have examined suggests that German policies are effective in stabilising employment in the short run without imposing burdensome costs on employers . . . we do not find any consistent difference between the medium-run responsiveness of German employment to changes in shipments and that in the corresponding US industry' (Abraham and Houseman 1993: 97). Whereas US employers relied predominantly on reductions in employment levels in reacting to demand fluctuations, German employers depend primarily on a reduction in average hours worked by employees. Notwithstanding these differences, Abraham and Houseman contended that there was little variation among the two countries in the extent to which labour input was reduced in response to a decrease in demand. However, they identified primary metals, automobiles, and non-electrical equipment as three industries in which employment and hours adjustment in Germany were far below that in the US.[1] In a previous study of industrial restructuring in the European steel industry, one of the authors, Susan Houseman, concluded that the especially strong protection for German workers in this industry, based largely on

---

[1] German employment and hours adjustment were also below the US in non-electrical equipment and stone, clay, and glass but the authors argue that a large part of the difference stems from differences in demand conditions in Germany and the US (Abraham and Houseman 1993: 98).

the strength of the powerful metalworkers' union IG Metall, inhibited employment adjustment in the medium term as well as investment and plant closure decisions (Houseman 1991). Abraham and Houseman suggested that a similar analysis may apply to the automobile and non-electrical equipment industries, where 'the very strong and somewhat radical metal workers' union' also plays an important role (Abraham and Houseman 1993: 99).

To fully assess the impact of employment protection measures on economic performance, however, it is insufficient to look at relatively short-term responses to competition ('medium term' is defined in the Abraham and Houseman study as a period of only one and a half years). Of considerable importance is the relationship between employment protection and measures to upgrade products and processes as part of a creative or innovative response to competition. Some scholars have highlighted the importance of job protection as one important element in a system of governance that gives workers the incentives and abilities to promote innovation precisely in the industries in which the unions, and especially IG Metall, are strong.

In the case of the steel industry, for example, Kathleen Thelen has argued that

[w]orks councils tolerate—indeed they encourage—rationalization investment, which they see as their only hope of making the remaining jobs 'krisensicher' (crisis-proof). Labor's influence on supervisory boards ensures that investment goes toward this end. This has meant, among other things, that industrial adjustment in the German steel industry has been adjustment more *within* as opposed to *out* of steel than for example in the United States. (Thelen 1991: 134, emphasis in original; see also Thelen 1987; Esser and Fach 1989)

In the automobile industry the German system of governance seems to have facilitated technological change compared with, for example, its British and American counterparts (Jürgens *et al*. 1993: 173–214). In his study of the automobile industry in the 1970s and 1980s, Wolfgang Streeck reported a 'successful adjustment to turbulent markets'. Specifically he pointed out that

[c]odetermination, with its peculiar rules of the game, has become the institutional core of what is best described as a firmly established productivity coalition between management and labor at the point of production. Prototypically in the automobile industry, codetermination has provided the basis for a trade union policy of cooperative productivism . . . The tendency of works councils in West Germany to identify with the economic fate of their firm because they are elected as representatives of an enterprise's entire work force is reinforced in the auto industry by a keen sense, shared by the external union, of exposure to a volatile and competitive world market. As a consequence, hardly anywhere is there greater willingness than among automobile trade unionists to think through and accept the consequences of labor-management cooperation. Together with the opportunities offered by the framework of industrial unionism and codetermination, this has given rise in the 1970s and 1980s to an interactive configuration of policies and institutional structures which appears to have formed a 'virtuous circle' ideally matched to, and indeed almost making inevitable, an industrial strategy of upmarket restructuring. (Streeck 1989: 128–9)

Other industry analyses, specifically on mechanical engineering, chemicals, and banking and finance, lend support to Streeck's analysis of the tendency of the German

system of governance to induce the adoption of strategies of 'diversified quality production' (Herrigel 1989; Allen 1989; Oberbeck and Baethge 1989). The importance
of these strategies to the performance of German industry is also suggested by
research on 'matched plants' across countries conducted by the National Institute in
the UK and by work coordinated by Michael Porter on 'The Competitive Advantage
of Nations' (Porter 1990).

While the German system of organizational control has played an important role
in sharing the gains and losses of the process of development, in doing so it has
proven most successful in advancing the interests of skilled, male German workers
in industries in which their representation is strongest and where the organizational
integration of their skills is critical to the competitive success of industrial enterprises. These workers gained most from the rising prosperity of the post-war decades.
The system was, however, much less of a boon to contingent members of the labour
force, those euphemistically described as *Gastarbeiter* (guest workers), as well as to
women. The importance of guest workers in the German labour force grew steadily
in the decades after the war to reach 8.1 per cent of total employment in 1970
(Giersch *et al.* 1992: 127). These workers have tended to be treated as a buffer stock
of flexible labour to insulate the domestic workforce from layoffs, as evidenced by
the higher rate of unemployment experienced by foreign workers in the latter part
of the 1970s and during the 1980s (Abraham and Houseman 1993: 124–5). The
account by Esser and Väth of the strategy of IG Metall toward the restructuring of
the steel industry is worth quoting at length:

The circle of those who were energetically defended was limited, and in itself carefully graded;
the top rank consisted of the most *efficient and productive nucleus* of the labour force, because it
is from here that the union recruited its membership predominantly. Next came the group of
old workers, highly threatened by redundancy and therefore to be conciliated by all possible
means of rhetoric. They were mostly old union members, with a higher interest in honourable
social programmes than in safe jobs. It was not the union's problem what happened to these
men when, after a life of hard work in the steel mills, followed by early retirement, the first
wave of euphoria had gone, and the feeling of uselessness set in. *Young employed* can also be
sure of provoking any amount of verbal welfare. Yet here again, it was not the concern of IG
Metall to help them really, when existing jobs had disappeared through rationalisation, and
recruitment to the steel plants had virtually ended. Guest workers were left without any union
protection and were therefore, as a rule, dismissed first, likewise those 'black sheep' who were
already in the bad books of personnel departments, shop-floor supervisors and works councillors, and whose poor work record gave good enough reasons for sacking. Briefly, IG Metall
accepted a reconstruction policy for the steel industry which was characterised by the need for
competitiveness on the international market, and it merely stressed the need for a *safety net* of
social programmes, retraining, further training, etc. IG Metall did not look for an alternative
to this logic. Instead it fully exploited the advantages of its strategy—without paying the
price; more precisely, the union, in company with the State and industry, made the fringe
groups of the labour force pay that price. (Esser and Väth 1987: 659; emphasis in original)

In times of recession foreign workers have often been 'persuaded' to return to their
native lands; indeed in 1983 the German government offered payments to foreign

workers who were unemployed or on short-time work if they left Germany with their families (Abraham and Houseman 1993: 125). Significant attempts have, however, been made to give these workers the chance to improve their employment opportunities, especially by encouraging them to participate in the dual training system; foreigners' share of apprenticeships increased from 2.8 per cent in 1985 to 6.7 per cent in 1990 although they are still under-represented in the apprenticeship system compared with their importance in the workforce (Winkelmann 1996: 663).

Nor have women directly participated in the gains of post-war economic development to the same extent as men. Their employment opportunities have, in general, been more limited than those available to men. The workforce participation rate of German women was, at around 40 per cent in the 1960s and 1970s, among the lowest in the advanced industrial economies. Moreover, the German women that did work were disproportionately concentrated in low-skilled jobs. This pattern undoubtedly reflects, at least in part, a lower average tenure than their male counterparts which, because of the emphasis on continued education as the means to promotion in the German employment system, is a particular handicap to women's career advancement (Abraham and Houseman 1993: 114–23).

7.5. Conclusion

In contrast to the US system of managerial control, the German post-war system of governance is best described as a contested form of organizational control. Codetermination of supervisory boards, works councils, inter-company shareholding, and the banks' relationships with industry, as shareholders and in the exercise of depositors' proxies, make it very difficult to pinpoint exactly where control resided in major German enterprises in the post-war decades. Who exercised control in particular German enterprises depended on such particulars as the articles of association, which defined the responsibilities of the various organs of the corporation, as well as the organizational structure that a holding company put in place to manage its participations, and in particular on the degree of integration with the operations of the parent company that such a structure entailed. But whatever the variations in corporate control across particular German enterprises, the institutions discussed above, as well as other elements of legal and financial regulation (Franks and Mayer 1990), ensured that control over the allocation of corporate resources and returns was an organizational phenomenon in the FRG in the post-war period.

Yet, especially in comparison with organizational control since the 1960s in Japan, organizational control in post-war Germany was contested for a number of reasons. First, the central foundations of pre-World War II managerial control—namely, bank–enterprise relations and inter-company shareholding networks—remained strong. Secondly, whereas lifetime employment and enterprise unionism—two key elements of the Japanese system of governance—fostered employee commitment to the enterprise, in Germany institutions such as unionism and the system of skill formation encouraged competing loyalties (Streeck 1996; Teague 1997). Finally, the German banks, although they bolstered financial commitment in the post-war decades, were always much more diversified beyond, and independent of, industrial finance than the main banks in Japan. Their business interests are, as a result, more independent of those of major German industrial enterprises.

In recent decades the institutional foundations of organizational control in Germany have proven to be more enduring than in the United States. Nevertheless various pressures have built up on the German system of corporate governance and are bringing the relationship between corporate control and economic performance to the fore in policy debates. The source of these pressures, the reaction to them by key interest groups in the German economy, and the effects that they have already had and are likely to have on German governance institutions, are the subjects of the next chapter.

8

The Emerging Challenges to Organizational Control in Germany

8.1. Introduction

In the previous chapter, I described how a system of organizational control was supported by the social institutions that persisted or developed in post-war West Germany. In recent decades the institutional foundations of organizational control in Germany have proven to be more enduring than in the United States. Nevertheless various pressures have built up on the German system of corporate governance that raise questions about its sustainability in its current form. Some of these pressures emanate from sources external to the operation of the domestic corporate economy, such as the processes of European integration and German reunification. The more powerful pressures, however, reflect financial and productive challenges that are integrally related to the evolving political economy of the German corporate sector.

First, pressures for financial liquidity have increased; as Germans have grown wealthier, they have been moving their savings out of bank deposits and into more market-based instruments, a trend that is likely to lead to increased demands for higher returns on corporate securities. These pressures, discussed in section 8.2, may well be amplified by the striking trend towards growing intergenerational dependence in West Germany and the concerns, real and manufactured, that have been evoked with respect to the economic viability of the extant system of pension provision. In section 8.3 I discuss the second formidable challenge to the German system of organizational control, which is that posed by international competition, especially emanating from Japan. The Japanese competitive challenge is fundamentally an organizational one since it confronts the social foundations on which German enterprises have successfully competed in the past even in high-quality niches in which they have previously been unrivalled.

Together, and in combination with forces external to the German economy, these structural changes in the German economy—the one financial, the other productive—may challenge the foundations of the post-war system of corporate governance. Section 8.4 documents some of the political responses to these challenges from key interest groups and, in particular, labour and financial interests in the German economy. In section 8.5 I conclude by drawing out some of the possible implications of these responses for the future of German corporate governance.

8.2. Financial Challenges to Organizational Control

In recent decades, financial commitment has proven to be more robust in Germany than in the United States but whether it will continue to be so is an open question. There are clear indications of an increasing emphasis on financial liquidity in the German system of governance which, if it gains momentum, may exacerbate the existing organizational problems in German industry. Growing systematic pressures for financial liquidity are rooted in the rising level of savings generated by the country's post-war economic success, pressures which are likely to grow as the trend toward intergenerational dependence increases in Germany.

The federal government controlled interest rates after the war, thus limiting interest rate competition not only among different sectors of the banking industry, but also from savings instruments provided by other financial enterprises (Francke and Hudson 1984: 81). The objective of this restriction was to stabilize the banking system and thus protect depositors. Its effect was seen in the channelling of the vast majority of German savings through the banks; although the formation of monetary assets was limited during the 1950s, about 75 per cent of these assets were channelled into the banking sector (Francke and Hudson 1984: 76).

As their incomes expanded, Germans were able to save more, and the success of public campaigns and state subsidies to promote saving led to the emergence of higher aggregate saving rates in Germany than in the US by the 1960s. Automatic wage deposits for workers helped mass consumer banking to become the major source of expansion in the banking business in the 1960s. Once restrictions on branch banking were removed in 1958, competition in the banking sector occurred primarily through the expansion of branch networks (Francke and Hudson 1984; Deeg 1991). In 1970, as Table 8.1 shows, claims against banks accounted for more than half of the financial assets of German households, and over three-quarters of these bank deposits were in savings accounts. In the 1950s and 1960s competition for the rapidly growing funds of German savers took place primarily among the savings banks, the private banks, and the cooperative banks. In 1970 the savings banks dominated the market with 58.8 per cent of total savings deposits; the credit cooperatives followed with 18.2 per cent and then came the private banks with 17.3 per cent (Oberbeck and Baethge 1989: 285).

During the 1970s, investors began to move out of bank deposits and into higher-yielding savings instruments. As Table 8.1 shows, the proportion of financial assets held as savings deposits in banks almost halved during the period from 1970 to 1992. Insurance investments increased from 13.3 per cent of private financial assets in 1970 to 18.5 per cent in 1992. The share of fixed-interest securities in financial assets also showed a substantial increase, from 7.7 per cent in 1970 to 20.9 per cent in 1992. In the 1980s and early 1990s mutual funds increased their share of private financial assets; by the end of 1993 they accounted for 6.3 per cent, up from 2 per cent at the end of 1980 (*Deutsche Bank Research Bulletin*, Jan. 1995: 8).

The absolute volume of private financial assets also expanded dramatically from 1970. Between 1972 and 1988 the financial assets of German households rose by

TABLE 8.1 Structure of financial assets of private households, Germany, 1970–1993 (% of total private financial assets)

Assets	1970	1992	1993 Unified Germany
Bank deposits	52.4	40.7	41.7
Cash and sight deposits	10.6	8.0	8.8
Time deposits	1.8	8.0	12.6
Savings deposits	39.1	19.4	20.3
Savings certificates	0.9	5.3	—
Savings and loan deposits	7.6	3.7	3.5
Insurance[a]	13.3	18.5	19.8
Fixed-income securities[b]	7.7	20.9	15.9
Stocks[c]	11.3	5.2	5.4
Investment fund certificates			6.3
Other receivables[d]	7.7	11.0	7.4

[a] Including life insurance and pensions.
[b] Including bond fund shares.
[c] Including stock fund shares.
[d] Including pension claims within the company.

Source: Deutsche Bank Research Bulletin, 9 Jan. 1995: 7.

290 per cent compared with an increase in their total income of 150 per cent. At the end of 1988, households had accumulated a massive DM2.6 trillion (gross) in financial assets, which amounted to nearly twice their annual disposable income (Deutsche Bank Research Bulletin, June 1989: 10). By the end of 1993, private households in Germany as a whole had financial assets amounting to nearly DM4.2 trillion; 94.5 per cent of these assets were held by West German households (Deutsche Bank Research Bulletin, Jan. 1995: 6).

The changes in the structure and level of German financial assets are striking in historical perspective and have been linked to the rapid growth in the holdings of institutional investors during the period from 1990 to 1995. Yet, the pressures for financial liquidity, although increasing rapidly, have to date proven much weaker than in the United States, which is primarily attributable to the fact that the German savings system has generated nothing approaching the vast liquid funds under management by US financial institutions; in 1995, for example, institutional investors in the United States held financial assets of US$11,871 billion compared with US$1,113 billion for their German counterparts (OECD 1997: 20).

8.2.1. The German System of Pension Provision

Pension funds account for a substantial proportion of the difference. Although there has been a significant increase since 1960 in personal provision for pensions in Germany through the accumulation of financial assets, the financial assets held by

German pension funds were, at US$65 billion in 1995, very low compared with their American counterparts, who had comparable holdings of US$4,156 billion (OECD 1997: 22). The difference is even more striking when one compares financial assets of pension funds as a percentage of GDP: in the US in 1995 the relevant figure was 59.8 per cent compared with 2.7 per cent in Germany. In Germany there are, moreover, restrictions on the proportions of the assets of pension funds and insurance companies that can be held in different types of financial instruments, which has limited the pressures for financial liquidity from this source. For example, the limit for domestic equities is 30 per cent (increased from a maximum of 5 per cent in 1990), and 6 per cent for foreign equities; in 1994, German pension funds put about 72 per cent of their assets in domestic bonds and only 9 per cent in equities (Queisser 1996: 14).

The difference in pension funds under management in Germany as compared with the US also reflects the way in which German employers fund the pensions that they provide to employees. Employer pensions were originally introduced as elements in the compensation packages offered to key workers to keep them with specific companies, mainly larger companies, when labour markets became tight from the mid-1950s. In more recent periods of relatively high unemployment, some German companies have reduced these benefits. Moreover, changes in German pension law in 1974, which allowed workers to transfer their pensions from one company to another, have reduced the effectiveness of this device for retaining workers. Nevertheless, these pensions still represent a significant accumulation of pension liabilities in the German economy; in 1993 the total pension obligations of companies amounted to c. DM460.6 billion (Queisser 1996: 12).

In the early 1990s, as Table 8.2 shows, about one-fifth of employer pension assets were in private pension funds (*Pensionskassen*). Employers and employees generally make contributions to these funds and the investment behaviour of these funds is regulated by the life insurance laws (Turner and Watanabe 1995: 97). Some employer pensions are funded by direct insurance (*Direktversicherungen*) through life insurance companies. Support funds (*Unterstützungskassen*) are another significant channel for employer pensions. These funds are legal entities that are financed by allocations of resources from the employer company but are legally separate from it. The funds are generally lent back to the employer company as an interest-bearing loan (Turner and Watanabe 1995: 97). As Table 8.2 indicates, these three channels together comprise just over 40 per cent of employer pension assets in Germany.

The remainder, nearly 60 per cent of the funds earmarked for the payment of company pensions, remain in the company as book reserves. As a company builds up its pension reserves (*Pensionrückstellung*), the increases in its pension liabilities are tax-deductible. Since enterprises are permitted to invest the funds allocated to pension obligations in the normal course of their businesses, this system in effect affords them a tax-effective means of borrowing from their employees; company pension funds were used to finance almost 5 per cent of the net investment of German producing enterprises in the period from 1980–9 and thus represent a more important source of finance for industrial enterprises than equity issues (Edwards and Fischer 1994:

TABLE 8.2 Allocation of employer pension assets in Germany,
1996 (Total volume, DM515bn)

Type of plan	Percentage of total pension assets
Book reserves	57
Private fund	22
Direct insurance	13
Support fund	8

Source: *Deutsche Bank Research Bulletin*, No. 2 (1998: 35).

TABLE 8.3 Sources of Retirement Income in Germany, 1992

Source	Percentage of retirement income
Social security	68.8
Public employer pensions	14.4
Private employer pensions	5.3
Other	11.7

Source: Schmähl (1994: 393).

54). For large manufacturing joint-stock companies (*Aktiengesellschaften* or AGs) provisions for pensions were even more important, accounting for nearly 15 per cent of
their net investment in the period 1970–85 (Edwards and Fischer 1994: 128). Major
German AGs have enormous pension reserves on their balance sheets; as Hauck put
it, 'Siemens has over DM 14bn of pension reserves and can be compared in this
respect with a good medium-sized life insurance company' (Hauck 1994: 557).
Although the importance of book reserves has fallen since 1981 from 67 per cent of
all occupational pension assets and, correspondingly, direct insurance has increased
its share from under 5 per cent in 1981 (Queisser 1996: 14), the accumulation of
book reserves nevertheless remains the prevalent practice with regard to German
employer pensions.

The final and most important reason for the differences between the Germany and
the US in accumulated pension funds under management is the relative importance
of the state pension system in Germany. As Table 8.3 shows, social security accounts
for nearly 70 per cent of the retirement income of German pensioners; in the US, by
comparison, social security contributes about 40 per cent of retirement income
(Turner and Watanabe 1995: 136). As a pay-as-you-go system, the German government pension system generates no reservoir of surplus funds to be allocated. Instead,
almost 75 per cent of the financing for the system comes from employee and employer
contributions on the basis of earnings up to a ceiling of 1.8 times the average gross
earnings of all insured individuals; the remainder is paid by the federal government
out of general revenues (World Bank 1994: 361).

Since 1960 there has been a steady increase in the contribution rate required to finance the pay-as-you-go pension system; it has risen from 14 per cent in 1960 to 20.3 per cent in 1997 (Deutsche Bundesbank, Sept. 1997: 42). A further increase in the contribution rate to 21 per cent in 1998 was forestalled only by the emergency measure agreed in April 1997 to raise VAT by one point to 16 per cent. The levy is expected to rise still further in the decades to come as growing life expectancy and a decline in fertility contribute to a 'double ageing' process in Germany. The OECD has forecast that by 2040 pension costs in Germany will amount to an enormous 18 per cent of GDP (OECD 1996b).

8.2.2. The Pressures of Early Retirement

Demographic trends are not, however, the only source of increased pressure on the financing of the German pension system. They are compounded by labour market pressures. All major OECD countries have experienced a strong decline in labour supply by the elderly but the German participation rate for older people is now among the lowest of the major OECD countries. It is just over half that of the comparable US figure and much lower than the Japanese rate. Some scholars have attributed the striking German trend to the structure of the state pension system, which provides generous incentives to retire and, until recently, did not decrease with age in a manner which was actuarially 'fair' (Börsch-Supan 1991).

The low average retirement age also reflects German corporate behaviour, specifically the use by employers of inducements to early retirement as a means of contracting their workforces (see Chapter 7). During the 1980s the restrictions on the use of the early retirement scheme for unemployed workers were eased through a lengthening of the maximum period for receipt of unemployment benefits. For workers aged 54 or more, for example, the maximum period had, by 1987, been increased from 12 months to 32 months. Thus companies could take advantage of the scheme to retire workers who were as young as 57 years and four months (Abraham and Houseman 1993: 27). By 1984 6 per cent of new retirees qualified under the early retirement scheme for unemployed workers, up from less than 2 per cent in 1974 (Abraham and Houseman 1993: 27).

In 1984 the government introduced a new scheme to permit early retirement for private sector workers who reached the age of 58 during the years 1984 to 1988 or who were already over 58. The employer was required to pay the early retiree at least 65 per cent of his previous gross income until he became entitled to collect a state pension (at 63 years of age for men and 60 for women). The proposal was intended as a temporary measure to ease the unemployment situation (*European Industrial Relations Review* (*EIRR*), 120: 9–10; 125: 7–9). It was tied explicitly to this objective by allowing the employer to claw back more than half of his payment to the retired worker if the vacated job was filled by a registered unemployed person. The scheme did not, however, prove very popular, seemingly because the early retirement scheme for unemployed persons was financially more attractive to employers (Abraham and Houseman 1993: 27).

Early retirement schemes for the unemployed remained a relatively low-cost means for employers to reduce their workforces notwithstanding the government's attempts to shift some of the costs of these programmes from the social security funds to individual employers. Since 1982, companies have been obliged to reimburse the Federal Labour Office for unemployment benefits paid to older workers whom they have 'fired' and who are waiting to take early retirement, unless this would be a threat to the company in light of its precarious economic situation (Bosch 1990: 36). Many companies using these schemes did, however, claim an exemption on the grounds that they were in economic distress (Abraham and Houseman 1993: 27).

In recent years early retirement due to unemployment has risen sharply. About 190,000 people, or 21 per cent of all those making pension claims, applied for early pensions in 1994. In 1995 the number had increased to 290,000 and in that year alone the cost to the system of early pension claims was DM69 billion, of which DM37 billion was paid by the statutory contributory pension funds, DM27 billion was paid from unemployment insurance, and DM5 billion was paid by employers (*EIRR*, 272: 24–6). The process of German reunification has been an important additional contributor to the growing burden of early retirement in the 1990s. As part of this process the German welfare system, including the pension scheme, was extended to cover the whole country. The restructuring of industry in the East has left many older workers jobless and claims for pensions in the East because of unemployment increased from 373 in 1992 to more than 180,000 in 1995 (*EIRR*, 272: 24–6).

Disability pensions have also grown in importance since the definition of disability was broadened in 1969 by the German courts. In 1995 those in receipt of disability pensions accounted for about 26 per cent of all pensioners (Queisser 1996: 8). The German system now makes provision for occupational and general disability. The former applies when a person's earning ability falls by more than 50 per cent. Successful claimants under this scheme qualify for two-thirds of the benefits under a normal pension. General disability pension benefits are equivalent to normal pension benefits and are paid to those who are considered to be permanently incapable of earning a basic income (Queisser 1996: 8).

The importance of early retirement and disability pensions increases the pressures on the pension system beyond what the growing old-age dependency ratio would imply. In 1994, only 29 per cent of new pension benefits awarded were paid to those retiring at 'normal' retirement age (Queisser 1996: 18). More generally, how Germany deals with the problem of supporting more and more people in old age will have critical implications for the sustainability of financial commitment in the German economy. The growing concerns that have been expressed in Germany about the funding of pensions suggest that if the evolution toward financial liquidity in Germany is to get a major push in the near future it will come from changes in the pension system.

When corporations are successful in their innovative investment strategies they can generate returns that can help to fund not only an expanding number of well-paid and stable employment opportunities but also, directly or indirectly, the retirement system. A conflict between the allocation of corporate returns to employment and retirement can arise, however, when, on the retirement side, retirees (both present and future) demand higher incomes and on the employment side, corporate decision-makers face a new competitive environment in which investments in productive resources do not generate the returns they did in the past. As demands for financial liquidity grow in Germany, there is also growing evidence that German corporate enterprises are being confronted with unprecedented competitive challenges even in market segments that they previously dominated.

8.3. Productive Challenges to Organizational Control

Industries that had already contracted, like steel, shipbuilding, coal-mining, and consumer electronics (Bosch 1990: 54), were hit by new job losses in the early 1980s. For example, employment in iron and steel fell from 624,000 in 1979 to 473,000 in 1991 and in shipbuilding from 60,000 in 1979 to 34,000 in 1991 (OECD 1996b: 142). In contrast, production and employment expanded in sectors of particular German strength. During the period from 1979 to 1991, employment increased from 971,000 to 1,077,000 in non-electrical machinery (excluding office and computing machinery), from 876,000 to 963,000 in transport equipment, from 923,000 to 987,000 in metal products, from 996,000 to 1,118,000 in chemical products, and from 578,000 to 677,000 in electrical machinery (excluding radio, TV, and communication equipment) (OECD 1996b: 142–3).

The success of these industries contributed to Germany's strong export position during this period (Carlin and Soskice 1997). As a whole, the German economy continued to grow during the 1980s and the reunification process prompted a further upsurge in economic performance around 1989. However, unemployment rose substantially in the early 1980s, although it remained at a lower level than in the United States for most of the decade, and much lower than in most other European countries. By the end of the 1980s, confidence in the ability of the 'Rhenish system of capitalism' to deliver economic performance without sacrificing social cohesion was running at an all-time high (Albert 1991).

When the dust settled in the early 1990s, however, it became clear that throughout the 1980s the competition that German enterprises faced on international product markets had intensified further. Besides the structural problems that reunification posed, key industrial sectors in the former West German economy seemed to confront systematic challenges from international and, in particular, Japanese competition. By 1992 the German economy had plunged into its worst recession since World War II. Among the industries that were worst hit were automobiles and machine tools, the great bastions of German post-war industrial strength.

Employment in the motor vehicles industry had increased from 699,000 in 1979 to 823,000 in 1991. Exports had more than doubled in current DM prices during the same period. All of the West German car producers had increased their production in the 1980s and were hit heavily by the slump that followed the decade of expansion. VW and Opel reduced production by 25 per cent, Audi by 31 per cent, Ford by 30 per cent, and BMW by 12 per cent in 1993/4. Only Mercedes-Benz managed to increase sales by launching a new series but the successful introduction of luxury cars by Toyota and Nissan suggested that the sustainability of this German company's success could not be taken for granted.

Concerns about the German automobile industry's competitiveness had already been heightened by the publication in 1991 of a German-language version of *The Machine that Changed the World*, the MIT comparative study of the auto industry, particularly when it was revealed that the European plant held up to unfavourable scrutiny for its low productivity was Daimler-Benz's most important assembly plant (Womack *et al.* 1990). Other symptoms of serious underlying problems were to be found in the rapid growth of automobile imports to Germany during the 1980s; for example, the share of Japanese brands in total German car registrations had risen from 10.4 per cent in 1980 to 25.3 per cent by 1991 (Sachwald 1994: 65). More-over, a substantial proportion of German export gains in the 1980s had been won in European markets that were still relatively protected from Japanese competition (Keck 1993: 136).

The machine tool industry also faced serious challenges from foreign competitors. The traditional competitive advantage of German machine tool producers had been based on their ability to produce high-quality customized machines for which cost considerations were secondary in influencing demand. By the 1990s, however, Japan-ese competitors had succeeded in developing their standard machines so that they could perform many functions previously possible only with highly specialized machines (Schumann *et al.* 1994; Herrigel 1996: 37). Symptoms of emerging com-petitive problems were discernible in the 1980s. Although the German share of export markets held steady during the 1980s, German enterprises were weak in the most rapidly expanding markets for machine tools; in 1988, German producers accounted for only 9.3 per cent of machinery imports by south-east Asian newly industrialized countries (NICs) compared with 50.4 per cent from Japan and 26.4 per cent from the US (*Deutsche Bank Bulletin*, Jan. 1991: 3). Between 1991 and 1993 the value of German machine tool production fell from DM17 billion to DM12 billion (*Economist*, 16 Oct. 1991, 16 July 1994). Despite a recovery of orders in 1994, Japanese machine tool makers maintained a considerable cost advantage over their German competitors.

As Table 8.4 shows, the economics of German machine tool producers had been deteriorating relative to their Japanese competitors for some time. Japanese produc-tivity, measured by value added per employee, was double that of German machine tool companies throughout the 1980s (Englmann *et al.* 1994: 37). In part, the dif-ference can be attributed to the longer hours worked by the Japanese; in 1990 hours worked per employee in Japan were 2,197 compared with 1,604 in Germany. But the Japanese performance also reflected their success at integrating human and physical resources to generate continuous innovation (Finegold *et al.* 1994: 23).

In general in machine-based industries, where process innovation has been impor-tant in driving down costs, the Japanese, in particular, have been able in recent years to generate organizational learning that has permitted them to move into progres-sively higher-quality market segments at lower unit costs, even in industries such as

TABLE 8.4 Comparative performance of German and Japanese machine tool companies, 1980–1989 (per employee, thousands of DM)

	1980	1985	1989
German enterprises			
Sales	109	138	174
Staff expenditure	45	55	64
Value added	55	63	77
Japanese enterprises			
Sales	315	391	447
Staff expenditure	48	59	67
Value added	119	147	166

Source: Adapted from Englmann et al. (1994: 37).

precision machine tools and luxury automobiles in which the Germans were previously unrivalled. Some of the industries in which the Germans were competitively strong, and which have historically been considered stable technology, have been transformed by the Japanese, who have leveraged their flexibility at the enterprise level as a basis for continuous innovation (Schumann et al. 1994; Herrigel 1995, 1996: 36).

The key organizational advantage of Japanese companies relative to their German competitors seems to be their capacity to achieve cross-functional integration on the shop floor as well as in management structures. German enterprises, like their Japanese counterparts and in contrast to most American companies, have in the post-war period attained considerable success in organizing the hierarchical integration of technical skills. However, two key features of the German system that facilitated hierarchical integration—specialized skills among production workers and functional divisions within the managerial organization—impeded cross-functional integration (Schumann et al. 1994: 643–64; Herrigel 1995, 1996: 38–43; Jürgens and Lippert 1997).

The weaknesses of the German system of organizational integration in facilitating cooperation across functions seems to be rendering them vulnerable to international competition. Herrigel argues that the problems with the German system are apparent in the development of new products:

Each time a new product or a new technology is introduced—as opposed to an old one that is customised for a customer—the various roles that each of the categories of skill and management will play in the production and development of the new product must be bargained out. Each currently existing cluster of expertise and institutional power, naturally, wants to participate; each has its own ideas and solutions; each defends its turf against encroachments from the others; each takes for granted that it should have a legitimate place in the new arrangement within the firm. Electrical masters and technicians, for example, will fight with mechanical ones both on the shop-floor and in the design studios over different kinds of technical or manufacturing solutions to problems that have direct consequences for the amount and character of work that each will have to do and on the overall value that their role within the firm will contribute to the value of the product. (Herrigel 1996: 42)

These problems in achieving cross-functional integration are difficult to overcome within the extant institutional context. Herrigel describes the day-to-day obstacles to such a transformation as forming a dynamic process of 'self-blockage' which involves all stakeholders, be they workers or managers, who have entrenched interests to protect. He argues that

[f]ew producers, large or small, have had success up until now in being able to overcome the opposition of entrenched groupings of skilled workers threatened with the loss of status through incorporation into teams that deny the boundaries of former jurisdictional specializations or of independent departments, reluctant to have their functional areas of power within the firms redefined and diluted through recomposition with other areas. It is difficult, after all, to tell workers and managers who with considerable legitimacy understand themselves as having contributed significantly to the traditional success of high quality manufacturing in Germany that their roles have become obstacles to adjustment. (Herrigel 1996: 43)

There continues to be debate about the extent of the current problems with German work organization as the basis for generating higher-quality, lower-cost products. In their recent study of the German pump industry—which accounted for 25 per cent of output and exports in general industrial machinery, one of Germany's critical manufacturing sectors—David Finegold and Karin Wagner found evidence which suggests that functional segmentation is a significant barrier to improving performance in the current competitive climate. Yet, they caution against excessive gloom in assessing the implications for the viability of the German system of work organization. They contend that there are countervailing strengths of that system 'that have the potential to help firms develop a new, distinctive German production model' (Finegold and Wagner 1998: 469).

If that transition is to occur, however, there is a need for a widespread commitment among employers, workers, and unions in Germany to overcome existing organizational barriers to continuous innovation. In all of the industries in which they have previously been highly effective, German enterprises are currently able to produce and to export quite successfully. They are likely to continue to be able to do so for some time, despite intensified competition, because of the depth of organizational capabilities that reside in these companies. But continuity on the basis of existing capabilities may ultimately be the undoing of the market strength of German enterprises if a strategy of business-as-usual stands in the way of the organizational reform that is necessary if German enterprises are to recreate the foundations on which they can compete effectively in the future.

8.4. Responses to the Governance Challenges

The financial and productive challenges outlined above interact directly with each other through the influence of the growing strains in financing pensions on indirect labour costs and the effect on pension obligations of the use of early retirement as an instrument of industrial rationalization. In combination, these pressures may well challenge the institutional foundations of the post-war system of corporate governance. By analysing how those with substantial interests in the allocation of German corporate revenues have responded to the financial and productive challenges that confront the German economy, we can gain some insight into their possible implications for the German system of governance.

8.4.1. Responses to the Productive Challenges

From the early 1980s there were growing concerns within the German labour movement about the continued reliance on early retirement schemes as a peaceable means of contracting the workforce. These arrangements were becoming more difficult in industries in which employment had been falling for some time, like steel, ship-building, coal-mining, and consumer electronics, because the pool of eligible workers had diminished. There were also concerns that the government was going to tighten the eligibility requirements for these schemes and make them more expensive for individual companies. Employers also seemed less and less willing to use temporary measures, such as short-time work, because they increasingly regarded the challenges that German enterprises confronted as structural problems (Bosch 1990: 35–6). Moreover, with unemployment on the rise from the early 1980s it was clear that, to generate broad-based prosperity, much more was required than a preservation of existing jobs; new jobs had to be created.

Led by IG Metall, the German trade unions responded to this situation by launching a major campaign for shorter weekly working hours; they demanded the introduction of a thirty-five hour week without any reduction in pay. When negotiations over working time between the employers' organization and the union broke down, IG Metall struck for shorter hours. The 1984 strike was the worst in the history of the Federal Republic. It lasted for nine weeks and involved about 455,000 workers (Baethge and Wolf 1995: 240).[1] The strike was concluded when the employers agreed to reduce average working hours to 38.5 a week.

From the unions' perspective, an important unintended consequence of the 1984 strike was the decentralization of negotiations over the allocation of working time to the plant level;[2] in return for agreeing to shorter hours, employers were allowed to meet the 38.5-hour target only for the average worker in an enterprise. The growing importance of works councils in negotiating working time complemented a more general increase in the relative importance of the works council in the bargaining process induced by the ongoing reorganization of German enterprises associated with the introduction of new technologies (Katz 1993).

The Works Constitution Act of 1972 gave works councils information rights, but not codetermination rights, with respect to rationalization measures undertaken by

---

[1] 58,000 workers were officially on strike, 147,000 were locked out, and 250,000 were out of work due to a lack of supplies (Baethge and Wolf 1995: 240).

[2] Another unintended consequence was the change in regulations on social insurance payments made during strikes, which made it much more costly for a union to take industrial action.

employers. The councils could, however, use their codetermination rights in other areas to exert an indirect influence on the process of technological change (Müller-Jentsch 1995; Thelen 1991: 184). In practice, works councils displayed varying capacities to deal with the growing complexity of their tasks and, in particular, with the process of technological change. In many cases, worker representatives' involvement was limited to negotiating with management about plans that had already been developed for the organization of work (Altmann 1992: 368–70, 377–8). Works councils, especially in small and medium-sized enterprises, often found themselves overwhelmed by the increasing demands placed on their capacities and resources. Not only did they lack the basis on which to resist employers' demands, they also lacked strong incentives because of concerns among works councillors that such resistance would lead to a loss of jobs for themselves and the workers they represented (Müller-Jentsch 1995).

In the 1980s the German unions began to take a much more critical stance toward technological initiatives put forward by managers.[3] In its annual report for 1982 IG Metall made the following statement:

> The economic boom in the Federal Republic in the first twenty-five years of its existence was founded on a fundamental consensus between the unions, employers, and the government. The unions did not fundamentally challenge rationalization and new technology; through their collective bargaining and worker protection policy they were able to reap for their members the fruits of productivity gains in the form of wage increases, working time reduction, and job and health protection. Developments in recent years make this social consensus more and more fragile . . . Rationalization in recent years has been at the expense of workers, in the growth of mass unemployment and worsening working conditions. (IG Metall, *Geschäftsbericht*, 1980–2: 413, quoted in Thelen 1991: 193)

As unemployment rose in the 1980s, such concerns increased and qualitative issues attracted more and more attention in the labour movement. These concerns were heightened by the fact that plant-level negotiations between employers and works councils, to adapt industry-level contracts to local conditions, led to uneven benefits across the workforce as skilled workers were kept on for longer hours at the expense of shorter hours for the less skilled (Thelen 1991). There were also fears in the labour movement that managerial technological initiatives, or more precisely, their organizational ramifications, would undermine the basis for labour representation (Turner 1991: 113).

Initially, the unions tried to influence the evolving interaction between technology and organization in an indirect way through their support for a 'training offensive' to promote increased training and retraining for workers. They also facilitated an overhaul of the structure and content of traditional apprenticeship programmes to take account of recent technological developments (Baethge and Wolf 1995: 247). In pushing for high levels of training throughout the 1980s the unions hoped that the availability of qualified workers would convince employers to reorganize work in ways that would allow them to use their skills (Streeck 1989). The federal

---

[3] For a history of IG Metall's technology policy, see Thelen (1991: ch. 8).

government and the state governments also increased their support for apprenticeship training during this period. They appealed to companies to take on apprentices, implicitly threatening to mandate such training vacancies otherwise (Winkelmann 1996: 663); whereas the number of apprenticeships available had been 5 per cent below the demand for these places in 1984, by 1989/90 there was a surplus of 11 per cent (Casey 1991: 206).

One example of the unions' more aggressive approach to training was their promotion of employment plans to replace the traditional social plans. The latter had dealt with mass redundancies in a way that was 'largely defensive or reactive; they do not intervene directly in the mechanisms of the labour market in the event of redundancies, but have mainly been focused on promoting external mobility, which at most cushions the negative effects'; by contrast, employment plans were intended 'by means of training and diversification measures, to act on the "root of the evil" and remove the need for redundancies' (Bosch 1990: 37). In practice, these plans were to prove far less successful than their originators had hoped, primarily because of the absence of a serious commitment from employers (Bosch 1990; Thelen 1991: 139).

More generally, the effectiveness of the unions' training initiatives was undermined by the ongoing changes in production technologies, and the difficulties for the dual system in keeping abreast of them, as evidenced by shortages of production workers with requisite computer skills. As a result, investments in further training became increasingly important as the basis for the competitive advantage of German enterprises (Mahnkopf 1991: 68). In contrast to initial vocational training, which is heavily regulated and relies on extensive worker involvement through unions' role in governing the system and works councils' participation in the implementation of training within enterprises, further training is to a much greater extent at the discretion of employers. The trend toward increased further training meant that

the *public* control of initial training is losing its formative function for the occupational biography of the participants. In the future, further training measures organized at plant level, i.e. by *private* economic interest, will decide the distribution of social status, incomes, social privileges and social recognition. Thus, private firms can determine, on the basis of profitability considerations, which groups of employees will receive additional qualifications and who must obtain them during or outside working hours by way of a 'voluntary' commitment. (Mahnkopf 1991: 77; emphasis in original)

To be in a position to do more than merely ratify managerial decisions about investments in skill formation, the unions had to go beyond their traditional channels of representation. In 1984 the Deutscher Gewerkschaftsbund (DGB) launched a 'Codetermination Initiative' which had as its goal the direct participation of employees in the design of their work in a humane manner (Altmann 1992: 378; Fricke 1986). IG Metall took the lead in formulating a position on labour participation in decisions about the development and utilization of technology. Its strategy emphasized the importance of local involvement, and it relied heavily for its implementation on the cooperation of works councils. The role of the union was seen as providing works councillors with training and materials on issues relevant to technological change based on real-world experiences in selected model plants. The programme was also designed to educate works councils about the range of economically viable forms of work organization in order to encourage them to take a more pro-active stance on these issues with employers. By the late 1980s, IG Metall had developed a coherent vision of work organization called *Gruppenarbeit* or 'group work' (Thelen 1991: ch. 8; Turner 1991).

These initiatives met with some limited success in the late 1980s although the majority of employers displayed little interest in group work and were resistant to extending workers' codetermination rights over the development and utilization of technology. In 1989, when the Works Constitution Act was amended to specify more clearly the consultation and information rights of workers with respect to the introduction of new technology, the main employers' organization, the BDA, complained that West German workers and their representatives already had more rights to information, consultation, and codetermination than anywhere else in the world and to extend them would interfere unduly with managerial decision-making. The amendment did not, however, provide workers with codetermination rights over the introduction of new technology and for that reason was criticized by the unions.

One can certainly find examples of German companies that took an 'anthropocentric' approach to technological change during the 1980s but the predominant approach during this period seems to have been a 'technocentric' one (Altmann 1992: 367; Altmann *et al.* 1992). The main objective of restructuring efforts in German companies during the 1980s was the development of factory automation. By the end of the decade a widespread diffusion of the components of computer-integrated manufacturing systems had occurred in German enterprises although they had not by then been integrated into anything approaching the technocratic dream of a 'factory of the future' (Köhler and Schmierl 1992; Jürgens *et al.* 1993).

The appetite of German employers for technological rather than organizational strategies to deal with intensified international competition is reminiscent of the responses of leading American managers in the 1980s. Arguably, German managers, who are much more likely than their American counterparts to be technically trained, were even more attracted to technological 'solutions' to organizational problems. The attempt by Daimler-Benz to become an 'integrated technology concern' by diversifying its operations into aerospace, aircraft, and other sectors that were deemed to be 'technologically related' to its traditional businesses in automobiles and trucks is a well-known example of such a fetish.

German employers also displayed increasing concerns about the costs of production, and, in particular, the labour costs associated with doing business in Germany. The unions had traditionally countered the employers' arguments by pointing to the highly skilled German workforce and the export market success of German industry. As Germany's competitive position showed signs of deteriorating in the 1990s, however, this argument was rejected by employers, who warned that German companies would be forced to relocate production abroad if drastic action was not taken. In the words of Hans-Peter Stihl, President of the Association of German Chambers of Industry and Commerce, and the owner of Andreas Stihl, a chainsaw manufacturer near Stuttgart: 'We have a cost crisis that has caused something of a structural crisis. Either German unions will accept substantial reductions in incomes and wages or we will lose more jobs. We also have the possibility of moving more jobs abroad' (*New York Times*, 13 Feb. 1996).

The recent trends in foreign direct investment (FDI) into and out of Germany have been taken as evidence by many commentators that companies have been voting with their feet on the declining attractiveness of Germany as a place to do business. FDI by German companies has been rising rapidly since the 1980s; from 1984 to 1995 the direct investment of German enterprises abroad rose at an average annual rate of 17.5 per cent from US\$50 billion to US\$300 billion. Inward FDI, according to the German balance of payments, was much lower; during the period from 1984 to 1995 total inward investment amounted to just over US\$36 billion (Deutsche Bundesbank 1997: 64, 71).

It is, however, unlikely that the cost of German labour is the main reason for these trends in FDI.[4] The regional distribution of the stock of German enterprises' FDI, and, in particular, the fact that it is almost identical to that of German exports, suggests that German companies are investing abroad to secure market access. That is, in fact, what has been reported as the main reason for investing abroad in surveys of German employers (Deutsche Bundesbank 1997: 66 n. 5). Despite increases in the US and south-east Asia, German FDI continues to be heavily concentrated in European countries, which have somewhat lower labour costs than in Germany but can hardly be classified as low-wage countries (Heiduk and Hodges 1992; Dicken 1998: 55). The changing of the guard in eastern Europe has, however, created lower-wage location possibilities closer to home for German enterprises than heretofore. In 1995 Germany's direct investment in central and eastern European countries amounted to DM4.2 billion, which, although increasing, constitutes just over 7 per cent of German FDI as a whole and is also being driven, to an appreciable extent, by market-access considerations; the expansion of trade with these countries has already provided German-based exporters with lucrative export opportunities, especially in mechanical and engineering products, road vehicles, and chemical products (Deutsche Bundesbank, July 1996: 35).

German companies have also been investing abroad to gain access to foreign research capabilities. This is particularly true for the German chemicals industry, which accounted for 34 per cent of Germany's manufacturing FDI in 1994 (Dicken 1998: 55). Moreover, the ongoing process of European integration and the general propensity towards globalization strategies in business circles has persuaded many German service companies, banks, and insurance companies, as well as those operating in the wholesale and retail trades, of the value of acquisition strategies designed to build up an international presence; these services companies accounted for more than 60 per cent of total German FDI in 1994, up from less than 40 per cent in 1985 (Dicken 1998: 54–5).

---

[4] For an expression of this view by Heinrich von Pierer, the chairman of Siemens, see *Financial Times*, 16 Feb. 1996: 17.

The sustained appreciation of the Deutschmark has made all of these FDI strategies relatively cheap for German enterprises. The strength of the Deutschmark is undoubtedly also part of the explanation for the relatively low level of inward FDI. Statistical discrepancies are another. In contrast to the figure of US$36 billion reported in the German balance of payments as the cumulative total of direct investment imports from 1984 to 1995, a comparable figure of US$118.9 billion is reported by the balance of payments of investor countries. On the basis of these revised figures, as the Deutsche Bundesbank put it, 'Germany's position as a recipient country of international direct investment appears in a much more favourable light' (Deutsche Bundesbank 1997: 72; *Financial Times*, 14 July 1997: 7).

On balance there is little support in the evidence on foreign direct investment for the contention that high costs have been driving companies out of, or keeping them away from, Germany. Whatever the real reasons for their international strategies, however, some German employers have used the fact of a deficit in FDI, and other arguments about declining German cost competitiveness, to take a much harder line on labour costs at home. In December 1993, Gesamtmetall, the metalworking employers' association, took the unprecedented action of cancelling their collective agreement with IG Metall. The action was largely symbolic because the agreement lasted only until the end of 1993 but it was widely interpreted as a signal of a shift by employers to a more aggressive stance toward labour (Baethge and Oberbeck 1995).

German employers have railed against collectively bargained wage increases and have called instead for plant-level agreements. There had, in fact, already been a strong trend in that direction before the early 1990s (Katz 1993), but it rapidly gained momentum when the German economy went into recession in 1993. In general, the recession has prompted a process of concession bargaining at the plant or company level (Sadowski, Schneider, and Wagner 1994: 534). *Standortsicherungs* (location-guaranteeing) agreements have become widespread at the plant and enterprise levels; their common feature is the concession of a reduction in labour costs by the works council or union in return for a guarantee of employment security. These agreements differ substantially, however, with respect to their details. Some are focused primarily on cost-cutting; others include more pro-active measures to improve long-term competitive performance (Jürgens 1997).

Employers claim that they cannot afford to keep high-cost German workers employed given the intense competition that they face on international product markets. According to a survey conducted by the Institut der deutschen Wirtschaft of average hourly labour costs in manufacturing in the world's leading economies, West Germany is leading the pack. Wage increases, however, play a smaller role in Germany's relative position than one would imagine from employers' rhetoric. During the period from 1970 to 1994, the country with the lowest wage increases was the US; Switzerland and Germany were the countries with the second lowest rate of growth of pay! One reason for the growth in hourly labour costs was a rise in indirect labour costs, mostly due to increased social security contributions; in absolute terms West Germany had the highest indirect costs of all of the countries surveyed.

But the relative increase was also substantially attributable to the appreciation in the value of the Deutschmark rather than an increase in domestic costs as such (*EIRR*, 259: 13).

In and of themselves international labour cost comparisons do not say anything definitive about the competitiveness of a country, a region, or a nation. German companies have in the past paid relatively high wages and still managed to be competitive on international markets (Carlin and Soskice 1997). Bringing productivity into the picture to calculate unit labour costs is one way of getting a more accurate reading of competitiveness. A 1993 report by the research institute DIW contended that only twice in the last 25 years—in 1970/1 and in 1992—did German unit labour costs rise faster than the average for other industrialized countries. For the remainder of that period, the increase in German unit labour costs was below that of its competitors (*EIRR*, 241: 14). Employers argue, however, that productivity no longer compensates for high German labour costs. According to a survey by the employers' research institute IW, in the period 1985–92 unit labour costs—calculated on the basis of exchange rates against the Deutschmark—rose by 30.2 per cent in Germany, or more rapidly than in almost any other of the major trading nations included in the survey. The IW did acknowledge that the relative increase had more to do with the growing strength of the Deutschmark than with an increase in domestic costs but, whatever the reason, it argued, the fact was that Germany had the highest unit labour costs of any major industrial nation (*EIRR*, 241: 13–17).

Studies conducted at the industry level generally support the view that the key symptom of the competitive challenge facing German industry is found in productivity rather than cost differences. In the automobile industry, for example, average gross value added per employee was DM92,000 per year in Germany during the period from 1981 to 1990 compared with DM131,000 in Japan (Roth 1997: 123). Productivity differences do not, however, explain competitive problems; they are symptoms of them. Moreover, they are only useful in understanding relative competitiveness when studied over the long term. To the extent that enterprises pursue developmental strategies, short-term productivity often has to be sacrificed in the expectation of achieving long-term gains. Once companies move away from traditional ways of doing business, once they start transforming technologies and organizations, productivity measures become muddy, and sometimes quite inaccurate, measures of potential competitive strength.

To really get at the nature of the competitive challenges confronting German enterprises necessitates studying the bases on which companies compete with each other on international product markets. The explanation for the productivity differences between German industry and Japanese industry, as I have already noted, seems to be organizational. Thus, although wage restraint and increased working hours may well be elements of a creative response by German enterprises to competitive challenges, they are unlikely to be enough to lay the foundations for sustainable prosperity in the German economy. It remains an open question whether those with powerful interests in the extant system of governance have the requisite abilities and incentives to bring about organizational transformation in the German economy.

Certainly there is no consensus on how organized labour should proceed. The stronger unions, like IG Metall, have always expressed concerns that, left to their own devices, works councils would contribute to a segmentation of the workforce by consolidating the interests of insiders. But the unions face a similar dilemma themselves. Birgit Mahnkopf casts the current situation facing the unions in pessimistic terms. On the one hand, they run the risk of being denounced as barriers to progress if they obstruct employer strategies. On the other hand, a 'skill-oriented' modernization strategy risks strengthening social inequalities further by entering into 'an ideological alliance between the "hard-working" and "successful" against the "indolent" and "incapable"' (Mahnkopf 1991: 77). As unemployment grows and cuts into union membership, however, even the most powerful unions are displaying a defensive pragmatism in response to employer strategies.

German employers have certainly shown that they are willing to tackle what they consider to be the excessive wages and insufficent working hours of German employees even when it involves confrontation with the unions, as happened, for example, in 1996 over the issue of sick pay. Nor have wage restraint and productivity gains stopped the unprecedented wave of corporate layoffs that began in Germany in 1991. What is not clear, however, is whether employers have the abilities and incentives to recognize and confront the organizational foundations of German industry's competitive problems. Indeed, to focus on technology and labour costs, as many German managers have been wont to do, is to obscure the nature of the problem. In recent years, however, there seems to have been growing recognition among employers of the need for organizational transformation. In the automobile industry, in particular, 'the lean production revolution' which got under way in Germany in 1991 forced a recognition of the importance of organizational issues for enterprise performance. To date, progress in confronting these issue has been patchy, as is evident from Jürgens' recent evaluation of the development of teamwork in the automobile industry:

In the more than five years since the adoption of lean production by German companies, major differences in the degree of emphasis on teamwork have become evident. Some manufacturers have achieved almost full integration of their workforces into teams, while others . . . are in a pilot stage. The differences cannot be explained by blockades and controversies in the industrial relations arena, however. Rather, operations managers often hesitate to introduce far-reaching changes, while top-level managers have other priorities. (Jürgens 1997: 111)

If the German system of governance faced only productive challenges, one could have some confidence that consensus could be achieved to promote the social transformation necessary to regenerate the organizational foundations of innovation in German enterprises. The confluence of productive and financial challenges, however, makes the achievement of this outcome much less likely. It provides the scope for those with interests in financial liquidity to use their growing power to live off what has been accumulated in the productive economy in the past rather than to restrain their claims in order to permit the reallocation of resources necessary to develop the organizations required to strengthen the innovative dynamic in the German economy.

8.4.2. Responses to the Financial Challenges

Trends in Pension Reform   To date the initiatives undertaken by the government to improve the funding situation in the state pension scheme have focused on making adjustments within the framework of the pay-as-you-go pension system. The most important legislative initiative to date is the Pension Reform Act of 1989 (which took effect in 1992). It was motivated by the expectation, based primarily on projections of demographic ageing, that contribution rates would have to rise to unsustainable levels in the early decades of the next century to support the extant pension system. The act raised the statutory retirement age to 65 by 2001. It was also intended to make early retirement more difficult in the future. If workers wished to retire earlier they would have to take a reduction in their pension of 3.5 per cent per annum (compared with a reduction of 6.6 per cent per annum in the US) but from 2001 the earliest age at which they can retire will be set at 62 years (Schmähl 1993).

The effectiveness of the 1992 reform of the pension system was dependent on enterprises' employment strategies and conditions in the labour market more generally. However, the major workforce reductions in West German industry in the 1990s, as well as the ongoing process of restructuring in East Germany, increased the demands for pension benefits as claims for early retirement due to unemployment continued to rise. Rising unemployment also reduced the number of contributors to the system. Notwithstanding the reform, therefore, the contribution rate had to be increased to make up the shortfall.

It was in this context that new legislation, to deal explicitly with early retirement, was introduced in August 1996. The law aimed to raise the minimum early retirement age for men in steps from 60 to 63 over the period from 1997 to 1999. Employees who want to retire before 63 years of age will have to accept an annual cut of 6.3 per cent in their pension for every year taken before that age. Men aged 55 years and more by February 1996 were exempted from the provisions of the law, as were women, employees with disabilities, and employees in the iron and steel industry under certain circumstances. The reform also introduced measures to encourage employees over the age of 55 to work on a part-time basis prior to retirement; workers can halve their working hours and receive 70 per cent of their incomes. Employers are required to pay only for the hours worked; the unemployment insurance fund makes up the difference if the employer hires another employee to work the half-job made available (*EIRR*, 272: 24–6).

The contribution rate to finance the statutory pension scheme was increased again in 1997 and the Kohl government proposed the introduction in 1998 of the draft of a new Pension Reform Bill which was originally slated for 1999. The draft included a proposal to eliminate the early retirement pension for unemployed workers and for women in 2012. Instead, the right to early retirement would only be granted to those who have paid contributions for at least 35 years, the option would only be available from the age of 62, and a reduction in pension benefits of 3.6 per cent per annum would have to be borne by the retiree. The draft also proposed a reduction in the contribution rate by increasing the federal grant and a substantial tightening of the eligibility requirements for disability pensions (Deutsche Bundesbank 1998: 42–6).

As yet the reforms of the German pension system that have occurred do not constitute a major rethinking of the pension system. Proposals for a fundamental overhaul of the German pension system—for example, the replacement of the existing statutory pensions by a flat-rate minimum pension and/or a change from the pay-as-you-go system to a funded pension scheme—were mooted in Germany around the time of the 1989 legislative reform. They were, however, put forward primarily by academics and were not taken seriously by mainstream parties in the political debate. All of the political parties, except the Green Party, supported the reform, as did the trade union and employer organizations (Schmähl 1993: 42).

The pressures are, however, increasing. The current financing problems are serious and worsening. They are, moreover, directly linked to the *Standort* debate. The previous government was certainly concerned about the *Standort* issue; in September 1993 it published a report called 'Securing Germany's Future as an Economic Base' in which Chancellor Kohl warned of the consequences of rising labour costs, falling working hours, and longer holiday entitlement on Germany's international competitiveness (*EIRR*, 241: 13–17). Since 1982, Kohl's governments had undertaken various legislative initiatives, such as the Employment Promotion Act of 1985, in a concerted attempt to deregulate the labour market, and on issues of labour market policy had in general lined up with employers. Pension reform is, however, even more of a political minefield. Kohl trod carefully in this area and, as a result, drew the wrath of the more right-wing employers, who accused the government of putting off an overhaul of the pension system.

The SPD and the Greens, in contrast, made the issue of pension reform a central part of their election campaigns in September 1998. One proposal that received considerable attention was the imposition of an energy tax to fund state pension obligations. Since taking office, however, it has proven difficult for the Red–Green coalition to agree on the appropriate direction for reform. Gerhard Schroeder's government has put a brake on the cutbacks to the state pension that were due to take effect in January 1999 but as yet no concrete proposals have been made about pension reform (*Pensions and Investment*, 2 Nov. 1998: 16).

The likelihood of radical measures being introduced is being given an added impetus by policy initiatives in the European Union. In its attempts to promote the mobility of capital and labour across European borders, the EU has identified retirement provision as one of the key obstacles to achieving this objective (Mortenson 1992: 6). With a view to removing this obstacle, it has been developing policy proposals that, if introduced, will make private pension provision much more attractive than heretofore, as is evidenced by the recent proposal for a directive to liberalize the EU pension fund market. Multinational companies have been exerting pressure on the European Commission to develop such a directive but they have also been threatening to take the issue to the European Court of Justice if the Commission does not comply with their demands. The directive has been stalled with the resignation of the Commission in early 1999 but it is likely to be pushed through in the near future ('Upheaval in Brussels Delays Pensions Reform', *Financial Times*, 22 Apr. 1999).

Whatever their source, significant changes in the German pension system would undoubtedly entail some move to funding, whatever the merits of such an approach for equitable retirement provision. The legislative framework for a new personal pension vehicle was introduced by the Third Financial Market Promotion Act, which took effect in mid-1998. However, these pension funds were not accorded any tax incentives, making them very little different in practice from ordinary mutual funds ('Pinning Hopes on Pension Reform', *Euroweek*, Apr. 1998). A Pension Reform Commission established by the former Kohl government recommended a move to funded employer pensions along US and British lines but these proposals were not translated into reform prior to the government's losing office. The Red–Green coalition has not yet published any guidelines on the subject although it has stated that 'state pensions will remain the decisive pillar' of pension provision in Germany.

There are, moreover, some signs that employer pensions may be moved out of company financing into market-based instruments. In early 1996 Deutsche Bank purchased equities to the value of $330 million—nearly 15 per cent of its pension book reserve—and allocated them to a pension fund managed by an asset management subsidiary. In late 1997 Deutsche Shell AG announced that it would create a DM2 billion fund in an attempt to generate higher returns from its pension assets. The company expects to earn an average annual return of 7 per cent on investments in stocks and bonds compared with the current rate of 3 per cent that it is generating from holding the funds in cash.

The implications of any move to market financing of pensions for the financial system and, in particular, for pressures for financial liquidity would be substantial. According to Josef Wertschulte, a director of Bayerische Hypotheken- und Wechsel-Bank, 'Pension funds could total between DM1,600 bn and DM2,000 bn in 10 years if the right legal and tax conditions were created. This would double the size of the present equity market' (*Financial Times*, 17 Feb. 1997: 20). The comparative and historical evidence on the relationship of the stock market to the process of economic development in the advanced industrial economies does not suggest that such a deepening of the German equity market would lead to an increased allocation of funds to productive investment. To the contrary, it would more likely promote escalating demands for financial liquidity among those with accumulated financial assets and could, as a result, undermine the social conditions necessary to support the development and utilization of productive resources (Lazonick and O'Sullivan 1997*b*, 1997*c*).

Germany's Impatient Financial Enterprises   There are key players in the German economy who have significant incentives to support pressures for greater financial liquidity. Of particular importance are the interests of major financial enterprises operating in Germany. All three sectors of the banking industry—the savings banks, the cooperative banks, and the private banks—have been active participants in 'the battle over the piggy bank' which has been under way in Germany in recent decades

(Oberbeck and Baethge 1989: 287). Indeed, Germany has one of the most extensive banking networks in the world and in recent decades competition among German banks has rapidly intensified. By the end of the 1970s the major insurance companies had also become formidable competitors for the savings of German people. Competing for savings has provided these financial enterprises with strong incentives to promote liquidity in the German economy.

Arguably, the large private banks—Deutsche Bank, Dresdner, and Commerzbank, the alleged 'patient capitalists' of the German economy—have particularly strong incentives to support higher returns on financial assets. They have less to lose than the savings and cooperative banks (with a combined total of 80 per cent of savings deposits) through the disintermediation that has already resulted and will continue to result from the widespread introduction of market-based savings instruments (Deutsche Bundesbank 1991). Moreover, with their access to high-income Germans through their retail networks, and their experience in securities markets at home and abroad, they are well positioned to exploit the profit potential of this business. Reflecting these incentives, they have already been very active in the introduction of these new savings instruments and in attempting to promote an 'equity culture' in Germany.

Deutsche Bank, for example, has been leading the campaign to induce reserves off company balance sheets into pension funds controlled by professional asset managers. In 1996, Deutsche Bank Research published a report that called for a shift 'From Pension Reserves to Pension Funds' which provoked much discussion and controversy in Germany. At the end of 1997, the German banking association submitted draft legislation on employer pension funds that called for the management of pension funds by external money managers as well as favourable tax treatment for externally funded pension provision.

It is not just the banks that have a stake in greater financial liquidity in the German economy; German insurance giants like Allianz have also been eyeing the increased business opportunities in asset management that would be available to them if there were a greater trend toward financial liquidity in the German economy. Allianz has substantial holdings in other financial enterprises—for example, it owns 22 per cent of Dresdner Bank and 26 per cent of Munich Re—and so its increased interest in asset management is likely to have important implications for the future of the German financial sector (*Euromoney*, Jan. 1997: 41–8).

The incentives of these financial enterprises to stimulate demands for higher financial returns in Germany are reinforced by similar trends towards heightened competition in other segments of their business. The overhaul of the regulatory framework of the German financial markets that has occurred since the mid-1980s has facilitated the intensification of competition in the German financial sector (Deeg 1996; Story 1997). For example, Deutsche Bank dominated the market as the syndicate leader for new issues in the post-war period. From the early 1980s, however, more banks won access to the stock exchange as dealers, and competed successfully for such a role (Deeg 1991: 201). The intensification of competition in this segment of the banking business was seen in the rush to float the shares of medium-sized enterprises during a boom in the German stock market in the late 1980s. The boom was fuelled by the success of these companies and the excitement about the prospects of reunification for German industry. So vigorous was the competition among German financial institutions for this initial public offering business that when the market slumped in the early 1990s and a number of companies encountered substantial difficulties, the banks were charged with floating companies that were not 'borsenfähig' (ready for the stock market) (*Institutional Investor*, Nov. 1993).

In the late 1980s and early 1990s, the leading German banks, especially Deutsche Bank and Dresdner Bank, seemed confident that they could compensate for slimmer margins in their domestic business by turning themselves into global investment banks. They have, however, encountered serious setbacks in the pursuit of that strategy. Deutsche Bank, in particular, has run into a series of expensive obstacles. Deutsche Bank bought the British investment bank Morgan Grenfell in 1989 but ran into serious problems with the integration of its operations in the mid-1990s. An asset management fraud in the London operation raised serious questions about the German bank's internal controls and senior executives in Frankfurt assumed control of the British operation. In the meantime, Deutsche Bank embarked on another strategy to build its investment banking business when it paid enormous amounts of money to poach teams of top investment bankers from its rivals, including Frank Quattrone from Morgan Stanley and Edson Mitchell from Merrill Lynch, along with their respective teams. The German bank was heavily criticized by its competitors for inducing pay inflation. As it turned out, the strategy was a failure. It proved extremely difficult to integrate the highly paid recruits into the Deutsche Bank organization, and most of them have already left. Meanwhile, competition had intensified in Deutsche Bank's domestic market and it found itself in a weak position with respect to its US competitors even on its home turf; in 1997 it ranked only sixth in Germany among merger and acquisition (M&A) advisers behind US banks like J. P. Morgan and Goldman Sachs. Moreover, in December 1997, Merrill Lynch hired Werner Fassbender, the chief of M&A at Deutsche Morgan Grenfell.

Deutsche Bank has spent huge amounts of money in what to date looks like a distinctly unsuccessful strategy. Group profits have been declining in recent years and in 1997, the investment banking and equity trading activities were reported to have made a loss (*Global Finance*, Apr. 1998). In January 1998 the bank announced that it was about to undertake a major restructuring, the cost of which was estimated to be an additional $1.9 billion, and that it would refocus its efforts on its domestic market. When, later in 1998, Deutsche Bank announced that it would acquire Bankers' Trust for $10.1 billion, a premium of $2.6 billion on its market value, and that it would pay an additional $400 million to keep Bankers' Trust's top executives in place for the early months of the integration, the financial markets were shocked. As one analyst put it, 'It's like the Titanic. One hour after hitting the iceberg, you can still go to the bar and ask for a whiskey on the rocks, but this ship won't make port' (Crispin Odey, London hedge fund manager, quoted in *Global Finance*, Apr. 1998: 33). In April 1999, Jürgen Krumnow, Deutsche Bank's chief financial officer, resigned from the *Vorstand*, reportedly because he strongly disagreed with the decision of Rolf Breuer, the speaker of the *Vorstand*, to acquire Banker's Trust and more generally with his strategy of expanding into investment banking ('Deutsche Bank Loses Chief of Financing,' *Wall Street Journal Europe*, 22 Apr. 1999: 13).

Deutsche Bank's bid looks like a defensive move to regain lost ground, even in Germany, by using the strengths of Bankers' Trust in asset management, high-yield bonds, and derivatives. However that strategy turns out in practice, the level of competition in German finance is likely to increase still further as Deutsche Bank, and other German banks, struggle to regain business and profits in the German market. To characterize these companies as 'patient capitalists' seems particularly misguided in the 1990s. Indeed, it has arguably long been a misnomer. The Big Banks, for example, have never been shy about advancing their profit interests and have done well from their post-war acquiescence in a system that provided German enterprise with financial commitment largely because of restrictions on competition, both among savings instruments and in the securities markets. As Germans have grown wealthier and competition for their savings has intensified, however, the banks increasingly see their interests as being better achieved by promoting financial liquidity rather than financial commitment.

A symptom of this change is the weakening of bank–industry linkages over the last two decades. The private banking sector as a whole has reduced its seats on the supervisory boards of the 100 largest AGs from 162 in 1974 to 104 in 1989. They have also reduced their direct shareholdings; the number of companies in which banks held at least 10 per cent of the shares (directly or indirectly) fell from 129 in 1976 to 86 in 1986 and the number on which they controlled a blocking minority of more than 25 per cent fell from 86 to 45 (Deeg 1991: 201). In the 1990s, the reduction of banks' industrial holdings has gained pace. The major commercial banks, especially Deutsche Bank, have made no secret of the fact that they would like to receive higher returns from these holdings either by managing them more actively or by selling them. Until recently, the German tax system has put a brake on the latter option; a major capital gains tax liability would accrue on most of these holdings because they have been held by the banks for so long. As the banks have come under increasing financial pressures in their own businesses, however, that barrier is no longer prohibitive.

In 1997, for example, Deutsche Bank reduced to zero its stakes in a number of important German companies including AMB, Bayersiche Vereinsbank, and Karstadt, and substantially reduced its stakes in other leading companies like Continental and Metallgesellschaft. Apparently, the premia paid for these shares was sufficiently high to compensate Deutsche Bank for the tax liability incurred on the transactions. In December 1998, the bank issued euro-denominated bonds, exchangeable into Allianz ordinary shares. The hugely successful issue allowed Deutsche Bank to sell off some of its holdings of Allianz shares—its stake in Allianz was reduced from 10 to 8.3 per cent in the process—at a substantial premium and to defer the tax liability until the bonds are exchanged. Later the same month, in what is regarded as a prelude to a more shareholder-value-oriented strategy toward the management of its share portfolio, Deutsche Bank announced that it would move its remaining stakes in other German companies into a group of newly formed, tax-efficient, asset management subsidiaries. Other major German financial enterprises have been following Deutsche's lead. In February 1998, for example, Allianz issued an exchangeable bond to monetize approximately half of its stake in Deutsche Bank. Dresdner has announced that it is moving its portfolio of shareholdings into an asset management subsidiary that will be managed at arm's length from the rest of the bank.

The Big Banks' involvement in the hostile takeover bid launched by Krupp for Thyssen in March 1997 is also suggestive of a shift in their orientation. The head of Krupp, Gerhard Cromme, had already made history in 1991 as the first German businessman to successfully conclude a major hostile takeover when his company bought out the Hoesch steel enterprise (*The Economist*, 22 Mar. 1997: 80). As *The Economist* described him, Cromme is 'much liked by western investment bankers in Frankfurt, who see him as a champion of new-style Germany, committed to shareholder value and transparent accounts—as well as a future filled with juicy fees for them' (*The Economist*, 8 Nov. 1997). Deutsche Morgan Grenfell and Dresdner Kleinwort Benson were Cromme's advisers and reputedly provided Krupp with a credit line of DM18 billion through their parent banks, Deutsche Bank and Dresdner Bank respectively. That the banks were also involved with Thyssen, not least because of the proxy votes that they hold in this diffusely held company, got them into some hot water. In general, the bid was denounced by Thyssen management, the unions, and local politicians. Krupp was persuaded to drop its bid although the companies agreed to merge their carbon steel businesses. In November 1997, however, Thyssen dropped its objections and the two companies agreed to a friendly merger (*The Economist*, 8 Nov. 1997: 69–70; *Der Spiegel*, 48 (1997): 124–5).

To date, notwithstanding the concerted efforts by financial enterprises to promote demands for higher yields among broad sections of the German population, they have had limited though growing success. The stock market is already highly liquid but largely because of the influential role played by foreign investors, some of whom, however, are Germans recycling their money through international financial markets to avoid domestic taxes. But the market is not, as yet, very deep. Notwithstanding changes in the structure of German savings in recent decades, equity holdings as a percentage of private financial assets remain low in international terms (*Deutsche Bank Bulletin*, 9 Jan. 1995: 9). The appetite of German households for equities, however, has been rapidly increasing in recent years. The proportion of Germans owning shares increased from 5.4 per cent in the early 1990s to 7.6 per cent in 1995 and then again to 8.8 per cent in 1997 (*Deutsche Bank Bulletin*, Jan. 1995: 9; *The Economist*, 6 Dec. 1997).

If the trend toward financial liquidity continues, and particularly if it gains a major boost from reforms of the pension system, it is plausible that German financial enterprises may find willing allies in the country's corporate managers attracted by the possibilities of enriching themselves. A striking example of a senior German manager who has in recent years marketed himself as an exemplar of a new breed of tough and entrepreneurial German executives is the chairman of Daimler-Benz, Jürgen

Schremmp. Until recently, Daimler-Benz was pursuing a grand strategy to become an integrated technology concern under the leadership of its previous chairman, Edzard Reuter, and with the support of Deutsche Bank, the company's leading share-holder. In 1995, however, Reuter was replaced by Schremmp following the announce-ment of an enormous loss of DM5.7 billion, the largest sustained by a German company in the post-war period.

Schremmp's stated objective as chairman is to transform the company to make shareholder interests the number-one priority. Among the changes that have been justified as 'maximizing shareholder value' are the transfer of work valued at DM1 billion to suppliers in Asia to eliminate 8,800 jobs at Daimler-Benz Aerospace (Dasa), the dismantling of the loss-making AEG industrial goods subsidiary, and the with-drawal of financial support for Fokker, Daimler's Dutch aircraft subsidiary (*Financial Times*, 11 Apr. 1996: 11; *The Economist*, 16 Mar. 1996). In April 1996 the company announced the introduction of a share-option incentive scheme for 170 of its senior executives to ensure that their personal financial interests coincide with those of its shareholders (*Financial Times*, 2 Apr. 1996, 24 Apr. 1996). The company's works councils apparently supported the plan but the employee representatives on the supervisory board, with one exception, objected to it. In explanation of their stance, one member of the board, Bernhard Wurl, a senior official of IG Metall, said that they were afraid that the company's share price would assume overriding significance if the executives had options and that job losses would be increased in attempts to get profits up. But the plan brought kudos from the Anglo-American business press, as exemplified by an article in the *Financial Times*:

the case for seeking to establish a closer alignment between the interests of owners and man-agement is not difficult to make here. One of the disadvantages of a bank-dominated corpo-rate system is that banks may have a greater interest in promoting size rather than profitability. It is certainly striking that Deutsche Bank, the biggest shareholder in Daimler-Benz, was inti-mately involved in the disastrous conglomerate strategy pursued by Mr Schrempp's predeces-sor, Mr Edzard Reuter. (*Financial Times*, 9 Apr. 1996)

The statement omits to mention that not only was Deutsche Bank a supporter of Daimler's 'disastrous conglomerate strategy', so too was Jürgen Schrempp! Nor does it recognize that the incentives of Deutsche Bank and other financial enterprises in Germany have changed considerably in recent decades. Indeed, Deutsche Bank had pipped Daimler-Benz to the post by a week when it announced the first large-scale executive share-option scheme in the German corporate economy (*Financial Times*, 24 Apr. 1996).[5]

Senior German managers seem to be increasingly influenced by what is happen-ing overseas, especially in the US corporate economy, and they display a growing propensity to adopt practices that until recently were regarded as anathema in German business circles. The ostensible role of these 'innovations', from executive stock options to stock buybacks, is to improve the efficiency of the German corpo-

---

[5] Continental, the tyre company, and BHF-Bank have run small-scale option schemes for some time.

rate economy to allow it to compete better in an integrated European economy and a tougher global economy. There are, however, reasons to doubt that executives' true motivations are, in fact, so noble. Moreover, to the extent that they are really trying to build stronger capabilities to develop and utilize productive resources within the corporations they control, some of their methods seem to be of doubtful efficacy.

Some German chief executives are clearly motivated by the opportunities for their own self-enrichment which comes with the type of restructuring that they are pushing through. A mere six months after Daimler had made its generous stock option award to its senior managers, 75 per cent of them had cashed in on the current stock price. Notwithstanding all of the talk of the importance of 'pay for performance' that accompanied the introduction of options, Daimler had 'overlooked' the importance of locking their recipients into the success of the company.

The Daimler–Chrysler merger has also thrown the issue of executive pay in Germany into sharp focus. The deal was, at the time it was undertaken, the largest industrial merger and the largest cross-border merger ever. In fact, however, although described as a merger of equals, the transaction really represented a takeover of the US company by its German counterpart. Yet, the Chrysler senior executives can hardly be cast as unfortunate victims, since they were outrageously compensated for their relative loss of power. Thirty of Chrysler's top executives received $395.8 million in cash and stock options in the new company to divide up among themselves. Robert Eaton, Chrysler's CEO, received $3.7 million in cash, $66.2 million in Daimler–Chrysler stock, options on an additional 2.3 million of the new company's shares, some of which he was allowed to cash in within six months, the remainder inside of twelve months, and the promise of a 'golden parachute' to the tune of $24.4 million, if the stress of being an underling to Schrempp proves too taxing to be endured.

Compared to his US counterparts, Schrempp himself, making nearly $1,000,000 a year, looks like a pauper. Yet, if the Germans are now firmly in charge of the new company, especially as a number of high-ranking Chrysler executives have left with their nest eggs in hand, it looks as if the American ethos may come to dominate the otherwise German company. A spokesman for the German side noted, 'We've always said we have to make our pay structure here more competitive internationally . . . But obviously you cannot adopt the US system from day one' (Daimler spokesman Eckhard Zanger, quoted in *Asian Wall Street Journal*, 7 Aug. 1998: 2).

There are, undoubtedly, other reasons besides their own enrichment that explain why German corporate executives are waxing lyrical about the merits of shareholder value. With German companies involved in unprecedented levels of merger activity as acquirers and targets, getting the stock valuation up seems to be a critical means of maintaining control in the wave of corporate restructuring under way. Indeed, there is no doubt as to why Daimler was the driving force behind the merger with Chrysler if one looks at their relative stock valuations in the period leading up to the deal. If Daimler has been an aggressor, other German companies are attempting to boost their stock valuations to avoid being targets. The German banks are a good example, as *Business Week* pointed out in April 1999:

These days, investors judge banks on a Europewide basis, so the Germans' faltering strategies and anemic profits don't measure up. And the more stock the shareholders dump, the more vulnerable Germany's banks. As rivals build clout with megamergers, the Germans' weak share prices mean that they can't afford to make deals with successful prospective partners elsewhere in Europe, let alone in the US Unless the Germans focus on boosting their stock, they'll wind up the losers in the bank wars raging across the Continent.

Clearly the importance of highly valued stock as a merger currency or a deterrent against undesirable bidders provides German executives with significant incentives to sing to the tune of shareholder value. Yet, given the historical problems of corporate overextension, compounded by the challenge of integrating companies embedded in different national economies, it is open to serious question whether the restructuring of German corporations that is being driven by the merger market will raise their productive capabilities.

8.5. Whither German Corporate Governance?

The new managerial rhetoric of shareholder value at leading German companies such as Daimler-Benz, Hoechst, and Veba is certainly striking in historical perspective but, at this point, it is difficult to assess its likely implications for the German system of corporate governance as a whole. Many Germans, and continental Europeans in general, are sanguine about the possibilities of these types of behaviour taking hold among German managers. And within German companies, even those that are most strident in their proclamations of their conversion to shareholder value, corporate resource allocation processes are only beginning to be overhauled to accord with its logic.

Nevertheless, it is dangerous to dismiss such rhetoric as grandstanding or faddish. The analysis which I have presented here suggests that the confluence of structural changes in the financial and productive spheres has created the conditions under which a formidable challenge to the extant system of German corporate governance might be mounted. Moreover, the US experience of corporate governance in recent decades is an instructive one. Today the United States is regarded as a bastion of liquid financial markets. Yet, market control over the allocation of corporate resources is a relatively new phenomenon in US history. Until the 1980s, organizational control dominated, ensuring committed finance to American corporate enterprises. One of the most important lessons which the recent history of American corporate governance teaches us is that, in the face of unprecedented productive and financial challenges to an extant system of corporate governance, 'organization men' can be induced to be ardent proponents of shareholder value, at least with appropriate incentives for self-enrichment.

If it is too early to tell how the current contest for corporate control will conclude in Germany it is apparent that in studying the evolution of the German system of corporate governance there are a number of critical relations to watch. One is the relationship between senior German managers and the rest of the corporate organization. To the extent that they are increasingly segmented from the people they manage, share prices will undoubtedly become more and more important as an incentive either for their personal gains through stock options or for their empire-building through mergers and acquisitions. The second critical relationship for shaping the evolution of German corporate governance is that between older generations who depend on retirement income and the rest of German society. To what extent will a social solution be found to remedy the ills of the German pension system, or will there be a push to greater individualization of pension provision with the greater resort to the financial markets, and the equity markets in particular, that such a strategy would almost inevitably entail? Thirdly, there is the relationship between labour and the rest of German society. An important difference between Germany and the US is that if German managers try to follow their American counterparts down the path to shareholder value, they will have to contend with a politically powerful labour movement. Already the German advocates of shareholder value have been attacked by workers and their representatives, at least for their more blatant attempts to introduce 'casino capitalism'.

A strong labour movement does not, however, ensure that the foundations of sustainable prosperity will be regenerated in Germany. Perhaps the biggest risk that the German system of corporate governance now faces, given the productive and financial challenges it confronts, is that German labour and financial interests will insist on pursuing their own independent strategies to extract returns from industrial enterprises without any consideration of whether those returns will be forthcoming in the future. If this were to happen German corporate governance would dissipate into a 'stakeholder economy' in which different interest groups fight for their claims to corporate returns without any concern for whether these returns are sustainable. Alternatively, the existing system of governance may provide the possibility for the coordination of financial, labour, and managerial interests to develop a new system of organizational control that allows a regeneration of the basis for sustainable prosperity in the German economy.

Conclusion

Empirical analysis of the US and German systems of corporate governance highlights the prevalence of organizational control across industry and over time. In both cases, the institutional foundations for organizational control were laid in the late nineteenth century. Yet the comparison of the systems of governance reveals that the institutional foundations of organizational control have taken very different forms in both of these countries, with important economic and political repercussions. Furthermore, governance institutions in both the US and Germany have evolved substantially, so that in both cases the essence of organizational control has changed considerably over the course of the twentieth century.

That the allocation of resources in the US and German corporate economies has been shaped by governance regimes which can be characterized as systems of organizational rather than market control during the most vigorous periods of their development poses a serious historical dilemma for shareholder theory given the importance that it ascribes to the free flow of economic resources from one use to another. Moreover, the empirical problems that the shareholder theory confronts when considered as a holistic perspective on the appropriate governance of corporate enterprises are also reflected in analyses of the economic effects of mechanisms advocated by financial economists to increase the control of financial markets over corporate resource allocation and, as a result, to limit the discretion of corporate managers to act other than in the interests of shareholders. Notwithstanding the vigour with which the efficacy of these mechanisms is asserted by proponents of shareholder theory, there is, as I have discussed in Chapters 5 and 6, a striking dearth of unambiguous empirical evidence to support their theoretical claims and much that casts considerable doubt on their validity.

The empirical problems of the shareholder theory of governance are rooted in the limitations of its theoretical framework. To understand how corporations should be governed to generate economic performance in a dynamic economy necessitates an analysis of corporate governance that is rooted in an understanding of the relationship between corporate resource allocation and innovation. Far from providing an analysis of that relationship, the shareholder theory of corporate governance, taking its lead from neoclassical economics, makes no attempt to deal with innovation and its implications for resource allocation. The central problem with shareholder theory is that it is based on a concept of economic activity as the allocation of scarce resources to alternative uses, where the productive capability of these resources, and the alternative uses to which they can be allocated, are given. Yet, how returns to investment are generated within the economy cannot be understood without analysing the process through which resources are developed as well as utilized within the economy. Financial economists make no attempt to deal with innovation and its implications for resource allocation. Instead, they assert that shareholders are entitled to lay claim to the rewards that investments generate without analysing how these investments might yield returns.

In recognizing the need for an analysis of wealth creation as the foundation for a theory of corporate governance, the stakeholder theory provides a much better starting point for an analysis of the institutional foundations of corporate resource allocation in dynamic economies. Yet, at least to date, the stakeholder theory of governance has not succeeded in delving deeply into the question of how corporations allocate resources to generate innovation. In analysing the stakeholder theory I have focused on what I regard as the most sophisticated articulation of the perspective, that advanced by Margaret Blair, who makes the case for a corporate governance process that allocates returns to 'firm-specific' assets. But Blair provides no analysis of the process that generates 'firm-specific' assets. That is, she asserts that these assets can generate 'quasi-rents' but without explaining where the opportunities to create such rent-generating assets might come from or under what conditions they will generate returns. Consequently, the stakeholder perspective provides no analytical basis for understanding why corporate economies that at one time and place were capable of generating prosperity on the basis of investments in the knowledge and experience of certain groups of people become incapable of doing so when conditions in the environment in which they compete change. As is evident from the empirical analysis of the US and Germany, it is imperative that we have a theoretical framework for understanding these issues if we are to understand the evolving relationship between corporate governance and economic performance over the *longue durée*.

An additional problem with the stakeholder perspective as a guide to the reality of corporate governance is that it sees returns as attaching to specific human and physical assets, and views the claims to these assets as being based on investments that individual shareholders and employees make. The assumptions that both investment in and returns from productive investments attach to individuals, even when these factors of production are combined in firms, preclude an analysis of the organizational character of corporate investment and corporate returns. As a result, as I emphasized in Chapter 2, the stakeholder theory provides no analytical basis for dealing with the fact that in all systems of corporate governance there are insiders and outsiders to the process of innovation and wealth creation. The differences between the access of various participants in the corporate economy to learning opportunities and rewards do not seem to be reducible to differential incentives to make investments in firm-specific assets. Rather, they are more plausibly explained as a consequence of the abilities and incentives of strategic decision-makers to commit resources to processes that can generate organizational learning. The stakeholder perspective has no conception of strategic control, primarily because it has no theory of the firm other than as a combination of physical and human assets which for some reason—labelled 'firm-specificity'—happen to be gathered together in a particular company. As in neoclassical theory, actual investment decisions are made by individual actors, with shareholders investing in physical assets and employees investing in human assets. That perspective, however, ignores the fact that in the US and

Germany, and indeed in most corporate economies, corporations themselves, not individuals, have been the most critical source of investment in these assets.

There is one additional perspective on corporate governance that has been advanced in the contemporary debates by a number of business school academics, most notably Michael Porter, to which I referred in Chapter 3 as a 'managerial control' perspective (Porter 1992; see also Thurow 1988). Unlike the shareholder or stakeholder theories it makes innovation central to its concept of corporate resource allocation. The proponents of managerial control recognize that the competitive success of the corporate enterprise depends on investments in innovation which entail specialized in-house knowledge, and which require time, and hence financial commitment, to achieve their developmental potential. Thus they argue that managers need discretion to allocate corporate resources, which they are only assured if they have access to 'patient capital' that will enable them to see their investments in productive resources through to competitive success.

The managerial control perspective is full of words such as 'capabilities', 'knowledge', 'skills', 'learning', 'factor creation', and 'innovation' as sources of 'sustained competitive advantage' for the enterprise. That orientation alone sets it apart from the shareholder theory, and brings the proponents of managerial control into much closer contact with the real world. But the fundamental problem with the managerial control perspective, which has made it vulnerable to critiques from shareholder advocates, is that it does not connect to a theory of innovation and investment. The proponents of managerial control provide no systematic explanation of the conditions under which managers will make investments that promote innovation and generate returns and those under which such investments will not be made. Thus they provide no response to allegations that corporate managers have grown 'fat and lazy'.

Furthermore, focused as it is on what existing managers think and do rather than how they are integrated into, or segmented from, the productive organizations in which they invest, the managerial control perspective provides no analysis of the social foundations of innovation and economic development. From the perspective of managerial control, what determines whether or not an enterprise invests in innovation is the 'mindset' of the strategic manager as an actor in a social environment that includes organizations and institutions. What determines the mindset of the manager is rarely addressed. Lacking such an analysis of the social foundations of managerial control, the perspective provides little basis on which to understand the institution and exercise of corporate control across countries with different social structures, as well as the manner in which the incentives and abilities of those who do exercise corporate control evolve over time in ways that may impede rather than enhance the process of innovation in the corporate economy.

What I have attempted to do in this book is to confront the central analytical problem of the leading theories of corporate governance by developing an alternative theory of corporate control that is based on a systematic integration of the economics of innovation and corporate resource allocation. Specifically, the organizational control theory of corporate governance that I have presented tries to come to terms with the reality of a resource allocation process which is, at once, developmental, organizational, and strategic. It seeks to explain how, at any point in time, a system of corporate governance generates institutional conditions that support (1) the commitment of resources to irreversible investments with uncertain returns; (2) the integration of human and physical resources into an organizational process to develop and utilize technology; and (3) the vesting of strategic control within corporations in the hands of those with the incentives and abilities to allocate resources to innovative investments. It also provides a framework for analysing the relationship between institutions of corporate governance and innovation across different business activities, and, within business activities, over time.

In the empirical analysis of the structure and evolution of the US and German systems of corporate governance, I have tried to illustrate the advantages of the organizational control theory for understanding the complex interaction between institutions of corporate governance and economic performance across countries and over time. I have argued that it is only by taking seriously the dynamics of enterprises and economies that we can hope to understand the relationship between corporate governance and corporate performance as it has existed and as it is evolving. That is not to say, however, that the empirical work I have presented herein comes close to achieving that objective. There is a need for much more detailed empirical analysis in order to understand the economic logic of systems of corporate governance. In particular, one can identify the need for further research at three different levels of analysis.

First, economists need to learn much more than we currently know about the incentives and abilities that shape organizational learning processes in enterprises. There are serious limitations to understanding these issues associated with the dominant way of thinking about corporate organizations. One shortcoming is that in analysing the economics of organizations, most economists have emphasized the study of incentives to the exclusion of what is arguably much more important, the economics of the process through which firms develop capabilities. That bias comes at a major cost for our understanding of how firms actually work, as Richard Langlois and Nicolai Foss recently pointed out:

The emphasis in the literature [that is, the mainstream literature on the economics of organization] on misaligned incentives obscures, in our view, the fundamental role that institutions (including the firm) play in qualitative coordination, that is, in helping cooperating parties to align not their incentives but their knowledge and expectations. All recognize that knowledge is imperfect and that most economically interesting contracts are, as a consequence, incomplete. But most of the literature considers seriously as coordinating devices only contracts and the incentives they embody. It thus neglects the role—the potentially far more important role—of routines and capabilities as coordinating devices. Moreover, the assumption that production costs are distinct from transaction costs and that production costs can and should always be held constant obscures the way productive knowledge is generated and transmitted in the economy. (Langlois and Foss 1999: 206)

To remedy the shortcomings of current research on the economics of organization, the challenge is not to throw out incentive issues and focus exclusively on how firms develop their capacity to innovate. Indeed, one could argue that certain heterodox economists, in focusing exclusively on the development of the internal capabilities of the firm to the neglect of the incentives of participants in these firms, have created theories that give accounts of firm behaviour and organization just as biased as those of mainstream economists of organization (Nelson and Winter 1982; see Coriat and Weinstein 1995 for a critique). The challenge is to integrate the analysis of incentives and capabilities in the study of enterprise behaviour.

There is more to achieving such a synthesis than mixing the state of the art on the economics of innovation with the dominant literature on economic incentives. There is a second limitation associated with the way in which most economists conceptualize incentives that makes their work of questionable value for understanding how enterprises provide people with incentives to participate in organizational learning processes. Research on the provision of incentives in firms has to date been dominated by analysis based on the assumption that all relations between individuals which are relevant to understanding their economic behaviour can be understood as arm's-length exchanges or contracts between economic actors, each of whom is ultimately motivated by his desire to maximize his own self-interest. Indeed, most of the mainstream literature on economic incentives focuses on a subset of self-interested contractual relationships described as agency relationships (the study of which is, as I have noted, the foundation for the shareholder theory of corporate governance).

Agency theory analyses economic incentives in situations in which a person (the principal) delegates a task which affects his own welfare to another person (the agent). The principal and agent are assumed to have divergent interests so that the agent cannot be expected to act in the best interests of the principal. What makes the agency relationship economically interesting is that the agent is assumed to have more information than the principal (hidden information) and/or the principal is assumed to be unable to perfectly observe the task that the agent performs (hidden action). The basic incentive problem that emerges in these situations derives from the fact that the principal has no assurance that the agent will take actions that maximize the principal's welfare. The agent's point of view in these situations was captured well by Mark Twain: 'Well, then, says I, what's the use of learning to do right when it's troublesome to do right and ain't no trouble to do wrong, and the wages is just the same?' Most of the economic literature on incentives has addressed itself to the task of making sure that 'the wages is not just the same' by designing contracts to compensate agents in ways that align their interests as closely as possible with those of the principals.

That agency theory has become so dominant as a framework for thinking about the provision of incentives in firms cannot be attributed to an accumulation of compelling empirical support for its arguments; such evidence does not exist. In a recent review of the mainstream literature on incentives and firms, Canice Prendergast, himself a contributor to that literature, began with the statement that '[i]ncentives are the essence of economics. Despite many wide-ranging claims about their supposed importance, there has been little empirical assessment of incentive provision for workers' (Prendergast 1999: 7). Having reviewed the empirical evidence that does exist, Prendergast concluded that

[t]he available evidence suggests that incentives do matter, for better or for worse. It is much less clear, however, whether the theoretical models based on this premise have been validated in the data. The true test of agency theory is not simply that agents respond to incentives, but that the contracts predicted by the theory are confirmed by observed data. Here the literature has been less successful. The literature on the trade-off between risk and incentives has had mixed results. (Prendergast 1999: 56)

Hardly a ringing empirical endorsement of what has become the overwhelmingly dominant framework for thinking about incentives in economics and increasingly in other disciplines too! It is, therefore, not surprising that those less friendly to the mainstream literature on the economics of organization have been more forthright in expressing their doubts that the essential relationships which make firms work can be understood as agency, or even contractual, relationships.

In an article on 'Organizations and Markets', Herbert Simon contended that '[t]he attempts of the new institutional economics to explain organizational behavior solely in terms of agency, asymmetric information, transaction costs, opportunism, and other concepts drawn from neoclassical economics ignore key organizational mechanisms like authority, identification, and coordination, and hence are seriously incomplete' (Simon 1991: 42). Simon goes on to say that '[g]ood answers to the policy questions that face all industrialized societies depend on having empirically sound theories of the behavior of large organizations. Such theories cannot be developed from the armchair. They call for fact-gathering that will carry researchers deep into the green areas, the organizations, that dominate the terrain of our economic systems' (Simon 1991: 43). The need for a richer analysis of organizational incentives is certainly of vital necessity to a richer understanding of corporate governance. In a similar, although more caustic, vein, Charles Perrow emphasizes the need for a broader enquiry into organizational behaviour which has been occasioned by 'the challenge that economists have presented by their foray into the world of organizations, a challenge that resembles the theme of the novel and movie *The Invasion of the Body-Snatchers*, where human forms are retained but all that we value about human behavior—its spontaneity, unpredictability, selflessness, plurality of values, reciprocal influence, and resentment of domination—has disappeared' (Perrow 1986: 41).

There are, of course, those who have responded to these challenges or indeed who have been engaged in broader analyses of organizational behaviour since before agency theory was ever developed. Yet, one should be careful about overstating how much of the extant research in social theory can be used, at least in its current form, to shed light on the economics of incentives in large corporate enterprises. Much of it does not focus directly on the economics of the enterprise. Even economic sociology, the field of enquiry from which one might expect a richer analysis to emerge, and one which has made considerable intellectual progress in the last two decades, has, as yet, failed to provide a compelling analysis of the relationship between organizations and economic performance. Neil Fligstein, someone who has himself made important contributions to the burgeoning literature on economic sociology, described the hole that needs to be filled in our understanding in a recent review in the *American Journal of Sociology* of an edited volume by Alfred Chandler, Franco Amatori, and Takashi Hikino on *Big Business and the Wealth of Nations* (Chandler, Amatori, and Hikino 1997):

We [in economic sociology] have excellent theoretical and empirical studies of the myriad ways in which social relationships and governments have shaped the development of particular organizations and markets. We even have the beginnings of a comparative study of capitalist societies and societies in transition from socialism to market economies.

But economic sociologists have failed to demonstrate systematically why various social arrangements are or are not consequential for economic growth and development. We have skirted the question of efficiency and more or less fallen back on the argument that the world is more contingent than economics would allow. (Fligstein 1999: 902)

If more empirical research is needed to uncover the manner in which incentives and abilities influence and are shaped by business organizations, a research agenda that seeks to understand the relation between corporate governance and innovation also requires comparative studies of resource allocation and competitive performance of corporate enterprises in particular industries operating in different social environments. As I have already noted, research on the relationship between the process of innovation and corporate governance has been limited to date because the leading theories of corporate governance do not systematically integrate an analysis of the economics of innovation. But it has also been neglected because most of the empirical research on innovation has ignored issues of corporate control (see, for example, Nelson 1993; Freeman and Soete 1997; Mowery and Rosenberg 1998).

Finally, more empirical research is required to understand the institutions of corporate governance as they have emerged in different countries and as they have evolved and continue to change over time. In the literature on corporate governance, the treatment of these issues has been too superficial, partly because much of the empirical analysis of systems of corporate governance has not been sufficiently historical (for an exception, see Roe 1994) or comparative. There has therefore been a tendency to assume that the contemporary structure of corporate control has long characterized the economy in which it has been instituted and that it has, as a result, somehow proven itself in terms of its capacity to support the generation of prosperity. Such assumptions, as we have seen in the case of the US in particular, can in fact be extremely misleading. Another tendency in the corporate governance literature is to use classifications such as 'Anglo-American', 'Rhenish', 'Continental European', 'outsider', and 'insider' systems of governance that, by putting countries with quite distinct systems of corporate governance into the same box, arguably obscures rather than reveals the relationship between corporate governance and economic performance.

The French system of corporate governance, for example, is often classified with its German counterpart as a representative of a continental European model of governance. There are certainly important similarities between the two systems, most notably the importance of cross-shareholding. Yet, their institutional differences, particularly with respect to the role of the state in the corporate sector and the relations between senior corporate executives and the rest of the corporate organization, are arguably more important. In the post-war decades, these institutional differences led to important variations between the two countries' corporate economies in terms of who made corporate investment decisions, what kinds of investments they made, and how the returns from those investments were distributed. Notwithstanding recent waves of privatization in France, as well as extensive reorganization of the internal structures of French corporations, the French system of corporate governance is still quite different from its German counterpart. As a result, the pressures that the extant system of governance in France has faced in recent years are somewhat different from those that have confronted the German system. The future evolution of French corporate governance in response to those pressures is also likely to be distinguished from the future trajectory of German corporate governance (O'Sullivan 1999).

If more empirical research is needed to allow us to delve deeper into the economics of corporate governance, we must also overcome the neglect, and indeed in many cases the obfuscation, of the politics of corporate governance. To recognize the central role that organizational control has played in the corporate governance systems of advanced industrial economies is to recognize that the politics of corporate governance is neither an anomaly in successful economies nor separable from issues of efficiency and wealth creation. Rather, it is inherent in systems of corporate governance that generate innovation and development because of the social autonomy of enterprises which these systems support.

The politics of corporate governance is, perhaps, most obvious with respect to how corporate returns are allocated to, for example, higher wages, dividends, or reinvestment. Even more important, however, is the politics that surround what types of investments are made in the corporate economy. Corporate investments have a critical influence on the manner in which resources are developed and utilized. The kinds of investments that corporations make determine what productive capabilities are developed and, therefore, who is included in the process which generates wealth in the economy. For example, even when corporate strategists are willing and able to commit resources to innovative activities, there is no assurance that they will do so in a way that maximizes the breadth and depth of the skill base which is integrated to a process of organizational learning. Innovation may be based on an exclusive learning process—the strategic development of the abilities and incentives of a narrow collectivity of insiders—or an inclusive learning process—strategic investments in the abilities and incentives of a broad-based group of insiders. In general, how corporate control is vested and exercised thus influences the availability and quality of employment opportunities in the corporate economy as well as patterns of social inclusion and exclusion that go beyond the corporate enterprise. The incentives and abilities of those who are endowed with strategic control over corporate investment are thus of central importance in any economy in which corporations play a major role. That innovation is an organizational rather than a 'purely' financial process means that those who exercise corporate control exercise a form of social control. What right do they have to control corporate resources? What defines the boundaries of their power? These are questions for which we still need answers, and as corporations extend their reach further and further throughout the world, these questions are more compelling now than ever before.

An economy in which corporations are central cannot adequately be understood as a 'market' economy that allocates resources to its best alternative uses. As I have emphasized throughout this book, the cumulative, collective, and uncertain character of the innovation process means that the innovative enterprise is a social organization. The accumulation of resources within a corporation to be allocated to alternative uses today reflects, to a considerable extent, processes of innovation that occurred in the past. The economic problem for the corporate enterprise and the economy in which it is embedded is to allocate these resources to processes of innovation in the present that can generate returns to the enterprise and the economy in the future. The mode of corporate control that a society puts in place to resolve this economic problem must be based on an understanding of the corporate enterprise as a social organization which develops and utilizes the productive resources on which the sustainable prosperity of the economy relies.

It is because the innovative enterprise is a social organization and because business corporations have been so important to the innovation process that the key questions of corporate governance—who controls the allocation of corporate resources? what investments do they make? and how are the returns on these investments distributed?—have become, and must remain, foci of public debate. At stake is not just the economic performance of the corporate enterprise but also the sustainable prosperity of the economy as a whole. What mode of organizational control can allocate corporate resources to generate prosperity for the enterprise and the economy? What types of corporate investments in the productive resources can enhance the productive capabilities of enterprise employees and the population more generally? How should different groups of people in the enterprise and in the economy benefit from the returns on these investments so that the enterprise remains a viable economic entity and the economy enjoys sustainable prosperity? These questions concerning the relation between the enterprise and the economy, and ultimately between the economy and society, are not easy to answer. But, as reflected in the narrowness of the academic and public debates on corporate governance to date, the effort to find answers that fit the needs of a modern democratic society has barely been made. My hope is that the theoretical and historical arguments I have presented in this book will help, in some small way, to make the public debates on these central social issues much more penetrating and informed than has thus far been the case.

References

AAMA (American Automobile Manufacturers' Association) (various years), *World Motor Vehicle Data*, Detroit: Government Affairs Division of the AAMA.

ABELSHAUSER, W. (1982), 'West German Economic Recovery, 1945–1951', *The Three Banks Review*, 135: 34–53.

ABRAHAM, D. (1981), *The Collapse of the Weimar Republic: Political Economy and Crisis*, Princeton, NJ: Princeton University Press.

ABRAHAM, K., and HOUSEMAN, S. (1993), *Job Security in America: Lessons from Germany*, Washington, DC: Brookings Institution.

AGRAWAL, A., JAFFE, J., and MANDELKER, G. (1992), 'The Post-merger Performance of Acquiring Firms: A Re-examination of an Anomaly', *Journal of Finance*, 47: 1605–21.

ALBERT, M. (1991), *Capitalisme contre capitalisme*, Paris: Seuil.

ALCHIAN, A., and DEMSETZ, H. (1972), 'Production, Information Costs and Economic Organization', *American Economic Review*, 69: 777–95.

ALLEN, C. (1989), 'Political Consequences of Change: The Chemical Industry', in P. Katzenstein (ed.), *Industry and Politics in West Germany: Toward the Third Republic*, Ithaca, NY: Cornell University Press, 157–84.

ALMEIDA, B. (1998), 'European High Technology: Strategy, Learning, and Competition in Aircraft Engine Manufacturing', mimeo.

ALTMANN, N. (1992), 'Unions' Policies towards New Technologies in the 1980s—An Example from the Metal Industry', in N. Altmann, C. Köhler, and P. Meil (eds.), *Technology and Work in German Industry*, London and New York: Routledge, 361–84.

ALTSCHULER, A., ANDERSON, M., JONES, D., ROOS, D., and WOMACK, J. (1986), *The Future of the Automobile: The Report of MIT's International Automobile Program*, Cambridge, Mass.: MIT Press.

American Management Association (various years), *Survey on Downsizing and Assistance to Displaced Workers*, New York: American Management Association.

ANTONELLI, C. (1997), 'The Economics of Path-dependence in Industrial Organisation', *International Journal of Industrial Organization*, 15: 643–75.

ARNOLD, H., and FAUROTE, F. (1919), *Ford Methods and the Ford Shops*, New York: The Engineering Magazine Company.

ARROW, K. (1964), 'The Role of Securities in the Optimal Allocation of Risk Bearing', *Review of Economic Studies*, 91: 91–6.

——(1974), *The Limits of Organization*, New York: Norton.

——and DEBREU, G. (1954), 'Existence of an Equilibrium for a Competitive Economy', *Econometrica*, 22: 265–90.

ASQUITH, P. (1983), 'Merger Bids, Uncertainty and Shareholder Returns', *Journal of Financial Economics*, 11: 51–83.

——BRUNER, R., and MULLINS, D. (1983), 'The Gains to Bidding Firms from Merger', *Journal of Financial Economics*, 11: 121–40.

——MULLINS, D., and WOLFF, E. (1989), 'Original Issue High Yield Bonds: Aging Analysis of Defaults, Exchanges, and Calls', *Journal of Finance*, 44: 923–52.

ATLESON, J. (1993), 'Wartime Labour Regulation, the Industrial Pluralists, and the Law of Collective Bargaining', in N. Lichtenstein, and H. J. Harris (eds.), *Industrial*

Democracy in America: The Ambiguous Promise, Cambridge: Cambridge University Press, 142–75.

BAETHGE, M., and WOLF, H. (1995), 'Continuity and Change in the "German Model" of Industrial Relations', in R. Locke, T. Kochan, and M. Piore (eds.), *Employment Relations in a Changing World Economy*, Cambridge, Mass. and London: MIT Press, 231–62.

BAKER, D., and Mishel, L. (1995), 'Profits Up, Wages Down: Workers' Losses Yield Big Gains for Business', Economic Policy Institute press release.

BAKER, G. (1992), 'Beatrice: A Study in the Creation and Destruction of Value', *Journal of Finance*, 47: 1081–1119.

——and SMITH, G. (1998), *The New Financial Capitalists: Kohlberg Kravis Roberts and the Creation of Corporate Value*, New York: Cambridge University Press.

——JENSEN, M., and Murphy, K. (1988), 'Compensation and Incentives: Practice vs. Theory', *Journal of Finance*, 43: 593–616.

BALDERSTON, T. (1991), 'German Banking between the Wars: The Crisis of the Credit Banks', *Business History Review*, 65: 554–605.

BALDWIN, C., and CLARK, K. (1994), 'Capital-budgeting Systems and Capabilities Investments in US Companies after the Second World War', *Business History Review*, Spring: 73–109.

BANZ, R. (1981), 'The Relationship between Return and Market Value of Common Stocks', *Journal of Financial Economics*, 9: 3–18.

BARY, A., 'Today's Nifty Fifty. Memories of the 1970s Raise a Question: Are these Giants Worth It?', *Barron's*, 15 Mar. 1999: 21–2.

BASKIN, J.B., and MIRANTI, P., Jr. (1997), *A History of Corporate Finance*, New York: Cambridge University Press.

BECKER, G. (1975), *Human Capital: A Theoretical and Empirical Analysis, with special reference to education*, 2nd edn., New York: National Bureau of Economic Research.

BELL, S. (1940), *Productivity, Wages, and National Income*, Washington, DC: Brookings Institution.

BENINGTON, H.D. (1983), 'Production of Large Computer Programs', *Annals of the History of Computing*, 5: 350–61.

BERLE, A. (1925), 'Problems of Non-par Stock', *Columbia Law Review*, 25: 43–63.

——(1926), 'Non-voting Stock and "Banker's Control"', *Harvard Law Review*, 39: 673–93.

——(1931), 'Corporate Powers as Powers in Trust', *Harvard Law Review*, 44: 1049–74.

——(1932), 'For Whom Corporate Managers are Trustees', *Harvard Law Review*, 45: 1365–72.

——(1968), 'Property, Production and Revolution: A Preface to the Revised Edition', preface to *The Modern Corporation and Private Property*, rev. edn., New York: Harcourt, Brace and World.

——and MEANS, G. (1932), *The Modern Corporation and Private Property*, New York: Macmillan.

BERLE, B.B., and JACOBS, T.B. (eds.) (1973), *Navigating the Rapids, 1918–1971: From the Papers of Adolf A. Berle*, New York: Harcourt Brace Jovanovich.

BEST, M. (1990), *The New Competition: Institutions of Industrial Restructuring*, Cambridge, Mass.: Harvard University Press.

BHAGAT, S., SHLEIFER, A., and VISHNY, R. (1990), 'Hostile Takeovers in the 1980s: The Return to Corporate Specialization', *Brookings Papers on Economic Activity: Microeconomics*, special issue, 1–84.

BLACK, B. (1998), 'Shareholder Activism and Corporate Governance in the United States', in P. Newman (ed.), *The New Palgrave Dictionary of Economics and the Law*, New York: Stockton Press, 459–65.

——and COFFEE, J. (1994), 'Hail Britannia? Institutional Investor Regulation under Limited Regulation', *Michigan Law Review*, 92: 1997–2087.

——and Gilson, R. (1998), 'Venture Capital and the Structure of Capital Markets: Banks Versus Stock Markets', *Journal of Financial Economics*, 47: 243–77.

——(1992), 'Agents Watching Agents: The Promise of Institutional Investor Voice', *UCLA Law Review*, 39: 811–93.

BLAIR, M. (1993), 'Financial Restructuring and the Debate about Corporate Governance', in M. Blair (ed.), *The Deal Decade: What Takeovers and Leveraged Buyouts Mean for Corporate Governance*, Washington, DC: Brookings Institution, 1–18.

——(1995), *Ownership and Control: Rethinking Corporate Governance for the Twenty-first Century*, Washington, DC: Brookings Institution.

BORRUS, M., ERNST, D., and HAGGARD, S. (forthcoming), 'Cross-border Production Networks and the Industrial Integration of the Asia-Pacific'.

——and ZYSMAN, J. (1997), 'Wintelism and the Changing Terms of Global Competition: Prototype of the Future?' Berkeley Roundtable on the International Economy Working Paper 96B.

BÖRSCH-SUPAN, A. (1991), 'Aging Populations: Problems and Policy Options in the US and Germany', *Economic Policy*, 12: 103–39.

BOSCH, G. (1990), *Retraining—Not Redundancy: Innovative Approaches to Industrial Restructuring in Germany and France*, Geneva: International Institute for Labour Studies.

BOUND, J., CUMMINS, C., GRILICHES, Z., HALL, B., and JAFFE, A. (1982), 'Who does R&D and Who Patents?', National Bureau of Economic Research Working Paper.

BRANCATO, C. (1997), *Institutional investors and corporate governance: best practices for increasing corporate value*, Chicago: Irwin Professional.

BREEDEN, D., GIBBONS, M., and LITZENBERGER, R. (1989), 'Empirical Tests of the Consumption-oriented CAPM', *Journal of Finance*, 44: 231–62.

BROCKSTEDT, J. (1984), 'Family Enterprise and the Rise of Large-scale Enterprise in Germany, 1871–1914: Ownership and Management', in A. Okochi, and S. Yasuoka (eds.), *Family Business in the Era of Industrial Growth: Its Ownership and Management*, Tokyo: Tokyo University Press, 237–67.

BRODY, D. (1993), *Workers in Industrial America: Essays on the Twentieth Century Struggle*, 2nd edn., New York: Oxford University Press.

BROOKS, J. (1987), *The Takeover Game*, New York: E. P. Dutton.

BROSSMAN, M., and TATMAN, M. (1998), 'SEC's Amendments to Shareholder Proposal Rules are a Victory for Shareholder Advocacy', *Employee Benefits Journal*, Dec., 20–3.

BRUSONI, S., and PRENCIPE, A. (1999), 'Modularity in Complex Product Systems: Managing the Knowledge Dimension', Complex Product Systems Innovation Centre (University of Sussex and University of Brighton) Working Paper no. 57.

BUCHANAN, J. (1994), 'Increasing Returns: An Introductory Summary', ch. 1 in J. Buchanan, and Y. Yoon (eds.), *The Return to Increasing Returns*, Ann Arbor: University of Michigan Press, 3–13.

BULL, C., and ORDOVER, J.A. (1987), 'Market Structure and Optimal Management Organisations', *Rand Journal of Economics*, 18: 480–91.

BULLOCK, M. (1983), 'The Small Research-based Company Phenomenon in the USA', *Multinational Business*, 1: 22–7.

BURTLESS, G. (1999), 'Growing American Inequality: Sources and Remedies', *Brookings Review*, 17(1): 31–5.

BYGRAVE, W., and TIMMONS, J. (1992), *Venture Capital at the Crossroads*, Cambridge, Mass.: Harvard Business School Press.

BYRNE, J. (1993), *The Whiz Kids: The Founding Fathers of American Business—and the Legacy they Left us*, New York: Currency Doubleday.

CALVERT, M. (1967), *The Mechanical Engineer in America, 1830–1910*, Baltimore, Md.: Johns Hopkins University Press.

CAMPBELL-KELLY, M., and ASPRAY, W. (1996), *Computer: A History of the Information Machine*, New York: Basic Books.

CARLIN, W., and SOSKICE, D. (1997), 'Shocks to the System: The German Political Economy under Stress', *National Institute Economic Review*, Jan., 57–76.

CAROSSO, V. (1970), *Investment Banking in America*, Cambridge, Mass.: Harvard University Press.

CASE, JOSEPHINE YOUNG, and CASE, EVERETT NEEDHAM (1982), *Owen D. Young and American Enterprise: A Biography*, Boston: David R. Godine.

CASEY, B. (1991), 'Recent Developments in the German Apprenticeship System', *British Journal of Industrial Relations*, 29: 205–22.

CHANDLER, A., Jr. (1962), *Strategy and Structure: Chapters in the History of the Industrial Enterprise*, Cambridge, Mass.: MIT Press.

——(1977), *The Visible Hand: The Managerial Revolution in American Business*, Cambridge, Mass.: Harvard University Press.

——(1990), *Scale and Scope: The Dynamics of Industrial Capitalism*, Cambridge, Mass.: Harvard University Press.

——(1997), 'The United States: Engines of Economic Growth in the Capital-intensive and Knowledge-intensive Industries', in A. D. Chandler, F. Amatori, and T. Hikino (eds.), *Big Business and the Wealth of Nations*, Cambridge and New York: Cambridge University Press, 63–101.

——and TEDLOW, R. (1985), *The coming of managerial capitalism: a casebook on the history of American economic institutions*, Homewood, Ill.: R. D. Irwin.

CHANDLER, L. (1970), *America's Greatest Depression, 1929–1941*, New York: Harper and Row.

CICCOLO, J.H., Jr., and BAUM, C.F. (1985), 'Changes in the Balance Sheet of the US Manufacturing Sector, 1926–1977', in B. Friedman (ed.), *Corporate Capital Structures in the United States*, Chicago: University of Chicago Press, 81–109.

CLARK, K., and FUJIMOTO, T. (1991), *Product Development Performance: Strategy, Organisation, and Management in the World Auto Industry*, Cambridge, Mass.: Harvard Business School Press.

COASE, R. (1937), 'The Nature of the Firm', *Economica*, 4: 386–405, repr. in Williamson, and Winter (1993), 18–33.

COFFEE, J. (1991). 'Liquidity versus Control: The Institutional Investor as Corporate Monitor', *Columbia Law Review*, 91: 1277–1368.

COOK, W. (1913), *Treatise on the Law of Corporations Having a Capital Stock*, 7th edn., Boston: Little, Brown.

CORBETT, J., and JENKINSON, T. (1996), 'The Financing of Industry, 1970–1989: An International Comparison', *Journal of the Japanese and International Economies*, 10: 71–96.

CORDINER, R. (1952), 'The Challenges to Management', GE internal publ., Sept., quoted in *Professional Management at General Electric*, vol. 1, p. 75.

——(1956), *New frontiers for professional managers*, New York: McGraw-Hill.

COWAN, R. (1983), *More work for mother: the ironies of household technology from the open hearth to the microwave*, New York: Basic Books.

CRINGELY, R. (1996), *Accidental Empires: How the boys of Silicon Valley make their millions, battle foreign competition, and still can't get a date*, Reading, Mass.: Addison-Wesley.

CUSUMANO, M. (1985), *The Japanese Automobile Industry*, Cambridge, Mass. Cambridge, Mass.: Council on East Asian Studies, Harvard University.

CUTLER, D., POTERBA, J., and SUMMERS, L. (1989), 'What Moves Stock Prices?', *Journal of Portfolio Management*, Spring: 4–12.

DANIEL, K., HIRSHLEIFER, D., and SUBRAHMANYAM, A. (1998), 'Investor Psychology and Security Market Under- and Overreactions', *Journal of Finance*, 53: 1839–85.

DAVID, P. (1975), *Technical choice, Innovation and Economic growth: Essays on American and British Experience in the Nineteenth Century*, New York: Cambridge University Press.

DAVIDSON, P. (1988), 'Financial Markets, Investment, and Employment', in J. Kregel, E. Matzner, and A. Roncaglia (eds.), *Barriers to Full Employment*, London: Macmillan, 73–92.

DEANE, P. (1978), *The Evolution of Economic Ideas*, Cambridge and New York: Cambridge University Press.

DEBREU, G. (1959), *The Theory of Value*, New York: Wiley.

DEEG, R. (1991), 'Banks and the State in Germany: The Critical Role of Subnational Institutions in Economic Governance', unpubl. Ph.D. dissertation, MIT.

——(1996), 'German Banks and Industrial Finance in the 1990s', Discussion Paper of the Wissenschaftszentrum Berlin, FS I 96–323.

DERTOUZOS, M., LESTER, R., SOLOW, R., and the MIT Commission on Industrial Productivity (1989), *Made in America: Regaining the Productive Edge*, Cambridge, Mass.: MIT Press.

DEUTSCHE BUNDESBANK (various years), *Monthly Report of the Deutsche Bundesbank*.

DEWING, A. (1934), *A Study of Corporation Securities, and their Nature and Uses in Finance*, New York: Ronald Press.

DIAL, J., and MURPHY, K. (1995), 'Incentives, Downsizing, and Value Creation at General Dynamics', *Journal of Financial Economics*, 37: 261–314.

DICKEN, P. (1998), *Global Shift: Transforming the World Economy*, 3rd edn., New York: Guilford Press.

DIERICKX, I., and COOL, K. (1989), 'Asset Stocks Accumulation and Sustainability of Competitive Advantage', *Management Science*, 35(12): 1504–15.

DIWAN, R., and CHAKRABORTY, C. (1991), *High Technology and International Competitiveness*, New York: Praeger.

DODD, E.M. (1932), 'For Whom are the Corporate Managers Trustees?', *Harvard Law Review*, 45: 1145–63.

DODD, P. (1980), 'Merger Proposals, Managerial Discretion and Stockholder Wealth', *Journal of Financial Economics*, 8: 105–37.

——and RUBACK, R. (1977), 'Tender Offers and Stockholder Returns: An Empirical Analysis', *Journal of Financial Economics*, 5: 351–73.

DORFMAN, N. (1983), 'Route 128: The Development of a Regional High Technology Economy', *Research Policy*, 12: 299–316.

DORN, P.H., 'Learning from Lemons', *Datamation*, 15 Jan. 1985: 72–4, 76, 78, 80.

DOSI, G. (1982), 'Technological Paradigms and Technological Trajectories', *Research Policy*, 11(3): 147–62.

——(1988), 'Sources, Procedures, and Microeconomic Effects of Innovation', *Journal of Economic Literature*, 26: 1120–71.

DOW, G. (1987), 'The Function of Authority in Transaction Cost Economics', *Journal of Economic Behaviour and Organisation*, 8: 13–38.

DRI/McGRAW-HILL (1996), *The Globalization of the Semiconductor Industry*, New York: DRI/McGraw-Hill.

DRUCKER, P. (1949), *The New Society: The Anatomy of the Industrial Order*, New York: Harper Bros.

DULMAN, S. (1989), 'The Development of Discounted Cash Flow Techniques in US Industry', *Business History Review*, 63: 555–87.

DYAS, G., and THANHEISER, H. (1976), *The Emerging European Enterprise: Strategy and Structure in French and German Industry*, Boulder, Colo.: Westview Press.

DYSON, K. (1986), 'The State, Banks and Industry: The West German Case', in A. Cox (ed.), *State, Finance and Industry: A Comparative Analysis of Post-war Trends in Six Advanced Industrial Countries*, Brighton: Wheatsheaf, 118–41.

ECKAUS, R.S. (1963), 'Investment in Human Capital: A Comment', *Journal of Political Economy*, 71: 501–5.

EDQUIST, C. (ed.) (1997), *Systems of Innovation: Technologies, Institutions and Organisations*, London: Cassell.

EDWARDS, F. (1996), *The New Finance: Regulation and Financial Stability*, Washington, DC: AEI Press.

EDWARDS, J., and FISCHER, K. (1994), *Banks, Finance, and Investment in Germany*, Cambridge and New York: Cambridge University Press.

——and OGILVIE, S. (1996), 'Universal Banks and German Industrialisation: A Reappraisal', *Economic History Review*, 49(3): 427–46.

EISTERT, E., and RINGEL, J. (1971), 'Die Finanzierung des Wirtschaftlichen Wachstums durch die Banken: Eine Quantitativ-empirische Untersuchung für Deutschland, 1850–1913', in W. Hoffmann (ed.), *Untersuchungen zum Wachstum der deutschen Wirtschaft*, Tübingen: Mohr, 345–62.

ENGLMANN, F., HEYD, C., KÖSTLER, D., and PAUSTIAN, P. (1994), 'The German Machine Tool Industry', in Finegold *et al.* (1994), 23–68.

ESSER, J. (1990), 'Bank Power in West Germany Revised', *West European Politics*, 13(4): 17–32.

——and FACH, W. (1989), 'Crisis Management "Made in Germany" ': The Steel Industry', in P. Katzenstein (ed.), *Industry and Politics in West Germany: Toward the Third Republic*, Ithaca, NY and London: Cornell University Press, 221–48.

——and VÄTH, W. (1987), 'Overcoming the Steel Crisis in the Federal Republic of Germany, 1975–83', in Y. Mény, and V. Wright (eds.), *The Politics of Steel: Western Europe and the Steel Industry in the Crisis years (1974–1984)* (Berlin: de Gruyter).

FAMA, E. (1970), 'Efficient Capital Markets: A Review of Theory and Empirical Work', *Journal of Finance*, 25: 383–417.

——(1991), 'Efficient Capital Markets: II', *Journal of Finance*, 46: 1575–1617.

——(1998), 'Market Efficiency, Long-term Returns, and Behavioral Finance', *Journal of Financial Economics*, 49: 283–306.

——and FRENCH, K. (1992), 'The Cross-section of Expected Stock Returns', *Journal of Finance*, 47: 427–65.

————(1996), 'Multifactor Explanations of Asset Pricing Anomalies', *Journal of Finance*, 51: 55–84.

——and JENSEN, M. (1983), 'Separation of Ownership and Control', *Journal of Law and Economics*, 26: 301–25.

——and MILLER, M. (1972), *The Theory of Finance*, Hinsdale, Ill.: Dryden Press.

FARBER, H. (1997), 'The Changing Face of Job Loss in the United States', *Brookings Papers: Microeconomics*, 55–142.

FELDENKIRCHEN, W. (1983), 'Capital Raised and its Use by Mechanical Engineering Firms in the Nineteenth and Early Twentieth Centuries', in W. Engels, and H. Pohl (eds.), *German Yearbook of Business History*, Berlin and New York: Springer, 19–55.

——(1985), 'Zur Finanzierung von Grossunternehmen in der chemischen und elektrotechnischen Industrie Deutschlands vor dem Ersten Weltkrieg', in R. Tilly (ed.), *Beitrage zur quantitativen vergleichenden Unternehmensgeschichte*, Stuttgart: Klett-Cotta, 94–125.

——(1988), 'Concentration in German Industry, 1870–1939', in H. Pohl, and W. Treue (eds.), *The Concentration Process in the Entrepreneurial Economy since the Late Nineteenth Century*, Stuttgart: Franz Steiner, 113–46.

——(1991), 'Banking and Economic Growth: Banks and Industry in Germany in the Nineteenth Century and their Changing Relationship during Industrialisation', in W. Lee (ed.), *German Industry and German Industrialisation*, London and New York: Routledge, 116–47.

FELDMAN, G. (1992), 'Banks and Banking in Germany after the First World War: Strategies of Defence', in Y. Cassis (ed.), *Finance and Financiers in European History, 1880–1960*, Cambridge and New York: Cambridge University Press, 243–62.

FERGUSON, C. (1988), 'From the People Who Brought You Voodoo Economics: Beyond Entrepreneurialism to US Competitiveness', *Harvard Business Review*, 66(3): 55–62.

——and MORRIS, C. (1994), *Computer Wars: How the West can Win in A Post-IBM World*, New York: Times Books.

FINEGOLD, D., and WAGNER, K. (1998), 'The Search for Flexibility: Skills and Workplace Innovation in the German Pump Industry', *British Journal of Industrial Relations*, 36: 469–88.

——BRENDLY, K., LEMPERT, R., HENRY, D., and CANNON, P. (eds.) (1994), *Machines on the Brink: The Decline of the US Machine Tool Industry and Prospects for its sustainable Recovery*, Santa Monica, Calif.: Rand Corp.

FISHER, F., McKIE, J., and MANCKE, R. (1983), *IBM and the US data processing industry: An economic history*, New York: Praeger.

FISHER, I. (1913), 'The Impatience Theory of Interest', *American Economic Review*, 3: 610–18.

——(1930), *The Theory of Interest*, New York: Macmillan.

FLAMM, K. (1988), *Creating the computer: government, industry, and high technology*, Washington, DC: Brookings Institution.

FLIGSTEIN, N. (1990), *The transformation of corporate control*, Cambridge, Mass.: Harvard University Press.

——(1999), 'Review Essay: Chasing Alfred Chandler', *American Journal of Sociology*, 104: 902–5.

FLORIDA, R., and KENNEY, M. (1988), 'Venture Capital, High Technology and Regional Development', *Regional Studies*, 22: 33–48.

————(1990), *The Breakthrough Illusion: Corporate America's Failure to Move from Innovation to Mass Production*, New York: Basic Books.

FLYNN, J.T. (1934), *Security Speculation: Its Economic Effects*, New York: Harcourt, Brace.

FORTUNE, Editors of (1951), *USA: The Permanent Revolution*, New York: Doubleday.

——(1956), *The Executive Life*, New York: Doubleday.

FOULKES, F. (1980), *Personnel Policies in Large Nonunion Companies*, Englewood Cliffs, NJ: Prentice-Hall.

FOY, N. (1975), *The sun never sets on IBM*, New York: Morrow.

FRANCKE, H.-H., and HUDSON, M. (1984), *Banking and Finance in West Germany*, London: Croom Helm.

FRANKS, J., and MAYER, C. (1990), 'Capital Markets and Corporate Control: A Study of France, Germany and the UK', *Economic Policy*, 10: 191–231.

FRANKS, J., and MAYER, C. (1996), 'Hostile Takeovers and the Correction of Managerial Failure', *Journal of Financial Economics*, 40: 163–81.

FREEMAN, C. (1974), *The Economics of Industrial Innovation*, Harmondsworth and Baltimore: Penguin.

——(1994), 'The Economics of Technical Change', *Cambridge Journal of Economics*, 18: 463–514.

——and SOETE, L. (1997), *The Economics of Industrial Innovation*, 3rd edn., Cambridge, Mass.: MIT Press.

FRICKE, W. (1986), 'New Technologies and German Co-determination', *Economic and Industrial Democracy*, 7: 541–52.

FRIEDMAN, L. (1973), *A history of American law*, New York: Simon and Schuster.

FRUHAN, W., Jr. (1979), 'General Electric Company', in W. Fruhan, *Financial Strategy: Studies in the Creation, Transfer, and Destruction of Shareholder Value*, Homewood, Ill.: R. Irwin, 149–79.

FUNK, J. (1992), *The Teamwork Advantage: An Inside Look at Japanese Product and Technology Development*, Cambridge, Mass.: Productivity Press.

GALBRAITH, J.K. (1967), *The New Industrial State*, Boston: Houghton Mifflin.

GALL, L., FELDMAN, G., JAMES, H., HOLTFRERICH, C.-L., and BUSCHGEN, H. (1995), *The Deutsche Bank, 1870–1995*, London: Weidenfeld and Nicolson.

GAUGHAN, P. (1996), *Mergers, Acquisitions, and Corporate Restructurings*, New York: John Wiley and Sons.

GERUM, E., STEINMANN, H., and FEES, W. (1988), *Der mitbestimmte Aufsichtsrat: Eine empirische Untersuchung*, Stuttgart: C. E. Poeschel.

GESSLER COMMISSION (1979), 'Grunsatzfragen der Kreditwirtschaft', *Scheifenreihe des Bundesministerium der Finanzen*, 28: 231–45.

GIERSCH, H., PAQUÉ, K.-H., and SCHMIEDING, H. (1992), *The Fading Miracle: Four decades of market economy in Germany*, New York and Cambridge: Cambridge University Press.

GILDER, G. (1988), 'The Revitalisation of Everything', *Harvard Business Review*, May–June: 49–61.

GILSON, R., and KRAAKMAN, R. (1991), 'Reinventing the Outside Director: An Agenda for Institutional Investors', *Stanford Law Review*, 43: 863–906.

GISPEN, K. (1989), *New Profession, Old Order: Engineers and German Society, 1815–1914*, Cambridge: Cambridge University Press.

GLICKMAN, M. (1994), 'The Concept of Information, Intractable Uncertainty, and the Current State of the 'Efficient Markets' Theory: A Post-Keynesian View', *Journal of Post-Keynesian Economics*, 16: 325–49.

GOETZMANN, W., and JORION, P. (1997), 'A Century of Global Stock Markets', NBER Working Paper Series, no. 5901.

——and MASSA, M. (1998), 'Index Funds and Stock Market Growth', NBER Working Paper Series, no. 7033.

GOMPERS, P. (1998), 'Venture Capital Growing Pains: Should the Market Diet?', *Journal of Banking and Finance*, 22: 1089–1104.

——and METRICK, A. (1998), 'Institutional Investors and Equity Prices', NBER Working Paper Series, no. 6723.

GORDON, D., EDWARDS, R., and REICH, M. (1982), *Segmented Work, Divided Workers: The Historical Transformation of Labor in the United States*, Cambridge and New York: Cambridge University Press.

GORT, M. (1962), *Diversification and integration in American industry: A study*, Princeton, NJ: Princeton University Press.

GRAHAM, M. (1986), *RCA and the Videodisc: The Business of Research*, Cambridge and New York: Cambridge University Press.

GREENWOOD, R. (1974), *Managerial decentralization: a study of the General Electric philosophy*, Lexington, Mass.: Lexington Books.

GROSSMAN, S., and HART, O. (1980), 'Takeover Bids, the Free-rider Problem and the Theory of the Corporation', *Bell Journal of Economics*, 11: 42–64.

————(1988), 'One Share, One Vote, and the Market for Corporate Control', *Journal of Financial Economics*, 20: 175–202.

HALL, B. (1994), 'Corporate Restructuring and Investment Horizons in the United States, 1976–1987', *Business History Review*, 68(1): 110–43.

——and Liebman, J. (1997), 'Are CEOs Really Paid like Bureaucrats?', NBER Working Paper 6213.

HARCOURT, G.C. (1972), *Some Cambridge Controversies in the Theory of Capital*, Cambridge: Cambridge University Press.

HAROLD, G. (1938), *Bond Ratings as an Investment Guide: An Appraisal of their Effectiveness*, New York: Ronald Press.

HARRIS, H.J. (1982), *The Right to Manage: Industrial Relations Policies of American Business in the 1940s*, Madison, Wisc.: University of Wisconsin Press.

HARRISON, B. (1994), *Lean and mean: the changing landscape of corporate power in the age of flexibility*, New York: Basic Books.

HART, O. (1995), 'Corporate Governance: Some Theory and Implications', *Economic Journal*, 105: 678–98.

HAUCK, M. (1994), 'The Equity Market in Germany and its Dependency on the System of Old Age Provisions', in T. Baums, R. Buxbaum, and K. Hopt (eds.), *Institutional Investors and Corporate Governance*, Berlin and New York: de Gruyter, 555–64.

HAYEK, F. (1945), 'The Use of Knowledge in Society', *American Economic Review*, 35: 519–30, repr. in Nishiyama and Leube (1984), 212–24.

——(1984), 'Competition as a Discovery Procedure', in F. Hayek, *New Studies in Philosophy, Politics, Economics, and the History of Ideas*, Chicago: University of Chicago Press (1978), 179–90, repr. in Nishiyama and Leube (1984), 254–65.

HAYES, R., and ABERNATHY, W. J. (1980), 'Managing our Way to Economic Decline', *Harvard Business Review*, July–Aug.: 67–77.

HBS (Harvard Business School) (1994), 'Saturn: A Different Kind of Car Company', Case No. 9-795-010.

HEISLER, J. (1994), 'Recent Research in Behavioral Finance', *Financial Markets, Institutions and Instruments*, 3(5): 76–105.

HERDING, R. (1972), *Job Control and Union Structure*, Rotterdam: Rotterdam University Press.

HERMAN, E., and LOWENSTEIN, L. (1988), 'The Efficiency Effects of Hostile Takeovers', in J. Coffee, L. Lowenstein, and S. Ackerman (eds.), *Knights, Raiders, and Targets: The Impact of Hostile Takeovers*, Oxford: Oxford University Press.

HERRIGEL, G. (1989), 'Industrial Order and the Politics of Industrial Change: Mechanical Engineering', in P. Katzenstein (ed.), *Industry and Politics in West Germany: Toward the Third Republic*, Ithaca, NY: Cornell University Press, 185–220.

——(1995), *Industrial Constructions: The Sources of German Industrial Power*, New York and Cambridge: Cambridge University Press.

HERRIGEL, G. (1996), 'Crisis in German Decentralised Production', *European Urban and Regional Studies*, 3(1): 33–52.

HERZ, D.E. (1990), 'Worker Displacement in a Period of Rapid Job Expansion, 1983–1987', *Monthly Labor Review*, May, 21–33.

HEW (Health, Education, and Welfare Department of the US Government) (1973), *Work in America: Report of a Special Taskforce to the Secretary of Health, Education, and Welfare*, Cambridge, Mass.: MIT Press.

HILFERDING, R. (1981), *Finance Capital: A Study of the Latest Phase of Capitalist Development*, London: Routledge and Kegan Paul.

HIRSHLEIFER, J. (1965), 'Investment Decision under Uncertainty: Choice-theoretic Approaches', *Quarterly Journal of Economics*, 79: 509–36.

HOFFMAN, M. (1972), 'The Conglomerate Mergers', in C. Gilbert (ed.), *The Making of a Conglomerate*, Hofstra University Yearbook of Business, ser. 8, vol. 3, Hempstead, NY: Hofstra University Press, 1–39.

HOFFMANN, W. (1959), 'Die unverteilten Gewinne der Kapitalgesellschaften in Deutschland, 1871–1957', *Zeitschrift für die gesamte Staatswissenschaft*, 115: 271–91.

——GRUMBACH, F., and HESSE, H. (1965), *Das Wachstum der deutschen Wirtschaft seit der Mitte des 19 Jahrunderts*, Berlin: Springer-Verlag.

HOLLAND, M. (1989), *When the Machine Stopped: A Cautionary Tale from Industrial America*, Boston: Harvard Business School Press.

HOLTFRERICH, C.-L. (1986), *The German Inflation, 1914–1923: Causes and Effects in International Perspective*, Berlin: de Gruyter.

HORWITZ, M. (1977), *The Transformation of American Law, 1780–1860*, Cambridge, Mass.: Harvard University Press.

——(1985), 'Santa Clara Revisited: The Development of Corporate Theory', *West Virginia Law Review*, 88: 173–224.

HOUNSHELL, D. (1997), 'Why Corporations Don't Learn Continuously: Waves of Innovation and Desperation at Ford Motor Company, 1903–1996', mimeo.

HOUSEMAN, S. (1991), *Industrial restructuring with job security: the case of European steel*, Cambridge, Mass.: Harvard University Press.

HURST, J.W. (1970), *The Legitimacy of the Business Corporation in the Law of the United States, 1780–1970*, Charlottesville, Va.: University Press of Virginia.

IBER, B. (1985), 'Zur Entwicklung der Aktionarsstruktur in der Bundesrepublik Deutschland, 1963–1983'. *Zeitschrift für Betriebswirtschaft*, 55: 1101–19.

IVERSON, K., with VARIAN, T. (1998), *Plain Talk: Lessons from a Business Maverick*, New York: Wiley.

JACKSON, T. (1997), *Inside Intel: Andy Grove and the rise of the world's most powerful chip company*, New York: Dutton.

JACOBY, N. (1969), 'The Conglomerate Corporation', *The Center Magazine*, 3: 41–53.

JACOBY, S. (1985), *Employing Bureaucracy: Managers, Unions, and the Transformation of Work in American Industry, 1900–1945*, New York: Columbia University Press.

——(1997), *Modern Manors: Welfare Capitalism since the New Deal*, Princeton, NJ: Princeton University Press.

JENSEN, M. (1978), 'Some Anomalous Evidence regarding Market Efficiency', *Journal of Financial Economics*, 6: 95–102.

——(1986), 'Agency Cost of Free Cash Flow, Corporate Finance, and Takeovers', *American Economic Review*, 76: 323–29.

——(1988), 'Takeovers: Their Causes and Consequences', *Journal of Economic Perspectives*, 2(1): 21–48.

——(1989), 'Eclipse of the Public Corporation', *Harvard Business Review*, 67(5): 61–74.

——(1993), 'The Modern Industrial Revolution Exit and the Failure of Internal Control Systems', *Journal of Finance*, 48: 831–80.

——and MURPHY, K. (1990), 'Performance Pay and Top Management Incentives', *Journal of Political Economy*, 98(2): 225–64.

——and RUBACK, R. (1983), 'The Market for Corporate Control: the Scientific Evidence', *Journal of Financial Economics*, 11: 5–50.

JOHNSON, T., and KAPLAN, R. (1987), *Relevance Lost: the rise and fall of management accounting*, Boston, Mass.: Harvard Business School Press.

JORDE, T., and TEECE, D. (1990), 'Innovation and Cooperation: Implications for Cooperation and Antitrust', *Journal of Economic Perspectives*, 4(3): 75–96.

JÜRGENS, U. (1997), 'Germany: Implementing Lean Production', in T. Kochan, R. Lansbury, and J. P. MacDuffie (eds.), *After Lean Production: Evolving Employment Practices in the World Auto Industry*, Ithaca, NY and London: ILR Press, 109–16.

——and LIPPERT, I. (1997), 'Schnittstellen des deutschen Produktionsregimes— Innovationshemmnisse im Produktentstehungsprozeß', in WZB, *WZB-Jahrbuch*, Berlin: WZB, 65–94.

——MALSCH, T., and DOHSE, K. (1993), *Breaking from Taylorism: Changing Forms of Work in the Automobile Industry*, New York and Cambridge: Cambridge University Press.

KALDOR, N. (1972), 'The Irrelevance of Equilibrium Economics', *Economic Journal*, 82: 1237–55.

KAPLAN, S. (1989), 'Management Buyouts: Evidence on Taxes as a Source of Value', *Journal of Finance*, 44: 611–32.

——and STEIN, J. (1993), 'The Evolution of Buyout Pricing and Financial Structure in the 1980s', *Quarterly Journal of Economics*: 313–57.

KATZ, H. (1993), 'The Decentralization of Collective Bargaining: A Literature Review and Comparative Analysis', *Industrial and Labor Relations Review*, 47: 3–22.

KAUFMAN, A., and ENGLANDER, E. (1993), 'Kohlberg Kravis Roberts and Co. and the Restructuring of American Capitalism', *Business History Review*, 67: 52–97.

——ZACHARIAS, L., and KARSON, M. (1995), *Managers vs. Owners: The Struggle for Corporate Control in American Democracy*, New York: Oxford University Press.

KAYSEN, C. (1959), 'The Corporation: How Much Power? What Scope?', in E. Mason (ed.), *The Corporation in Modern Society*, New York: Atheneum, 85–105.

KECK, O. (1993), 'The National System for Technical Innovation in Germany', in R. Nelson (ed.), *National Innovation Systems: A Comparative Analysis*, New York: Oxford University Press, 115–57.

KELLER, M. (1989), *Rude Awakening: the rise, fall and struggle for recovery of General Motors*, New York: Morrow.

KELLY, G., KELLY, D., and GAMBLE, A. (eds.) (1997), *Stakeholder Capitalism*, Basingstoke: Macmillan.

KENNEY, M., and FLORIDA, R. (1993), *Beyond Mass Production: The Japanese System and its Transfer to the US*, New York: Oxford University Press.

KENNICKELL, A., STARR-McCLUER, M., and SUNDÉN, A. (1997), 'Family Finances in the US: Recent Evidence from the Survey of Consumer Finances', *Federal Reserve Bulletin*, 83(1): 1–24.

KIRZNER, I. (1985), *Discovery and the Capitalist Process*, Chicago: University of Chicago Press.

—— (1989), *Discovery, Capitalism, and Distributive Justice*, Oxford: Basil Blackwell.

—— (1997), 'Entrepreneurial Discovery and the Competitive Market Process: An Austrian Approach', *Journal of Economic Literature*, 35: 60–85.

KLINE, S., and ROSENBERG, N. (1986), 'An Overview of Innovation', in R. Landau, and N. Rosenberg (eds.), *The Positive Sum Strategy: Harnessing Technology for Economic Growth*, Washington, DC: National Academic Press, 275–305.

KNIGHT, F. (1971), *Risk, Uncertainty and Profit*, Chicago: University of Chicago Press.

KOCH, A.R. (1943), *The Financing of Large Corporations, 1920–39*, Cambridge, Mass.: National Bureau of Economic Research.

KOCHAN, T., KATZ, H., and McKERSIE, R. (1986), *The Transformation of American Industrial Relations*, New York: Basic Books.

KOCHERLAKOTA, N. (1996), 'The Equity Premium: It's Still a Puzzle', *Journal of Economic Literature*, 34: 42–71.

KOCKA, J. (1971), 'Family and Bureaucracy in German Industrial Management: Siemens in Comparative Perspective', *Business History Review*, 45: 133–56.

—— (1973), 'Entrepreneurs and Managers in German Industrialisation', in P. Mathias, and M. Postan (eds.), *Cambridge Economic History of Europe. Vol. 7, pt. 1, The Industrial Economies: Capital, Labour, and Enterprise*, Cambridge: Cambridge University Press, 578–89.

—— (1980), 'The Rise of the Modern Industrial Enterprise in Germany', in A. Chandler, and H. Daems (eds.), *Managerial Hierarchies: Comparative Perspectives on the Rise of the Modern Industrial Enterprise*, Cambridge, Mass.: Harvard University Press, 77–116.

KOGUT, B. (ed.) (1993), *Country Competitiveness: Technology and the Organising of Work*, New York and Oxford: Oxford University Press.

KÖHLER, C., and SCHMIERL, K. (1992), 'Technological Innovation—Organisational Conservatism', in N. Altmann, C. Köhler, and P. Meil (eds.), *Technology and Work in German Industry*, London and New York: Routledge, 142–59.

KONIG, W. (1993), 'Technical Education and Industrial Performance in Germany: A Triumph of Heterogeneity', in Robert Fox and Anna Guaghini (eds.), *Education, Technology and Industrial Performance in Europe, 1850–1939*, New York: Cambridge University Press, 65–8.

KRAFCIK, J. (1988), 'Triumph of the Lean Production System', *Sloan Management Review*, 30(1): 41–52.

KUHN, T. (1962), *The Structure of Scientific Revolutions*, Chicago: Chicago University Press.

LANE, C. (1989), *Management and Workers in Europe*, Aldershot: Edward Elgar.

LANGLOIS, R. (1986), 'Rationality, Institutions and Explanation', in R. Langlois, *Economics as a Process: Essays in the New Institutional Economics*, Cambridge and New York: Cambridge University Press, 225–55.

—— and FOSS, N. (1999), 'Capabilities and Governance: The Rebirth of Production in the Theory of Economic Organization', *Kyklos*, 52: 201–18.

—— and STEINMÜLLER, W.E. (1998), 'The Evolution of Competitive Advantage in the Worldwide Semiconductor Industry, 1947–1996', mimeo.

LATSIS, S. (1972), 'Situational Determinism in Economics', *British Journal for the Philosophy of Science*, 23: 207–45.

LAWRENCE, P. (1980), *Managers and Management in West Germany*, New York: St Martin's Press.

LAZONICK, W. (1990), *Competitive Advantage on the Shop Floor*, Cambridge, Mass.: Harvard University Press.

—— (1991), *Business Organization and the Myth of the Market Economy*, New York: Cambridge University Press.

——(1992), 'Controlling the Market for Corporate Control', *Industrial and Corporate Change*, 1(3): 445–88.

——(1998), 'Organizational Learning and International Competition', in J. Michie, and J. G. Smith (eds.), *Globalization, Growth, and Governance: Creating an Innovative Economy*, Oxford: Oxford University Press, 204–38.

——and O'SULLIVAN, M. (1996), 'Organisation, Finance, and International Competition', *Industrial and Corporate Change*, 5(1): 1–49.

————(1997*a*), *Corporate Governance and Sustainable Prosperity*, New York: Jerome Levy Economics Institute.

————(1997*b*), 'Finance and Industrial Development: Japan and Germany', *Financial History Review*, 4(2): 113–34.

————(1997*c*), 'Finance and Industrial Development: The United States and the United Kingdom', *Financial History Review*, 4(1): 7–29.

————(1997*d*), 'Big Business and Skill Formation in the Wealthiest Nations: The Organizational Revolution in the Twentieth Century', in Chandler *et al.* (1997), 497–521.

LEBERGOTT, S. (1976), *The American economy: income, wealth, and want*, Princeton, NJ: Princeton University Press.

LESLIE, S., and KARGON, R. (1996), 'Silicon Valley: Frederick Terman's Model for Regional Advantage', *Business History Review*, 70: 435–72.

LEVEN, M., MOULTON, H., and WARBURTON, C. (1934), *America's Capacity to Consume*, Washington, DC: Brookings Institution.

LEVY, H. (1935), *Industrial Germany: A Study of its Monopoly Organisations and their Control by the State*, Cambridge: Cambridge University Press.

LICHTENBERG, F., and SIEGEL, D. (1990), 'The Effects of Leveraged Buyouts on Productivity and Related Aspects of Firm Behavior', *Journal of Financial Economics*, 27: 165–94.

LICHTENSTEIN, N. (1995), *The most dangerous man in Detroit: Walter Reuther and the fate of American labor*, New York: Basic Books.

LIEFMANN, R. (1977), *Cartels, Concerns and Trusts*, New York: E. P. Dutton.

LINN, S., and ROZEFF, M. (1986), 'The Corporate Sell-off', in J. Stern, and D. Chew (eds.), *The Revolution in Corporate Finance*, New York: Basil Blackwell, 428–36.

LINTNER, J. (1965*a*), 'Security Prices, Risk, and Maximal Gains from Diversification', *Journal of Finance*, 20: 587–615.

——(1965*b*), 'The Valuation of Risky Assets and the Selection of Risky Investments in Stock Portfolios and Capital Budgets', *Review of Economics and Statistics*, 47: 13–37.

LITTLER, R.M.C. (1946), 'Managers Must Manage', *Harvard Business Review*, 24: 366–76.

LOASBY, B. (1976), *Choice, Complexity, and Ignorance: An Inquiry into Economic Theory*, Cambridge and New York: Cambridge University Press.

——(1989), *The Mind and Method of the Economist: A Critical Appraisal of Major Economists in the 20th Century*, Aldershot: Edward Elgar.

LOCKE, R. (1989), *Management and Higher Education since 1940: The influence of America and Japan on West Germany, Great Britain, and France*, New York: Cambridge University Press.

LONG, W., and RAVENSCRAFT, D. (1993), 'The Financial Performance of Whole Company LBOs', Center for Economic Studies, Bureau of Economic Analysis Discussion Paper CES 93-16.

LOTH, D. (1958), *Swope of G.E.*, New York: Simon and Schuster.

LUNDVALL, B.-A. (ed.) (1992), *Towards a Theory of Innovation and Interactive Learning*, London: Pinter.

MACHER, J., MOWERY, D., and HODGES, D. (1998), 'Reversal of Fortune? The Recovery of the US Semiconductor Industry', *California Management Review*, 41(1): 107–36.

McKELVEY, M. (1996), *Evolutionary Innovations: The Business of Biotechnology*, Oxford and New York: Oxford University Press.

McKITRICK, F. (1994), 'The Stabilization of the Mittelstand: Artisans in Germany from National Socialism to the Federal Republic, 1939–1953', unpub. Ph.D. thesis, Columbia University.

MAGAZINER, I., and REICH, R. (1982), *Minding America's Business: The Decline and Rise of the American Economy*, New York: Vintage.

MAGENHEIM, E., and MUELLER, D. (1988), 'Are Acquiring Shareholders Better Off after an Acquisition?', in J. Coffee, L. Lowenstein, and S. Ackerman (eds.), *Knights, Raiders, and Targets: The Impact of Hostile Takeovers*, Oxford: Oxford University Press, 171–93.

MAHNKOPF, B. (1991), 'The "Skill-oriented" Strategies of German Trade Unions: Their Impact on Efficiency and Equality Objectives', *British Journal of Industrial Relations*, 30(1): 61–81.

MALATESTA, P. (1983), 'The Wealth Effects of Merger Activity and the Objective Functions of Merging Firms', *Journal of Financial Economics*, 11: 155–81.

MALERBA, F. (1985), *The Semiconductor Business: The Economics of Rapid Growth and Decline*, Madison, Wisc.: University of Wisconsin Press.

MALKIEL, B. (1987), 'Efficient Market Hypothesis', in J. Eatwell, M. Milgate, and P. Newman (eds.), *The New Palgrave: A Dictionary of Economics*, London: Macmillan, 120–3.

MALONE, M. (1985), *The Big Score: the billion-dollar story of Silicon Valley*, Garden City, NY: Doubleday.

MANNING, B. (1958), review of Joseph Livingston, *The American Stockholder*, *Yale Law Journal*, 67: 1477–85.

MARGLIN, S. (1974), 'What Do Bosses Do? The Origins and Functions of Hierarchy in Capitalist Production', *Review of Radical Political Economics*, 6: 33–60.

——(1979), 'Catching Flies with Honey: An Inquiry into Management's Initiatives to Humanize Work', *Economic Analysis and Workers' Management*, 13: 473–88.

MARKOVITS, A. (1986), *The Politics of the West German Trade Unions: Strategies of Class and Interest Representation in Growth and Crisis*, Cambridge and New York: Cambridge University Press.

MARKOWITZ, H. (1959), *Portfolio Selection: Efficient Diversification of Investments*, New York: Wiley.

MARSH, T., and MERTON, R. (1986), 'Dividend Variability and Variance Bounds Test for the Rationality of Stock Prices', *American Economic Review*, 76: 483–98.

MARSHALL, A. (1948), *Principles of Economics*, 8th edn., London: Macmillan.

MAURICE, M., SELLIER, F., and SILVESTRE, J.-J. (1986), *The Social Foundations of Industrial Power*, tr. Arthur Goldhammer, Cambridge, Mass.: MIT Press.

MAYER, C., and ALEXANDER, I. (1990), 'Banks and Securities Markets: Corporate Financing in Germany and the United Kingdom', *Journal of the Japanese and International Economies*, 4: 450–75.

MEANS, G. (1930), 'The Diffusion of Stock Ownership in the United States', *Quarterly Journal of Economics*, 44: 561–600.

MEHRA, R., and PRESCOTT, E. (1985), 'The Equity Premium: A Puzzle', *Journal of Monetary Economics*, 15: 145–62.

MERRILL LYNCH ADVISORY SERVICES (1994), *Mergerstat® Review*, Chicago: W. T. Grumm & Co.

MICHIE, R. (1987), *The London and New York Stock Exchanges, 1850–1914*, London and Boston: Allen and Unwin.

MINTZBERG, H. (1998), 'Managing Quietly', mimeo.

MIROWSKI, P. (1989), *More Heat than Light: Economics as Social Physics, Physics as Nature's Economics*, Cambridge and New York: Cambridge University Press.

MISES, L. VON (1949), *Human Action: a treatise on economics*, New Haven, Conn.: Yale University Press.

MISHEL, L., BERNSTEIN, J., and SCHMITT, J. (1999), *The State of Working America, 1998–99*, Ithaca, NY: Cornell University Press.

MIT COMMISSION ON INDUSTRIAL PRODUCTIVITY (1989), *The Working Papers of the MIT Commission on Industrial Productivity*, 2 vols., Cambridge, Mass.: MIT Press.

MIYAZAKI, K. (1995), *Building Competences in the Firm: Lessons from Japanese and European Optoelectronics*, New York: St Martin's Press.

MONKS, R., and MINOW, N. (1991), *Power and Accountability*, New York: Harper Business.

MONOPOLKOMMISSION (1978), *Fortschreitende Konzentration bei Grossunternehmen*, Baden-Baden: Nomos-Verlagsgesellschaft.

MONTGOMERY, D. (1987), *The Fall of the House of Labor*, Cambridge and New York: Cambridge University Press.

MORCK, R., SHLEIFER, A., and VISHNY, R. (1988), 'Characteristics of Targets of Hostile and Friendly Takeovers', in A. Auerbach (ed.), *Corporate Takeovers: Causes and Consequences*, Chicago: National Bureau of Economic Research, 101–36.

————(1989), 'Alternative Mechanisms of Corporate Control', *American Economic Review*, 79: 842–52.

MOSSIN, J. (1966), 'Equilibrium in a Capital Asset Market', *Econometrica*, 34: 768–83.

MOWERY, D. (1986), 'Industrial Research, 1900–1950', in Bernard Elbaum and William Lazonick (eds.), *The Decline of the British Economy*, New York: Oxford University Press, 189–222.

——and LANGLOIS, R. (1996), 'Spinning Off and Spinning on (?): the Federal Government Role in the Development of the US Computer Software Industry', *Research Policy*, 25: 947–66.

——and ROSENBERG, N. (1993), 'The US National Innovation System', in R. Nelson (ed.), *National Innovation Systems: A Comparative Analysis*, New York and Oxford: Oxford University Press, 29–75.

————(1998), *Paths of Innovation: Technological Change in 20th Century America*, Cambridge and New York: Cambridge University Press.

MÜLLER-JENTSCH, W. (1986), *Soziologie der industriellen Beziehungen: Eine Einführung*, Frankfurt: Campus-Verlag.

——(1995), 'Germany: From Collective Voice to Co-management', in J. Rogers, and W. Streeck (eds.), *Works Councils: Consultation, Representation, and Cooperation in Industrial Relations*, Chicago: University of Chicago Press, 53–76.

MÜNCH, J. (various years), *Vocational Training in the Federal Republic of Germany*, Berlin: European Centre for the Development of Vocational Training.

MURPHY, K. (1985), 'Corporate Performance and Managerial Remuneration: An Empirical Analysis', *Journal of Accounting and Economics*, 7: 11–42.

MYERS, S. (1984), 'Finance Theory and Financial Strategy', *Interfaces*, 14(1): 126–37.

NADER, R. (1965), *Unsafe at any speed: the designed-in dangers of the US automobile*, New York: Grossman.

NAVIN, T., and SEARS, M. (1955), 'The Rise of a Market for Industrial Securities', *Business History Review*, 29(2): 105–38.

NELSON, R. (1959), *Merger Movements in American Industry, 1895–1956*, Princeton, NJ: Princeton University Press.

——(1990), 'US Technological Leadership: Where Did it Come from and Where Did It Go?', *Research Policy*, 19(2): 117–32.

——(1991), 'Why Do Firms Differ and How Does It Matter?', *Strategic Management Journal*, 12: 61–74.

——and WINTER, S. (1977), 'In Search of Useful Theory of Innovation', *Research Policy*, 6(1): 36–76.

————(1982), *An Evolutionary Theory of Economic Change*, Cambridge, Mass.: Harvard University Press.

——and WRIGHT, G. (1992), 'The Rise and Fall of American Technological Leadership', *Journal of Economic Literature*, 30: 1931–64.

NEUMANN, F. (1944), *Behemoth: The Structure and Practice of National Socialism, 1933–1944*, New York: Oxford University Press.

Nishiyame, C., and Leube, K. (eds.) (1984), *The Essence of Hayek*, Stanford, Calif.: Hoover Institution.

NOBLE, D. (1977), *America by Design: Science, Technology, and the Rise of Corporate Capitalism*, New York: Knopf.

NSF (National Science Foundation) (1998), *Science and Engineering Indicators*, Washington, DC: NSF.

OBERBECK, H., and BAETHGE, M. (1989), 'Computer and Pinstripes: Financial Institutions', in P. Katzenstein (ed.), *Industry and Politics in West Germany*, Ithaca, NY: Cornell University Press, 275–306.

O'DRISCOLL, G., and RIZZO, M. (1985), *The Economics of Time and Ignorance*, Oxford and New York: Basil Blackwell.

OECD (Organisation for Economic Cooperation and Development) (1993), *Private Pensions in OECD Countries: The United States*, OECD Social Policy Studies, no. 10, Paris: OECD.

——(1994), *Manufacturing Performance: A Scoreboard of Indicators*, Paris: OECD.

——(1996a), 'Ageing Populations, Pension Systems, and Government Budgets: Simulation for 20 OECD Countries', OECD Working Paper no. 168, Paris: OECD.

——(1996b), *The OECD STAN Database for Industrial Analysis, 1975–1994*, Paris: OECD.

——(1997), 'Institutional Investors', in OECD, *Statistical Yearbook*, Paris: OECD.

——(1999), *OECD Principles of Corporate Governance*, Paris: OECD.

OKIMOTO, D., SUGANO, T., and WEINSTEIN, F. (1984), *Competitive Edge: The Semiconductor Industry in the US and Japan*, Stanford, Calif.: Stanford University Press.

OLDFIELD, H. (1998), *King of the Seven Dwarfs: General Electric's Ambiguous Challenge to the Computer Industry*, Los Alamitos, Calif.: IEEE Computer Society Press.

OLNEY, M. (1991), *Buy now, pay later: advertising, credit, and consumer durables in the 1920s*, Chapel Hill, NC: University of North Carolina Press.

O'SULLIVAN, M. (1997), 'Strategy and Learning at General Electric, 1892–1970', paper presented at the Business History Conference, Glasgow, July 1997.

——(1999), 'French Corporate Governance: History and Recent Developments', INSEAD working paper.

O'TOOLE, J. (1996), *Forming the Future: Lessons from the Saturn Corporation*, Cambridge, Mass. and Oxford: Basil Blackwell.

OWEN SMITH, E. (1994), *The German Economy*, London and New York: Routledge.

PACKARD, DAVID (1995), *The HP Way: How Bill Hewlett and I Built our Company*, New York: Harper Business.

PASINETTI, L. (1977), *Lectures on the Theory of Production*, London: Macmillan.

PATCH, E. (1995), *Plant Closings and Employment Loss in Manufacturing: The Role of Local Conditions*, New York: Garland.

PAVITT, K. (1988), 'A Critique of Tushman and Anderson's Chapter', in A. Pettigrew (ed.), *The Management of Strategic Change*, Oxford and New York: Basil Blackwell, 123–7.

——(1994), 'Key Characteristics of Large Innovating Firms', in M. Dodgson and R. Rothwell (eds.), *The Handbook of Industrial Innovation*, Aldershot: Edward Elgar, 357–66.

PENROSE, E. (1995), *The Theory of the Growth of the Firm*, 3rd edn., Oxford and New York: Oxford University Press.

PERROW, C. (1986), 'Economic Theories of Organization', *Theory and Society*, 15: 11–45.

PIORE, M.J. (1982), 'American Labor and the Industrial Crisis', *Challenge*, 25, Mar.–Apr.: 5–12.

POHL, H. (1982), 'On the History of Organisation and Management in Large German Enterprises since the Nineteenth Century', in W. Engels and H. Pohl (eds.), *German Yearbook of Business History*, Berlin and New York: Springer, 439–71.

——(1984), 'Forms and Phases of Industry Finance up to the Second World War', in W. Engels and H. Pohl (eds.), *German Yearbook of Business History*, Berlin and New York: Springer, 75–94.

PORTER, M. (1987), 'From Competitive Advantage to Corporate Strategy', *Harvard Business Review*, 65(3) (May–June): 43–59.

——(1990), *The Competitive Advantage of Nations*, New York: Free Press.

——(1992), *Capital Choices: Changing the Way America Invests in Industry*, Washington, DC: Council on Competitiveness.

POTERBA, J., and SAMWICK, A. (1995), 'Stock Ownership Patterns, Stock Market Fluctuations, and Consumption', *Brookings Papers on Economic Activity*, 2: 295–372.

POUND, J. (1992), 'Beyond Takeovers: Politics comes to Corporate Control', *Harvard Business Review*, 70(1) (Mar.–Apr.): 83–93.

POZEN, R. (1994), 'Institutional Investors: The Reluctant Activists', *Harvard Business Review*, 72(1) (Jan.–Feb.): 140–9.

PRENDERGAST, C. (1999), 'The Provision of Incentives in Firms', *Journal of Economic Literature*, 37(1): 7–63.

PUGH, E. (1995), *Building IBM: Shaping an Industry and its Technology*, Cambridge, Mass.: MIT Press.

QUEISSER, M. (1996), *Pensions in Germany*, Washington, DC: World Bank.

RAINES, J.P., and LEATHERS, C. (1996), 'Veblenian Stock Markets and the Efficient Markets Hypothesis', *Journal of Post-Keynesian Economics*, 19: 137–52.

RAISER, T. (1988), 'The Theory of Enterprise Law in the Federal Republic of Germany', *American Journal of Comparative Law*, 36: 111–29.

RAVENSCRAFT, D., and SCHERER, F. (1987), *Mergers, Sell-offs and Economic Efficiency*, Washington, DC: Brookings Institution.

REHDER, R. (1994*a*), 'Is Saturn Competitive?', *Business Horizons*, Mar.–Apr.: 7–15.

——(1994*b*), 'Saturn, Uddevalla and the Japanese Lean Systems: Paradoxical Prototypes for the Twenty-first Century', *International Journal of Human Resource Management*, 5(1): 1–32.

REHFELD, B. (1997), 'Low-cal CalPERS', *Institutional Investor*, internat. edn., 22(3): 107–16.

REICH, N. (1979), 'Auswirkungen der deutschen Aktienrechtsform von 1884 auf die Konzentration der deutschen Wirtschaft', in J. Kocka and N. Horn (eds.), *Recht und Entwicklung der Grossunternehmen im 19. und frühen 20. Jahrhundert*, Göttingen: Vandenhoeck and Ruprecht, 255–71.

REINGANUM, M. (1981), 'A New Empirical Perspective on the CAPM', *Journal of Financial and Quantitative Analysis*, 16: 439–62.

RETTIG, R. (1978), 'Investitions- und Finanzierungsverhalten deutscher Grossunternehmen, 1880–1911', unpub. Ph.D. thesis, University of Münster.

RIESSER, J. (1931), *The German Great Banks and their Concentration in connection with the Economic Development of Germany*, Washington, DC: National Monetary Commission.

RIPLEY, W. (1927), *Main Street and Wall Street*, Boston: Little, Brown.

ROACH, S. (1998), 'Global Restructuring: Lessons, Myths, and Challenges', Morgan Stanley Dean Witter, International Investment Research, Special Economic Study.

ROBINSON, E.A.G. (1931), *The Structure of Competitive Industry*, Cambridge: Cambridge University Press.

ROBINSON, J. (1933), *The Economics of Imperfect Competition*, London: Macmillan.

ROE, M. (1994), *Strong Managers, Weak Owners*, Princeton, NJ: Princeton University Press.

ROLL, R. (1994), 'What Every CFO Should Know about Scientific Progress in Financial Economics: What is Known and What Remains to be Resolved', *Financial Management*, Summer: 69–75.

ROSEGRANT, S., and LAMPE, D. (1992), *Route 128: Lessons from Boston's high-tech community*, New York: Basic Books.

ROSENBERG, N. (1994), *Exploring the Black Box: Technology, Economics, and History*, Cambridge and New York: Cambridge University Press.

——and NELSON, R. (1994), 'American Universities and Technical Advance in Industry', *Research Policy*, 23: 323–48.

ROSENBLOOM, R., and CUSUMANO, M. (1987), 'Technological Pioneering and Competitive Advantage: The Birth of the VCR Industry', *California Management Review*, 29: 51–76.

ROSKAMP, K. (1965), *Capital Formation in West Germany*, Detroit: Wayne State University Press.

ROSS, S. (1973), 'The Economic Theory of Agency: The Principal's Problem', *American Economic Review*, 63: 134–39.

——(1997), 'Germany: Labor's Perspective on Lean Production', in T. Kochan, R. Lansbury, and J. P. MacDuffie (eds.), *After Lean Production: Evolving Employment Practices in the World Auto Industry*, Ithaca, NY and London: ILR Press, 117–36.

ROTHSCHILD, E. (1974), *Paradise Lost: the Decline of the Auto-Industrial Age*, New York: Vintage.

RUMELT, R. (1974), *Strategy, Structure, and Economic Performance*, Boston: Harvard Business School Press.

——(1982), 'Diversification, Strategy, and Profitability', *Strategic Management Journal*, 3(4): 359–69.

SACHWALD, F. (1994), *European Integration and Competitiveness: Acquisitions and Alliances in Industry*, Aldershot: Edward Elgar.

SADOWSKI, D., SCHNEIDER, M., and WAGNER, K. (1994), 'The Impact of European Integration and German Unification on Industrial Relations in Germany', *British Journal of Industrial Relations*, 32: 523–37.

SAH, R., and STIGLITZ, J. (1986), 'The Architecture of Economic Systems: Hierarchies and Polyarchies', *American Economic Review*, 76: 716–27.

SAHLMAN, W., and STEVENSON, H. (1986), 'Capital Market Myopia', *Journal of Business Venturing*, 1(1): 7–30.

SASS, S. (1997), *The Promise of Private Pensions: The First Hundred Years*, Cambridge, Mass. and London: Harvard University Press.

SAXENIAN, A. (1991), 'Institutions and the Growth of Silicon Valley', *Berkeley Planning Journal*, 6: 36–57.

——(1994), *Regional Advantage: culture and Competition in Silicon Valley and Route 128*, Cambridge, Mass. and London: Harvard University Press.

SCHARFSTEIN, D. (1988), 'The Disciplinary Role of Takeovers', *Review of Economic Studies*, 55: 185–99.

SCHATZ, R. (1983), *The Electrical Workers: A History of Labour at General Electric and Westinghouse, 1923–60*, Champaign-Urbana, Ill.: University of Illinois Press.

SCHERER, F.M., and ROSS, D. (1990), *Industrial Market Structure and Economic Performance*, 3rd edn., Boston: Houghton Mifflin.

SCHMÄHL, W. (1993), 'The "1992 Reform" of Public Pensions in Germany: Main Elements and Some Effects', *Journal of European Social Policy*, 3(1): 39–51.

——(1994), 'Perspectiven der Alterssicherung in Deutschland', *Wirtschaftsdienst*, 74(8): 390–5.

SCHREYOGG, G., and STEINMANN, H. (1981), 'Zur Trennung von Eigentum und Verfugungsgewalt', *Zeitschrift für Betriebswirtschaft*, 51: 533–58.

SCHUMANN, M., BAETHGE-KINSKY, V., KUHLMANN, M., KURZ, C., and NEUMANN, U. (1994), *Trendreport Rationalisierung: Automobile Industrie, Werkzeugmaschinenbau, Chemische Industrie*, Berlin: Sigma.

SCHUMPETER, J. (1928), 'The Instability of Capitalism', *Economic Journal*, 48: 361–86.

——(1939), *Business Cycles*, vol. 1, New York: McGraw Hill.

——(1947), 'The Creative Response in Economic History', *Journal of Economic History*, 7: 149–59.

——(1949), 'Economic Theory and Entrepreneurial History', in Research Center in Entrepreneurial History, Harvard University (ed.), *Change and the Entrepreneur*, Cambridge, Mass.: Harvard University Press, 63–84.

——(1951), *Ten Great Economists: From Marx to Keynes*, New York: Oxford University Press.

——(1975), *Capitalism, Socialism and Democracy*, New York: Harper Torchbooks.

——(1996), *The Theory of Economic Development*, New Brunswick, NJ: Transaction Publishers.

SCHWAB, S., and THOMAS, R. (1998), 'Realigning Corporate Governance: Shareholder Activism by Labor Unions', *Michigan Law Review*, 96: 1018–94.

SCHWARZ, J. (1987), *Liberal: Adolf Berle and the Vision of a New American Era*, New York: Free Press.

SCIBBERAS, E. (1977), *Multinational Electronic Companies and National Economic Policies*, Greenwich, Conn.: JAI Press.

——(1981), *Technical Innovation and International Competitiveness in the Television Industry*, Stanford, Conn. Omega.

SEAGER, H. (1912), 'The Impatience Theory of Interest', *American Economic Review*, 2: 835–7.

SEARS, J. (1929), *The New Place of the Stockholder*, New York: Harper and Brothers.

SERVOS, J.W. (1980), 'The Industrial Relations of Science: Chemical Engineering at MIT, 1900–1939', ISIS, 71: 531–49.

SHACKLE, G.L.S. (1970), *Expectation, Enterprise and Profit: The Theory of the Firm*, Chicago: Aldine.

SHACKLE, G.L.S. (1992), *Epistemics and Economics: A Critique of Economic Doctrines*, New Brunswick, NJ: Transaction Publishers.

SHARPE, W. (1964), 'Capital Asset Prices: A Theory of Market Equilibrium under Conditions of Risk', *Journal of Finance*, 19: 425–42.

SHILLER, R. (1981), 'Do Stock Prices Move Too Much to be Justified by Subsequent Changes in Dividends?', *American Economic Review*, 71: 421–36.

——(1990), 'Speculative Prices and Popular Models', *Journal of Economic Perspectives*, 4: 55–65.

SHLEIFER, A., and SUMMERS, L. (1988), 'Breach of Trust in Hostile Takeovers', in A. Auerbach (ed.), *Corporate Takeovers: Causes and Consequences*, Chicago: National Bureau of Economic Research, 33–56.

——and VISHNY, R. (1991), 'Takeovers in the '60s and the '80s: Evidence and Implications', *Strategic Management Journal*, 12: 51–9.

————(1997), 'A Survey of Corporate Governance', *Journal of Finance*, 52: 737–83.

SHONFIELD, A. (1965), *Modern Capitalism: The Changing Balance of Public and Private Power*, London: Oxford University Press.

SIEGEL, J. (1994), *Stocks for the Long Run: A Guide to Selecting Markets for Long-Term Growth*, Burr Ridge, Ill.: Irwin Professional Publishing.

——and THALER, R. (1997), 'The Equity Premium Puzzle', *Journal of Economic Perspectives*, 11: 191–200.

SIEGRIST, H. (1980), 'Deutsche Grossunternehmung vom späten 19. Jahrhundert bis zur Weimarer Republik', *Geschichte und Gesellschaft*, 6: 60–102.

SIMON, H. (1991), 'Organizations and Markets', *Journal of Economic Perspectives*, 5(2): 25–44.

SKLAR, M. (1988), *The Corporate Reconstruction of America, 1890–1916: The Market, the Law and Politics*, New York: Cambridge University Press.

SLICHTER, S. (1929), 'Current Labor Policies of American Industry', *Quarterly Journal of Economics*, 43: 393–435.

SLOAN, A. (1964), *My Years with General Motors*, New York: Doubleday.

SMYSER, W.R. (1992), *The Economy of United Germany: Colossus at the Crossroads*, New York: St Martin's.

SORGE, A., and STREECK, W. (1988), 'Industrial Relations and Technical Change: The Case for An Extended Perspective', in R. Hyman, and W. Streeck (eds.), *New Technology and Industrial Relations*, London: Basil Blackwell, 204–19.

——and WARNER, M. (1986), *Comparative Factory Organisation: An Anglo-German Comparison of Management and Manpower in Manufacturing*, Brookfield, Utah: Gower Publishing.

SPARKS, C., and GREINER, M. (1997), 'US and Foreign Productivity and Unit Labor Costs', *Monthly Labor Review*, Feb.: 26–49.

SPOTTON, B., and ROWLEY, R. (1998), 'Efficient Markets, Fundamentals, and Crashes: American Theories of Financial Crises and Market Volatility', *American Journal of Economics and Sociology*, 57: 663–90.

SRAFFA, P. (1926), 'The Laws of Returns under Competitive Conditions', *Economic Journal*, 36: 535–50.

STAELIN, D., et al. (1989), 'The Decline of US Consumer Electronics Manufacturing', MIT Commission on Industrial Productivity Working Paper.

STAUDOHAR, P., and BROWN, H. (1987), *Deindustrialization and Plant Closure*, Lexington, Mass.: Lexington Books.

STEIN, B. (1992), *A License to Steal: The Untold Story of Michael Milken and the Conspiracy to Bilk the Nation*, New York: Simon and Schuster.

STEVENS, W.H. (1926), 'Stockholders' Voting Rights and the Centralization of Voting Control', *Quarterly Journal of Economics*, 40: 353–92.

STORY, J. (1997), '*Finanzplatz Deutschland*: National or European Response to Internationalisation?', *German Politics*, 5: 371–94.

STREECK, W. (1989), 'Successful Adjustment to Turbulent Markets: The Automobile Industry', in P. Katzenstein (ed.), *Industry and Politics in West Germany*, Ithaca, NY: Cornell University Press, 113–56.

——(1992), *Social Institutions and Economic Performance: Studies of Industrial Relations in Advanced Capitalist Economies*, London and Newbury Park, Calif.: Sage Publications.

——(1995), 'German Capitalism: Does it Exist? Can it Survive?', Max Planck Institut Für Gesellschaftsforschung Working Paper No. 95.

——*et al.* (1987), *The Role of the Social Partners in Vocational Training and Further Training in the Federal Republic of Germany*, Berlin: CEDEFOP.

STRICKER, F. (1983), 'Affluence for Whom?—Another Look at Prosperity and the Working Classes in the 1920s', *Labor History*, 21: 5–33.

SUMMERS, L. (1986), 'Does the Stock Market Rationally Reflect Fundamental Values?', *Journal of Finance*, 41: 591–601.

SUSMAN, G.I. (ed.) (1992), *Integrating Design and Manufacturing for Competitive Advantage*, New York: Oxford University Press.

SUTTON, F., HARRIS, S., KAYSEN, C., and TOBIN, J. (1956), *The American Business Creed*, Cambridge, Mass.: Harvard University Press.

TARBELL, I. (1932), *Owen D. Young, a new type of industrial leader*, New York: Macmillan.

TEAGUE, P. (1997), 'Lean Production and the German Model', *German Politics*, 6(2): 76–94.

TEECE, D. (1986), 'Profiting from Technological Innovation', *Research Policy*, 15(6): 285–305.

——PISANO, G., and SHUEN, A. (1997), 'Dynamic Capabilities and Strategic Management', *Strategic Management Journal*, 18(7): 524–6.

THAKOR, A. (1990), 'Investment "Myopia" and the Internal Organisation of Capital Allocation Decisions', *Journal of Law, Economics and Organisation*, 6: 129–48.

THALER, R. (ed.) (1993), *Advances in Behavioral Finance*, New York: Russell Sage Foundation.

THELEN, K. (1992), *Union of Parts: Labour Politics in Postwar West Germany*, Ithaca, NY: Cornell University Press.

THIMM, A. (1981), 'How Far should German Codetermination Go?', *Challenge*, July–Aug.: 13–22.

THORP, W.L., and CROWDER, W. (1941), *The Structure of Industry*, Temporary National Economic Committee Monograph no. 27, Washington, DC: Temporary National Economic Committee.

TILLY, R. (1982), 'Mergers, External Growth, and Finance in the Development of Large-scale Enterprise in Germany, 1880–1913', *Journal of Economic History*, 42: 646–58.

TILLY, R. (1986), 'German Banking, 1850–1914: Development Assistance for the Strong', *Journal of European Economic History*, 15: 113–52.

TILTON, J. (1971), *The International Diffusion of Technology: The Case of Transistors*, Washington, DC: Brookings Institution.

TURNER, H., JR. (1985), *German Big Business and the Rise of Hitler*, New York: Oxford University Press.

TURNER, J., and WATANABE, N. (1995), *Private Pension Policies in Industrialised Countries: A Comparative Analysis*, Kalamazoo, Mich.: Upjohn Institute.

TURNER, L. (1991), *Democracy at Work: Changing World Markets and the Future of Labor Unions*, Ithaca, NY and London: Cornell University Press.

TUSHMAN, M., and ANDERSON, P. (1988), 'Technological Discontinuities and Organizational Environments', in A. Pettigrew (ed.), *The Management of Strategic Change*, Oxford and New York: Blackwell, 123–7.

UN (1995), *World Population Prospects*, New York: United Nations.

US BOARD OF GOVERNORS OF THE FEDERAL RESERVE SYSTEM (various years), *Flows of Funds Accounts of the United States: Flows and Outstandings*, Washington, DC: US Board of Governors of the Federal Reserve System.

US BUREAU OF THE CENSUS (1976), *The Statistical History of the United States: from Colonial Times to the Present*, New York: Basic Books.

US BUREAU OF LABOR STATISTICS (1998), *Employee Tenure in 1998*, press release, 23 Sept. (http://stats.bls.gov/newsrels.htm).

US CONGRESS (various years), *Economic Report of the President*, Washington, DC: US Government Printing Office.

US DEPARTMENT OF COMMERCE (various years), *Statistical Abstract of the United States*, US Government Printing Office.

USEEM, M. (1996), *Investor Capitalism: How Money Managers are Changing the Face of Corporate America*, New York: Basic Books.

VAN TULDER, R., and JUNNE, G. (1988), *European Multinationals in Core Technologies*, Chichester: Wiley.

VEBLEN, T. (1904), *The Theory of Business Enterprise*, New York: C. Scribner's Sons.

——(1923), *Absentee Ownership and the Business Enterprise in Recent Times: The Case of America*, New York: B. W. Huebsch.

VENTURE ECONOMICS (1996), *Venture Capital Annual Review*, Boston: Venture Economics.

VITOLS, S. (1995), 'Are German Banks Different?', Wissenschaftszentrum Berlin Discussion Paper FS I 95-308.

VOGL, F. (1973), *German Business after the Economic Miracle*, New York: Wiley.

VON TUNZELMANN, G.N. (1995), *Technology and Industrial Progress: The Foundations of Economic Growth*, Cheltenham: Edward Elgar.

WALLICH, H. (1955), *Mainsprings of the German Revival*, New Haven, Conn.: Yale University Press.

WALTON, R. (1972), 'How to Counter Alienation in the Plant', *Harvard Business Review*, 50(6) (Nov.–Dec.): 70–81.

——(1975), 'The Diffusion of New Work Structures: Explaining Why Success didn't Take', *Organizational Dynamics*, 3: 3–22.

——(1979), 'Work Innovations in the United States', *Harvard Business Review*, 57(4) (July–Aug.): 88–98.

WEBER, A. (1938), *Depositbanken und Spekulationsbanken: Ein Vergleich deutschen und englischen Bankwesens*, Munich: Duncker and Humblot.

WEINSTEIN, M., and KOCHAN, T. (1995), 'The Limits of Diffusion: Recent Developments in Industrial Relations and Human Resource Practices', in R. Locke, T. Kochan, and M. Piore (eds.), *Employment Relations in a Changing World*, Cambridge, Mass.: MIT Press, 1–31.

WEISSKOPF, T., GORDON, D., and BOWLES, S. (1983), 'Hearts and Minds: A Social Model of US Productivity Growth', *Brookings Papers on Economic Activity*, 2: 381–450.

WELLHÖNER, V. (1989), *Grossbanken und Grossindustrie im Kaiserreich*, Göttingen: Vaudenhoeck and Ruprecht.

WENGENROTH, U. (1997), 'Germany: Competition Abroad—Cooperation at Home, 1870–1900', in A. D. Chandler, F. Amatori, and T. Hikino (eds.), *Big Business and the Wealth of Nations*, Cambridge and New York: Cambridge University Press, 139–75.

WHALE, P.B. (1930), *Joint-stock Banking in Germany: A Study of the German Creditbanks before and after the War*, London: Macmillan.

WHITE, E. (1997), 'Relying on the Power of People at Saturn', *National Productivity Review*, Winter: 5–10.

WHITMAN, R. (1997), 'Including Employment Practice Data in Proxy Statements', *New York Law Journal*, 6 Nov., 1–28.

WHYTE, W.F., JR. (1953), 'The Crown Princes of Business', *Fortune*, Oct.: 153.

WIGMORE, B. (1989), 'The Decline in Credit Quality of Junk Bond Issues', in P. Gaughan (ed.), *Readings in Mergers and Acquisitions*, Cambridge: Basil Blackwell, 171–84.

——(1997), *Securities Markets in the 1980s: The New Regime, 1979–1984*, vol. 1, New York and Oxford: Oxford University Press.

WILLIAMSON, O. (1985), *The Economic Institutions of Capitalism: Firms, Markets, Relational Contracting*, New York: Free Press.

——and Winter, S. (1993), *The Nature of the Firm: Origins, Evolution, and Development*, New York: Oxford University Press.

WILSON, J. (1985), *The New Venturers: Inside the High-stakes World of Venture Capital*, Reading, Mass.: Addison-Wesley.

WINKELMANN, R. (1996), 'Employment Prospects and Skill Acquisition of Apprenticeship-trained Workers in Germany', *Industrial and Labor Relations Review*, 49: 658–72.

WISE, G. (1979), 'On Test: Postgraduate Training of Engineers at General Electric, 1892–1961', *IEEE Transactions on Education*, vol. E-22, no. 4: 171–7.

——(n.d.), 'General Electric's Century', unpub. MS.

WOHLSTETTER, C. (1993), 'Pension Fund Socialism: Can Bureaucrats Run the Blue Chips?', *Harvard Business Review*, 71(1) (Jan.–Feb.), 78.

WOMACK, J., JONES, D., and ROOS, D. (1990), *The Machine that Changed the World*, New York: Rawson.

WORLD BANK (1994), *Averting the Old Age Crisis: Policies to Protect the Old and Promote Growth*, Oxford: Oxford University Press.

YOUNG, A. (1928), 'Increasing Returns and Economic Progress', *Economic Journal*, 38: 527–42.

Index